The Theater of Protest and Paradox:
Developments in the Avant-Garde Drama

The Theater
of Protest and Paradox

Developments
in the Avant-Garde Drama

Revised Edition

By George Wellwarth

NEW YORK UNIVERSITY PRESS   1971

REVISED EDITION, FIRST PRINTING

© 1964, 1971 BY NEW YORK UNIVERSITY

LIBRARY OF CONGRESS CATALOG CARD NUMBER: 64-16901

ISBN 0-8147-0432-8 (CLOTH)

0-8147-0433-6 (PAPER)

MANUFACTURED IN THE UNITED STATES OF AMERICA

ACKNOWLEDGMENTS

I should like to acknowledge the assistance and advice of Professor Leo Hamalian of City College of New York, Professor Myron Taube of Long Island University, Professors Robert Clements, Henry Popkin, and Oscar Cargill of New York University, Miss Louise Gruner, Mr. Kurt Hellmer, and my wife Marcia. Without their help and encouragement this book might not have been completed.

Several of the chapters in this book first appeared in somewhat different form as articles in the following journals: *Tulane Drama Review*, Spring, 1962 (Dürrenmatt and Frisch); *Tulane Drama Review*, Fall, 1963 (Ghelderode); *Drama Survey*, Winter, 1963 (Artaud); *Drama Survey*, Spring, 1962 (Genet); *Ararat*, Spring, 1961 (Adamov); *University of Kansas City Review*, Autumn, 1961 (Beckett); *Southern Speech Journal*, Fall, 1961 (Dennis); *Southern Speech Journal*, Fall, 1962 (Ionesco); *Texas Studies in Literature and Language*, Autumn, 1962 (Audiberti); *Quarterly Journal of Speech*, Autumn, 1963 (Hochwälder); *Literary Review* (published by Fairleigh Dickinson University, Teaneck, N.J.), Autumn, 1963 (New American Drama); the chapter on Alfred Jarry is reprinted from *Criticism, a Quarterly for Literature and the Arts*, Vol. IV, No. 2 (Spring, 1962) by permission of the Wayne State University Press. Permission of the editors of these periodicals, who hold copyright on these respective items, is gratefully acknowledged.

In Memoriam Erwin Wellwarth

1890-1948

PREFACE TO FIRST EDITION

THIS BOOK is a critical study of the extraordinary outburst of drama in the French, German, English, and American theaters since the end of the second World War. Ever since 1950, when Eugene Ionesco's first play *The Bald Soprano* was produced, the theater has been vibrant with the excitement of a new movement of artistic creation. In France this movement has taken the form of "avant-garde" theater or "theatre of the absurd," as Martin Esslin has more satisfactorily called it. In the German-speaking theater it has taken the form of the brilliantly constructed dramatic conundrums of the Swiss writers Friedrich Dürrenmatt and Max Frisch and the Swiss-based Austrian Fritz Hochwälder. England has seen the rise of the "angry young man," writers whose plays have a potentially high intellectual significance that is unfortunately smothered by the ineptness of their practical execution. In addition, England has produced the "neo-absurdist" theater of Harold Pinter and N. F. Simpson, that, although rather enigmatic and esoteric for the literalness of the Anglo-Saxon taste, will yet prove to be more lasting and significant than the angry-young-man drama. America alone has been unable to produce enough dramatists working at the same time in a sufficiently similar vein to be called a "movement." It has, however, produced a small number of remarkable, if uneven, individual playwrights, such as Edward Albee, Jack Gelber, Arthur Kopit, and, above all, Jack Richardson.

At first glance the plays written in French, English, and

German since the end of the second World War are entirely
dissimilar. It is the purpose of this book to explain the meanings of these plays, set them in their proper place in the history
of dramatic literature, and point out their basic similarities.
These similarities consist of a common theme (protest) and a
common technique (paradox). Since intellectual drama (as
distinct from box-office drama, which reflects popular social
mores) always reflects current philosophical trends, it is only
natural to find an outburst of profound dissatisfaction after a
great war. Just as the first World War produced the immature
frenzy of expressionism and the contemptuous rejection of
surrealism and Dada, so the second World War has stimulated
a philosophy of protest against the social order (in the English-
and German-speaking drama) and against the human condition (in the French-speaking drama and in a few English-
speaking ones). The protest no longer takes the form of hair-
clutching hysteria, as it did in so many of the World War I
dramas, but rather of a quiescent cynicism born of bitter experience. The cumulative knowledge of two World Wars in
less than half a century, not to mention sundry atrocities and
diverse obscenities thrown in every now and then as a bonus
from the gods, so to speak, has made of today's intellectuals
men without faith. They can no longer scream because they
can no longer hope. They can no longer speak directly to their
hearers because they can no longer believe that they are heard.
They can only express themselves indirectly in sardonic paradoxes.

In the French section I have endeavored to show that there
is a direct relationship between the avant-garde writers of today
and the dramatic principles of Antonin Artaud and Alfred
Jarry. The theatre of the absurd began, I believe, abruptly and
suddenly on the evening of December 10, 1896, with the first
performance of Alfred Jarry's *Ubu roi*. This play was the perfect
example of artistic primitivism, a play literally without forebears, totally uninfluenced by any previous work. The attempt

by some critics to relate *Ubu roi* to previous works by pointing
out that Jarry had obviously read these works because he men-
tions them in the play is futile and illogical. Literary influence
cannot be demonstrated by citing a reading list. Nor does a
thumbnail history of nonsense literature prove that the nonsense literature which Jarry composed and which is being
written today belongs in a literary continuum. Jarry's nonsense
is, as a matter of fact, entirely different, both in style and purpose, from previous nonsense literature. The German, English,
and American writers have more recognizable antecedents in
the conventional drama of ideas.

George Wellwarth

November, 1963

PREFACE TO REVISED EDITION

THE MOST important addition in this revised edition is the chapter on the new Spanish drama. In the years since the publication of the first edition I have had the good fortune to become acquainted with the extraordinary drama being written in Spain today by a group of authors who have remained virtually unpublished and unproduced because of censorship. Seven of their plays have already been published in English in my edition of *The New Wave Spanish Drama* (New York University Press, 1970), but this chapter is the first extended critical treatment of these playwrights. Because of the peculiar theatrical situation in Spain I have had to work in large part from manuscripts, but I would hope that my account of these authors will stimulate further interest in them in English-speaking countries so that more and more of their plays will be made available in published form.

The other chapters in the first edition have been brought up-to-date except for those dealing with authors who have not produced plays of sufficient importance for extended treatment since the last edition.

George E. Wellwarth

Binghamton, N.Y., 1970

xiii

CONTENTS

The New English Dramatists

The New English Dramatists

Hope Deferred

CONTENTS

The Theater of Protest and Paradox
Developments in the Avant-Garde Drama

The French-Speaking Drama

ALFRED JARRY
The Sower of the Avant-Garde Drama

ON THE EVENING of December 10, 1896, the Paris theater
world was shocked by an extraordinary and unprecedented
event. All the leading critics and members of the literary demi-
monde had assembled to see Lugné-Poë's Théâtre de l'Oeuvre
company perform Alfred Jarry's new play, *Ubu roi* (King Ubu),
at the Théâtre Nouveau. The curtain opened and Fermin
Gémier stepped forward to say a word that had never before
been pronounced on stage. The theater was never the same
again.

Thus began the avant-garde drama.

Alfred Jarry died in 1907 at the age of thirty-four. Thanks
in large measure to his own considerable ability for self-adver-
tisement, he was by no means entirely neglected during his
lifetime. Jarry's critical reputation, however, presents a rather
peculiar picture. While he was still alive, those who wrote about
him were, understandably enough, more concerned with his
personal peculiarities than with his works. After his death,
little of any significance was written about him for a long time.
There was a brief revival of interest in him during the short-
lived Dada movement of the early twenties; and Charles Chassé
unwittingly contributed to the Jarry legend by publishing a
book in which he accused him of plagiarizing the character of

1

Ubu from two old schoolfellows. In 1927 Antonin Artaud and Roger Vitrac founded the Théâtre Alfred Jarry for the production of avant-garde drama. In 1938 Artaud, the direct ancestor of the current avant-garde drama, laid down the rules for the new drama in *Le Théâtre et son Double* (The Theatre and Its Double). But it was not until the College of 'Pataphysics was founded by a group of Jarry disciples in 1948 that Jarry came back into his own. With the increased popularity of the current avant-garde drama—the drama of Ionesco, Beckett, Genet, Adamov, Audiberti, etc.—interest in Jarry has revived steadily as it has become evident that there is some similarity between the style of the new plays and that of the *Ubu* plays.

It will be necessary first to clear up what is meant by the term "avant-garde." Roughly speaking, the term means "out in front of everybody else." Now, a person who is out in front of everybody else is fully exposed to the fire of the enemy. Such intrepidity, whether fearless or merely foolhardy, is shocking to the timid, the cautious, and the prudent who comprise the majority; all the more so because the majority—instinctively and in all innocence—always considers its position sacred and inviolate. The power to *shock* is, then, the chief characteristic of the avant-garde drama and at the same time its chief source of strength.

Avant-garde drama has always been with us, and the modern avant-garde drama is merely the successor to, although not the lineal descendant of, the Robertsonian cup-and-saucer drama, the society drama of the Pinero-Jones axis (difficult though it may be now to realize that these were considered shocking in their day), and the Ibsen-Shaw social drama. The twentieth-century avant-garde drama is unlike any previous avant-garde drama. Previously the forefront was always created by means of a logical, if unexpected, development of some aspect of the currently popular drama. Thus the Robertsonian drama rose out of an increased emphasis on physical realism in stage production; the "Pinerotico-Jonesian" drama shocked because it introduced moral problems that had previously been thought unfit for public discussion; the Ibsen-Shaw drama shocked even more by actually discussing these moral problems seriously instead of just titillatingly skittering around them in the fey manner of Pinero and Jones. The current avant-garde drama, however, has no such respectable antecedents. It sprang into existence with explosive suddenness on the evening of December 10, 1896.

Jarry was one of the very few true primitives in the history of literature. Some critics have seen the influence of Rabelais in the tone of raucous vulgarity that pervades the Ubu plays,[1] but a common interest in scatology hardly proves influence. Others have professed to see Hamlet in Bougrelas, the vengeful son of the Polish king whom Ubu kills,[2] but—again—parody does not imply literary influence. No, Jarry was simply an anomaly. In the continuum of literary history he suddenly appears, mysteriously crystallized, as it were, out of the elements of his own uniquely slanted mind.

The superficial childishness of the Ubu plays should not prevent the reader from taking them seriously. That Jarry's mind remained in many essentials a child's in no way diminishes his importance as the originator of the scream of protest later to be decreed by Artaud the official theme of the avant-garde drama. Jarry never formulated a coherent philosophy: he presented everything with the simplicity and immediacy of a child slinging mud pies. With the intuition of genius he was able to perceive an elaborate philosophy that he did not have the intellectual staying power to work out and understand, and to which, consequently, he succumbed.

When Jarry wrote *Ubu roi*, he was rebelling not only against the outmoded conventions of the current drama, as the previous "avant-gardists" had done, but against absolutely everything. Jarry rebelled against all things, both physical and metaphysical, to the point where he had to invent a new "reality" beyond the physical and metaphysical worlds—and thus the calculated insanity of 'Pataphysics came into being. The inverted world of 'Pataphysics is important in the history of

1. For example, Roger Shattuck, *The Banquet Years* (New York: Harcourt, Brace & World, Inc., 1958), p. 204.
2. Martin Esslin, "The Theatre of the Absurd," *Tulane Drama Review*, IV (Summer, 1960), p. 7.

drama only in so far as it symbolizes Jarry's total rejection of
the world and the cosmos. Jarry, fortunately, was not a practical and active person, for he was the ultimate rebel who insisted on building up his own dream world after completely
rejecting all existing reality.

Jarry's revolt was both seminal and instinctive. The blasé
audiences of today are accustomed to hearing the most extreme
forms of verbal obscenity casually mentioned in everyday con-
versations. Consequently, obscenity as a symbol of protest
against the rigidities of convention has lost all effect. To us the
famous opening line of *Ubu roi* seems mildly amusing, perhaps even a little trite, and certainly innocuous. But in 1896
the public utterance of that one word "*merdre*" (slightly altered
to make it Jarryesque) had an absolutely cataclysmic effect. It
was a slap in the face of society. When Fermin Gémier uttered
the famous *mot d'Ubu* on that riotous night in 1896 the shock
was electric. It did not matter that the performance was marred
by continual catcalls and outbreaks of rioting, or that all the
respectable critics excoriated the play on the following morning, or that Jarry was taken seriously only by a small coterie
he had gathered round him, or that "Ubuism" had no direct,
immediate influence on the drama. The point was that the
word had been spoken, that the event had occurred. In the
theater, as in life, events are irreversible. Once something has
happened, it has happened; and once it has happened, it can
happen again. In art, setting the precedent is the important
thing. After the production of *Ubu roi* the theater could not
be the same again: *Ubu roi* had happened, and the totality of
theatrical experience had instantly and irretrievably been translated into a new perspective.

Ubu roi begins with the tremendous thunderclap of *le mot
d'Ubu*, which set the expectant first-night audience off into
a maniacal frenzy, if contemporary accounts do not exaggerate.
The word shocked propriety. But the rebellion implicit in the
utterance of the word on a public stage was a rebellion against
all society and, indeed, all life. It was an evocation of disgust
so deep that conventional language was powerless to express

it, and at the same time the very unconventionality of the word was a gesture of defiance itself. The various scatological references sprinkled through the play represent rebellion on its most instinctive and elementary level—that of a child's refusal to bow to bathroom training. The purpose is deeper, however. Jarry's protest against the human condition was primitive and untutored; it was protest based on blind nihilism. Jarry's urges are those of a blinkered colt champing at the bit: "*Cornegidouille!*" says Père Ubu at one point, "*Nous n'aurons point tout démoli si nous ne démolissons même les ruines!*" Even the ruins must be pulled down.

The cosmic malignity that hovers invisibly over the characters in present-day avant-garde dramas is tangible and personified in Jarry's plays. Instead of being a helpless pawn (like Vladimir and Estragon in *Waiting for Godot,* or the employee in Adamov's *La Parodie,* or Maurice in Genet's *Deathwatch*), Jarry's protagonist, Père Ubu, is dirty, treacherous, greedy, ungrateful, cowardly, and cruel. In other words, the grotesquely bloated but still human figure of Father Ubu has all the attributes of the cosmic malignant force that pervades the avant-garde drama. Present in Ubu's elaborate "disembraining" machine, in his impaling people he doesn't like, and in the offhand mass slaughters he constantly orders, is the cruelty that Artaud later wanted to put into drama to show man's subjection to the hostile powers of the universe.

The story of *Ubu roi* is basically a naïve childish fantasy. The play is Jarry's warped version of the typical fairy tale—a king killed by a wicked usurper, the young and virtuous rightful heir to the throne as avenger, battles fought between troops who resemble the little tin soldiers of a toy box, eerie (but not too eerie) "supernatural" events, a fight with a make-believe bear, and so on.

At the beginning of the play, Ubu, an ugly, dirty, smelly, and grotesquely fat person, is being urged by his wife to kill Wenceslas, king of Poland, and usurp the throne himself. Ubu was formerly king of Aragon but is now captain of Wenceslas's dragoons. On the following day King Wenceslas is butchered by Ubu and his supporters as he reviews a parade of his troops. Ubu immediately slaughters the remaining members of the royal family (except Bougrelas, the heroic heir, who escapes with his mother) and takes over the kingdom. Basically, Ubu's idea of ruling is to kill all the people who have any money so that he can have it all for himself. Thus we see a long procession of noblemen, judges, and financiers fall into the trap door of the "disembraining" machine. Once Ubu has gathered unto himself all the money (or, as he prefers to call it, the "phynances") in Poland, he sets out to fight the czar of Russia, who is determined to avenge his cousin Wenceslas. Ubu is routed in the battle and flees with two of his followers to a cave, where they kill a bear while Father Ubu perches on a high rock reciting a paternoster. After this, Ubu is joined by his wife, and off they sail for France.

Ubu cocu (Cuckold Ubu, written 1897 or 1898) shows us Ubu as a private man once again. Except that he is no longer king, nothing is changed. He is still the same totally self-centered juggernaut of evil, crushing everyone in his path—a naïvely personified symbol of cosmic maliciousness and cruelty. Jarry has Ubu describe himself exactly when he first appears as an interpolation in the early work *César-Antechrist: "Semblable à un oeuf, une citrouille ou un fulgurant météore, je roule sur cette terre où je ferai ce qu'il me plaira."* This is Ubu's constant watchword: he will do just as he pleases. Like the cosmic evil he represents, Ubu rolls over everyone in his path with the obliviousness of a robot-controlled tank. And so, when Ubu takes over the house of M. Achras, the harmless, bumbling student of polyhedrals, he cheerfully takes over everything and, after consulting his conscience, impales M. Achras. The scene with Ubu's Conscience is illuminating as an example of Jarry's satiric qualities. Ubu asks his Conscience whether he should kill M. Achras for insulting him. "Monsieur," his Conscience answers, "it is not proper for a civilized man to answer good with evil. M. Achras has sheltered you, M. Achras has opened his arms and his collection of polyhedrals to you, M. Achras, and so forth, is a very fine gentleman, completely inoffensive, and it would be a terrible thing and so forth to kill a poor old man who is incapable of defending himself." [3] That is enough for Ubu: he instantly decides to kill M. Achras since there is no danger in doing so. Jarry's humorous effects are usually achieved by this forced marriage of cynical satire and broad farce. He is not even averse to mixing a little playful criticism of the contemporary theater into his most farcical scenes. When Ubu is jammed half in and half out of the trapdoor through which M. Achras has planned to drop him, Jarry, with a little oblique mocking bow in the direction of Alfred de Musset, has him say, "*De par ma chandelle verte, il faut qu'une trappe soit ouverte ou fermée. La beauté du théâtre à phynances gît dans le bon fonctionnement des trappes.*" [4] The play as a whole is a hodgepodge of this kind of flippant ridicule. Jarry does not bother to get together a coherent plan of attack: he prefers to dance about and flick out an occasional jab. In the later avant-garde drama this technique becomes less haphazard, more purposeful; but the formlessness and illogicality of plot line remains and has become one of the avant-garde's identifying characteristics.

The one other complete Ubu play (Jarry had a tendency to insert elements of the Ubu plays into other works) is *Ubu enchaîné* (Ubu Enchained, published 1900). This play is unlike Jarry's other Ubuesque works in that it is earthbound. He switches here from the naïve cosmic defiance he originated to a form of social satire. *Ubu enchaîné* is as formless and haphazard as ever, but it is essentially a sarcastic spoofing of human nature. Jarry's point—and this too was taken up by the later avant-garde dramatists—is that human beings are unable to think straight (i.e., objectively) and consequently act in accordance with the perverted paradoxes to which their ways of thinking lead them. Thus the climax of the play comes when Pissedoux shouts, to the acclamation of the mob, "*La liberté, c'est l'esclavage!*" But we are getting ahead of ourselves. Jarry begins this spoof of human behavior by spoofing himself. Ubu steps forward, poises himself, opens his mouth, and says—nothing! Mère Ubu is aghast. "What!" she says, "You don't say anything

3. Alfred Jarry, *Tout Ubu* (Paris: Le Livre de Poche, 1962), p. 206.
4. *Ibid.*, p. 215.

Père Ubu? Have you forgotten the word?" ". . . I don't want to say the word," answers Ubu, "It's made too much trouble for me already." Mère Ubu is deeply grieved by her husband's stubborn refusal to utter the magic word. She reminds him that they are in France now and that this is no time to forget how to speak French. But Ubu will have none of it. He is determined to change his way of life. He has had enough of being a king and ruling over people: now he wants to work with his hands and become a slave. It does not prove so easy to change human nature, however. Even as a slave, Ubu is the same powerful mass as before. Even as "free men" under an anarchistic social system, the ordinary beings are helpless driven slaves.

Ubu starts out on his quest for slavery by joining the army (*l'armerdre*), which consists of three "free men" and a corporal. The free men demonstrate their "freedom" by always doing precisely the opposite of what they are told to do. The corporal can thus control them with complete effectiveness by simply telling them to halt when he wants them to move, to stand at ease when he wants them to snap to attention, and so forth. The free men are constantly proclaiming their freedom (*"Nous sommes les hommes libres. . . . Vive la liberté, la liberté, la liberté! Nous sommes libres"*) but are actually as enslaved as the automatons of a regular army. At the end of the play they quite naturally choose slavery because Ubu's adoption of it has made it appear "freer" than anarchy. Ubu himself succeeds in achieving the lowest rank of slavery—that of a galley slave. As the coast of France recedes, he assures Mère Ubu that they will surely be taken to some country extraordinary enough to be worthy of them, where they will be put on a trireme with at least four banks of oars.

The bare plot outlines of the Ubu plays give us no inkling of their real significance. Like the modern avant-garde dramas to which they gave birth, the Ubu plays mystify by their apparent simplicity. Audiences laugh and scratch their heads in bewilderment as they watch the Ubu plays or the avant-garde dramas because they feel that they are being hoaxed—that a lot of simple-minded nonsense is being jabbered at them by a tongue-in-cheek author who wants them to rack their brains in a futile attempt to uncover a nonexistent profound meaning. And having, as they think, found this out, they laugh derisively and congratulate themselves on their perspicacity.

As usual, the audience, whom Jarry called an obstacle to the advance of the theatrical art in his essay *"De l'inutilité du théâtre au théâtre"* has got hold of the wrong end of the paradox. The Ubu plays and the avant-garde drama *appear* to be simplicity disguised as profundity and are actually profundity disguised as simplicity. The simplicity is deceptive, just as the simplicity of *Alice in Wonderland* or the simplicity of the painter Henri Rousseau, with whom Jarry has often been linked, is deceptive.[5] Perhaps we can get some idea of the way in which Jarry conceals profundity under a facade of naïveté and childlike vulgarity by analyzing one of Rousseau's most famous paintings. *Le Rêve* (The Dream) shows a sleeping woman's dream of a primeval wilderness transformed into a child's picture-book jungle. A naked woman on a red couch is set in the midst of a jungle landscape in which we can see two lions, a snake charmer, and a mysterious disembodied eye. The lions stare with vaguely worried expressions out of brilliantly colored hothouse foliage, their round eyes giving them the fixed, staring look of stuffed toy animals. Behind them the fantastic dream figure of the snake charmer rises out of the thick shrubbery like a forgotten caryatid from some overgrown and crumbled temple. And brooding over all is the sinister slanted eye that peeps out of a gap in the foliage just above the edge of the dreamer's couch. The piled-up, random mélange of exotic plants simultaneously gives the impression of being a stifling mephitic nightmare vision and an innocent playroom wallpaper design. Like William Blake, Rousseau interpenetrated works with sinister meaning and naïve, instinctive playfulness. Jarry shared this faculty. Ubu has the large, carefree jollity and buoyancy always associated with excessive corpulence, and the sinister, cruel menace of total evil. He is at the same time a symbol of the oblivious malignity of the cosmos and an evocation of the pathetically ridiculous

5. I am indebted to Roger Shattuck's *The Banquet Years* for the suggestion of the Jarry-Rousseau connection. Professor Shattuck's book is far and away the best treatment of Jarry in English.

high-school physics teacher who served as his original model.[6]

This quality of innocence is lost in the works of the later avant-garde dramatists, who derived their theories from Antonin Artaud rather than directly from Jarry. Artaud took the essence of Jarry's philosophy and applied it to strictly theatrical matters. He attempted to transmit Jarry's intellectual system (the system of rebellion through paradox) in terms of the theater. Jarry himself had been primarily interested in the theater, but he had by no means concentrated his energies on it as single-mindedly as Artaud was to do. Jarry's sole purpose in life was to rebel, and this he did not only in his dramas but in his deliberately bizarre personal behavior and in his straight-faced advocacy of the "supreme science" of 'Pataphysics as well. 'Pataphysics ("the science of imaginary solutions, which symbolically attributes the properties of objects, described by their virtuality, to their lineaments") is Jarry's protest against the futility of thought. Reason and logic and scientific discovery can only bring us up to a certain point of knowledge; beyond that point the human mind is powerless. Since that point is the only point that really matters—the understanding of death—Jarry felt that all thought was self-defeating and ultimately ridiculous. The invention of 'Pataphysics, which is dedicated to the use of strict logic in order to arrive at senseless conclusions, was Jarry's way of satirizing faith in human endeavor. Jarry's personal habits were also dictated by his desire to rebel. He seemed to operate on the theory that the cultivation of deliberately bizarre behavior constituted a rebellion against existing modes of behavior. He was implying that socially acceptable behavior is as arbitrary as the behavior he improvised, and that his own eccentric deportment destroyed the validity of the conventional behavior. Thus he became a well-known figure in the Paris of the eighteen-

6. Ubu originated as a caricature of Monsieur Hébert, Jarry's physics teacher at the *lycée* in Rennes. Hébert seems to have been a classic example of a man choosing the wrong profession. As a teacher he appears to have been totally incompetent and utterly incapable of controlling his pupils. The fact that he was also extremely fat made him the perfect target for Jarry and his classmates, and they soon began writing puppet plays in which he appeared as Père Héb. These plays later formed the basis for the Ubu plays.

nineties because of his peculiar mannerisms. Jarry used to affect an "Ubuesque" way of talking in which each syllable was given an exactly equal stress so that he sounded like a slowed-down recording. He lived in incredibly cluttered apartments where he kept owls, and went about the streets of Paris with firearms ostentatiously displayed. His defeat of the French army compares with Felix Krull's defeat of his German draft board. He was finally discharged on grounds of ill-health after swallowing some acid, but the real reason was probably that the army simply felt that it could not cope with him any longer.

Jarry's greatest gesture of rebellion, however, was his alcoholism. There can be little doubt that he deliberately drank himself to death. Not long after his arrival in Paris, he must have made up his mind to make the supreme rebellious gesture of suicide. He chose alcohol as his medium because it was slow and because the immediate effects of the alcohol enabled him to carry on his eccentricities undisturbed by the restraints of his own personality. Alcohol freed him from himself temporarily; eventually it freed him permanently from the whole burden of his life. In a way it was a heroic death, for it was a death for a cause, and probably it was not as pleasant a one as the casual drinker might suppose. It was certainly not an insane or unreasonable death. Rebellion as Jarry saw it was a quest for total freedom and a protest against the ultimate enslavement, which is death. Jarry chose to rebel against the ultimate by systematically destroying himself. In this way he conquered—paradoxically; for, having consciously sentenced himself to death, having decided to control his own death, as it were, by deliberately bringing it on, he was able to be completely at liberty, completely contemptuous of all manifestations of social order during the period of life that was left to him.

Jarry was as much a rebel and innovator in the field of theatrical technique as he was in the field of personal behavior. He extended his philosophical rebellion against the status quo by suggesting that realism should be eliminated from the theater. He had no use for the theater of the eighteen-nineties, still based for the most part on the even-tempered technique of Scribe and Sardou, whose dramas aimed at an exact-as-possible imitation of contemporary reality in dialogue and in scenic effect. Just about the only contemporary play Jarry admired was Ibsen's *Peer Gynt,* which, in the France of 1896, was still considered wildly heretical because of its poetic expansiveness and its bland disregard of all the current canons of playwriting theory. Jarry himself wished to go back to a theater that frankly admitted it was theater, back to the self-confessedly unrealistic theater that had last been seen in Elizabethan and *commedia dell'arte* times. The oft-quoted letter Jarry wrote to Lugné-Poë about the staging of *Ubu roi* in 1896 is very illuminating in this respect:

> It would be interesting . . . to be able to stage the play . . . on the following lines:
>
> Mask for the chief character, Ubu . . .
>
> A cardboard horse's head which he would hang from his neck, as they did in the old English theater, for the only two equestrian scenes, all of whose details are in the spirit of the play, as I intended to make it a "guignol."
>
> Adoption of a single set, or rather of a plain backcloth, doing away with the raising and lowering of the curtain during the single act. A conventionally dressed character would appear, as in the Guignols, and hang up a placard informing the audience of the location of the scene. (Note that I am certain that the written placard is much more "suggestive" than scenery. Neither scenery nor supers could represent "The Polish Army marching in the Ukraine.")
>
> No crowds; these are a mistake on the stage and hamper the intelligence. Thus a single soldier in the Review scene, a single one in the scrimmage where Ubu says: "What a gang, what a retreat," etc.
>
> The adoption of an "accent," or rather, a special "voice" for the chief character.
>
> The costumes should give as little as possible the impression of local color or chronology (this renders better the idea of something eternal). They should preferably be modern, as the satire is modern; and sordid, to make the play appear more wretched and horrific.[7]

7. Wallace Fowlie, ed., *Four Modern French Comedies* (New York: G. P. Putnam's Sons, 1960), pp. 23–24.

Jarry is here advocating stylization and suggestion as the best means of dramatic communication. For years past, theater people had been committed to the theory that drama was enhanced by imitating real life as precisely as possible. Inevitably this had strangled the drama because plays that imitated reality as precisely as possible were necessarily confined for the most part to a tedious, standardized, repetitive routine of respectable drawing rooms, opulent and plush (though still respectable) bedrooms, and an occasional ballroom or fashionable restaurant. Only in such dramas as Ibsen's *Brand* and *Peer Gynt* was the full potential of the drama realized. Jarry's letter to Lugné-Poë is a sketch of the practical technique that would make the staging of such plays possible.

Artaud formulated a coherent theatrical philosophy on the basis of Jarry's practices and random theoretical remarks. Briefly, Artaud saw drama as a means of expressing rebellion against the human condition. For him all drama was an action that emanated from a perception of man's helplessness in a universe of which he could comprehend only that it was implacably hostile. On a cosmic level man's cry of defiance is only that of a mote whirled around in a trackless void; but on the microcosmic level of the drama, man's protest attains the significance granted to it by its more restricted context. Later this view was to be formulated in nondramatic terms by Albert Camus in his concept of the absurd—the contrast between man's baffled impotence and the apparent malignity of an inscrutable eternity. Camus, also, advocated protest and defiance as a means—the only means possible—of nullifying the cruelty of the cosmic power on a temporal level. In Jarry's dramatic microcosmos this protest takes a far more primitive and instinctive form.

The last of Jarry's Ubu plays closes as Père Ubu fades away into the middle distance. Seated on the galley bench in potbellied, mock-heroic defiance, shackles on his legs and sweep oar in his hands, Ubu looks like some grotesque parody of Napoleon on his way to Elba. Like Napoleon, too, Ubu was destined to return. The exile was temporary only. Ubu continued to lie in wait, ready to leap out from his distant Avalon and save the drama from the curse of a too precise mimesis. Every so often he would make forays back to his former haunts. Careful observers could have dimly perceived him skittering about rather uncertainly behind the scenes of the post-World War I German expressionistic drama, giving an occasional uncharacteristically timid tug on the strings of one of the "*über*marionettes." He came forward somewhat more boldly in the surrealistic drama of Apollinaire and the early Cocteau. With the excesses of Dadaism, which were, however, largely of a nondramatic nature, Père Ubu was once more thunderously in evidence. And, finally, when Antonin Artaud created the Théâtre Alfred Jarry in 1927, and when he published his collection of manifestoes, *Le Théâtre et son Double* in 1938, Père Ubu came into his own again. Fully rehabilitated, even respectable now, he has waddled back onto the stage and now pervades the avant-garde drama like some enormous intangible and interpenetrating influence. Ubu is back with us—to stay. The seed that Gémier sowed on that momentous evening in 1896 has finally taken root and sprouted. With that incredibly simple yet explosively destructive word, Jarry changed the whole course of the future dramatic continuum. Indeed, the theater would never be the same again.

ANTONIN ARTAUD
The Prophet of the Avant-Garde Theater

ONE OF THE more curious and paradoxical aspects of modern theatrical history is that trends in the drama have been started not by the playwrights but by the critics. The dramatist presents the thesis, but it is the critical commentator who presents the counterthesis that is necessary before the final synthesis of a new theatrical movement can be produced. The drama of the past (the ancient Greek plays, the Roman comedy, the medieval mysteries and moralities, the Elizabethan heroic play, the eighteenth century sentimental drama, the nineteenth century melodrama and well-made jigsaw puzzle play) was "written down" to its particular audience: it was designed to be immediately comprehensible to its spectators. If it was not, it suffered the relegation to the closet shelf. In modern times, however, the drama has become more intellectual and sophisticated; and although the goal still is, as it always has been, to communicate directly to the audience, it has become something mysterious and puzzling. The simplicity of the drama of the past was such that dramatic movements were not discovered until they were dead; today the complexity of the drama is such that dramatic movements must be discovered by the critic before they can come to life.

The contemporary avant-garde theater—the theater of Ionesco, Beckett, Adamov, and Genet—is for most people a theater of mystification. Many go to see the plays of these authors because it is currently the fashionable thing to do. Crowds of people sit in darkened theaters and stare incredulously at lighted stages where plays are performed. Much of the confusion caused by these apparently willfully obscure playwrights might be cleared up by a study of the source of the ideas that animate them. All of the plays of the current avant-garde experimental drama have a common source in the theories of Antonin Artaud (1896–1948).

The dramatic theories of Artaud, as outlined in his chief critical work, *Le Théâtre et son Double,* represent the counter-thesis to the thesis of Alfred Jarry's seminal work, *Ubu roi.* Together they lead to the synthesis of the twentieth century avant-garde drama. Before Artaud had formulated his theories, the very real significance of Jarry's drama had passed unnoticed; and indeed it is only very recently that Jarry has come to be recognized as something more than an infantile prankster. The situation is in many ways analogous to the start given the modern problem-play movement by Shaw's criticism of Ibsen, who had previously been shunted aside—by the British public at any rate—as a tasteless trouble-maker. The spectacular riot that took place at the opening of *Ubu roi* in 1896 instantly established Jarry as France's leading *enfant terrible.* The play itself, however, was brushed aside as a piece of wantonly mischievous nonsense. Only a very few critics had the perceptiveness to observe the significance behind Jarry's nebulous overlay of apparent nonsense. One of them was William Butler Yeats, who attended the first performance. Rather wistfully, Yeats recognized that what he had seen was an important and irrevocable step forward in the development of comedy. Speaking of himself and the writers of his school, he said, "After us, the Savage God." Yeats' characterization of Jarry's comedy, and the movement it would breed, as the comedy of "the Savage God" was one of those instinctive insights that mark the great critic. "The Comedy of the Savage God" might almost be a catch phrase to describe the whole avant-garde movement. It is doubtful whether Jarry himself realized the full extent of what he was starting. His play, like the plays of the avant-gardists who came after him, is a play of pure rebellion, a comedy of the Savage God remorselessly trampling over everything that exists. The avant-grade drama is the comedy of nihilism and despair.

It took a critic of Antonin Artaud's temperament to perceive the far-reaching implications of Jarry's play. He saw Ubu as a powerful destructive force that had eliminated forever the convention-bound "drama as entertainment" or "drama with a purpose," which had dominated the stage for so long. After Ubu, drama had to return to its primal origins as an atavistic folk rite.

As Artaud saw it, what was wrong with drama, as well as with all the other arts, was culture. By "culture" Artaud meant the overlay of artificialities that civilization had imposed upon human nature. The *essence* of human nature, its basic and intrinsic quality, had become obscured by the unreal formal masks —the socially acceptable behavior patterns arbitrarily imposed on us by custom and tradition. Since art is reality, the artist's task was to strip away the layers of artificiality and expose the core of reality that had been hidden for so long. To Artaud this core was pure emotion; and the emotion was latent, instinctual savagery. He perceived that men are, as they always have been, basically barbaric, that the thick protective wall of urbane, civilized behavior they have acquired through centuries of hiding from psychological self-realization is easily crumbled by a forceful appeal to irrational emotion.

Culture, then, must be swept away. Only the instinctive human desires (anger, hate, longing, the physical desires, etc.) are worthy of consideration by the artist. Everything must be elemental—culture and all it implies, including form in art, is out of harmony with instinctive human emotion. We can see from this the real significance of Jarry's Ubu figure. No longer a mere tasteless prank, he becomes, through Artaud's scheme, the prototype of the elemental figure unencumbered by inhibition or respect for the veneer of law and order. The mere existence of a figure like Ubu, whose heedless freedom makes "civilized behavior" look ridiculous, is a protest in itself. And once something has been made to look ridiculous, it can never carry the same authority again.

The apparent perverseness and obscurity of the avant-garde drama is a direct outcome of the Ubu figure and the subsequent Artaud theories. It is an inevitable result of the confusion created in the human mind by its acquired fear of instinct and its ingrained habit of analyzing action. The spectator is confused because he shies away from overt displays of his own instinctual self and because he tries to analyze, i.e., understand, instead of responding and participating emotionally. The vitality of this new drama, despite the puzzlement of the audiences, indicates that the old intensity of instinct is still there, though it has hitherto been stifled.

The function of the drama, according to Artaud, is two-fold: it must, by being consistently uninhibited, protest against the artificial hierarchy of values imposed by culture, and it must, by a "drama of cruelty," demonstrate the true reality of the human soul and the relentless conditions under which it lives.

The manner in which this violent attack on the everyday is to be accomplished involves a fantastic, larger-than-life callousness that enables the characters to disregard the amenities of social behavior, and a rejection of speech as a means of communication. Speech, according to Artaud, is nontheatrical; therefore, strictly speaking, it has no place in the theater. The paradox forming the basis of Artaud's system of theatrical practice is that instead of clarifying the meaning of drama, instead of using the various elements of the theater (scenery, lighting, costumes, stage movement, etc.) to make the plays easier to understand, it is necessary to make the plays less easy to understand in order to make them the more accessible to instinctive human emotion. What Artaud meant by this was that ever since the theater had descended (as he saw it) from ritual to art form, all the essentially theatrical elements—those elements that distinguish the theater from other forms of expression—had been subordinated to speech. Everything that has ever been done in the theater since ancient Greece has been predicated on the assumption that the function of the theater is communication through speech. But speech—communication of rational thoughts—is the very thing that does not and cannot distinguish the theater from anything else—which makes it, in short, merely a branch of literature. If rational communication through speech is really the ultimate goal of the theater, then, according to Artaud, there is no point at all in going to the enormous trouble and expense of producing a play: it is obviously enough simply to read it. One can obtain information from the written word just as easily as from the spoken. Theater, Artaud decreed, must be theatrical, and speech is not theatrical, but literary. Therefore we must concentrate exclusively on those elements of the theater peculiar to it alone.

Through the ages the true nature of the theater had become

obscured. The demands of society shaped theater into something national, even local, reflecting the current mores and points of view of particular segments of humanity rather than universal human feeling. In this way the rational, imitative theater came into being; and problem plays (dealing with some specific aspect of some specific society) or irresponsible comedies designed for superficial entertainment became the vehicles of theatrical expression. Artaud's theater was therefore a return to the original purity of drama.

Artaud did consciously what Jarry had done instinctively when he wrote *Ubu roi:* he went back to the most primitive forms of the theater. To Artaud, theater was something that had been perfect in its beginnings and had been degenerating ever since as a result of contamination by civilized convention. Artaud felt that the theater had originally been the medium through which men expressed their unconscious feelings—the mysterious, nonrational essence of their beings. Inevitably, the first step in Artaud's program was the destruction of the present-day theater. He rebelled against everything that the contemporary theater represented: against society, against convention, against modern dramaturgy, even against the physical structure of the theater itself. Artaud had no wish to compromise or modify: he did not have the temperament to slither deviously to his objective. Revolt, overthrow, and complete, merciless destruction were the steps he recommended. The new theater had to be created as it had been created in the first place—from its original motivating forces.

Artaud rebelled not only against current methods of production, but against the current matter of production as well. He wanted drama to return to its elemental beginnings—yes; but Artaud was not merely an intellectual purist or a passionate dramatic archaeologist with a fetish for restoring originals. His reason for going back to the original form of drama was his conviction that the drama was an expression of the human condition. Unlike the ceremonies of religious worship, in which man abased himself before a superior power with the object of propitiating it, the ritual of the drama was man's assertion of his dignity and independence and was therefore a defiance and *protest* against the superior power. In religious observances man is nothing; in the self-expression of drama he is everything. Both are forms of worship, for both recognize the existence of a superior power. To love and to bow down to that superior power is no more an acknowledgement of its power and superiority than to hate and defy it. And the latter course is the nobler course because it is the truer: man has a right to his own feelings and his own dignity as a being. Reasoning thus, Artaud arrived at his concept of a theater pervaded by a sense of cosmic powers and by an attitude on the part of actors and audiences that simultaneously implied awe and defiance. Like Jarry and like all the other avant-garde writers who came after him, Artaud looked at mankind in much the same way that Pascal did, although the latter drew radically different conclusions from his view: *"Condition de l'homme: inconstance, ennui, inquiétude."* The condition of man was such because of the unrelenting malignancy of the incomprehensible cosmic powers that govern him. Hence the theater, which reflects the condition of man, must be a "theater of cruelty."

Cruelty in the theater does not mean, as Artaud was careful to emphasize, mere sadism: it is the impersonal, mindless—and therefore implacable—cruelty to which all men are subject. The universe with its violent natural forces was cruel in Artaud's eyes, and this cruelty, he felt, was the one single most important fact of which man must be aware. This cruelty is seen to some extent as viciousness between human beings. But such scenes must be presented in a manner calculated to purge the spectator of the corresponding emotions in him rather than to arouse in him the desire to imitate. At the same time, the spectator must be made aware of the violence dormant within himself and the omnipotence of the forces outside himself: each theatrical performance must shatter the foundations of the spectator's existence. It must show the spectator his own helplessness in the presence of the awesome and ineluctable forces that control the world. The theater must entangle the emotions, for the majority of the people use their senses rather than their intellect. It must be *ecstatic*. It must crush and hypnotize the onlooker's sense. It must have the same effect on the audience as the dances of the whirling dervishes and the ritual incantations and ceremonies of black magic. Like these ceremonies, the theater must combine submission and mystic union with protest and defiance.

The natural consequence of all this is that theater must be spontaneous. Since theater for Artaud is essentially a primitive ritual, it draws the spectators into the vortex of emotion generated by the actors. Unlike the separated and dispassionate onlookers in the modern theater, the audience should always be like extras who are part of the performance.

If, then, theater is to be spontaneous, it must use only works inspired by the emotion of the moment. In his essay "No More Masterpieces," Artaud explains that all the so-called masterpieces of dramatic literature must either be eliminated or brought up to date. The scholar's slavish cringing before and the layman's passive acceptance of the classics have no place in the new theater. Artaud maintains that there is no reason whatever to suppose that a work can be equally valid at all times. Even if its theme is still as valid as it was in the time the work was written, its structure must be altered to bring it into close harmony with the feelings of a contemporary audience. Artaud attacked the faithful rendition of masterpieces as "bourgeois conformism"—that clapboard superstructure of civilized behavior so antipathetic to his atavistic spirit. "Bourgeois conformism" makes us confuse sublime ideas with the forms they have taken in time. What must be said must be said in a way that is immediately accessible to the masses: "It is idiotic to reproach the masses for having no sense of the sublime when the sublime is confused with one or another of its formal manifestations, which are, moreover, always defunct manifestations." [1] Thus, for example, the themes of Sophocles's *Oedipus*

1. Antonin Artaud, *The Theatre and Its Double*, translated by Mary C. Richards. Copyright © 1958 by the Grove Press, Inc. (New York: Grove Press, Inc., 1958), p. 74.

Rex are as sublime as ever, but the form in which Sophocles embodied them, i.e., the dramatic form peculiar to the needs of the ancient Greek theater, is not. Sophocles's stately language, for one thing, is inappropriate for the "rude and epileptic rhythm" of our time. Oedipus-Rex does have all the elements that Artaud requires in a play. The relentless cruelty of the implacable forces that control man, the violence of human nature, the defiance of common mores in the incest theme—all are there. But they mean nothing if presented in the archaic form and language of the ancient Greek drama:

> . . . a public that shudders at train wrecks, that is familiar with earthquakes, plagues, revolutions, wars; that is sensitive to the disordered anguish of love, can be affected by all these grand notions and asks only to become aware of them, but on condition that it is addressed in its own language, and that its knowledge of these things does not come to it through adulterated trappings and speech that belong to extinct eras which will never live again.[2]

This statement crystallizes Artaud's aesthetic theory. Form, as such, has no meaning for him. All that matters is the theme of the play and the technique by which it can be presented most effectively. Plays must be changed in form and language in order to make them clear to the public. The only objection that might be made against this is that form is self-evidently an integral part of a work of art. Change the form of Oedipus Rex and you no longer have Oedipus Rex. What you have is a different play on the same theme, like the modern reinterpretations of the classical drama by Sartre, Giraudoux, and Anouilh. Artaud's answer to this would be that if modernizing a play means destroying it, then it must be destroyed. In short, Artaud sees drama as a set of important themes floating around amorphously, ready to be shaped into whatever form the all-powerful metteur en scène (a combination of producer, director, and author in Artaud's system) wishes to give them.

2. Ibid., p. 75.

Artaud was above all a practical—and practicing—theater man. His theories may sound vague, but he described very specifically how he wanted them carried out in actual practice. Artaud maintained that a production should concentrate only on those aspects of the drama that are purely *theatrical*, i.e., that require the medium of the stage to be intelligible. Music, dance, plastic art, pantomime, vocal mimicry, lighting, and scenery fall into this category. When properly combined, they form what Artaud called the "poetry of space." Thus the "poetry of speech," which has always been the theater's chief medium of expression, is eliminated. This is not to say that Artaud intended to transform the theater into a vehicle for pure mime. Speech might still be used in the theater, but not for the communication of ideas and not in such a way as to make it an end in itself. Words can be used on the stage as sound *per se* —as intonations. As such, their purpose would no longer be to communicate thought, but to bring about an emotional effect. For example, a hoarse, rasping, aspirated roar might indicate a feeling of terror. Artaud's idea of the function of words is rather similar to that of Ionesco's Professor in *The Lesson*: "words charged with significance will fall, weighted down by their meaning, and in the end they always collapse, fall . . . on deaf ears." Like the Professor, Artaud would like to have only "purely irrational assemblages of sounds, denuded of all sense" floating allusively around at high altitudes, where they can charge the atmosphere with a pervading emotion, far above the "deaf ears" of the mind. Insofar as there is to be anything at all even remotely approaching the communication we are accustomed to in the ordinary theater, Artaud would like to convey to the onlookers a generalized impression of a state of mind rather than the communication of facts. Clearly this can only be managed by means of symbols—which on the stage would have to take the form of a formalized sign language. In this "unperverted pantomime" (a term Artaud uses to distinguish it from the type of pantomime ordinarily seen in the theater, which merely substitutes gestures for words as a means of communicating specific ideas) the gestures represent "ideas, attitudes of mind, aspects of nature" instead of words and sentences. As an example Artaud cites the oriental device of representing Night by a tree on which a bird that has already closed one eye is beginning to close the other. This evocation of images or states of mind rather than specific thoughts may be termed a macrocosmic approach to theatrical art rather than the microcosmic one now in use. Like all visionaries, Artaud always saw the large view, the ecstatic, all-embracing concept; thinkers and analyzers, on the other hand, always work through specific instances. In a sense, Artaud was going back to the intellectual method of the Scholastics, rejecting the reform of the inductively minded Renaissance thinkers.

In the drama of Artaud, the *metteur en scène* is responsible both for the text and for the manner of its presentation. The text as written has no authority whatsoever, and the *metteur en scène* is perfectly free to alter it at will. It is his business to transform the text into a set of "animated hieroglyphs" that will involve everyone's emotions. Artaud suggested that this can best be done by a technique of interpenetration of action and audience. That is to say, the old partition between action and audience, which was achieved by the artificial dividing line of the proscenium arch or the barrier of the front-row seats, must be eliminated. The stage will continue to exist, but a great part of the action will be carried on *in* the audience and all around it. Instead of the auditorium being lined-up in front of the stage, as in the theater of conventional design, or around the stage, as in the arena theater, *the stage will surround the audience.* In this way, the audience, seated on swivel chairs, will be encompassed by the action and will feel itself to be part of it instead of hovering over it like students at a surgical demonstration. The theatrical devices that will involve the audience will consist of music, lights, color, masks, and rhythmic physical movement. In addition, Artaud planned to insert novel devices that would serve as hieroglyphs indicating the supernatural forces surrounding man. These would include apparitions, effigies yards high dressed in costumes based on old ritual models, stereophonic sound, and "new and surprising objects." [3] Thus every play would be rewritten by the Supreme Godhead of the New Theater, the Director-Author or *metteur en scène*, in order to fit into the new hieroglyphic language of the stage. The stage will surround the audience, and the auditorium will resound to the eerie wails, the unearthly moans, and the nerve-rending screams of Artaud's apparitions. Often, instead of rearranging already existing plays, the *metteur en scène* will piece together a "drama" on some appropriately awe-inspiring theme as he goes along. A quote from Artaud's tentative repertoire for his new theater makes this clearer:

We shall stage, without regard for text:

1] An adaptation of a work from the time of Shakespeare, a work entirely consistent with our present troubled state of mind, whether one of the apocryphal plays of Shakespeare, such as *Arden of Feversham,* or an entirely different play from the same period.

2] A play of extreme poetic freedom by Léon-Paul Fargue.

3] An extract from the *Zohar:* "The Story of Rabbi Simeon," which has the ever-present violence and force of a conflagration.

4] The story of Bluebeard reconstructed according to the historical records and with a new idea of eroticism and cruelty.

5] The Fall of Jerusalem, according to the Bible and history; with the blood-red color that trickles from it and the people's feeling of abandon and panic visible even in the light; and on the other hand the metaphysical disputes of the prophets, the frightful intellectual agitation they create and the repercussions of which physically affect the King, the Temple, the People, and Events themselves.

---

3. For example, the Ubu figure, the "terrible cry" and "menace" in *Waiting for Godot,* the "awful presence" outside the room in *Endgame,* the growing body in Ionesco's *Amédée,* the loud speaker in Adamov's *La grande et la petite Manoeuvre,* Jarry's disembraining machine, the mausoleum in Genet's *The Balcony.*

6] A Tale by the Marquis de Sade, in which the eroticism will be transposed, allegorically mounted and figured, to create a violent exteriorization of cruelty, and a dissimulation of the remainder.

7] One or more romantic melodramas in which the improbability will become an active and concrete element of poetry.

8] Büchner's *Wozzeck*, in a spirit of reaction against our principles and as an example of what can be drawn from a formal text in terms of the stage.

9] Works from the Elizabethan theater stripped of their text and retaining only the accoutrements of period, situations, characters, and action.[4]

This list of tentative productions was never realized in fact. Artaud's only opportunity to put his theories into practice with absolute freedom came between 1927 and 1929, when he and Roger Vitrac ran their own theater, significantly named the Théâtre Alfred Jarry. Here he produced *Les Cenci*, which he adapted from the Shelley and Stendhal versions, several of Vitrac's plays, Strindberg's *Dream Play*, the third act of Claudel's *Partage du Midi* (acted as a farce), and several other things. But Artaud is not important as a mere transformer of other men's work. He was the catalytic agent for an entirely new drama that used the complex resources of the modern theater to express the age-old cry of fear and protest, the most elemental human impulse from the most primitive man to the present. Taking the sudden outburst of primitive elemental force that Jarry's *Ubu roi* projected into the theater as his starting point, Artaud continued to define a drama denuded of all the excess and essentially nondramatic elements which had accumulated around the art of the theater through the ages. Artaud's drama may be compared to the bare trunk of a tree stripped of all the shrubbery that usually obscures its reality; but the only tree that would have satisfied Artaud would have been Yggdrasil, the sacred, magical, awe-inspiring ash which penetrates to the center of the earth and to the core of life itself. From this tree sprang the modern avant-garde drama—

4. Artaud, *op. cit.*, pp. 99–100.

the plays of Beckett, Ionesco, and Adamov (who in 1947 called Artaud the greatest living poet), of Genet, Audiberti, and Jean Tardieu, and of the other avant-garde playwrights. All their plays are concerned with man's subjection to a malignant fate, all of them discard sociology and psychology as media for building characters, and all of them move in a purely theatric, dreamlike atmosphere. This dreamlike atmosphere (which becomes overt in plays like Adamov's *Professor Taranne*, Ionesco's *Victims of Duty*, and Beckett's *Embers*) is not accidental, but is rather the key to the whole technique. Artaud felt that men see themselves clearly only in dreams; and that it was through dreams that men could reach back to the primeval past when drama was born as the ritual observance of the myths whose creation is coeval with the beginning of human thought itself. Artaud's theory of the dream is allied to the Jungian theory, in which dreams bind men together through their demonstration of an inherited collective unconscious. Artaud opposed Freud's theory of dreams because it showed the effects of individually different psychoneurotic repressions—and so is closely allied to the modern drama of individual character analysis.

The use of the dream technique is basic to Artaud's drama. It enabled him to use speech in a purely theatrical and non-literary manner; and it enabled him to justify his use of visual communication through hieroglyphic symbols, which is the method by which dream communication takes place. It was through the use of the dream technique, too, that Artaud could present the apparitions, effigies, and other "shocks and surprises" which could bring the audience into the desired mystic union with one another, with the action, and with the cruel, primeval, juggernautlike forces governing the world.

ARTHUR ADAMOV
The Way Out of the Void

ARTHUR ADAMOV's early plays illustrate in their purest form the principles of the avant-garde drama. In all the dramas of the current avant-garde the purpose is protest against the hopelessness of the human condition and against the strictures imposed on the individual by society. The method by which this protest is conveyed is the method of paradox, in which a truth is presented by an exaggerated emphasis on its opposite.

Like most modern dramatists, Adamov has a thoroughly pessimistic outlook on life. His themes are the tyranny of parental love; the innate cruelty of the society in which we are forced to live; and the meaninglessness, futility, and confusion of everyday life.

The tyranny of parental love, which the avant-gardists consider one of the oppressions inherent in human existence, is treated by Adamov in *Les Retrouvailles* (The Recoveries, published 1955) and *Le Sens de la Marche* (this title cannot be translated as it contains two double meanings in the French— The Direction of the March, The Meaning of the Way). These two plays deal with, respectively, an amorphous mother image that literally forces the son back to a state of physical infancy; and with a son who rebels against a father and a father-substitute, finally killing the latter. *Les Retrouvailles* is a play of hopelessness whose final scene is strongly reminiscent of the scene in Strindberg's *The Father* in which the Captain reverts to an infantile state under the pressure of his nurse-mother. Beyond this grotesquely powerful final curtain scene, however, there is little of interest in *Les Retrouvailles*. *Le Sens de la Marche* is more in the mainstream of the modern avant-garde movement as a play of rebellion. In this often incoherent and badly constructed play the son carries on a rebellion against society, the army, love, and finally his father, a crotchety, demanding old man who, in all but actual physical appearance, is the traditional Xanthippo-Oedipal stage mother. The son finally purges himself of the poisonous parental influence by strangling his father's companion and alter ego in a fit of uncontrollable, instinctive, self-purifying rebellion.

Even in these thematically fragmentary plays Adamov follows the pattern of protest, which is the chief characteristic of the modern avant-garde drama.[1] He protests against the merciless cruelty of the world—a cruelty that is at once inhuman and superhuman, omnipresent in the external and immanent in the individual's inner world, an almost tangible entity in itself and at the same time an emanation of a greater, instinctively malicious entity. The purpose of the protest, as Camus has shown us in *The Rebel,* is to curtail the cruel power *by rebelling against it.* The power against which the protest is made is thwarted to an extent directly in proportion to the violence of the protest. The reason for this is the postulated theory that all power, whether temporal or metaphysical, is based upon an imbalance of strength and weakness which can never reach perfect equilibrium; but the delicately poised scale adjusts instantly to any change, so that a gain on one side automatically involves a corresponding loss on the other. Thus if the violence of the protest is sufficiently radical, as in the son's murder of the father-substitute in *Le Sens de la Marche,* the scale tips over entirely, and one particular aspect of the universal, all-pervading cruelty is triumphantly vanquished. In *Les Retrouvailles,* on the other hand, the son's protest is unsuccessful, and the play ends with the sudden and complete triumph of the forces of cruelty as the mother wheels her full-grown son off in a baby carriage.

The sense of cosmic cruelty that appears in Adamov's work is accompanied and balanced in most cases by a narrower, specifically human type of cruelty. The sense of helplessness that man experiences when confronted by the metaphysical world is intensified by his confrontation with the same helplessness and thwarted desire when he turns to his fellow men. Man becomes a dumb animal frustratedly bellowing back and forth across a

1. The best piece of scholarship on Adamov to appear in English so far is Martin Esslin's "Arthur Adamov: The Curable and the Incurable" in *The Theatre of the Absurd* (Garden City, N. Y.: Doubleday & Company, Inc., 1961), pp. 47–78.

crowded space that seems to him a void. Adamov has recorded for us how an ordinary street incident first made him aware of the dramatic possibilities of mutual solitude. He saw one day two young girls passing a blind beggar on the street. As they passed arm-in-arm, oblivious of the beggar, they sang a popular song of the day, the words of which went, *"J'ai fermé les yeux, c'était merveilleux"* (I closed my eyes; it was wonderful). As soon as he saw this, Adamov tells us, he said to himself, "That's theatre, that's what I want to do." [2] It is significant that this particular incident should have stimulated a modern dramatist, for it is exactly the opposite of what has always been thought dramatic. Here we have the absence of communication, the absence of human sympathy and emotion, and above all the absence of conflict. Adamov concentrates in his early plays (*La Parodie, L'Invasion, La grande et la petite Manoeuvre, Tous contre Tous*) on this impersonal type of drama in which the characters have no psychological individuality. These plays are a sort of mystic ritual dance between two magnets with the like poles constantly turned towards each other. Nothing decisive ever happens, except the inevitable, meaningless and reasonless death at the end, which represents the remerging of the human with the greater impersonal controlling power. During the play the characters move aimlessly in mutually exclusive spheres running on courses unfathomable to their occupants.

The theme of cruelty within the social system shows up in *Tous contre Tous* (All Against All, 1953) and *Paolo Paoli* (1957). In the earlier play the theme is treated in general symbolic terms; in the later one in specific, individual terms. *Tous contre Tous* is undoubtedly Adamov's best play. It is about the instinctive mutual enmity human beings display toward each other. The play is not so much an indictment of a social system which forces human beings to act in their habitual dog-eat-dog manner as an implication that the social system is a result of human nature. A social system, Adamov is saying, is no more than a conglomeration of individuals and

2. Arthur Adamov, *Théâtre* (Paris: Gallimard, 1955), II, p. 8.

their traits. The only rule the individual respects is the rule of self; therefore, the society in which he lives is an impersonal one where the law of self-preservation is the only guiding principle and treachery the accepted mode of conduct.

Briefly, *Tous contre Tous* concerns the persecution of a particular group of people within the society. These people are distinguished from the rest of their fellows by having a limp. They are used as scapegoats whenever a scapegoat is needed. Between these persecutions they are tolerated and even respected, since many of them show an ability to be even more unscrupulous than their straight-walking compatriots and are therefore more successful. The ironic thing is that the trait that supposedly distinguishes them from the rest of the populace—their limp—is by no means confined to them. There are plenty of people who limp but are not *réfugiés*, and plenty who do not limp but are *réfugiés*. Naturally the people who limp but are not really *réfugiés* are the ones who are the most rabid enemies of the *réfugiés*. The play as a whole may be described as a microcosmic view of treachery, hate, and double-dealing. The characters are driven to deceive each other and injure or betray each other by the impersonal, blandly mischievous power represented by the radio, whose announcements at the beginning of each scene determine the characters' actions. The characters are skeletal puppets, stripped bare of all dignity and feeling—obsessed only by their desire to survive at any cost.

As in all plays of rebellion, death is the great enemy. Here, though, the inevitably futile struggle against the onslaught of death does not produce the heroic protester, but a small, sneaking, sniveling, shameless schemer who tries to subvert death, to slide unnoticed away from it, to shove someone else into its jaws instead of defying it. As one reads the play, one feels only disgust and revulsion at such a picture of the human race. But it is a true picture; there is no doubt of that. Adamov explicitly states in his introduction to the play that it is an allegory of the Central European persecution of the Jews and of the attempt of many of those Jews to continue living their old lives at whatever price to their personal dignity.[3] The play ends—necessarily—with the brutal, violent and, above all, *senseless* death of all the main characters.

In *Paolo Paoli* Adamov again took up the theme of social cruelty he began in *Tous contre Tous*. This time, however, he has treated the matter in terms of specific individuals rather than in generalized terms.

Paolo Paoli shows the development in France of a state of mind that made World War I possible. In order to present this story Adamov has taken over a stage technique perfected by Bertolt Brecht in *Der Aufhaltsame Aufstieg des Arturo Ui* (The Preventable Rise of Arturo Ui). Each of the twelve scenes is preceded by a short "movie show" of pictures and extracts from newspapers, magazines, and speeches of the pre-World War I period. These provide an ironic contrast with the action that follows and serve to put that action into its proper historical focus. Adamov himself states that the purpose of the technique is to remind the audience how war was slowly but inevitably being prepared underneath the veneer of carefree and euphoric living.[4] The tragedy of the political events described in the screen projections is underlined by an accompaniment of contemporary popular songs, which slowly change to military marches as the play progresses. The idea is excellent, but the actual story of Paolo Paoli is simply dull. In turning from the general to the specific, Adamov has paradoxically lost the knack of telling a story in dramatic terms. The specific petty chicaneries of Paolo Paoli as he trades in butterfly bodies may be symbolic of a materialism that sacrifices esthetic values for commercial considerations, but they are not interesting in themselves. The continuous vacillation from faithfulness to adultery of Paoli's half-Catholic, half-Protestant, Franco-German wife may be symbolic of a moral degeneration which,

3. *Ibid.*, p. 14.
4. This remark does not appear in the French edition (Paris: Gallimard, 1957) but shows up in the prefatory note to Pierre Aron's German translation (Arthur Adamov, *Theaterstücke* [Darmstadt: Hermann Luchterhand Verlag, 1959], pp. [187]–320).

when raised to the social level, leads inevitably to war, but it is merely dull in itself. In *Tous contre Tous*, on the other hand, the generalized actions of the frankly symbolic characters are far more interesting because the audience is able to transfer them to its own specific experiences and observations.

Adamov's first two plays, *La Parodie* (The Parody, written 1947, performed 1952) and *L'Invasion* (The Invasion, written 1949, performed 1950), deal with the mutual isolation of human beings. The world depicted in these plays resembles the one envisioned by Leibnitz, who saw an endless rain of self-contained monads floating blindly down through space, accidentally bumping into each other now and then. However, since these monads are "windowless," the occupants have no more real contact with each other than the yolks of two eggs lying side by side with the shells touching. Whenever two of these drifting cells bump into one another, the persons inside are jarred, but they have no idea what has disturbed them. Consequently their reactions have absolutely nothing to do with the real facts of the situation. Even more often some undefined but malicious and invisible power reaches out and casually crushes a monad, so that the person inside is either killed or maimed.

La Parodie is, as the title indicates, a parody of human existence. There is no plot to speak of. The two leading characters, identified only as N and The Employee, represent, respectively, rejection and acceptance of life as it is. Both are destroyed in the end, so that Adamov appears to be saying that it does not matter what one's attitude to life is—that it is pointless indeed to bother having any attiude at all—since it all comes to the same thing in the end.

In his second play, *L'Invasion*, Adamov changed his method but not his theme. Instead of using type chracters in an undefined setting, as in *La Parodie*, he used specific people in a specific, realistic setting. But the idea remains the same: nobody listens to anybody else. Everyone lives wrapped up in the cocoon of his own personal absorptions. The title of the play refers to the "invasion" that human beings suffer through social obligations; through the presence of other people, who are in their turn absorbed in and weighed down by their own preoccupations; and through the constant pressure of inanimate external forces that can only with great difficulty be brought into harmony with the individual's inner life. All these influences work upon the individual like an insidious, creeping paralysis until he is completely stripped of his own character.

In *L'Invasion* the victim of this assault is a scholar who has decided to devote his whole existence to the endless task of editing and publishing the papers of his dead friend. In the opening scene he is eagerly attacking the piles of paper lying all over the room in utter confusion. As the play progresses, the piles of paper slowly become sorted and stacked away so that, at the end, the room is as neat as a business office. As this external tidying process advances, the victim's internal tidiness decreases in direct proportion. At the end, the scholar stands in the middle of his room, utterly confused among all the apparent neatness and order. He tears up all the papers, which constitute his life's work, and kills himself. Life has simply been too much for him, and so he leaves it. Instead of being permitted to cope with what interests him most in life, he is forced to take into account his mother, his wife, and her lover, a rival scholar who disagrees with his method of editing, and others. The solution is, of course, needlessly drastic, but Adamov has always been of the opinion that the solution to any human problem when it is presented in dramatic terms must be the ultimate solution. In Adamov the climax of a human event must always involve the relentless destruction of the hero. *L'Invasion*, then, is simply the drama of each person's isolation within himself and the impossibility of mutual adjustment.

La grande et la petite Manoeuvre (The Great and the Small Manoeuvre, 1950) and *Le Professeur Taranne* (Professor Taranne, 1953) are two dream plays in which, by means of a breakthrough into the subconscious world, the individual gains a momentary (and horrifying) glimpse of the world outside his monad. The inevitable result is that he is destroyed. The basic emotion running through both these plays is fear: the protagonist becomes gradually more and more conscious of the fact that every time he comes into contact with the outside world he will be hurt. In *La grande et la petite Manoeuvre* we have the picture of a harmless, terrified person caught between the active opposing factions of the modern world: between the rebels and the oppressors. This eternal victim, called "Le Mutilé," is constantly controlled by invisible voices, audible only to him, which tell him what to do and where to go. Every time he hears these voices he begins to tremble violently and feels impelled to go away. Whenever he comes back after obeying one of these mysterious orders, we find that he has lost a limb. At the end of the play he is an armless and legless cripple in a wheelchair. His gradual destruction has no reason: he is simply a victim of more powerful forces.

La grande et la petite Manoeuvre is an intensely bizarre allegorical dream about the cruelty of life; *Le Professeur Taranne* is an equally bizarre personal nightmare. Like its companion play, *Le Professeur Taranne* is about a man's amazed horror on discovering the obverse side of the world, the unseen one outside his cocoon. Professor Taranne is the epitome of self-centered harmlessness set down in the midst of an amorphous nightmare world inexplicably crystallized into reality. Both he and The Mutilated One undergo a long, slow, symbolic castration at the end of which they simply give up—human flies caught on the cosmic flypaper.

Professor Taranne's dream is that he, a famous savant, has been arrested because some children have accused him of walking around nude on the beach. The professor's explanation is essentially only an ineffective excuse for repeating assertions of his eminence in the scholarly world. But he finds that the things on which he has based his life mean absolutely nothing to anyone else. In the police station he goes up to several persons he knows well but is recognized by none of them. One person even mistakes him for his archrival, Professor Ménard. Immediately after his second encounter with the police, the professor is accused of scribbling obscenities on the walls of the bathing huts. As before, his bewildered explanation is cut short by the abrupt departure of the policemen, who suddenly lose interest in him. After this the professor receives an enormous map of a ship's dining room that shows him placed next to the captain in the seat of honor. While he is poring over this, he receives a letter from the foreign university where he has been a guest lecturer telling him that he will not be invited back because he has plagiarized Professor Ménard and because no one ever paid any attention to his lectures anyway. As the play ends, Professor Taranne hangs the map of the ship's dining room on the wall. It is seen to be a blank sheet of paper. Contemplating this sight with the ruminative attention of a scholar unhurriedly and carefully digesting a new discovery, the professor begins slowly to undress himself.

In *Le Ping-Pong* (Ping-Pong, 1955) the point of view is entirely changed. Adamov has abandoned the deterministic play for a more flexible, psychological drama. The characters are no longer helpless automatons but human beings endowed with free will. The people of *Ping-Pong* choose their own destiny and only they are to blame if, incapable of rebelling, they become the victims of superior *manmade* powers. Instead of a cosmic power to rebel against, the characters in *Ping-Pong* are given only a modest socioeconomic power to fight. The play is concerned with the reactions of two young students Arthur and Victor and the people around them to a pinball machine. The machine, which symbolizes money and prestige, can, of course, simply be left alone; one can play it or not, as one pleases. Nevertheless it has an absolutely irresistible attraction for the two young men and their friends. The flashing lights, the glistening steel balls, the jerking flippers, and the implacable bumpers draw them on like a magnet. They hang over the monstrous machine like degenerates over an opium pipe. The machine replaces religion; and the corporation, with "the Old Man" at the top, replaces the celestial hierarchy. The lust for money and the ephemeral prestige that comes with it has stifled all the formerly powerful spiritual values, Adamov is saying. But at the same time there is a choice in Adamov's philosophy now: one does not have to play. All the characters, however, devote the best part of their lives to the corporation. At the end of the play comes the scene which gives it its name.

In this scene, which Adamov wrote first and which he admits has no organic connection with the rest of the play,[5] Arthur and Victor, both old men now, play ping-pong. They begin to quarrel over the rules of the game, as they did in their younger days over the operation of the pinball machine, and finally wind up playing ping-pong without net or paddles. As Victor tries to leap in the air to bat the ball down with his bare hand, he falls dead.

Le Ping-Pong and *Paolo Paoli* mark an interesting evolution in the work of a typical avant-garde playwright. Like Ionesco, Adamov has abandoned the doctrinaire determinism of Antonin Artaud's faithful followers. Both Ionesco (*The Killer* and *Rhinoceros*) and Adamov have come around to the view that man, despite his admitted feebleness, can still struggle to *some* effect and therefore has moral responsibility. From here it is a direct step to the complete absorption with social responsibility that Adamov has shown in the anti-Gaullist sketches he published in 1958[6] and in his latest play, *Le Printemps 71* (Springtime '71, 1960). In the preface to this play about the Paris Commune, modeled partly on Brecht, whom Adamov has taken as his new mentor,[7] and partly on Büchner, Adamov states that by writing a historical play, "I was at last able to escape from those 'interiors' where I was suffocating, and to speak not only of the bourgeoisie, but of everyone, of those who make up the majority of people—that is to say, whether one likes it or not, of the proletariat." [8] With this step Adamov leaves the death-oriented hopelessness that is the avant-garde drama's chief philosophical standpoint and returns to a belief in the temporal hopes that exist in the illusion-laden world of social humanity.

5. Adamov, *Théâtre*, II, p. 17.

6. Arthur Adamov, Guy Demoy, and Maurice Regnaut, *Théâtre de Société (scènes d'actualité)* (Paris: Petite bibliothèque républicaine, 1958), pp. 9–52.

7. The old one was obviously Antonin Artaud despite Adamov's doubts about his influence on himself and on the subsequent theater in general. Cf. Arthur Adamov, "Parce que je l'ai beaucoup aimé . . . ," *Cahiers de la Compagnie Madeleine Renaud - Jean-Louis Barrault*, Nos. 22 and 23 (May, 1958), pp. 128–29.

8. Arthur Adamov, *Le Printemps 71* (Paris: Gallimard, 1961), p. [5].

Unfortunately, in his subsequent plays Adamov has emphasized the illusion rather than the humanity as he has adopted a more and more extreme leftist position. His enmity towards the pseudo-democratic political system of the West has, as is so often the case with people whose political "thinking" consists of a Pavlovian twitch rather than rational analysis, turned Adamov into a leftist reactionary. This transformation, unhappily, is not always one that makes the writer's thinking puerile and contemptible. An emotional reaction *should* produce puerile and contemptible thinking, but such is not invariably the case: when Adamov writes about the perversions of justice and decency committed by whites against Negroes in the South or in South Africa under the guise of law, as he does in *La Politique des Restes* (this is an ambiguous title, probably best translated as *The Politics of Garbage*, 1963), the wildest flights of outraged fancy are unable to surpass the recorded instances of reality. The damage here is to the writer's artistry even more than to his thinking since it produces a strident, argumentative tone that becomes irritating and even insulting to the reader or spectator who is not wholly in agreement with the author's views to begin with. Conversely, it may produce an atmosphere of suffocating boredom by its insistence on leaving nothing out, stifling the action of the play in tedious and often doctrinaire talk. Such is the case with *Sainte Europe (Holy Europe,* 1966), which starts out well enough—given Adamov's political views— with a prologue that juxtaposes St. Bernard of Clairvaux calling for the Second Crusade to a Nazi general calling for a crusade against "Asiatic" Bolshevism in 1941. This is paralleled in the musical accompaniment by a melange of Gregorian chants and "Deutschland über Alles." The central figure of the play is the Emperor Karl, a combination of Charlemagne, Charles V, and de Gaulle. Unfortunately, after this potentially excellent basic situation is established, the play peters out into a lot of talk irrelevant to the plot and a great deal of criticism and satire of de Gaulle, which may well be justified but is vitiated by being so obviously ill-tempered. This is equally true of *Off Limits* (1969—the original title is in English), an extremely chaotic play

about American reactions to the Vietnam War, which Adamov
says is based on his own experiences in the United States. Insofar as the play can be deciphered at all, it concerns two young
American pacifists and drug addicts who are both shot while
attempting to escape across the Mexican border so that the boy
can escape the draft. Adamov attempts to contrast their honesty
with the cynicism of a group of journalists and TV producers,
but the expression of his purpose loses itself in his indignation.

SAMUEL BECKETT
Life in the Void

SAMUEL BECKETT first came to the attention of the American public with the Broadway production of *Waiting for Godot* (En Attendant Godot, 1953) in 1956. The play received a sort of perverse notoriety because nobody was quite sure what it was all about. The public went to see it because Bert Lahr was in it (as Estragon) and because some cunning publicity work based largely on intellectual snob appeal had convinced them that going to see *Waiting for Godot* was the thing to do. The play thus received a longer run on Broadway than it had any right to expect, and Beckett's name suddenly became a well-known one in the American theater. Since then *Endgame* (Fin de Partie, 1957) and *Krapp's Last Tape* (1958) have been successful off Broadway, and Beckett's novels have been published by Grove Press. None of Beckett's works conforms to the orthodox literary form of its genre; none of them is easy to understand. One thing is obvious about them, however: they all appear to throw off a stark pessimism about human affairs that has rarely, if ever, been equaled in literature.

Naturally enough, a great deal of critical writing about Beckett has quickly appeared. This writing is disturbing, to say the least. Confronted with a writer who takes as uncomprisingly uncomfortable a viewpoint as Beckett, the critics have frantically tried to justify his existence by seeing signs of their own views in his works. The main point of the criticism is that Beckett could not possibly mean what he appears to mean because that would be very unpleasant indeed. In short, what is happening to Beckett is very much like what happened to Shaw: unable to face up to him, the critics have attempted to snuff him out by hailing him as a Member of the Establishment.

Perhaps the most curiously uncomprehending view of Beckett comes from Frederick Lumley. Lumley represents the reactions of the "pillar-of-society" theatergoer, who goes to plays to be entertained and to have his beliefs reaffirmed. It is surprising to see how outmoded this point of view has become in the few years since the first productions of Beckett, Ionesco, and the rest of the avant-garde dramatists. There is something amusingly anachronistic about Lumley's plaint: this is criticism from the vantage point of the English country garden satirized in Wilde:

> Even at the risk of sounding like a second Clement Scott writing on a new *Ghosts*, it seems to this writer that this play is more akin to a cesspool of the degradations of human souls than a tragedy of misfortune. Is there no limit to the depths to which man may descend and is there so little faith left in man that he must lie here forgotten? Will he never be given a resurrection, will we never again have new horizons opened to us through the nobility of man, and be able to enter a world not altogether unlike our own where there is no exploitation of facile optimism or morbid despair? [1]

Lumley's desire to run away from this world to a new stage world where man will be comfortably exalted is in itself a sub-conscious recognition of the truth of Mephistopheles's remark in Marlowe's *Dr. Faustus*, "Why this is hell, nor am I out of it." Lumley and the daily-newspaper reviewers are aware, at least, that the world of Beckett, even if it is a true world, is not the world they want to see. To the extent that they condemn it, they are honest critics. Honest also, if naïve and unrealistic, is the criticism of Bonamy Dobrée, the historian of eighteenth-century literature, who, in writing about *Waiting for Godot*, informs us that "it is time to affirm that anything that can be called art must ultimately be in praise of life, or must at least promote acceptance of life, thus indicating some values." [2] Less honest are the "romantic" critics. By romantic criticism I mean the quality of seeing what one would like to see rather than what is really there. An example of starry-eyed romanticism at its most extreme would be Kenneth Rexroth's reading of a

1. Frederick Lumley, *Trends in Twentieth Century Drama* (London: Barrie & Rockliff, 1960), p. 142.
2. Bonamy Dobrée, "The London Theatre, 1957," *Sewanee Review*, LXVI (Winter, 1958), p. 152.

plea for universal brotherhood into *Waiting for Godot:* "the comradeship of men, whether verminous tramps with unmanageable pants or Jim and Huck Finn drifting through all the universe on their raft—the comradeship of men in work, in art, or simply in waiting, in the utterly unacquisitive act of waiting—is an ultimate value, so ultimate that it gives life sufficient dignity and satisfaction." [3] According to Rexroth, Beckett is writing about only the last two hundred years when he writes about the sickness of society. His point is the same as Homer's—that we must accept the world on secular terms and believe in the brotherhood of man, represented by Vladimir and Estragon. [4] Leonard Pronko also emphasizes this quality of "togetherness" when he says that *Waiting for Godot* shows that the quality of friendship is the only solace human beings have on this earth. [5] Pronko sees *Endgame* as a picture of the disintegration of a human universe, [6] but he can still somehow conclude that Beckett's view of life is basically religious. [7] Following the same line of thought, Edith Kern sees *Waiting for Godot* as glorifying "the all-surpassing power of human tenderness," which, she feels, is a substitute for the real redeemer, who never comes and for whom men wait with forlorn hope. [8]

Worst of all, perhaps, is the attribution of Christian principles to Beckett. *Waiting for Godot* is particularly fertile ground for the symbol-seeker, and since there are undeniable references to God, Christianity, and the Bible in the play, it is quite easy to give it a religious interpretation with some judicious out-of-context quoting. Charles S. McCoy, Professor of Religion in Higher Education at the Pacific School of Religion, points out that "each interpreter runs the risk of merely reading into the

3. Kenneth Rexroth, "The Point is Irrelevance," *The Nation* (April 14, 1956), p. 328.

4. *Ibid.*

5. Leonard Pronko, *Avant-Garde* (Berkeley, Cal.: University of California Press, 1962), p. 39.

6. *Ibid.*, p. 47.

7. *Ibid.*, p. 54.

8. Edith Kern, "Drama Stripped for Inaction: Beckett's *Godot,*" *Yale French Studies,* No. 14 (Winter, 1954–1955), p. 47.

play his own point of view." [9] Having pointed out the trap,
he disregards it. He concludes, for example, that Godot *does*
come because the tree sprouts leaves in the second act, and a
tree is a symbol of the Cross and of life.[10] God(ot) is thus
immanent throughout the second act, but mankind is too willfully blind to see him. This is an ingenious interpretation, but
it ignores the overwhelming evidence of Beckett's lack of faith
to be found in his other plays and in his novels, as well as in
Waiting for Godot itself when looked at as a whole. The tree
is again plucked out by another Christian critic, who sees it
as the Tree of the Knowledge of Good and Evil, the Tree of
Life, the Cross, and the Tree of Judas. He concludes that *Waiting for Godot* is a "modern morality play on permanent Christian themes" and represents the "tension and uncertainty in
which the average Christian must live in this world." [11]

Another dangerous pitfall when dealing with a writer as
objective as Beckett is the biographical approach. Horace Gregory compares Beckett's characters to ancient Roman gladiators
because they live outside the conventions of society. Their
martyrdoms are not tragic, but anonymous. He attributes this
view to the effect on Beckett of being brought up as a Protestant
in southern Ireland, which gave him a feeling of alienation from
society.[12] The trouble with this interpretation is that it puts
the cart before the horse. Gregory starts out with a fact of
Beckett's life and concludes from this that certain attitudes
must be found in his works. But it is not true that Beckett's
characters must be social outsiders simply because he was
brought up as a social outsider. Beckett's men are not, as a
matter fact, outside the conventions of society: their actions
depict the inner reality of men in society. This biographical
method is taken one step further by Lionel Abel, who, noting
that Beckett used to be Joyce's secretary, postulates that Pozzo

9. Charles S. McCoy, "*Waiting for Godot*: A Biblical Appraisal,"
Religion in Life, XXVIII (Autumn, 1959), p. 595.

10. *Ibid.*, p. 602.

11. *Times Literary Supplement*, February 10, 1956, p. 84.

12. Horace Gregory, "Beckett's Dying Gladiators," *Commonweal*
(October 26, 1956), pp. 88–89.

in *Waiting for Godot* is a portrait of James Joyce and that Hamm in *Endgame* is a portrait of Joyce satirizing himself.[13]

All this is not to say that Beckett criticism, which is extremely voluminous by now, is uniformly on the wrong track. Ruby Cohn, in the best critical study of Beckett to appear so far, points out that Beckett's man lives in "a world that he did not make and that resists his efforts to make sense of it." [14] Charles Glicksberg agrees that pessimism and unrelieved meaninglessness are the main themes in Beckett's work.[15] And Rosette Lamont has said that "his theatre will remain as the ultimate expression of the despair of the atomic generation." [16]

Beckett's philosophical system, like that of so many of the current avant-garde writers, is based on a paradox. It is the concept that Thought (by which is meant logical thought, philosophical contemplation) is useless. Thought, says Beckett, can reveal nothing to us in the final analysis. All ultimate truth is forever beyond the compass of the human mind; and therefore truth does not, in effect, exist. It is this hopelessness and helplessness in an alien and incomprehensible universe that lead Beckett to the savage purity of his pessimism. Beckett makes Schopenhauer look like a gay optimist and Nietzsche like a devout believer.

The key passage for an understanding of Beckett's intellectual nihilism is the conversation about the four evangelists in *Waiting for Godot*. This passage has been inexplicably cited by at least one critic as proof of Beckett's Christianity. Vladimir tells Estragon that one of the two thieves crucified with Jesus was saved—according to one of the evangelists. Two of them say nothing about the matter, and the fourth says that both thieves cursed him. Vladimir becomes obsessed by the fact that although all four evangelists were there—"or thereabouts"—

13. Lionel Abel, *Metatheatre* (New York: Hill & Wang, Inc., 1963), pp. 135–36.
14. Ruby Cohn, *Samuel Beckett: The Comic Gamut* (New Brunswick, N. J.: Rutgers University Press, 1962), p. 225.
15. Charles I. Glicksberg, "Samuel Beckett's World of Fiction," *Arizona Quarterly*, XVIII (Spring, 1962), pp. 32–47.
16. Rosette C. Lamont, "The Metaphysical Farce: Beckett and Ionesco," *French Review*, XXXII (February, 1959), p. 328.

only one says that one of the thieves was saved. Why should the evangelist who says that one of the thieves was saved be believed rather than one of the others?

"Who believes him?" asks Estragon. "Everybody," answers Vladimir. "It's the only version they know."

And then we have Estragon's, and, I think, Beckett's verdict: "People are bloody ignorant apes."

Beckett is saying here that a precise and analytical discussion of religious problems leads only to confusion. All we find out is that the "ultimate truths" upon which we base the conduct of our lives and on which we rely as a source of moral justification for our actions are based on the flimsiest evidence and are often mutually contradictory. As the incident of the four evangelists shows, we cannot even begin to approach an understanding of the truths of religion—assuming that there are any such truths. If, then, we can know nothing about religion, which deals with such things as the origin of the world and the existence of human beings, it follows that we cannot really know anything about the world and the people on it either. The powers of the human mind are an illusion since they can tell us nothing about matters on which those things it apparently does understand ultimately depend. In short, all knowledge is an illusion and all things are pointless—in so far as the human mind is concerned.

The uselessness of thought and the consequent pointlessness of all human action appears again and again as a theme in Beckett's work. This is the crucial point upon which all of Beckett's thought rests: if the ultimate is meaningless, then the immediate is meaningless as well. The clearest statement of Beckett's belief in the uselessness of thought is in the tremendously effective scene of Lucky's tirade in *Waiting for Godot*. Beckett here implies that it is only in modern times that man has become impotent in thought and action. Man's increased "knowledge" has only served to make him aware of the uselessness of knowledge, the impossibility of certainty. Thus all that he has learned degenerates into a confused babble. Lucky's speech is a long, garbled stream-of-consciousness monologue which is a parody of logically connected utterance and scientific discourse. Just before his speech, Lucky goes through a weird dance called "The Net" which is expressive of bewilderment and impotence. Pozzo, Lucky's master, tells Vladimir and Estragon that Lucky used to dance farandoles, flings, brawls, jigs, fandangos, and hornpipes, but now he only dances this eerie, sinuous, tortured movement called "The Net." Similarly, Lucky "used to think very prettily once," but now he can only chatter away incoherently. Now there is only the numb impotence implied in Lucky's dance, his monologue, and his condition (he is a yoked beast of burden for his domineering master, Pozzo, the man who thinks he is created in God's image).

Beckett's belief in the uselessness of any attempt to arrive at a conclusion about anything can also be seen in the chess-game allegory in *Endgame* and *Murphy* (1938). Chess, the most logical of games, almost a symbol of logic itself, is made to look ridiculous in both works. The pure logic of the game is subverted, and the game becomes instead a blind, stupidly willful negation of logic. *Endgame*—the title may mean the playing out of the lives of the characters, the playing out of human existence, or the final moves of a fantastically perverted chess game—is a static ballet of two immovable pawns, a helpless king, and an aimlessly roving knight playing themselves into a hopeless stalemate. The climax of *Murphy* comes when Murphy plays a game of chess with a madman while working as an attendant in a lunatic asylum. In this game, which Beckett gives move by move in the text, every logical chess move is avoided. Only those moves that avoid an attack are used, and after about twenty moves the two players are back where they started, having moved all their pieces back (except the pawns, of course).

Beckett's early novel *Watt* (1953) is completely taken up with useless mental convolutions. Watt's interior monologues reduce the process of logical thinking to an absurdity. Watt is a servant in the house of a Mr. Knott and spends all his time worrying about the nature of his duties. How he ever gets anything done is a mystery, for his time seems to be wholly taken up with compulsively working out various combinations of ways in which he could do things. Everything that happens to Watt or to anyone he knows is minutely analyzed from all angles with obsessive diligence. Thus Watt figures out twelve ways in which Mr. Knott may have arrived at his peculiar method of eating; and we are given no less than thirty-six ways in which Mr. Knott can move around his room, the furniture of which can be arranged in twenty different ways—all of them described in detail.

Watt's thinking seems to be a way of passing time—not in the sense of amusing oneself, but in the sense of getting rid of life. It is a substitute for thought rather than thought itself. For Beckett this substitute makes as much (or as little) sense as the thing itself: "You would do better, or at least no worse," Molloy says, "to obliterate texts than to blacken margins, to fill in the holes of words till all is blank and flat and the whole ghastly business looks like what it is, senseless, speechless, issueless misery." Beckett looks at human knowledge *sub specie aeternitatis* and finds that it makes no sense when set beside the permanent incomprehensibles. His view of life is similar to the one expressed in Conrad's *Heart of Darkness:* "Droll thing life is—that mysterious arrangement of merciless logic for a futile purpose." The Beckettian man has achieved the degree of insight where all temporal concerns crumble, and nothing— or *Nothing*—is seen through the breach.

The force or forces that control the universe cannot be comprehended and appear to be unconcerned about humanity (Godot never comes; the *Endgame* players are alone). Therefore the concerns and actions of human beings are meaningless because they can have no ultimate goal. Occasionally Beckett seems to derive some sort of perverse comfort from this, as when he has the Unnamable say, "Nothing to do but stretch out comfortably on the rack in the blissful knowledge you are nobody for all eternity." Usually, however, Beckett's pessimism is intensified by his perception of the dreariness and pointlessness of life. The events of human existence have a monotonous sameness. Time is a succession of meaningless events that merge into each other so imperceptibly that they are indistinguishable. The whole world from the beginning of time to the present seems to Beckett like Tennyson's Land of the Lotos-Eaters—"a land where all things always seemed the same." Life goes on—and on—and on: infinite monotony, infinite torture. Everything is gray, as Clov tells Hamm in *Endgame*. The sun riseth no more—Beckett cannot even see the pitiful variety granted us by the Bible's supreme pessimist.

Endgame and *Waiting for Godot* are the best examples of Beckett's views on the monotony of life. The chief characters of both these plays—Vladimir and Estragon in *Waiting for Godot*; Hamm and Clov in *Endgame*—give one the idea that they are alive because they have to be. Objectively, they would like to die, but they are unable to kill themselves because the will to live (over which they have no control) is stronger than the will to die. And so they wearily occupy themselves with spinning out the skein of life, never daring to hope that some merciful Atropos will cut the thread for them. They play out the moves in their endless, aimless game with robotlike submissiveness.

"We're getting on," Hamm says with morbid self-satisfaction every time he and Clov complete another one of the eternally recurring episodes in their eternal farce.

"All life long, the same questions, the same answers," says Clov.

Only nature's cycles distinguish one period from another in Beckett's continuum of time. When Estragon and Vladimir return in the second act, the only difference in the dreary landscape is that the tree has flowered. It may be the next day, as they think. It may, however, also be the next month, or the next year, or it may be a thousand years later—it is always the same. The treadmill goes on, and Time turns upon itself like Vladimir's meaningless song about the dog that keeps eating and dying endlessly:

> A dog came in the kitchen
> And stole a crust of bread.
> Then cook up with a ladle
> And beat him till he was dead.
>
> Then all the dogs came running

And dug the dog a tomb
And wrote upon the tombstone
For the eyes of dogs to come:
A dog came in the kitchen
And stole a crust of bread.
Then cook up with a ladle
And beat him till he was dead.
Then all the dogs came running
And dug the dog a tomb (etc.)

Vladimir and Estragon just go on and on endlessly. They are faceless humanity slogging on through the dreary landscape with its blasted tree. They are always disappointed by Godot, whom they never see and whom they know only through his bland emissary, the boy. This boy always looks the same, but is always different. He brings reassurance of Godot's existence, although he himself really knows nothing about his supposed master and simply agrees that the image that the two tramps have built up for themselves is real. The allegory is inescapable —the boy might just as well appear in skullcap and cassock. Because there is "nothing to be done" in this world, Vladimir and Estragon arrive every day and numbly wait. Occasionally they hear a "terrible cry" and a "menace" from which they "cringe." This way they know that whether or not it is ever coming to them, whether it is GOD-ot or not, there is some superior and terrible power over them. The deterministic philosophy that underlies all of Beckett's work is most clearly exemplified in his drama.

In this colorless world where nothing significant happens, it is only natural that the people should be indistinguishable from each other as well. Beckett's characters are forever in search of the identity that will set them off from others, and of course they never find it. Molloy and Moran merge into one another and so do Mahood, Worm, and the pathetic Unnamable, who has not even got so much as a formal label to distinguish him. Beckett's five novels deal with five men who are trying to solve the problem of their own identity. In *Murphy*, the earliest, easiest to understand, and best of the novels, the "hero" ("antihero" would be a better term for Beckett's chief characters) is an expatriate Irish mystic whose peculiar custom it is to tie himself naked into a rocking chair with seven scarves and thus try to approach Nirvana. Murphy finally finds peace from pursuit in a job as a male nurse in a mental home. It is here that Murphy plays the chess game previously referred to with a mental patient significantly named Mr. Endon. At the end of the game Murphy peers into Mr. Endon's eyes and finds that the madman no longer sees him: the eyes are perfectly blank. In other words, Murphy discovers that he has ceased to exist in Mr. Endon's mind.

At the same time he forgets all his other acquaintances. He no longer exists in Mr. Endon's mind, and the people he knows no longer exist in his mind. His ceasing to exist in actual fact is therefore only a formality. Murphy goes to his room, ties himself into his rocking chair, and is annihilated by a gas explosion. Beckett's point is that if we exist in any sense at all, we exist in the minds of others and in our relationships with and effect on them. At some point in our lives however, we realize that we are unseen by others. Communication ceases. Each person is absorbed in himself, but he cannot exist unless he exists in someone else's mind. Ergo, he does not really exist. The reasoning is circular and therefore meaningless—like everything else.

Beckett's second novel *Watt* is about a compulsive manservant who feels impelled to build up an edifice of complicated reasoning about each trivial event in his life in order to prove to himself that he exists. Watt turns Descartes' straightforward logic into a paradox: "I think, therefore I am" becomes "I think, but do I exist?"

Beckett's later trilogy, *Molloy* (1951), *Malone Dies* (1951), and *The Unnamable* (1953), is composed of books written in the first person by men who are reminiscing at the end of their lives, trying to fasten upon some significant event so as to prove to themselves it was not all in vain. This is also Krapp's purpose in *Krapp's Last Tape*. None of them succeed. Molloy, Malone, and the Unnamable are essentially the same person. They are completely negative beings who have accomplished nothing.

This is not a condemnation of ineffective persons—Beckett's point is that no one has accomplished anything. Molloy, indeed, loses himself so completely that some omniscient force sends out a private detective to track him down and bring him back alive. The detective, Moran, does not find Molloy: he becomes him instead. Moran's possessions drop away from him, he loses contact with his comfortable, bourgeois home, his son deserts him; and then, when he is completely adrift in the middle of the forest, his legs become paralyzed. Like Molloy, Moran then has to drag himself hand over hand, inch by inch through the muck to his destination.

Malone is nothing and never was anything. He is writing down his reminiscences before dying, with a sort of sardonic self-satisfaction at his failure to turn up anything significant or even a little self-assertive in his vegetablelike past. Krapp does the same thing, but Beckett turns it into a touching piece of drama by making him lose his self-satisfaction. Instead of writing down his reminiscences, Krapp listens to them. Every year on his birthday he makes a tape recording of his thoughts about the past year. Now on his sixty-ninth birthday he listens to the tape he made exactly thirty years ago. On it he speaks of his one attempt to make love to a woman in a manner above the strictly animal level. He listens to the short, idyllic passage over and over as he realizes that it represents the one moment, in his otherwise meaningless and wasted life, that had some status as a true and significant experience. As the play ends, Krapp sits staring before him, listening once more to the inadequate description of his one love affair, overcome with helpless nostalgia for the one chance of genuine feeling he lightly tossed aside in the cynicism of thirty years before. The Unnamable, as we shall see, is hardly an individual even in the purely physical sense. He has no name for himself and constantly floats back and forth between Mahood and Worm, two characters that exist in his mind only.

Since no actions can mean anything, everything that man does is merely so much absurd pretension. The chief example of this is Hamm, the petty despot of *Endgame*, who rules not only over the bare-walled room which represents our accessible world but over the two garbage cans filled with the human refuse that created him. The inference, of course, is the vanity of human pomp and circumstance. Hamm's preoccupation with being in the center of the room is another instance of this, as is his grandiose self-pity when he wakes up at the beginning of the play ("Can there be misery loftier than mine?"). But the most marvelous example of all is the superbly ironic scene in which Hamm issues commands to his stuffed toy dog. The dog is not finished yet and has only three legs. Hamm, who is blind, asks Clov whether the dog is standing before him, "imploring" him. Clov assures him that it is, although the dog is, of course, lying on its side and is incapable of begging anyway. In the second act of *Waiting for Godot*, Pozzo's reappearance blind and helpless, after his domineering behaviour in the first act, is another case in point. Pozzo represents the masters of the earth, the omnipotent, in Act I, and his fall in Act II symbolizes the illusion inherent in even the greatest apparent power.

What all these things—the sameness of the human beings and their actions, the vanity of human ambition, the uselessness of thought—amount to is a pessimism deeper than any that has ever been put into words before. Throughout Beckett's work we can find evidence of his conviction that everything is hopeless, meaningless, purposeless, and, above all, agonizing to endure. Beckett's people are leveled off and merged into each other by being all more or less physically disabled—as if this were really the common condition of men on earth. In *Endgame* Nagg and Nell (Hamm's parents) are old and crippled and unable to climb out of their garbage cans. Hamm is blind and cannot stand. Clov cannot sit and, like Vladimir and Estragon in *Waiting for Godot*, has a constant nagging feeling of being unwell. Pozzo becomes blind and helpless and Lucky is dumb (during his one speech he is "thinking"). Molloy and his alter ego Moran both become paralyzed from the waist down. Malone is dying and cannot get up. Mrs. Rooney, in *All That Fall* (1957), is fat, senile, and dropsical, and her husband is blind. The Unnamable is an armless, legless hulk observing the world over the rim of a jar which hangs outside a restaurant, the proprietress of which feeds him and changes his sawdust once a week. And finally in *Watt* we have an account of the Lynch family, all twenty-eight members of which are crippled in one way or another.

As one plows through the catalog of the Lynches and their ailments, all minutely described, one feels that this is Beckett's view of the condition of all people: lameness is the natural state of man. Speaking of his mother, Molloy gives perhaps the most bitter and despairing of all Beckett's statements: "I know she did all she could not to have me, except of course the one thing, and if she never succeeded in getting me unstuck, it was that fate had earmarked me for less compassionate sewers." Surely disgust and loathing can get no further. Beckett's view of existence is summed up in Hamm's question, "Did you ever have an instant of happiness?" and Clov's answer, "Not to my knowledge"; and later in Hamm's despairing cry, "Use your head, can't you, use your head—you're on earth, there's no cure for that." Even in the comparatively cheerful early novels there are passages full of a biting misanthropy. The garden at the back of Mr. Knott's house in *Watt* is an example. Here Watt and Sam savagely kill the larks and robins, born and unborn, but affectionately feed the black rats with frogs, birds, or the rats' and frogs' own baby offspring. Sam states that he and Watt felt "closest to God" when they were feeding live baby rats to the voracious parent rats.

Beckett's subsequent plays have become more like experiments in pure form. Plot has been cut to a minimum, and the plays have come to resemble carefully constructed frames enclosing a void. The same development—or attrition—is visible in the novel *How It Is*. Beckett's pessimism has led him to concentrate his attention entirely on the self. The human mind and body are existential entities beyond which there is nothing but an alien Nature which Man has sought to neutralize through the creation of temporary artifacts. Man's isolation has led him to build castles in the air complete with implausible fairy tales to conceal from himself that what awaits him is an *oubliette*. Given these views of the self, the only thing left to observe is the process of gradual disintegration of the self. Beckett's writings have come to be formal expressions of the process of aging: attrition of mental powers, wasting of flesh: man as a dimly burning wick in an ever diminishing puddle of tallow—these are the themes of Beckett's later work. These later works are, consequently, less dramatic works than philosophical avatars of decay. We can see the process beginning in *Waiting for Godot*, of course—Beckett has always been rigidly consistent in his views. But it is not until *Happy Days* (1961) that the work has been pared down until it is practically pure form. In *Happy Days* Beckett has achieved a state of almost complete stasis on stage, a symbolic representation of Beckett's view of life. Winnie, buried to the waist in sand in Act I, to the neck in Act II, does not act: she is acted upon. The sand buries her, creeping up around her gradually, barely noticed by her as she goes on cheerfully chirping her way through her anaesthetizing daily routines, realizing only dimly that she is growing old. *Happy Days*—the title is a masterpiece of irony—is a play about aging. The two views we have of Winnie—in earlier stages she would be buried to her ankles and knees and Willie would be upright—show her in middle age and old age as life slips away, insidiously sapping her physical powers until she is sustained only by the illusions with which her inane babble numbs and soothes her "mind."

In *Play* (1964) the characters have passed beyond the end of "happy days." They are dead: three disembodied heads looking out of funeral urns. All action has stopped, of course; and the title of the piece becomes one with the form, as was to happen again later with *Film* (1967). In *Play* the characters—one man and two women—reminisce endlessly about the banalities of their sexual relationships in life. Here, as in the subsequent works, the text, like the action, becomes a paradigm for stasis so that these works resemble clocks running down to a few spasmodic ticks and then silence. This happens in the radio play *Cascando* (1963; the title is the present participle of the Italian verb *cascare*, to fall or stumble), which is, significantly, mostly a monologue by a man trying to write a story but petering out into nothingness. Similarly, in the television play *Eh Joe* (1967) we have the internal reminiscences of a man at the end of a misspent and meaningless life, an exact repetition of the Krapp theme with slight variations. The image that best illustrates all of Beckett's most recent work is that of an inward-turning spiral that must eventually reach the vanishing point—complete stasis. Eventually Beckett will no doubt feel moved to produce a work called *Period,* consisting of a dot at the end of a blank page.

Beckett has come around by quite another path to Blaise Pascal's conclusion that the condition of man is *"inconstance, ennui, inquiétude."* He sees man as a ridiculous mechanical puppet who, like the two figures in *Act Without Words, No. 2* (published 1960), responds to some persistent, merciless, and impersonal goad by going through the motions of everyday living, either morosely and lackadaisically or with the anesthetizing briskness and efficiency which leave no time for thought. Beckett has drawn one of the two possible conclusions from the perception that the universe is unknowable. The other conclusion—that the world as it is, is worthwhile for the simple reason that it is all that there is (that Being in any form is better than Nonbeing, in other words)—is Camus'. Beckett is the prophet of negation and sterility. He holds out no hope to humanity, only a picture of unrelieved blackness; and those who profess to see in Beckett signs of a Christian approach or signs of compassion are simply refusing to see what is there.

EUGENE IONESCO
The Absurd as Warning

WITH THE exception of Samuel Beckett, no present-day dramatist has caused such a varied spray of critical interpretations as Eugène Ionesco. The meaning of his plays is never explicit. His work is characterized, instead, by what may be termed a purposeful vagueness. His plays, in other words, are full of possible meanings, but void both of specific polemic purposes and of solutions. Ionesco is not committed to a point of view because he realizes that all points of view are useless. His plays are demonstrations of the incongruity between the human condition and the human being's desires. As such, they are true tragedies, for tragedy, as Ionesco himself points out, lies in the unbearable.[1] His plays are "demystifications." They strip the veils off man's everyday actions and expose the unbearable, tragic impasse beneath. Reality is tragic, Ionesco tells us, and it will always remain so, no matter what form the masks take. Committed playwrights, such as Arthur Miller or Bertolt Brecht (Ionesco's particular bête noire), are merely attempting the contemptibly superficial task of changing the masks.

It is this iconoclastic attitude that has caused Ionesco the greatest trouble with his critics. Unable to reconcile themselves to the idea of a generalized protest against the human condition or to a criticism of society that holds out no hope for improvement, the critics have produced all sorts of bizarre explanations. Richard Coe, in his excellent critical study, gives a run-down of some of the more *outré* of these. *The Lesson* is an allegory of national revolt against dictatorship, or it is an attack on the philistinism of female college students. *Victims of Duty* can be taken either as a Freudian dream-play, a satire on the Oedipus complex, or as a working-out of Hegelian dialectic. The killer's knife can mean death, or the impossibility of communication, or the perversion of logic, or the frustration

1. Eugène Ionesco, *Notes et contre-notes* (Paris: Gallimard, 1962), p. 7.

of bourgeois society, or the corruption of the police force.
Rhinoceros can be taken as a satire on fascism, communism,
trade unionism, or big business.[2]

The most virulent and typical critical outburst against
Ionesco was that initiated by Kenneth Tynan in *The Observer*
of June 22, 1958. After having fought for Ionesco's acceptance
in England, Tynan suddenly had doubts about the value of
plays that were not committed to some specific political point
of view. His dissatisfaction stemmed from the fact that Ionesco
no longer conformed to the left-wing social rebellion Tynan
had championed in the works of Osborne, Wesker, Kops, and
the rest of the "angry young men." Ionesco, of course, had
never conformed to it, but Tynan may well have been misled
into associating him with it by the use of the swastika armband
in *The Lesson* and by the apparent specific satire of English
bourgeois society in *The Bald Soprano*. Ionesco replied that a
work of art has nothing to do with doctrines.[3] He maintained
that the function of criticism is not to tell the author what he
should have said but to explicate and criticize what he *did* say.[4]
The Ionesco-Tynan controversy was not, as Martin Esslin would
have us believe, "brilliantly conducted on both sides." [5] It was
a brilliant vindication by Ionesco of the artist's right to be
judged on his own terms; and an attack on that right, uncomfortably reminiscent of the doctrinaire pronunciamentos of totalitarian state critics, by Tynan. Tynan seems to understand
Ionesco as little as does Thomas Barbour, who sees him simply
as a purveyor of telling stage effects and places him closer to
Oscar Hammerstein II and Joshua Logan, intellectually speaking, than to Beckett.[6]

Ionesco's plays fall easily into three subdivisions: the representative avant-garde, "theater of the absurd" plays; the "social

2. Richard Coe, *Eugene Ionesco* (New York: Grove Press, Inc., 1961),
p. 108.
3. *Notes et contre-notes*, p. 72.
4. *Ibid.*, p. 75.
5. Martin Esslin, *The Theatre of the Absurd* (Garden City, N. Y.:
Doubleday & Company, Inc., 1961), pp. 83–84.
6. Thomas Barbour, "Beckett and Ionesco," *Hudson Review*, XI
(Summer, 1958), p. 276.

warning" plays (*The Killer* and *Rhinoceros*); and the confessional plays (*The King Dies, The Aerial Pedestrian* and *Hunger and Thirst*). Like Beckett, Genet, Adamov, and the other authors of the French dramatic avant-garde, Ionesco bases his plays on the twin pillars of protest and paradox. The purpose of all of the plays of the dramatic avant-garde in general and of Ionesco's plays in particular is protest against the social order and the human condition. This protest does not take the form of a dispassionate rational criticism as in the traditional didactic drama with its implied attitude of aloof superiority; it is far more a chaotic and frenzied scream, the scream of a person who is trapped and knows it but who is determined to strain against his bonds to the last. The apparent absurdity of all of Ionesco's plays is actually an attempt to break through the confining borders of reality to a *beyond-reality* that, by its very existence, renders the everyday reality it protests against ridiculous by contrast. In other words, the seeming irrationality of the avant-garde drama is caused by the use of a technique that may be described as the selective exaggeration of reality in order to point up the ridiculousness of certain aspects of everyday reality, the *essential* ridiculousness of which usually passes unnoticed.

The technique of exaggerating selected aspects of everyday reality in order to demonstrate its pointlessness is the technique of paradox. Ionesco and the other avant-garde dramatists always show their truths by presenting their audiences with situations that conflict so strongly with commonly held ideas of the reasonable as to seem at first (or even second) glance senseless and absurd. The point is made all the stronger, once it has sunk in, by having initially masqueraded as apparent nonsense.

Ionesco's first play, *The Bald Soprano* (La Cantatrice Chauve, 1950), was the ground-breaker for the current avant-garde tradition on the stage. It illustrates, first of all, the dramatic technique which the avant-garde derived from Antonin Artaud; but, more important still, it illustrates the basic philosophical premise on which the whole avant-garde drama is based. This philosophical premise, the importance of which cannot be overestimated in a study of the avant-garde drama, is the concept of the absurd in human affairs. First appearing in a more or less unconscious form in the works of Alfred Jarry, it was continued in an equally instinctive and unreflecting vein by the surrealists and the Dadaists; but it was not until the appearance of Albert Camus' *The Myth of Sisyphus* that the "philosophy of the absurd" received a conscious and rational formulation.

Briefly stated, Camus' "philosophy of the absurd" says that human existence is unintelligible. Man lives in the world but understands neither it nor his own function in it. He is a displaced alien in what must ultimately appear an incomprehensible void to him. Man functions in this wilderness by anesthetizing himself to reality with various specious, artificial beliefs; by immersing himself in a comforting routine that gives him the illusion of having some significance; and by deluding himself into believing that he is not alone. It is the self-appointed task of the avant-garde dramatists to debunk these beliefs and to shock people into a realization of the *absurdity* of their position.

Ionesco concentrates mainly on showing his audiences the mutual isolation of human beings and the meaninglessness of the daily actions which constitute the major portion of their existence on earth.

The story of *The Bald Soprano* is unimportant in itself. We see an English living room in which an English couple are carrying on a parody of an English after-dinner conversation. They are visited by another English married couple, who cannot make up their minds whether they know each other or not, and by an incongruously but unmistakably Gallic fire chief. The action of the play consists simply of the characters sitting there and talking what appears to be utter nonsense. Ionesco has himself stated that the play's English setting is purely coincidental. He happened to be studying the language and the ridiculousness of the expressions in his Assimil-method phrase book struck him so forcibly that he was inspired to write the play.[7]

Ionesco uses the device of nonsense speech as a means of showing one aspect of the absurdity of everyday life through the breakdown of semantics. Since everyday life, whether absurd or not, depends for its coherence entirely on the coherence of speech patterns, it follows that if our speech patterns are absurd, everyday life in general is absurd *as far as we are concerned* (it is possible that to an individual the world does not appear absurd, but since he has no means of communication with other people except through intrinsically senseless speech patterns, it follows that his view is actually nonexistent in practice). Even if the world appears ordered and coherent to *everyone*, Ionesco is saying, it is still absurd because each person is trapped inside his own individual cell by the inadequacies of his means of communication. The only possible type of communication is the indirect method of paradox.[8]

Ionesco begins his attack on linguistic meaning right at the beginning of the play in the first stage direction. Here, in the description of the Smiths' living room, the word "English" is used seventeen times in a passage of seventy-five words—an average of once every four and a half words. Here we see that no word can retain its meaning under the stress of constant irrelevant usage. As soon as the curtain rises, Ionesco's point is made clearer by the "conversation" between Mrs. Smith and her husband, in which the truisms of everyday speech are repeated until they become ludicrous. When Mr. Smith finally does consent to join the conversation, it is only to comment on the death and burial of one Bobby Watson. This whole passage is a hilarious indictment of the illusion of human iden-.

7. Coe, *op. cit.*, pp. 45–47.
8. Wallace Fowlie, *Dionysus in Paris* (New York: Meridian Books, 1960), pp. 230–31, suggests that the theme of *The Bald Soprano* is the guilt of the aged couple, who have made a failure of marriage. This may well be the theme, or one of the themes, of *The Chairs* and of *Amédée*, but in *The Bald Soprano* the relationship of the Smiths is not described thoroughly enough for us to make an assertion one way or the other about their happiness. They seem quite content with their existence.

tity. The Bobby Watsons in the story proliferate until everyone seems to be called Bobby Watson. The individual's pride in his own uniqueness is vain: to other persons he is just another manifestation of each person's projected self.

Following this dialogue between the Smiths we have an apparently equally meaningless dialogue between their guests, the Martins. The Martins's problem is that, even though they have been introduced to us as man and wife, they don't know each other. During the course of their conversation they discover that they both come from Manchester, that they came up to London at the same time in the same compartment of the same train, and that they are staying on the same floor in the same hotel and, in fact, are occupying the same room and sleeping in the same bed. All these coincidences fail to convince them that they know each other and it is only when they discover that they each have a daughter with one white eye and one red one that they decide that they are probably man and wife. From a purely farcical standpoint the whole scene irresistibly reminds one of the recognition scene in *Cox and Box*. From a more serious standpoint, however, we see a typical couple, married for some years, who do not know each other. What Ionesco is saying—once more—is that people are isolated, people never *really* know each other, even when they are living together in the closest possible relationship. We always know only our illusions of each other. Cast-iron as the Martins's reasoning seems, it is instantly destroyed by the maid, who tells the audience that the Martins are not really man and wife because his child has a white right eye and a red left eye and hers has a red right eye and a white left eye. The point of the maid's interpolation seems to be that even the most closely knit chain of reasoning is futile. This perception that reason is essentially inadequate and at the same time the only form of thought available to us is the original basis for the philosophy of the absurd. The passage discussed here is analogous to Lucky's speech in *Waiting for Godot*, which is a parody of logic and scientific speech. Lucky's tirade is a long and confused jumble of tag ends of scientific discourse that gradually degenerates into an utterly incoherent babble. The enormously involved chains of reasoning made up for the most trivial purposes by the protagonist of Beckett's *Watt* are another example of this comment on the inadequacy of human thought processes. *The Bald Soprano* also breaks up into an incoherent nonsense babble at the end as all the characters scream snatches of familiar sayings and quotations at each other. As this shouting match fades away, the lights come up again on the same scene as at the beginning of the play. The meaningless monotony continues ad infinitum and ad nauseam.

Ionesco's next play was *The Lesson* (La Leçon, 1951). Here he shows us a private lesson given by an elderly professor to a young girl preparing, somewhat intrepidly, for her "total doctorate." At first the professor is the typical absent-minded pedagogue and the young girl is the confident and glib pupil. Gradually the roles reverse: the professor becomes confident, positive, overbearing; the girl timid, uncertain, and mentally paralyzed. Finally, the professor, enraged at the girl's stupidity, stabs her. When he realizes that the girl is dead, the frightened professor calls his maid to help him. Totally undisturbed by the dead body, which, as she casually remarks, is the fortieth that day, the maid calms the professor down. When he suggests that forty coffins might cause comment, she tells him that nobody will make awkward enquiries: the people are used to such sights. The professor, who has now reverted to the childlike timidity he displayed at the beginning of the play, is finally reassured when the maid pins "an armband with an insignia, possibly the Nazi swastika" on him. As the two accomplices carry the body out, the doorbell rings again, announcing the day's forty-first luckless visitor.

The interesting thing about *The Lesson* is the complete reversal of viewpoint as the play progresses. At the beginning, the play is purely realistic: a new pupil visits her tutor for her first lesson. The language is perfectly ordinary and intelligible. In fact, except for an occasional momentary hop into the facetious, like the business about studying for all the doctorates at once and the professor practically tying himself into knots with amazed delight when the pupil gives Paris as the capital of France, the first part of the play is so natural as to be almost banal. The play thus follows the regular formula of most of Ionesco's plays: an opening scene of everyday banality succeeded by a breakthrough into the fantastic by emphasizing the banality, as if Ionesco were a dentist probing a nerve incessantly until a transition to a new realm of pain occurs. In *The Bald Soprano* he accomplished this by the cumulative illogicality of the dialogue; in *The New Tenant*, by the endless piling on of the furniture; in *Jack*, by the bridegroom's demand for more and more grotesqueness in his bride; and here, in *The Lesson*, by reversing the personalities of professor and pupil as the former becomes carried away by his meaningless lecture.

What Ionesco is saying, by the professor working himself up into a homicidal frenzy as he gabbles his hysterical tirade on Neo-Spanish and its related identical tongues, is that the more wild, senseless, illogical, inane, and irrational words become, the more powerful—and, of course, the more dangerous —they become. As the professor raves about Neo-Spanish and Sardanapolitan, his power over his pupil increases until finally he kills her. The allegory is obvious: the insidious deadliness of the professor's speech is precisely analogous to the equally insidious deadliness of the rhetoric used by the Nazis—and nothing was more appalling about the Nazi era than the extent to which the German intellectuals (the teachers, the artists, all those, in short, whose task it is to guard the truth) willingly used their powers to pervert the truth, to give falsehood the appearance of truth.[9] Ionesco's professor perverts language, which, as he himself says, is more important than anything else, for it is the medium through which truth is expressed. As the words lose meaning, they become deadlier: the professor's frenzied gabble and Hitler's hysterical ravings—which were not only meaningless but unintelligible as well—are one and the same. Semantic anarchy equals moral anarchy.

9. Esslin (in *The Theatre of the Absurd*, p. 96) suggests that *The Lesson* deals with the sexual nature of all power and with the interdependence of language and power. This is true up to a point, but the most obvious examples available to Ionesco of sadism—sexual or otherwise—and of corruption through misuse of language cannot be ignored as a specific source of inspiration.

After the production of *The Chairs* (Les Chaises) in 1952 Ionesco began to be more widely known. It is in this play that he is most successful in achieving that abstract quality, that breaking-up of conventional theatrical forms, which he states he was striving for in his drama. *The Chairs* is the story of a very old couple who have invited a large crowd to the island on which they live so that the husband may impart the wisdom he has accumulated during ninety-five years. His plan for saving the world is to be communicated by a professional orator. The guests, all invisible, keep arriving, until finally the stage is filled with chairs. The old man announces that the orator will present his messianic secret to the audience; then he and his wife commit suicide by throwing themselves out of the window. As soon as they are gone, the orator indicates that he is deaf and dumb.

Ionesco's point here is the impossibility of communication between human beings. The empty chairs onstage, occupied by an invisible audience, parallel the seats of the theatre in which the play is produced. Although the audience of Ionesco's play may really exist visibly, the chairs which they occupy might just as well be empty because communication is an illusion.* By his own definition of tragedy ("For the unbearable there is no solution, and only the unbearable is true [i.e., tragic] theater") *The Chairs* is Ionesco's most tragic play. Nothing could be more "unbearable" and at the same time finely ironic, than the orator's impotence. The vague, incomprehensible maunderings of the two old people are suddenly knitted together by the superbly dramatic device of the vaunted orator's desperate attempt to speak. Life, Ionesco is saying, is a hell in which each person is imprisoned in his own separate sound-proof cubicle, invisible and inaudible to everyone else. All so-called communication is illusory: the only person we really communicate with all the time is ourself.

Victims of Duty (Victimes du Devoir), first produced in 1953, is a satire on conventionality, particularly conventionality

---

* I am indebted to my former student Miss Patricia Doughty for this suggestion.

in the theater. The play, subtitled a "pseudo-drama," begins, as is usual with Ionesco, in that citadel of banality, a *petit bourgeois* home. Choubert and his wife, a perfectly ordinary middle-class couple, are discussing the news. Suddenly, apropos of nothing, Choubert begins a Socratic disquisition on the modern drama. The classification of all drama that has ever been written under the heading of "thriller" is at least refreshing:

CHOUBERT: What do you think of the modern theatre: What are your ideas on the drama?

MADELEINE: You and your theatre! It's an obsession, you'll soon be a pathological case.

CHOUBERT: Do you really think something new can be done in the theatre?

MADELEINE: I've just told you there's nothing new under the sun. Even when there isn't any.

CHOUBERT: You're right. Yes, you're right. All the plays that have ever been written, from Ancient Greece to the present day, have never really been anything but thrillers. Drama's always been realistic and there's always been a detective about. Every play's an investigation brought to a successful conclusion. There's a riddle, and it's solved in the final scene. Sometimes earlier. You seek, and then you find. Might as well give the game away at the start.

MADELEINE: You ought to quote examples, you know.

CHOUBERT: I was thinking of the Miracle Play about the woman Our Lady saved from being burned alive. If you can forget that bit of divine intervention, which really has nothing to do with it, what's left is a newspaper story about a woman who has her son-in-law murdered by a couple of stray killers for reasons that are unmentioned . . .

MADELEINE: And unmentionable.

CHOUBERT: The police arrive, there's an investigation and the criminal is unmasked. It's a thriller. A naturalistic drama, fit for the theatre of Antoine . . . Come to think of it, there's never been much evolution in the theatre.

MADELEINE: Pity.

CHOUBERT: You see, the theatre's a riddle, and the riddle's a thriller. It's always that way.

MADELEINE: What about the classics?

CHOUBERT: Refined detective drama. Just like naturalism.[10]

At this point a detective actually does appear. The rest of the play is concerned with his frantic attempt to force Choubert to give him some entirely nonsensical information. It all ends as the detective, who is forcing Choubert to swallow chunks of stale bread in order to "plug the gaps in his memory," is killed by a huge, black-bearded character named Nicholas d'Eu. This d'Eu sounds off with a few more of Ionesco's opinions on the theatre:

D'EU: The theatre of my dreams would be irrationalist . . . Inspiring me with a different logic and a different psychology, I should introduce contradiction where there is no contradiction, and no contradiction where there is what common-sense usually calls contradiction. We'll get rid of the principle of identity and unity of character and let movement and dynamic psychology take its place. We are not ourselves. Personality doesn't exist. Within us there are only forces that are either contradictory or not contradictory . . . The characters lose their form in the formlessness of becoming. Each character is not so much himself as another . . . As for plot and motivation, let's not mention them. We ought to ignore them completely, at least in their old form, which was too clumsy, too obvious—too phony, like anything that's too obvious—No more drama, no more tragedy: the tragic's turning comic, the comic is tragic, and life's getting more cheerful.[11]

10. Eugène Ionesco, Three Plays: Amédée, The New Tenant, Victims of Duty, translated by Donald Watson. Copyright © 1958 by the Grove Press, Inc. (New York: Grove Press, Inc., 1958), pp. 119–20.

11. Ibid., pp. 157–59.

In Choubert's statements we have a perfectly explicit account of Ionesco's view of all drama other than his own; in d'Eu's statement, we have his account of what he feels drama ought to be. *Victims of Duty* is, however, not merely an academic discussion of the drama. It is also a horrifyingly nightmarish picture of the ordinary man's unthinking subservience to the conventions of society. All of us are victims of duty: Choubert and Madeleine, victims of the detective's official authority; the detective, victim of a higher level in the official pecking order; and even Nicholas d'Eu, the intellectual rebel, falls victim to "duty" the moment he has eliminated the detective. He takes over the dead man's functions, and poor Choubert has to get on the treadmill again.

Victims of Duty was first produced in February, 1953. Almost exactly a year later, Ionesco's next play, *Amédée, or How to Get Rid Of It* (Amédée, ou Comment s'en Débarrasser), was performed. Amédée is a mousey little playwright who never seems to get anywhere—his average output is in the vicinity of one line every few years. Fifteen years before the play starts, a young man visited Amédée and his wife, Madeleine. He never left the apartment alive—Amédée can't quite remember whether he killed him in a fit of jealousy or whether the young man just died—and his body, perfectly preserved, has been reposing in the best bedroom ever since. The trouble with the body is that it is more than perfectly preserved: not content merely to ward off putrefaction, it is actually growing all the time. In short, the body is suffering from "Geometrical Progression, the incurable disease of the dead." During the play the disease switches from the chronic stage to the acute, and we have the spectacle of the body steadily advancing across the stage until it fills practically the whole playing area, and Amédée and his wife are squeezed uncomfortably into a corner.

Amédée finally makes up his mind to get rid of the body, and late at night Madeleine lowers it down to him through the window, much as one might lower an enormously long, soggily limp salami. Amédée drags the body through the deserted streets leading to the river. Before he gets there, however, he meets an American soldier and from that point on everything goes wrong. The whole town wakes up: dogs start barking, windows open, whistles blow, trains start rolling, the police show up, fireworks are detonated, comets and shooting stars appear in the sky. Amédée, panic-stricken, rolls the body around his waist for more convenient carrying. Soon he is completely wrapped up in this coil of flesh, and then, "a surprising thing happens. The body wound round Amédée's waist seems to have opened out like a sail or a huge parachute; the dead man's head has become a sort of flowing banner . . . Amédée is flying up out of reach of the policeman. The banner is like a huge scarf, on which the head of the dead man is drawn, recognizable by the long beard, etc." [12] Slowly Amédée and the dead man float into the celestial regions, thoughtfully scattering such earthly dross as shoes and cigarettes as they go.

The rolling up and carrying away of the body, accompanied as it is in its later stages by fireworks, shooting stars, comets, police whistles, and so forth, is a hilarious parody of the funeral procession with all the empty pomp and circumstance reduced to flippant ribaldry. The ascent of Amédée with the body is, of course, a burlesque of the traditional ascent to Paradise. One is irresistibly reminded of Little Eva and her more sublime though no less ridiculous *Himmelfahrt*.

Amédée is the most allusive and obscure of Ionesco's works. The meaning, of course, hinges on the central symbol of the growing body. Is it a symbol of the ever greater and greater encroachment of death on our lives? As the body grows, our span of life becomes smaller (Amédée's living space shrinks), and decay sets in as we grow older (toadstools sprout in the apartment). Or is it a symbol of the unsuccessful and now dead love of Amédée and Madeleine, the forever doomed "love" of the poet and dreamer for the hard, acquisitive, unsentimental woman? [13] My own feeling is that this play foreshadows Ionesco's feelings about death, which he was to treat in his two intensely subjective and confessional plays *The King Dies*

12. *Ibid.*, p. 73.
13. Esslin, *op. cit.*, p. 108.

and *The Aerial Pedestrian.*

Ionesco's next play, *Jack, or Submission* (Jacques, ou la Soumission, 1955), is purely a study in dramatic surrealism. Stylistically it is a throwback to *The Chairs.* The story of a young man who has to submit to the conventions of family and society by confessing that he likes roast potatoes, it is Ionesco's demonstration of the evils of *not* rebelling. The actions we go through in submitting to *our* social conventions, Ionesco is saying, are as ridiculous as the ones Jack is made to go through; and very possibly he is right. Once Jack has submitted, he is introduced to his future bride, a young lady with two noses, whom he refuses on the rather bizarre ground that she is not ugly enough. He is then offered one with three noses, whom he finally accepts, though not without some preliminary grumbling about her inadequate repulsiveness.

In *The New Tenant* (Le Nouveau Locataire, 1957), a man hires a room on the top floor of a house. His furniture is delivered, and two moving men bring it up. They bring up a great deal of furniture and then they bring up more—and more—and more—and more. When they can't fit any more in, they leave it on the stairs and finally on the street in front of the house. Then reports pour in that the gentleman's furniture is blocking traffic, stopping up the subway, damming up the Seine: the whole country becomes paralyzed. Meanwhile the gentleman has ensconced himself in a little cubbyhole just large enough to hold him. Walled in on all sides by furniture, he disappears from view; and as the play ends we hear his muffled voice ordering the movers to put out the light. The room is plunged into darkness, and the gentleman has indeed gone back as far as he can go.

The nameless tenant is another Mr. Zero. He constructs a mechanistic womb for himself in terms of everyday banality and creeps into it. He is back in the cocoon; nothing will trouble him anymore. Similarly, the furniture chokes off all traffic and totally engulfs the country. In other words, not only is the tenant insulated is against the necessary troubles of the world, but everyone else as well. The paralyzing flood of furniture is a symbol of the deliberately created wall of banality (television, movies, pulp magazines, picnics, cocktail parties, etc.) with which modern man desperately seeks to shut himself off from the necessity of thinking.

In *The Killer* (Tueur sans Gages, 1959) and *Rhinoceros* (1960) Ionesco emerges more and more concretely as a playwright of rebellion against social conformity. The abstract and seemingly frivolous qualities of his earlier plays are gone and we see an Ionesco who has become more topical, more socially conscious, more polemic—in short, more *worried*. It is as if he had suddenly realized that his pleas for the independence of the human spirit, his condemnations of slavishness and conformity to the artificially created and tyrannically imposed "ideals" of society were not coming across and that there was no time to lose.

The Killer gives us a picture of a termite-infested society about to collapse of its own rot. Everything is drab and lusterless in this modern society, mildewed from the "moral damp" that seeps in everywhere. It has not always been this way, however. Bérenger, the timid, ineffectual little Everyman who is the protagonist of the play, can vaguely remember a time when things were different: "once upon a time there was a blazing fire inside me. The cold could do nothing against it, a youthfulness, a spring no autumn could touch; a source of light, glowing wells of joy that seemed inexhaustible. Not happiness, I mean joy, felicity, which made it possible for me to live. . . . Must be centuries ago . . . or perhaps only a few years, perhaps it was yesterday." [14] And now he thinks he has suddenly recovered this wonderful period of his youth, of humanity's youth. Within the cold, unfriendly city in which he lives he has found a "radiant city" where the sun always shines and where it never rains (no "moral damp") and where everything is always in bloom. This "radiant city" has been designed and built by the Architect, one of those omniscient puppeteer-bureaucrats so frequently encountered in the modern avantgarde drama. The "radiant city," however, is beautiful only on

14. Eugène Ionesco, *The Killer and Other Plays*, translated by Donald Watson (New York: Grove Press, Inc., 1960), p. 20.

the surface. Ionesco seems to be contrasting the hopefulness and energy—above all, the individuality—of people before the present with the bureaucratic age, symbolized by the Architect and his flawed, machine-made, preplanned (and therefore essentially drab) "radiant city." For this city is rotten at the core. It is haunted by a ruthless killer who murders two or three persons every day. These killings, the Architect explains to the horrified and disillusioned Bérenger, are always accomplished in the same way: the killer, dressed as a beggar, pursues his victim until they come to an ornamental pool in the middle of the radiant area. Here the killer offers to show his victim the "picture of the colonel." For some reason this is always irresistible, and the victim is pushed into the pool while he is absorbed in the picture. Men, women, and children meet death in this way; only members of the civil service are immune.

After making this shattering discovery, Bérenger hurries home. As he does so, he goes from illusion to reality: the scene in the "radiant city" is played on a brightly lit bare stage, but Bérenger's house is reproduced with deliberately ponderous realism. When he gets home, Bérenger finds Eduard, a tubercular and deformed friend of his, waiting for him. This Eduard, it turns out, has a briefcase full of pictures of the colonel. His explanation is that someone once sent them to him and that he had forgotten all about them—not being the nosey type, he has not looked into his briefcase lately. Bérenger immediately urges Eduard to rush off with him to the police. Eduard, however, leaves the briefcase in the room. The next scene is devoted principally to Bérenger's frantic search for the missing briefcase. Eduard, who is totally unconcerned about the murders, offers no help at all. This is played against a background of a fantastic political harangue given by "Mother Peep" to her "geese." Mother Peep's speech, like the Professor's in *The Lesson*, is an example of the perversion of words. It is a parody of a totalitarian campaign speech and is wildly applauded by the listeners. The point is that a goose-stepping society like the one Mother Peep is trying to create doesn't think—it permits insidious influences like the killer to operate.

At the end of the play Bérenger finally meets the killer, who turns out to be a puny, deformed, one-eyed dwarf. Bérenger, in a long speech to the killer, who never says a word, tries to find some ground for condemning him. But every time he brings up an argument against the killer, he finds some specious justification for the other side. Next he tries to exhort the killer to lead a better life, and finally he tries to exterminate him. But he is helpless: "how weak my strength is against your cold determination, your ruthlessness! And what good are bullets against the resistance of an infinitely stubborn will!" [15] He lets his pistols drop as the killer slowly advances on him, knife in hand.

Ionesco's theme is the moral spinelessness of society, personified in men like Bérenger, the perfect types of Eliot's "hollow men." Bérenger's powerlessness against the killer is, as Ionesco says, due to his own "rather commonplace morality." Bérenger has nothing to stand on; in spite of himself he keeps finding arguments to justify the killer's actions. Having no belief of his own, he represents a society that no longer has any right to defend itself against evil because it is not convinced that it is better than the evil opposing it. And the canker that has been rotting society, according to Ionesco and all the other playwrights of protest in the dramatic avant-garde, is the deindividualizing caused by the Mother Peeps and their gospel of the "disalienation of mankind" and the "mystification of the demystifiers"—of the suppression of the individual and the exaltation of the lie.

Bérenger endures another Calvary in Ionesco's next play, *Rhinoceros*, which is philosophically a continuation of *The Killer*. Once more Ionesco is concerned with the problem of the suppression of individuality in modern society. Mother Peep's geese are simply changed into rhinoceroses. But where Mother Peep's geese play a purely complementary part, providing a sort of ironic background mood music to Bérenger's doomed quest for justice, the animals of *Rhinoceros* are the

15. *Ibid.*, p. 108.

main feature. *The Killer* is a generalized protest against complacency about the ever-present elements of evil that pervade
society. *Rhinoceros*, like *The Lesson*, is an obvious commentary
on the disintegration of reason and morality under a totalitarian
state. Only those unfamiliar with the history of Nazism will
be at all puzzled by its allegory.

Unlike *The Killer*, *Rhinoceros* has no moral: it is a simple
horror story. A rhinoceros (or man in a brown shirt with a
bizarre-looking insignia on his right arm) appears and kills a
cat. Everyone is horrified. No one does anything about it. Soon
more and more rhinoceroses begin to appear on the streets,
roaring discordantly and trampling on things. Bérenger's best
friend suddenly turns green, develops a leathery skin, and
grows a horn above his nose. "We must rebuild the foundations
of our existence. We must return to primordial integrity," the
new party member tells Bérenger. Soon Bérenger's other associates join up. A fellow worker comes to tell him that their
boss has become a rhinoceros: " 'We must move with the
times.' Those were his last human words." Then the fellow
worker joins up too: "My duty requires me to follow the example of my superiors and fellow workers for better or for
worse." The discordant roaring of the rhinoceroses turns into
a barbarically rhythmic marching song; their undisciplined
rampaging turns into the measured tramp of the goose step.
Finally Bérenger is left alone with his fiancée. Then she too
leaves him. Alone, he wavers. But then, as the rhinoceroses
advance on him, he pulls himself together, and, realizing that
only he is left of all the humans in his town, he screams *"Je ne
capitule pas!"* as the curtain falls. Bérenger's willful, stubborn
(even, from a certain point of view, unreasonable and stupid)
defiance raises him, congenital nonentity though he is, to a
level of selfless heroism given to few men to attain. With that
magnificent cry, at once a defiance and a curse, which he utters
at the end, Bérenger pulls himself up to the level of the universal rebel described by Camus. For the sake of justice, humanity, and decency—above all, for the sake of the highest
virtue of all, the virtue of moderation—Bérenger sacrifices himself despite all the specious dictates of reason. His act of sym-

bolic rebellion is useless on the immediate, primary level, but it is nonetheless an act of faith in the independence of the human spirit and as such serves to testify against and undermine the tyranny that kills him.

The parallel between the situations of *Rhinoceros* and the gradual acceptance, through complacency and expediency, of the Nazi hooliganism as the ordinary and correct way of life by the German *petite bourgeoisie* is obvious. Ionesco's play is both a warning and a castigation; with regard to the former, it is probably no coincidence that the play is set in France.

In his latest plays Ionesco turns to a frankly confessional style of writing. In his excellent article, "The Inner and the Outer Reality," Richard Schechner points out that all of Ionesco's plays are autobiographical and confessional.[16] His early plays are externalizations of deeply personal obsessions, which, "like Kafka's, . . . are public coin, at least for this moment in history."[17] His success and growing importance brought him a measure of self-confidence and personal security, which in turn led to a greater involvement in immediately temporal affairs.[18] This led to the *engagé* plays, *The Killer* and *Rhinoceros*. As a result of his success he has come to have a sense of satisfaction with life and a love of all its aspects, without at the same time relinquishing his deeply rooted pessimism. He eats, he sleeps, he loves; and whereas before he did these things automatically, he now wallows in sensuous enjoyment of them. Like Camus, he has come to realize that life is all that there is; that death is the only real enemy. These plays are an expression of his fear of death. It would not be too rash to predict that Ionesco has reached his final phase—that all his future work will be concerned with this obsession. Like all great artists, he has at last come to grips with the only true reality and with the most unbearable and insoluble—and therefore the most tragic—subject.

16. Richard Schechner, "The Inner and the Outer Reality," *Tulane Drama Review*, VII (Spring, 1963), p. 187.
17. *Ibid.*
18. *Ibid.*, p. 206.

The King Dies (Le Roi se meurt, 1962) is a long, completely static one-act play. Donald Watson has pointed out that the characteristic aspect of Ionesco's art is the inflation of situation into the source of dramatic action.[19] The static situation viewed from every angle thus replaces plot. *The King Dies* takes place in a mythical kingdom, ruled over by King Bérenger I. Bérenger, the worried Everyman with whom Ionesco identifies in *The Killer* and *Rhinoceros*, is thus exalted and made the king of his own shadow world, just as each man is the king, the supreme figure, in his own personal world. Bérenger has not made much of a success of his reign. Under his heedless mismanagement his kingdom has shrunk to the point where it can be traversed from one end to the other in a few paces. It is inhabited exclusively by old men, congenital cretins, mongoloid idiots, and hydrocephalics. His palace is ghostly and run-down, somewhat like the palace in Ghelderode's *Escurial*. Bérenger himself is quite unaware of all this. He comes on full of vigor, greets his two wives, and prepares to bumble through another day. This is the day when at last he becomes aware of his life, by being made aware of his death. Marguerite, his embittered first wife, and the court physician (who is also the court executioner, bacteriologist, and astrologer) inform him that he will die in one-and-a-half hours, "at the end of the play." The rest of the play is taken up with Bérenger's gradual realization that he will in fact die, his desperate fight against that realization, and his progressive physical and mental deterioration. At the end he is only an incoherently babbling hulk of flesh, whose transition into total annihilation is barely noticeable.

The play is full of allusive touches. Ionesco plays with the concept of time: Bérenger has lived hundreds of years and he has lived only a few minutes. When one thinks of death and eternity, all time is the same. Marguerite seems at times like one of the implacable Fates. At others, she seems to be the hate that complements the intense love of Marie, the second wife. The real power of the play, however, resides in the poignancy

19. Donald Watson, "The Plays of Ionesco," *Tulane Drama Review*, III (Fall, 1958), p. 53.

of the emotion and the intensity of the repulsion with which Bérenger faces the prospect of his own annihilation. Like Ionesco, like modern man generally, Bérenger does not have the consolations of religion. Death means oblivion to him. Total disintegration of all that exists, as far as he is concerned. The thought that all will be as if he had never been is unbearable to King Bérenger. Like every man, Bérenger is his own universe, and the thought of its destruction fills him with horror:

Without me, without me. They'll laugh, they'll joke, they'll dance on my grave. I will never have existed. Ah, let them remember me. Let them weep, let them despair. Let them perpetuate my memory in all the history books. Let everyone know my life by heart. Let everyone re-live it. Let the students and the scholars have no other subject of study but me, my kingdom, my exploits. Let them burn every other book, let them destroy all the statues, let them put mine in all the public places. My image in all the ministries, all the police stations, all the internal revenue offices, all the hospitals. Let them name all the airplanes, all the ships, all the motor cars, and all the push-carts after me. Let all the other kings, warriors, poets, tenors, and philosophers be forgotten and let there be no one but me in everyone's mind. One single baptismal name, one single family name for everyone. Let them learn to read by spelling out my name: B-é-Bé, Bérenger. Let me be on the images and on all the millions of crosses in all the churches. Let them say Masses for me, let me be the Host. . . . Let them call on me for ever and ever, let them pray to me, let them implore me.[20]

In *The Aerial Pedestrian* (Le Piéton de l'air, 1963) Bérenger has recognizably become Ionesco again. He is a French dramatist who has given up writing for the theater because, as he reluctantly explains to an importunate newspaper reporter, "I

20. Eugène Ionesco, *Le Roi se meurt* (Paris: Gallimard, 1963), pp. 79–80.

am paralyzed since I know I must die." [21] As he leaves his house, a German bomber left over from the war blows it to bits. Bérenger then demonstrates his ability to fly, an ability that everyone has, though its use has been forgotten. Schechner suggests that flying may be a metaphor for the creative act itself.[22] I incline to the view that it is a metaphor for the act of living with full awareness. Bérenger's flight gives him a panoramic view of the earth. When he lands, he describes a landscape ravaged by bombs, by fire, and by ice. It is a vision of the earth as it might be after Armageddon, a writhing mass of fiercely striving, dismembered bodies, overcome by the implacable forces of Nature. Schechner suggests that this vision may be the postnuclear landscape.[23] More probably it is Ionesco's view of the inner reality of the earth and the people on it here and now.

Ionesco's latest play *Hunger and Thirst* (Le Soif et le Faim, 1966) continues the line opened up by the two immediately preceding plays. Once again he gives us here a play dealing with his own obsessions about life and death. Like *The Aerial Pedestrian*, it is based to a great extent on some of his own dreams, a fact that accounts at once for the apparent obscurity of much of these two plays as well as for their long stretches of dramatic aridity. Nevertheless, despite its inchoate form, *Hunger and Thirst* is an important play and deserves close analysis. The play is in three episodes, corresponding to the usual acts, entitled "The Flight," "The Rendezvous," and "The Black Masses of the Good Inn." In the first episode Jean and his wife are in the act of moving back into a damp and gloomy basement apartment from a spacious, light-filled one. Exactly why they are doing this is not made clear, although Jean registers vociferous disapproval. His wife—the ever-cheerful type— takes no notice of Jean's objections and goes gaily ahead with plans for brightening the room, drying the walls, and making a cosy nest of the place. Finally Jean flees, exasperated beyond

21. Eugène Ionesco, *Théâtre* (Paris: Gallimard, 1963), III, p. 128.
22. Schechner, *op. cit.*, p. 216.
23. *Ibid.*, p. 217.

endurance by her insistence on always looking on the bright side of everything. In the second episode Jean is on a high plateau full of light. Here he is supposed to meet a woman, although he cannot describe her or remember where he saw her last or be sure whether he is really supposed to meet her. In the third and by far the longest episode Jean, exhausted by his long trek through barren plains and walls of fog, comes to an inn staffed by men dressed as monks. The inn is and is not an inn: it is described as looking like a combination of monastery, prison, and military barracks. Here the "monks" assuage Jean's almost bottomless hunger and thirst and then show him a play in which two of the "monks" play starving prisoners who are forced to renounce their beliefs in order to get food. At the end Jean sees a dream vision of his wife and daughter welcoming him to an idyllic garden but learns that he must serve the "monks" an eternity before he can leave.

Much of the meaning of this must inevitably remain obscure, as all dreams must to those not in empathy with the dreamer. Nevertheless, it seems to me that the play is clearly connected to the two preceding ones. *The King Dies* and *The Aerial Pedestrian* dealt with death; *Hunger and Thirst* deals with life. Like Camus, Ionesco believes that life is all that there is and we must therefore make the best of it—such as it is. And it is not much. Man's life is really a death-in-life because man has no freedom. All through life man—if he is not one who instinctively accepts his lot—is thwarted, and at the end he realizes that the earthly paradise is really the bondage of everyday life against which he rebelled in the first place. In a world of despair, the best of all possible worlds may well be the one that seemed at first intolerable.

Ionesco seems to associate the words "hunger" and "thirst" with freedom, and to feel the paradox that freedom exists only in the imagination, that it is effectually lost as soon as it is gained. In one of his interviews with Claude Bonnefoy he makes the following distinction between freedom as enjoyed by those who have it and freedom as enjoyed by those who long for it: "Freedom is consumed every day along with the café-croissant and the glass of beer in all the bistros of Paris and Saint-Germain-des-Près; it's such an everyday thing there that no one thinks about it much anymore; the intellectuals of the eastern countries feel its absence, its necessity: they hunger and thirst for freedom; . . . the poets of the East give freedom a new virginity; they make us understand it, they make us understand . . . that we are free. Not entirely . . . we have less spiritual freedom, less imaginative power." [24] Thus to seek freedom, as Jean does in the play, is vain. When he begins his search he is already at his goal.

In the first episode he seeks to escape from the sameness of married life and family responsibilities to find "freedom" and "self-realization." Ionesco is portraying a generic and eternal marriage here, not a specific one: Jean's wife says that "I have known him for so long, since the beginning of the world. I am joined to him for eternity. Why does he call that being enchained?" [25] Instead of the boundless and undefined freedom that Jean longs for, she recommends imagination or doing the best with what one has: "From early morning look to the evening that will bring peace: it will come. During the night dream of the glory of the dawn." [26] And again: "Nourish yourself with your desires and drink from the cup of hope." [27] But Jean will have none of it, and, like Longfellow's foolish young man, rushes out overcome with the spirit of "Excelsior!" to seek his freedom.

In the second episode he comes to the high, clear plateau he has always imagined as the seat of his elusive freedom. Here he has a rendezvous with the ideal woman, but the woman does not come and he cannot describe her. Ironically, the only building on the plateau that Jean associates with freedom is a museum whose statues Jean plans to show his beloved when she comes. The only other characters in this episode are the two

---

24. Claude Bonnefoy, *Entretiens avec Eugène Ionesco* (Paris: Pierre Belfond, 1966), p. 106.
25. Eugène Ionesco, *Théâtre IV* (Paris: Gallimard, 1966), p. 95.
26. *Ibid.*, p. 94.
27. *Ibid.*

museum guards, who are almost as mummified as the exhibits they keep watch over and can think of nothing but their lunch while listening stolidly to Jean's ecstatic descriptions. Jean is free at this point, theoretically; but his inability to remember anything or to be exact in his descriptions of what he has seen is indicative of his inability to do anything with his freedom.

In the third episode Jean comes to the inn that looks like a combination prison, monastery, and barracks. Here sinister ceremonies, or "black masses," are practised. As the black mass is a reversal of the sacred ceremony, so the rituals practised by the false monks of the "good" inn are all mockeries of reality. They pretend hospitality but are really seeking to entrap their guest; they wash his feet, a sign of humility, but are really preparing to dominate him; they speak of Jean's freedom to go but station an armed guard at the door to prevent his leaving. The central incident in this episode is a lengthy scene from a play (there are 29 other scenes, we are told) involving two prisoners named Brechtoll and Tripp, atheist and believer, respectively. These are shown being systematically starved until they break down and renounce their beliefs: Brechtoll is given soup only after he prays to God for it, Tripp only after he renounces God. This scene is extremely difficult to interpret. It could mean that deeply held beliefs are meaningless because they are abandoned in the face of physical need. Or it could mean that the freedom to think openly and publicly, like all freedom, is merely something held by permission of the temporal (i.e., political) powers. Brechtoll, besides being an atheist, is also a socialist, and the "monks" on his side of the stage are robed in red; the ones on Tripp's side are in black. The names are so unusual that one is tempted to interpret them: Brechtoll seems to be a combination of the names of Brecht and Toller; Tripp seems to be an evocation of "tripartite" since he is clearly portrayed as a Christian believer. At the end of the play within a play Jean is shown a vision of his wife and child and realizes that that is where he wants to be and where he should have stayed. His search for an illusory freedom has brought him nothing: "Everything I wanted vanished as I approached it, everything I wanted to touch was blighted. As soon as I stepped on to a sunny field, the sky clouded over. I was never able to enjoy myself. The grass withered beneath my feet, the leaves on the trees yellowed and fell to earth as soon as I looked at them! Whenever I wanted to drink at the clearest spring, the water became tainted and disgusting." [28] And now, in one of Ionesco's typical nightmare endings, he is trapped at the inn, forced to work off the cost of all the food and drink he has consumed. As the play ends, Jean rushes around frantically serving food and drink to the "monks" as they chant the endless number of hours he must serve them.

We can see from this examination of Ionesco's plays that the main themes of his early plays (1950–1953) are (i) the paradox of the isolation of the individual in the midst of his fellows; and (ii) the paradox of the ultimate meaninglessness of the actions, which, taken together, constitute the sum of human existence. In the plays of his second period (*The Killer* and *Rhinoceros*) Ionesco abandoned the view of pessimistic fatalism in which man is a helpless puppet futilely and despairingly hammering against incomprehensible forces that always overwhelm him. Instead of the doctrinaire determinism which he derived from Antonin Artaud, Ionesco gave man a certain amount of free choice within the context of his temporal life. He thus made man morally responsible for his actions. With moral responsibility human existence once more took on meaning. Human actions once again became significant because they could be shown to have foreseeable results. Ionesco made the transition from preoccupation with ultimates, which is so characteristic of absolutists such as Artaud, to a concern for immediate, if relative, results—in other words, to the limited rebellion of Albert Camus, which concentrates on an individual ethical protest designed to bring about a relative alleviation of the human condition within the foreseeable future. In his latest (and probably last) phase, Ionesco has openly become an intensely personal writer. *The King Dies* and *The Aerial Pedestrian* are about Ionesco's preoccupation with his own

28. *Ibid.*, p. 165.

finiteness; *Hunger and Thirst* about the limits of possibility in life. Here again the influence of Camus can be discerned. In the future Ionesco must either find some sort of peace in philosophical speculation, as Camus did, or (as he has threatened in *The Aerial Pedestrian*) stop writing altogether.

JACQUES AUDIBERTI
The Drama of the Savage God

ONE OF THE marks of a great critic is his ability to grasp the significance of a particular work of art. To understand the meaning of a work is sufficiently difficult in itself; but to be able to place a work of art into its historical perspective upon first seeing it is a gift granted to few. The fact that he was totally unable to understand the work makes Yeats's remark about Jarry's *Ubu roi* all the more impressive. Most people dismissed Jarry as either a hoaxer or a psychopath, but Yeats had the critical perceptiveness to see that his play changed the whole course of creative thought in the theatre. "After us," he wrote, "the Savage God!" [1] More than twenty years later Antonin Artaud was to prove the truth of Yeats's prophecy; and more than twenty years after Artaud wrote *Le Théâtre et son Double* Jacques Audiberti was to write a series of plays with the Savage God—the malignant power of the cosmos—as protagonist. [2]

Awareness of and protest against the power of the Savage God is a characteristic of all current avant-garde drama. A sense of the twisted malignity of the universe hovers over all the plays of Ionesco, Beckett, Genet, and Adamov, but only in certain of the plays of Jacques Audiberti does this presence attain the stature of an invisible protagonist permeating the work.

Jacques Audiberti does not belong wholeheartedly to the avant-garde school of drama, and his plays look a little strange in the company of Ionesco, Genet, et al. With most avant-garde dramas, as soon as the curtain rises there is an instant assault on form and language which shocks the audience and forces it

1. William Butler Yeats, *Autobiography* (Garden City, N. Y.: Doubleday & Company, Inc., 1958), pp. 233–34. I am indebted to Professor Roger Shattuck's *The Banquet Years* for leading me to this reference.
2. Jacques Audiberti was born at Antibes in 1899 and is known in France primarily as a poet and novelist. He has published several volumes of poetry (e.g., *La beauté de l'amour, La pluie sur les boulevards, Race des hommes, Rempart, Des tonnes de semence, Toujours, Vive guitare*) and fifteen novels, the best known of which is probably *La Nâ*.

out of the conventional dramatic frame of reference. Audiberti does not operate in this way. His plays look superficially like perfectly ordinary plays in an unusual or exotic setting. All of these plays, however, have some peculiar, even fantastic, twist in the story that renders them unintelligible as ordinary melo-drama. The whole secret of understanding Audiberti's drama —and, indeed, most avant-garde drama—is not to expect to understand the plot as such. Ordinarily, the plot of a play is a carefully planned, logical, incident-by-incident account of what the play is about; and a discussion of the "meaning" of the play is identical with a discussion of the "meaning" of the plot. In the avant-garde drama, on the contrary, the plot is either a seemingly haphazard conglomeration of illogically connected incidents or a perfectly ordinary story with one or two un-expected insertions which suddenly make it unintelligible in the context of ordinary dramatic conventions. The point of all this is that in the avant-garde drama the plot is unimportant per se. The avant-gardist never tries to tell a story. Instead, he uses incidents to illustrate a theme. When Ionesco, for example, has the hero of *Jack* browbeaten into asserting that he likes roast potatoes, he is not writing a story about a young man be-ing browbeaten into asserting that he likes roast potatoes, which would be senseless. He is writing about a young man being forced to submit to ridiculous and arbitrary conventions (hence the use of the fantastic example of eating roast potatoes) by family pressure. Similarly, Beckett is not writing about the activities of two aimless vagrants in *Waiting for Godot*: their aimless meanderings are illustrative of the pointlessness and hopelessness of human existence. Precisely *what* Vladimir and Estragon do is not important at all. Precisely *what* Jack is forced to submit to is not important either. What is important is that the incidents serve to clarify some general theme. In the avant-garde drama, plot is relegated to a position of literally no importance whatsoever; only the theme matters. It is neces-sary, therefore, when studying the avant-garde drama to *dis-regard* the actual incidents of the play and apprehend instead the general theme of the author. Then one can observe how the incidents of the play, which may at first have seemed to be willfully meaningless, serve to illustrate the theme.

The two principal themes that Audiberti derives from Antonin Artaud are (i) the conflict between paganism and Christianity and (ii) the presence of a primordial spirit of evil in human affairs.

In Audiberti's eyes, as in Artaud's, paganism represents a purer state of mind than Christianity. Paganism was the first religion. It was a result of man's spontaneous, unsophisticated, unreasoned reaction to the powers of Nature. It was therefore far more real than the artificial, civilized, reasoned religion that Christianity represents. Paganism was a natural, instinctive reaction; Christianity is merely a patchwork of afterthoughts laid over the reality of human nature, which it stifles for the sake of social convenience. Anything that takes the human being away from his inborn reality is evil; and since in Audiberti's eyes the human being is evil to begin with, it follows that all artificial religions represent greater gradations of evil. The simplicity of instinctive human nature represents the best of all possible worlds in a universe where all possible worlds are bad.

Audiberti's second point—the pervading presence of evil in all human affairs—is usually expressed through his obsession with the idea of the controlling power of sex. He feels that in his sexual activities the human being comes closest to being an animal. With this emphasis on sex Audiberti pares all men down to one common level and gets rid of the artificial social distinctions that serve to differentiate people from each other in the traditional drama. All of Audiberti's characters are animalistic (with the exception of the myth characters in *Pucelle* and *Opéra parlé*); and there are no good animals in Audiberti's world. All of them are stained with the mark of an evil spirit. There is another, less obvious, reason for the emphasis Audiberti places on sex and that is the assumption that the act of intercourse merges us with Nature and therefore brings us nearer to the primordial evil. This view leads him to a sort of Manichean dichotomy between flesh and spirit with the flesh always conquering and leading inevitably to disaster.[3]

3. Leonard C. Pronko (in *Avant-Garde* [Berkeley, Cal.: University of California Press, 1962], p. 188) sees Audiberti's plays as pantheistic: man is pure only when he remerges with nature.

The conflict between paganism and Christianity, which runs through all of Audiberti's plays, is treated overtly only in *Quoat-Quoat* (1946) and *Opéra parlé* (Spoken Opera, published 1956). In *Quoat-Quoat*, for example, Audiberti is talking about the latent power in the primeval myths that formed the human character far back in prehistoric times, long before the advent of the skin-deep, artificially superimposed pseudomyths by which we live now. To illustrate this theme he sets his story on a ship bound from France to Mexico about one hundred years ago. Amédée has come on board in the guise of a young scholar in search of Mexican archaeological antiquities. But the captain informs him that he is aware that Amédée is really a French spy sent to discover the whereabouts of the late Emperor Maximilian's hidden treasure. He reads him the pertinent section from the law of the high seas which provides that any accredited espionage agent found entering into a relationship with a woman on board ship must be shot. Immediately afterwards, Amédée is caught making love to the captain's daughter and is sentenced to be shot by the overjoyed captain, who gets a bonus for each corpse. While he is awaiting the dawn, Amédée is visited by a wild-looking Mexican woman who offers to rescue him by means of a magic stone belonging to the ancient Mexican god Quoat-Quoat. Amédée refuses and insists on accepting the fate to which his actions have delivered him. He hands the woman and her magic stone over to the captain. Finally a third woman, a rather bedraggled, gypsylike hag, shows up and announces that she is the real spy and that Amédée was just an innocent decoy to divert suspicion from her. Amédée is now free since he is no longer subject to laws governing the behavior of spies on the high seas. He refuses, however, to avoid the fate to which he sincerely thought his actions had led him. Locking the captain and the real spy into the cabin, he rushes on deck and has himself shot by the firing squad. As the curtain falls, the captain raises the stone of Quoat-Quoat preparatory to annihilating the ship.

The important point in this apparently extremely confused plot is that Audiberti undoubtedly wishes us to believe that as the curtain falls the captain destroys his ship and everyone on it with the stone of the ancient god Quoat-Quoat. This does not mean that Audiberti literally believes in the existence of a childish black magic, but rather that he feels that the modern world represented by the ship, with its weblike overlay of arbitrary legal minutiae, is still basically at the mercy of the turbulent atavistic forces that originally molded the human spirit. To both Artaud and Audiberti the true expression of human nature is the phenomenon of the Malay native running amok, slashing without regard through the gradually woven net of "civilized" conventions. Only Amédée in a sense escapes. Although he too dies, he dies by his own choice, by making an existential decision and declining any longer to be bound up and batted back and forth by directions that do not concern him as a separate individual. Amédée is the rebel-hero of whom Camus speaks. He finds his death—and, paradoxically, his freedom at the same time—by taking his stand and saying thus far will he permit himself to be driven and no further. At some point one must rebel against the net of convention, and if the rebellion results in death, *tant pis*.

In *Opéra parlé* Audiberti again writes of his belief in the latent power of paganism. Here he describes the eclipse of paganism by Christianity as being a voluntary and temporary one. Set in the ninth century, A.D., the play tells of the cutting of a straight highway through the depths of a forest in eastern France. This straight road symbolizes the ascendancy of Christianity, with its mute promise of a definite destination at the end, over the mysterious tangled forest of druidic paganism. It is the triumph of the ordered over the arcane, of the highway over the labyrinth. The builder of the highway has under his care a young girl who had been entrusted to him by the Grand Master of the Pagan order. As the play opens, the Grand Master appears again and takes "a stone both visible and invisible" from between the girl's eyes:

> THE MASTER: Give back to me the stone both visible and invisible which shimmers between your eyes. . . . Little by little you will lose your power. You will become weak. You will become mild. You will become a woman.[4]

4. Jacques Audiberti, *Théâtre* (Paris: Gallimard, 1956), III, p. 110.

This act deprives her of her powers as a pagan goddess. She is now no longer free to merge with the woods and the waters and to communicate with the animals, for she must marry a Christian and subjugate herself and all that she represents to him. The holy oracles have spoken, the Grand Master tells her: for a time the people will wish to live according to the laws of the clerics:

> After the forest, the highway. After the star, the church. After the girl, the woman. . . . For a time the Gascons and the Saxons and all the nations will live according to the law clerical, canonical, episcopal, pontifical.[5]

But the Church of Christ will fall in its turn as well and then the pagan gods will come back from their eclipse. Meanwhile the young goddess must marry a Christian. She obeys and marries Baron Massacre, who embodies the bloody, vengeful, unnatural aspects of Christianity; but the pagan spirit cannot be entirely subjugated. While the girl loses her powers and becomes the wife of the baron, her real lover, a previously exemplary military officer, turns his back on Christianity in disgust at this unjust and incongruous union and becomes a sort of Robin Hoodlike outlaw specializing in the destruction and plunder of churches and monasteries. At the end all three protagonists are killed, as befits the conventions of the tragic melodrama that Audiberti uses as his framework for this story on the theme of the immortality of the pagan spirit.

Audiberti's plays about the latent force of the pagan spirit in the modern world do not mean that he himself believes in paganism. His point is that the essence of paganism is freedom from arbitrary, socially initiated coercion and that it is therefore closer to the Nature from which man originally sprang and from which he derives his true being. Paganism is not good in itself: it is merely *natural* and therefore inevitable. There is no absolute good in Audiberti's cosmos—only absolute evil and the comparative good that is to be found in not attempting to act against one's nature. In so far as men drift away from their origins, they become progressively more evil. This is the basis

5. *Ibid.*, p. 113.

of the series of plays Audiberti has written about the problem of evil in society.

His first play of this type, and probably his best-known play, is *Le Mal court* (The Evil Runs, 1947). As usual, the plot is unimportant in itself, serving only to illustrate the theme, which is that of the omnipresence and inexorable force of evil. Audiberti uses a conventional fairy-tale plot: beautiful young princess, daughter of an impoverished king, goes to marry rich young king; wicked cardinal intervenes and prevents marriage for political reasons; beautiful young princess heartbroken, etc., etc. Audiberti carries his classic fairy-tale formula only up to a point: the rich young king does not throw the wicked cardinal into an oubliette so that he can marry the beautiful young princess at the end. Instead, the princess, Alarica, finds as the play proceeds that she is, and always has been, ringed around with evil and deceit. Her illusions about the goodness of life and the decency and trustworthiness of people drop from her one by one in a series of painful shocks. She discovers that her projected marriage had been secretly abandoned a long time ago and that she is being used as a decoy so that the young king can make a politically more advantageous match. Even her old and faithful nurse is in the plot. There is absolutely nobody she can trust. Everyone is self-seeking, corruptible, and dishonest because everyone is living and ordering his existence within the context of an artificial and corrupt society. As the series of shocks she is obliged to undergo bludgeon her into an awareness of the true nature of the world, Alarica realizes that she must make her compromise with it if she is to survive as something other than a pawn. She determines to fight evil with evil—to let "the evil run." She deposes her amiable, bumbling old father, disregarding his pleas for filial respect, and resolves to rule with complete ruthlessness. If everything is evil, then the most evil wins.

If evil in *Le Mal court* takes the form of personal deceit, in *La Fête noire, La Logeuse,* and *Les Naturels du Bordelais* Audiberti links it with sex. Sex is for Audiberti a manifestation of elemental Nature. As such it is evil in itself, but evil also arises from its repression, from its transformation in society to something artificial and therefore perverted. This state of affairs brings about a paradox: evil is implicit in repression and perversion, and evil also comes when the long repressed force of sex inevitably breaks out with cyclonic savagery. In this latter form, Audiberti's sex is analogous to Artaud's plague—the heedless emotional whirlwind that takes the human being back into the long-abandoned racial subconsciousness, his only true reality.

Audiberti's most explicit statement of this theme and at the same time far and away his best play is *La Fête noire* (The Black Feast, 1948), which is also the most successful and faithful dramatization of the theories of Antonin Artaud. *La Fête noire* takes place in a wild and mountainous region of southern France, where Felicien, the hero of the piece, is the local doctor. Felicien's one desire is to win the love of a woman. But this is precisely the one thing that always eludes him. As the unnatural repression builds up in him, Felicien becomes a sort of perverted superman figure, a symbol of the masculine drive, the motor force behind men's actions, hemmed in by the restrictions imposed on its free outpouring by the laws of civilized society. Audiberti sees Felicien as Superman Bound—and bound so effectively that his ineluctable force can emerge only in a horribly twisted form, maliciously revenging itself on the culture that has fettered it. Felicien's pent-up fury escapes from him and, like an angry genie at last released from his bottle, takes the form of an evil beast that roams the country literally ripping open any woman it meets. At first this ecstatic and elemental fury spends itself on the women who have rejected Felicien, but gradually it eludes his control and becomes an independent scourge to punish all women for their disavowal of sex. This Jack the Ripper-like scourge is not to be taken literally, of course: it is the embodiment of Artaud's "plague," the instinctive force that the drama should express.

The second act of the play is a semifarcical parable about the killing of the beast. The whole countryside is up in arms as a result of the outrages committed, and Felicien is appointed leader of the hunt. The "beast" is cornered in a small square in front of a mountain-side shrine. Hundreds of people have turned out to watch the slaughter, which is to be blessed by a

high-ranking prelate. The "beast" is driven on and turns out
to be only a broken-down old goat. The goat is then cere-
moniously killed with much blowing of trumpets and sprinkling
of holy water, and the only person who recognizes the "beast"
for what it is and has the courage to say so is driven off by
the soldiers. Just as the bells are beginning to toll in celebration
of the death of the "beast," word comes that another girl has
been ripped apart in a neighboring village, but nobody takes
any notice of this: the "beast" has been officially killed; therefore, any further evidence of its presence is to be ignored.

Audiberti's parable here concerns the gradual suppression
by the Church of the natural human sex drives. Through its
ritual and liturgy the Church has tried to stifle the natural
human impulses and mold the human spirit to an artificial ideal.
But this molding process has inevitably been as unsuccessful as
the killing of the "beast" in the play. The continual repetition
of the forms and rituals, as well as the living repression of Nature in the celibacy of the clergy, has had the effect of numbing the senses of the arbiters of civilized behavior; and, having
officially decreed the beast dead, they can afford to take no
notice of its continued depredations beyond the range of their
comforting incense.

At the end of the play Audiberti changes the atmosphere
of his parable from farce to irony. Felicien has become world-
famous as the slayer of the beast. All the governments of the
world have decorated him, learned societies consult him, graduate students write theses on the habits of the Black Beast.
Felicien has grown rich by selling relics of the beast: he is just
about to dispose of the beast's eleven thousandth tooth. In
short, the beast has become a sort of religious cult. Alleged
pieces of the beast are revered in all the royal courts of the
world and are solemnly preserved and studied in all the great
universities. The priests eagerly abet Felicien's sale of dogs'
and cows' teeth as relics of the True Beast. But the beast has
in fact now become real and out of its creator's control: at the
end it destroys Felicien himself.

La Fête noire is important in the history of the modern
avant-garde drama because it is the most perfect realization of

Artaud's theories. Not only does Audiberti use the "plague" (in the form of the destructive beast) as his binding theme, but he also follows Artaud's specifications for involving the spectators in the vortex of emotion. Just before the "beast" is led in to be killed, Audiberti has the following stage direction:

> Brouhaha. The ground shakes under the audience's seats. Green leaves fly through the auditorium. At the back of the stage a hairy, sallow face floats by. It will be quite easy to bring about this rapid apparition.[6]

Here Audiberti directly follows Artaud's suggestions for encircling the audience and involving it in the action:

> Every spectacle will contain a physical and objective element, perceptible to all. Cries, groans, apparitions, surprises, theatricalities of all kinds, . . . concrete appearances of new and surprising objects, masks, effigies yards high, . . . A direct communication will be re-established between the spectator and the spectacle, between the actor and the spectator, from the fact that the spectator, placed in the middle of the action, is engulfed and physically affected by it. . . . The hall will be enclosed by four walls, without any kind of ornament, and the public will be seated in the middle of the room, on the ground floor, on mobile chairs which will allow them to follow the spectacle which will take place all around them.[7]

Audiberti continues his "actualization" of myths in *La Logeuse* (The Landlady, written 1954) and *Les Naturels du Bordelais*,[8] the only other two plays he has written which have any significance as avant-garde dramas. In *La Logeuse* Audiberti uses the Circe myth as the basis for a story about matriarchal domination. In modern life Circe becomes Mme. Cirqué, the

6. Jacques Audiberti, *Théâtre* (Paris: Gallimard, 1952), II, p. 73.
7. Antonin Artaud, *The Theater and its Double*, translated by Mary C. Richards. Copyright © 1958 by the Grove Press, Inc. (New York: Grove Press, Inc., 1958), pp. 93–96.
8. The several punning implications of this title are untranslatable. The literal translation would be *The Natives of the Bordelais* (the area around Bordeaux); it was first published in 1952.

owner of a rooming house, who transforms her male lodgers into slaves. Her husband, for example, was formerly a high-ranking government official, but now he spends all his time at home making ladies' hats. During the play Mme. Cirqué is arrested for hiding a fugitive from justice (her daughter's fiancé, whom she had egged on to commit a robbery). While she is away, all her men return to their former lives and live together in happy comradeship, their one fear that she will return. And return she does, having put her spell on the police inspector who had originally trapped her by pretending to be hypnotized by her charm. Now he is hypnotized in reality and helplessly joins the other swine in Mme. Cirqué's female-dominated household-world.

Les Naturels du Bordelais is easily Audiberti's most confusing play. Here he takes the theme of the destructiveness of sex one step further. Under Mme. Cirqué the men are figuratively turned into swine by the sexual force that radiates from her. In *Les Naturels* the characters are *literally* turned into animals. Just as surrender of the mind turns the characters of Ionesco's *Rhinoceros* into rampaging horned beasts, so a constant preoccupation with sex, a surrender of the mind to the animalism of the body, turns the characters of Audiberti's play into insects. Audiberti is, of course, referring here not to natural, unrepressed sex, but to the sickly, perverted, sexual preoccupation of modern society.

Audiberti has written several other plays, notably *Pucelle* (1950) and *L'Effet Glapion* (The Glapion Effect, 1959), but they are not significant in the history of the avant-garde movement. Both *Pucelle* and *L'Effet Glapion*, which has been mentioned for Broadway production, are about Audiberti's belief that true reality lies in the fantasies and not in the actual everyday experiences of people. More recently Audiberti has concentrated on writing radio plays.

It is extremely difficult to form any judgment of Audiberti's work. Some of his plays exemplify more perfectly than any others the theories of the twentieth-century avant-garde drama. However, Audiberti is primarily a poet, and he frequently goes off into lyric flights that are there for their own sake rather than for the play's. As a playwright he is distinctly out of his element. His plays are written as if he had carefully read Artaud and had deliberately followed his method in constructing them. They are like textbook examples of the avant-garde drama—lifeless, dry, dispassionate, carefully dovetailed, and laboriously planed. Yet despite his lucid approach, Audiberti is difficult to understand, perhaps more difficult than any other avant-garde dramatist. Writers like Ionesco and Beckett are difficult to understand because their meaning is implied rather than stated. Audiberti's obscurity is caused not by his meaning being implied, but by its being abstruse. Like most poets whose minds work easiest in the channels of symbolist verse, Audiberti is essentially a mystic; and mysticism on the stage is hopelessly out of place. The essence of stage writing is clarity, while the essence of mystical writing is its arcane quality. The apparent obscurity of Ionesco, Beckett, and Genet can instantly be made clear by good stage production: the obscurity of mysticism cannot.

JEAN TARDIEU
The Art of the One-Act Play

"THE PROBLEM, in my opinion, does not lie in knowing whether the theatre of the future will be 'realistic' or not, but rather in the discovery of new forms and in the unceasing search for new ways of expression." [1] These words by Jean Tardieu help to explain the remarkable series of one-act plays that he has published in the last few years.

The one-act play has always been a sort of theatrical lame dog. After the seventeenth century *entremés*, its most popular period was during the nineteenth century, when almost every full-length play was preceded by a one-act play and often followed by one as well. These short plays were usually farces. They were never taken very seriously by anyone, neither by the managers, nor by the players, nor by the audiences, nor (consequently) by the ill-paid hacks who wrote them. It was generally understood that the prologue served merely to give "fashionable" latecomers the satisfaction of creating a disturbance without at the same time missing any part of the main attraction. The epilogue, similarly, let the world of fashion serenely sweep out during a play instead of shuffling out with the crowd at the end and at the same time gave the glassy-eyed die-hards in the low-priced seats the illusion of having had their money's worth. Since those days the prestige of the one-act play has not risen appreciably. During the twentieth century it has usually been either a children's play or an adolescents' play or a play by someone too lazy to write a full-length play. The annual anthologies are carefully avoided by all theater people except high-school drama directors.

Tardieu has given the one-act form new meaning by realizing that it is inadequate for the treatment of any one theme. To take a theme or to preplan a story and then to try and squeeze it into the confines of the one-act form results inevitably in failure. The one-act play must be a self-contained entity.

1. I am indebted to M. Tardieu for this definition of his work.

Instead of treating a "subject" (i.e., a theme or a planned story), it should treat an "object" (i.e., a thing, a given problem, or situation). In other words, instead of writing drama *de*ductively (by starting with a theme or philosophical concept and working in toward a specific plot situation designed to illustrate it), Tardieu writes *in*ductively (by starting with a specific plot situation and letting it effloresce at will until the ramifications of the action touch upon some larger theme, even if only allusively). Tardieu confines himself to the given situation or concrete object about which he has decided to write, never once bringing in any subsidiary motifs. In this way he has given new life to the one-act form and hopes to complete a "well-tempered clavichord" of the one-act experimental drama.[2]

Tardieu's plays may be divided into two classes: the serious and the experimental-linguistic. The first class consists of miniature expositions of the principles of the avant-garde drama. They deal with the chief philosophical preoccupations of the avant-garde school: man's state as a powerless atom in a reasonless void, and, on a temporal level, the enslavement of the human mind, such as it is, by social pressure.

Tardieu's early plays are a strange combination of his interest in poetic language, his instinctive and natural faith in life, and his rationalized philosophy of despair. His characters seem to float in a mysterious and hostile immensity, in a void pulsating with implied menace, where they can feel "the stillness of an implacable force brooding over an inscrutable intention." And yet, unlike the other avant-garde dramatists, Tardieu sometimes holds out hope. There is hope for man if he can forget his cosmic context and concentrate on love: at certain moments Tardieu seems to be that paradoxical hybrid, a pessimistic romantic. This attitude can be seen most clearly in the early play *Le Sacre de la Nuit* (The Rite of Night, written 1948), in which two young people observe the depth of the sky and the night and fasten upon each other in the immensity:

> THE MAN: . . . The demons and the gods are in flight. You have merged with the immensity of the night,

2. Interview with the author.

you have entered into communion with the innocence of
the world. Be happy in this shower of light and honey and
freshness. Be reborn, pure and adorned for love, carried on
the wings of motionless time, weightless in my adoring night.
Come!
*(The man rises. He and the woman slowly advance towards
each other. When they reach the middle of the stage, they
take each other's hands and go slowly towards the right.)*
    THE WOMAN: I will go with you along the road
without an ending.[3]

All of these early plays of Tardieu's are little more than
pastiches, exercises in the creation of a *mood* (as distinct from
a situation or an action) on the stage. His first play, *Qui est là?*
(Who Is There?, written 1947, performed 1949), perfectly
compresses into the one-act form all the principles of the avant-
garde drama, as set forth by Antonin Artaud. Artaud decreed
that drama should strip man of the façade of illusion that
society erects around him and show him in his *real* context—
a helpless and insignificant being in an immense and hostile
nothingness. Artaud describes this nothingness through his
twin symbols of cruelty and the plague. The void is evil and
preys on men; and man's consciousness of it drives him into a
sort of atavistic delirium, symbolized in the drama by irrational
behaviour and "unexpected happenings." Thus, in *Qui est là?*
we have an ordinary family—father, mother, and son—who sit
in a harshly lit, almost bare room. The trappings of "civilization"
are deliberately avoided. The members of the family are not
identified by name: they are thoroughly depersonalized so that
they could be anybody. This is in accordance with Artaud's idea
that what we call individual personality is merely a superficial
gloss and the drama should seek to portray the elemental quality common to all men. In Tardieu's play the members of the
family are sitting around their dinner table when a woman
suddenly materializes, and, like one of the mythic Norns,
gives vague warnings of danger. Immediately afterwards the

3. Jean Tardieu, *Théâtre de Chambre I* (Paris: Gallimard, 1955), p.
31.

father is strangled by a "hired murderer" (hired by whom? The malign cosmic forces, presumably); and the mother and son, looking out of the window, see a landscape covered with dead. It is as if they were looking out on a scene by Hieronymus Bosch. The father emerges from this blanket of cadavers, which stifles the earth from above instead of fertilizing it from below, but he is not alive. He tells us that the man in all of us is dead but that one day he *will be*. As he makes this prediction, light floods the scene, and Tardieu ends his play on the "hollow man" theme with an expression of hope.

La Politesse Inutile (Useless Courtesy, written 1947, performed 1950), Tardieu's second play, has the same theme as *Qui est là?* but in a more restricted form. Again Tardieu is talking about the invisible, unsuspected line that separates man from reality. Within the magic circle of his illusions man feels secure, comfortable, self-respecting. He never understands that he is in a circle until he inadvertently steps across the incredibly thin line of its circumference or until some external influence invades his territory. When this happens man feels like a goldfish who has flipped out of his bowl or like one whose bowl is suddenly disturbed by a groping human hand. In *La Politesse Inutile* a respected professor, self-satisfied, a symbol of comfortable security, is visited by a sinister, shabby character who slaps him and leaves, threatening to return. The professor's habitual self-assurance can never again be the same, for he now knows he is as vulnerable as a toy balloon in a maze of capriciously moving spikes.[4]

Tardieu's most successful effort so far to depict the relationship between man and the universe is *L'A.B.C. de notre vie* (The A.B.C. of Our Life, 1959). In this long one-act play we see an ordinary man go through the motions of a typical day while a chorus of men and women provide a muted ac-

---

4. The professor figure as a symbol of self-assurance and comfortable respectability has also been used by Arthur Adamov in *Le Professeur Taranne*. Taranne suddenly finds that his academic reputation is gone and that nobody recognizes him. There is also a close thematic relationship between *La Politesse Inutile* and Edward Albee's *The Zoo Story*.

companiment of everyday sounds. The stage is divided into two parts, the young man on one side, the chorus on the other. While the young man—Tardieu calls him the "protagonist"— describes the various emotions he feels as he goes through his day, the chorus provides an undertone of murmured words which can be understood only occasionally and which fades away into a vox humana obbligato during the protagonist's speeches. In addition to these two forces, which complement each other like the scales of a balance, there are two characters named Monsieur Mot and Madame Parole who stand in the middle, so to speak, and comment on the action. Their comments consist mostly of strings of consecutive polysyllabic words from the dictionary, and they have the double function of providing comic relief and giving us Tardieu's own tongue-in-cheek view of the action. The play's purpose, and, indeed, the purpose of Tardieu's work as a whole, is summed up in the prologue's speech:

> Here begins the symphony of the great city,/A symphony without music, composed of murmurs, words, and cries,/ Here, before the break of day,/The sleeping citizens play out their churning dreams./One man among many slowly awakes./He wants to find again his childhood dream: his freedom in the wind, the trees, the sea . . . /But the vast murmur of the city/Will not let him escape. See him there/Caught up by the relentless multitude,/Bound to History and to the immediate event,/To something of which he is unaware, which happens far away from him./Love alone can be reborn, ever virginal and ever new/As on the first day of the world . . . / . . . No, Man cannot escape his fellow man,/For he is all he knows/And the murmur which lulls him to sleep/After so much trouble and torment/Is his own—the ocean of words,/Monotonous and devoid of sense/Like the sound of the wind among the trees.[5]

5. Jean Tardieu, *Poèmes à Jouer* (Paris: Gallimard, 1960), pp. [17]–18.

Most of Tardieu's plays are a satiric protest against the enslavement of the human mind by social pressure. We see this idea running through play after play and growing automatically and unconsciously out of Tardieu's "given situation." It is seen most clearly in *Le Guichet* (translated as The Information Bureau, 1955), the simplest and dramatically most effective of Tardieu's plays. Here Tardieu deals with the supreme position that bureaucracy has blandly assumed in modern society. Faced with the bureaucratic official, the ordinary individual automatically adopts the condition of a cocoon on a roller coaster. In Tardieu's cosmos the filing cabinet is God and the filing clerk is its prophet. The frightening aspect is that the ordinary man makes no attempt to fight. On the contrary, he has complete faith, and, once he feels himself *en rapport* with the official, he curls up with relief and allows himself to be rushed into the dark, comfortable maw that awaits him. There are only two characters in *Le Guichet*: the information-bureau official and the inquirer. The latter comes in to inquire about train departures and is instantly enmeshed in the bureaucratic net. He is given a tag numbered 3640 and told to wait, although he is the only person there. When the official has got through scratching himself and listening to the weather report, he calls the little man and asks him his name, his place and date of birth, profession and marital state. Then he examines his tongue and the palms of his hands. All this goes down on a file card before the inquirer can get a word out of his mouth. Finally it becomes the client's turn to ask some questions. It turns out that he has come to the information office much as an ancient Greek might have come to the Delphic oracle. Not only does he want to know when his train leaves —he also wants to know which train he should take. At first the official refuses to advise the man on the ground that it is not his business to do so. The inquirer is crushed by this unexpected rebuff:"And I wanted so much to get some advice, to find out what I should do . . . what I should do . . . what direction I should take . . . ! Yes, I would so much like to know what direction I should take . . . in life . . . and above all

. . ." [6] This speech is ominously interrupted by the loudspeaker saying, *in a far-away and dreamlike voice*, "Passengers for all directions, get ready, please . . . Attention, all passengers . . . your train is leaving . . . your train, your automobile, your horse is leaving in a few minutes . . . Attention! . . . Attention! . . . Get ready!" [7] The official, thawed by the man's pitiful state, decides to help him. He gets the little man to admit that he is really seeking "*Une femme du genre 'femme de ma vie.'* " The omniscient filing system steps in:

> THE OFFICIAL: Wait a moment while I consult my files. Let's see, your name begins with M and ends with T . . . good . . . (*He leafs through his cards*) Here we are. A brunette answering to the name of Rita Caraquilla crossed the street at 3:45 p.m. heading in a south-westerly direction. Is that the one?
>
> THE MAN: I don't think so. The woman of my life would be more blonde . . . blonde shading to chestnut . . . Between the two, in short.
>
> THE OFFICIAL: All right, perhaps it's this one then: Miss Rose Plouvier, modest . . . No, sorry: Modiste, will cross the porch of the building across the street tomorrow at 9 a.m. She will be going to visit a customer, Mrs. Couchois, who . . .[8]

But this isn't the right one either. The little man's "femme de ma vie" does not appear to exist. He then progresses to more complex questions: What does the official think of his way of living (he is advised to give up newspapers and black coffee); what will be his destiny in life (he is told he doesn't have one); and, finally, when will he die? The official takes his horoscope and then amiably tells him he will die in a few minutes—in fact, as soon as he leaves the office. Hopelessly, the man leaves. We hear a terrific crash and a scream. The official listens attentively. There is neither satisfaction nor regret in his attitude:

6. Jean Tardieu, *Théâtre de Chambre I*, pp. 77–78.
7. *Ibid.*, p. 77.
8. *Ibid.*, pp. 79–80.

only the quiet assurance of a mechanic who knows a car will stop if someone steps on the brake. He returns calmly to his file cards. I have treated *Le Guichet* at some length because I feel that it is the best example of Tardieu's theories of play-writing in practice, because it is a perfect example of what a one-act play ought to be, and because it deals with a dramatic theme that is constantly becoming more important.

In *Le Guichet* Tardieu has taken a simple, objective every-day situation, that of a man making inquiries in an information office. Everyday situations are not in themselves dramatic. The only thing that is dramatic is the *special* situation, the unusual twist in the everyday situation, the sudden entrance of the bizarre or ironic into the humdrum milieu. The introduction of the unusual and unexpected into the ordinary situation sharpens it, gives a point to what was pointless, and directs that point at the jarred consciousness of the audience. In other words, realistic situations can only be made dramatic by in-serting unrealistic elements. There never has been a "realistic drama." Every so-called "realistic drama" has been rendered dramatic by internal contrast with the unrealistic (that which does not constitute an element of ordinary everyday life). There is no such thing as a *tranche de vie* play. Any slice or sliver of anyone's life may be very interesting, as Thornton Wilder tells us, but no play purporting to present an ordinary, unadorned, unadulterated slice of life has ever been read seriously all the way through. M. Tardieu flavors his slice of life with a type of urbane irony and perverse humour commonly and erroneously attributed to his countrymen as a class by critics who rely on time-honored generalizations as a substitute for thought. Actu-ally this quality is peculiar to M. Tardieu and a select inter-national group of other highly gifted thinkers. Tardieu's twist is that the client seeks information about his destiny, and his bombshell is that the information bureau is fully informed about his destiny—indeed, even appears to control it.

Tardieu sees the human race as pressed down flat by the weight of the social institutions that it has itself built up. Men-tally, man has no initiative any more: he has been mangled and pounded by his mechanistic masters until his mind resembles nothing so much as a piece of very gelatinous head cheese. Physically, man is a neurotic, timid, ulcer-ridden mouse with a ring through his nose. The tragedy is that he has been brought to a state where his one wish is not to break the ring but to hook it to something—anything. The official is no better off, of course: he is merely a robot without knowing it. He is not seeking to hook his ring on to a machine: he has already been wholly fused into one.

The theme of human helplessness against authority occurs again and again in Tardieu's works. In *La Société Apollon* (The Apollo Society, 1955) he satirizes, on the surface at least, the gushy enthusiasm of the more ridiculous type of art worshipper. An amateur art-lovers' club pays a visit to a sculptor's studio. The sculptor is not at home, so the club leader, a bony, bucktoothed lady with a voice like an off-key English horn, proceeds to explain the various freshly created *objets d'art* scattered around the studio. An imposing arrangement of wires, cranks, and hooks in the middle of the studio attracts her attention, and she points out its "beauties" to her gawking acolytes. The object's marvelous form, ethos, and various other *"un je ne sais quoi"* attributes are faithfully admired and commented upon with the required knowledgeable air. The bubble has to be burst, of course; and pretty soon the sculptor enters and explains. The much-admired centerpiece is his "great invention, the universal kitchen machine." All one need do is dump the raw material into the hopper, turn the crank, and the finished product is spewed out at the bottom. His eyes aglint at the prospect of making a sale, the "master" passes out investment brochures to his now outraged visitors. One after another they dodge out of the door. Finally the "master" is alone, but he is so enraptured with the sacred fire that he fails to notice it. As the lights fade out, he stands before a jumble of squiggles on the wall and explains that it is an ear-washing machine for dogs.

La Société Apollon is more than just a cheap laugh at the poor defenseless incompetents who moon around Bohemian neighborhoods. Tardieu is trying to tell us (what is obvious enough but cannot be repeated too often) that the sheeplike stupidity of the art club members in following their donkey of a cicerone, though harmless and amusing in itself, is symptomatic of an unhealthy condition of the modern mind. In Tardieu the modern mind—the mind, that is, of the ordinary man-in-the-street—craves irresponsibility and therefore willingly and uncritically, almost by now instinctively, abases itself before the first vague semblance of authority that it encounters.

In *Conversation-Sinfonietta* (1951) Tardieu's effect, though less immediate, is none the less powerful. The scene is a broadcasting studio. The orchestra members have no instruments. Instead, they speak the phrases of ordinary everyday life as the conductor's baton directs them. The baton comes down, points, and "Good morning, good morning, good morning," the bassos mumble. "How do you do? How do you do? How do you do? You're looking well today," the tenor chimes in. The soprano simpers, "Oh, do you really think so?" And so on, and so on, and so on. The "orchestra" runs through all the petty phrases of an ordinary day at the conductor's command. That is all there is to it; but as the play goes on the speakers become more and more the puppets of authority and the conductor's baton looms ever larger as a symbol of the omnipotent cosmic meaninglessness that jiggles them into motion and stills them at will.

In *Un Geste pour un autre* (One Way For Another, 1951) Tardieu satirizes the ordinary conventions of behavior in polite society. He exposes the basic meaninglessness of the little automatic gestures required by society simply by inventing a society the same as ours in all respects except that these gestures are reversed. Admiral Sepulchre has discovered the Nameless Archipelago. He describes it as a place where there are many beautiful cities newly built in the most modern styles thanks to their previous destruction in bombing attacks; where there are completely free citizens protected by an omnipresent police force; where there are peaceful customs defended by a militia armed to the teeth; and where there is a stable parliament founded upon constantly unstable opinions. In short, as he puts it, all the trappings of Progress are there. But this country, so much like ours from a political standpoint, has completely different social customs. The point, of course, is that one set of customs will do as well as another, and therefore both are pointless. In the Nameless Archipelago, when a guest arrives at a party, he puts a hat on and takes his shoes and socks off, making the hostess a present of the latter. Then he kisses her foot. During the party the guests amuse themselves by coughing and spitting and insulting each other. The fact that this latter habit is becoming more prevalent at parties in our own society is one proof of the validity of M. Tardieu's theme. Perhaps we will soon be coughing and spitting and doing gymnastics at our parties too.

The essence of Tardieu's formula for the one-act play is that the selected situation must be carried to its logical conclusion. Thus in *Le Guichet* he takes the situation of a man making inquiries as far as it can go; in *Le Meuble* (The Piece of Furniture, 1954), a play about an answering machine that shoots its questioners if they catch it making mistakes, he takes the situation of an "infallible" machine as far as it can go; and in *La Serrure* (The Keyhole, 1955) he takes that good old French institution, the strip tease, as far as *it* can go. *La Serrure* is a sophisticated *grand guignol* skit shot through with a macabre humour. A timid little pervert comes to a whorehouse in order to see a woman undress. He is strictly a voyeur—personal contact with the woman does not interest him. The madam arranges matters so that he can watch one of her girls undress through a huge keyhole. We are given to understand that this occasion is the culminating point of the man's life—something he has been looking forward to and working for since an early age. Ecstatically the man watches the woman strip naked, but she does not stop. She takes out her eyes, pulls off her lips, peels off her flesh. Finally, when only a skeleton is left, the man drops dead. The madam appears again in the darkened room, looks down at the body, and says, *à voix très basse, presque en chuchotant* (in a very low voice, almost a whisper), "Je pense . . . que le monsieur . . . est satisfait." ("I trust . . . the gentleman . . . has no complaints.")

Tardieu's satires on mechanistic society are counterbalanced by another group of plays dealing with the peculiarities of meaning. This subject appears to fascinate Tardieu, and he has written a nondramatic book, *Un Mot pour un autre* (One Word for Another, 1951) on it as well. In *La Sonate* (The Sonata, written 1952, performed 1955), probably his best-known play, three men sit on stools on a bare stage and talk dreamily, rhythmically, meaninglessly. Tardieu tries to imitate the musical sonata form in this play, using words as sounds. *Eux seuls le savent* (They Alone Know It, 1952) is a satire on obscure drama. A group of highly nervous and intensely vague characters drifts in and out of a drawing room and discusses the advisability of choosing the "first possibility" rather than the "second possibility." *Il y avait Foule au Manoir, ou Les Monologues* (Party at the Manor, or The Monologues, 1951) satirizes, rather belatedly, the conventions of nineteenth-century melodrama. Since there is never more than one person on the stage, the whole play consists of a succession of asides. The best and most significant of Tardieu's "linguistic" plays is undoubtedly *Les Amants du Métro* (The Lovers in the Metro, 1952). In this play Tardieu brings together the two subjects that chiefly preoccupy him when he is not concerned with the avant-garde leitmotiv of human helplessness in the void. The two subjects are romantic love and the linguistic basis of communication. In *La Sonate, Eux seuls le savent,* and *Les Monologues* Tardieu has tried to show that the perversities of language render it inadequate as a means of communication. This is even more clearly demonstrated in *Oswald et Zénaide, ou Les Apartés* (Oswald and Zénaide, or The Asides, 1951), where the characters relate to each other purely by means of formal clichés while they tell their real thoughts in asides. In *Les Amants du Métro* we see two young lovers meeting on a bustling Paris Metro platform. Their exuberance and joy in each other is expressed as they waltz around the stage to their own word-music,[9] "*Un, deux, trois, amour. Un, deux, trois, toujours.*" The roar of the

---

9. A term that might be applied to all of Tardieu's attempts to demonstrate the rhythmic quality of language, e.g., in *Conversation-Sinfonietta, La Sonate, Rythme à trois temps,* and *Ce que parler veut dire.*

trains and the conversation of the other travelers, oblivious, for the most part, of the lovers, provide the orchestral obbligato. The speeches of the lovers do not make any particular sense ("You are?" "I am." "I was nothing. You came. I am." "We are." "We will be." "I want to be you." "You are me."), but they understand each other completely. Their words, which would be meaningless or silly to anyone else, make sense to the lovers because they are emotionally *en rapport*. But they quarrel, of course; and as soon as they do, they are unable to communicate. Each goes off into his own one-track-minded self-justifications, and the power of language, the only means we have to transmit meaning, becomes an absurdity: "It's you who is no longer you!" "Oh, that's too much! It's you who is no longer me!" "But what? But why? But what is it?" "You know very well that!" "That what?" Tardieu's point is that language, i.e., communication, is only possible through *feeling*. When two people feel for each other, they understand each other. Mutual trust and feeling bridge the gap between people: language merely carries the messages across the bridge. Rational meaning in language is not the important thing, since each person's reason is subjective: the important thing is that the language beat the *dreivierteltakt* between the two dancers. When the lovers lose each other completely, they become totally incoherent, each one struggling against the barrier that language has now become between them: "Yes, I you!" "I you never, me!" "Yes, you me!" "It's you who!" "Me who what?" "When then?" "Nowhere!" "Where then?" "Never!" In the second scene, which takes place in a crowded Metro car, the lovers are reunited after he has fought his way to her through a row of passengers, and the play ends to the sound of their verbal waltz tune.

Tardieu's experiments with drama purely as language are carried to their furthest point in *Rythme à trois temps* (Rhythm in Threes, 1958) and *Une Voix sans personne* (A Disembodied Voice, 1958). These are "skeletal" plays in which Tardieu has trimmed off all the appurtenances of the ordinary play and left only the bare essentials. He shows us in these plays that effective drama can exist without action—with sight and sound

alone. In *Rythme à trois temps, ou Le Temple de Ségeste*
(Rhythm in Threes, or The Temple of Segestus), Tardieu attempts to give the *atmosphere* of a deserted Greek ruin in Sicily
by having an off-stage voice give a poetic description of the
scene while six young women, representing the six columns at
the front of the temple, execute a slow, stately ballet. As they
move together they speak lines that merge with the off-stage
commentator's to give the impression of "a countryside motionless as if fixed in eternity." [10] In *Une Voix sans personne* Tardieu
has cut the scope of the drama even further. There are no
actors—only an off-stage voice and a room. The room is fully
furnished, and the voice describes the life that has gone on in
it as the light gradually fades away.

These "linguistic" plays are not in themselves (that is, with
respect to their content) as important as the plays I have discussed previously, but they do illustrate equally well the technique Tardieu has developed for the one-act play. Tardieu uses
the one-act play to present a single situation. What Tardieu
has shown us is that we must not try to squeeze a full Aristotelian action into the short play form. The one-act play with a
complete plot is as unwieldy as a bagatelle in sonata form.

10. Tardieu, *Poèmes à Jouer*, p. [85].

MICHEL DE GHELDERODE
The Theater of the Grotesque

AMONG MODERN dramatists Michel de Ghelderode
stands by himself. If we must have a classification for him, then
he can most nearly be compared to that group of novelists who
have concentrated on the creation of a fictional world of their
own, a microcosm in which to reflect their view of human behavior in the world as a whole. Like William Faulkner with
his Yoknapatawpha County, Charles Dickens with his nineteenth century London, or James Joyce with his Dublin,
Ghelderode has created an enclosed world that reflects and
comments upon the larger world outside. Ghelderode's world
is medieval Flanders, and his view of the world can best be
described as savagely grotesque. His plays are sadistic caricatures
shot through with a ribald scatological humor which reminds
one of the pictures of his countrymen Hieronymus Bosch and
Pieter Breughel and of the anonymous woodcuts of the danse
macabre. Indeed, Ghelderode has specifically set some of his
plays in a fictitious "Breughellande" where the painter's grotesque and ribald creations come to life. In all of his plays, with
the exception of those written on specifically Biblical themes
and set in the Holy Land, there is this quality of the painted,
frozen grimace suddenly animated. Several of Ghelderode's plays
are actually written for marionettes, and in these the sense of
moment-to-moment transformation from still picture to moving picture is intensified. The marionettelike quality is retained
in Ghelderode's plays for actors, which give the impression less
of continuous movement than of a series of static tableaux in
which the characters switch from one bizarre position to another, their faces seemingly permanently stretched into a sort
of hysterical frozen rictus, their bodies reminding us more of
Bosch's semihuman, basilisklike creatures than of human beings.
Figures based upon a concentrated exaggeration of one particular physical trait recur constantly. His characters, like spite-
fully caricatured puppets, are all lopsided in one direction: either
enormously fat or unbelievably cadaverous, shriveled into de-

formed lumps of scabrous flesh (Ghelderode is particularly fond of inserting fiendish dwarfs into his plays) or stretched into lanky, stilt-supported scarecrows, saintlike guileless fools (a rare type in Ghelderode), or exaggeratedly sinister figures like the danse-macabre personifications of Death that he uses so frequently.

No better introduction to the atmosphere of the "Ghelderode country" could be given than this typical stage direction from *Marie la Misérable,* a modern miracle play that Ghelderode wrote in 1952 to be performed before the Church of St. Lambert in Woluwe, near Brussels:

> . . . enter an extraordinary procession to the sound of cacophonous music which is at the same time arhythmic and infinitely nostalgic—the music of some other, barbaric world, played upon baroque instruments. . . . This musical dragon (actually a camouflaged automobile with its headlights on containing a jazz band whose instruments have been altered to appear as if they did not belong to any particular period and whose Negro players have been disguised to look unreal) . . . pulls a ship, a sort of fourteenth century vessel —the Ship of Fools of the medieval moralists—with a raised forecastle and quarter-deck constituting practicable platforms. The mast, in the center, has only shreds of sail attached to it. Grim-looking black pavilions ornament the mast and poop. The quarterdeck is surmounted by a sort of arched ruin in which can be seen an admiral's skeleton. It is drinking and holding on its knees a woman covered with leprous sores. She has no nose and is naked under a shroud. Several scrawny and spastic couples are dancing together in front of the ship with signs of mutual disgust, as if they were fighting a merciless combat: a savage frolic, with the women's hair hanging down to their waists and flying round their rigid, sallow faces and the young men dressed in shrouds, their jaws bound shut with strips of cloth, dancing like robots to the hypnotic music. Their faces express disgust and dread, their dance shows the battle of the sexes. The middle of the ship is occupied by people wearing devil

masks, pigs' snouts, animal muzzles, elephant trunks, asses' ears—a swarming menagerie, clucking, bellowing, whistling . . .[1]

Here we have a typical scene from the world of Ghelderode— fantastic, grotesque, bizarre, hypnotic: a subtle combination of the danse macabre with the lusty vulgarity of a Flemish peasants' kermess.

We can find this curious combination of demonism with ribaldry in all of Ghelderode's Flemish plays. As in the painting of Breughel, the world is seen as a place where the Devil is in control and moral perversity reigns. As in Breughel, this perversity takes the form of aimlessness and distraction in idle pursuits. Only the very few, like Marie la Misérable, see the purpose of life clearly and accomplish it through faith. Ghelderode's plays are almost all preoccupied, directly or indirectly, with Catholicism. However, their Rabelaisian attitude toward religion is not so much derisive of holy matters as a demonstration of his belief that sin has overcome the earth and that man's energies, instead of being concentrated on religion itself, are scattered and misdirected to the diabolic perversions of religion.

Several of Ghelderode's plays are taken *directly* from Breughel's paintings. Among these are *Les Aveugles* (The Blind Men, written 1933), *La Pie sur le Gibet* (The Magpie on the Gallows, written 1935), and *Le Cavalier Bizarre* (The Strange Rider, written 1920). The first of these is a short sketch inspired by Breughel's painting "The Parable of the Blind," now in the Museo Nazionale, Naples. Breughel's picture shows six blind men walking along one behind the other and about to tumble into the ditch into which their leader has already fallen. Breughel based his picture on the Biblical proverb, "they be blind leaders of the blind. And if the blind lead the blind both shall fall into the ditch." [2] In Breughel's picture, as in Ghelderode's world, the blind men are the helpless victims of a system perverted by the Devil's ascendancy. If the Devil were not in

1. Michel de Ghelderode, *Théâtre.* Copyright © Editions Gallimard (Paris: Gallimard, 1955), IV, pp. 288–89.
2. Matthew, XV:14.

control of the world, the men would not be blind, there would be no treacherously placed ditch for them to fall into, and they would not be instinctively led to disaster anyway, but rather to the church in the background of the picture. The literal presence of the Devil and his cohorts was a real concept to Breughel, as it undoubtedly is to Ghelderode as well. But Ghelderode makes the plan of the picture somewhat harsher. In Ghelderode's world the Devil makes men perverse: they are the victims not of their alien surroundings but of their own twisted and willful natures. The characteristic of the damned in religion, after all, is that they heed the promptings of the Devil instead of the voice of God. Ghelderode's blind men (reduced to three, presumably for convenience of staging) are pilgrims on the way to Rome, where they believe they have now arrived, although they have actually been wandering around in circles for weeks and are still in Flanders. A one-eyed man warns them that they are in dangerous country and offers to lead them to a monastery where they will be safe. The blind men refuse to believe him and scornfully reject his help. They trudge off and are swallowed up in a bog. Breughel's blind men are merely comically ducked in a ditch, but Ghelderode's deliberately turn down an offer of salvation and die.

In *La Pie sur le Gibet* Ghelderode has again dramatized a Breughel painting. "The Merry Way to the Gallows," now in the Darmstadt Museum, simply shows a gallows on a hill overlooking a countryside of extraordinary beauty. A magpie sits perched on top of the gallows, and a group of holidaying peasants is heedlessly dancing up the hill. Breughel here effects a double comment on the unfeeling stupidity of mankind, first in placing the gallows against a background of such idyllic tranquillity and secondly in having the peasants ignore both the beauty and the ugliness in the throes of their loutish dance. Ghelderode changes all this into a rollicking yet savagely contemptuous farce. The magpie becomes a sort of cynical croaking commentator on the action which here concerns a real execution. The peasants come dancing up to the gibbet and then are replaced by a group of pompous officials (Ghelderode's professional men are invariably caricatured) who have come to hang

Tyl Ulenspiegel. The strange location of the gibbet is now explained. The new ruler, wishing to temper justice with mercy, has decreed that death is to be made as pleasant as humanly possible for the condemned. They are to be hanged only after being permitted to get drunk on the best vintage wine. The ceremony is to be performed on a pink gibbet with a golden rope, and as the condemned man's eyeballs are extruded from his head by the force of strangulation his last view is to be of the most beautiful piece of countryside in Flanders. The condemned man drops dead just before he is to be hanged, and when the officials examine the body they find it is not Tyl Ulenspiegel at all. As the magpie croaks derisively, the carousing peasants return and the curtain falls.

Le Cavalier Bizarre is another short play and, if not directly taken from a Breughel painting like the two preceding ones, is inspired by the Flemish master's art. In his preface to the play Ghelderode states that his characters are taken from the brush of Breughel or the burin of Jacques Callot. A group of old people are living together in a large, dormitorylike room at a medieval Flemish hospice. They hear ghostly bells where none are supposed to be heard; one of them looks out of the window and sees a huge knight with large bells on his horse's bridle approaching. He says the horseman is Death, and the old people, believing him, go into a wild, kermesslike dance—their "last fling"—and then babble out their sins. They look like peaceful and innocent grandparents, and it is hard to imagine them once young and lusty and straight-backed. But the shriveled and bent old woman had sold her body when she was a beautiful young girl, one of the men had stolen, another fornicated tremendously, another had committed sacrilege, and still another had sinned so much that he feels only the pope in person could absolve him. After getting their sins off their chests, the ancients cease resigning themselves to their fate: "We want to live, no matter how—sick, suffering, covered with sores and vermin—but living!" [3] The whole thing ends with the watcher's revelation that Death has not come for them at all but has carried off

3. Michel de Ghelderode, *Théâtre* (Paris: Gallimard, 1952), II, p. 21.

a newborn child from another part of the hospice; and the audience is left in doubt as to whether the whole story proceeded from the watcher's imagination or not. The play ends with "a spasmodic dance of ancients, their mouths open, their fists clenched, like rigid marionettes." [4] After a moment's self-realization Ghelderode's ancients, teetering on the brink of death, fall back into the distraction from reality that is so typical of his people.

Demonism and Rabelaisianism are undoubtedly the two keynotes of Ghelderode's work: his plays combine the perversion of religious or political functions with scatological farce. Although the scatology often seems to be dragged in with willful vulgarity, it is really an extremely effective (because shocking) way of showing the author's disgust with the manner in which the world and the people in it have worked out. This element, too, Ghelderode seems to have got from Breughel, whose pictures, even the most idyllic ones, are full of hidden little scenes of defecation, urination, and animalistic fornication.

Two of Ghelderode's best plays, as yet unpublished in English, are *La Balade du Grand Macabre* (The Grand Macabre's Stroll, written 1934) and *Magie Rouge* (Red Magic, written 1931). In both of these ribald and unrestrained farces the demonism which suffuses Ghelderode's world takes the form of the primal satanic sin of belief in one's own divinity. In Ghelderode's view this leads to the creation of what may, literally, be described as monsters—persons who have become so obsessed by one of the more perverse possible phases of human character that they become in fact dehumanized personifications of it. This is, of course, essentially the same philosophy of dramatic construction as Ben Jonson's "humor" theory, except that Jonson uses it with satiric intent (i.e., he laughs at it from a position of superiority, thus implying that improvement is possible), while Ghelderode presents it as a literal picture of the world gone mad. Ghelderode's world is not populated by a few fools, as Jonson's is, but is collectively foolish.

In *Magie Rouge* Ghelderode has been influenced in about

4. *Ibid.*, p. 25.

equal parts by Molière's *L'Avare* and Jonson's *The Alchemist.*
Hieronymus is Sir Epicure Mammon taken seriously. He is
avarice personified. He has the primary characteristic of the true
obsessive in that he will not hesitate to sacrifice his own comfort
to feed his obsession. For example, although he has a young and
attractive wife (he himself being a filthy and unattractive old
man in the best Molière tradition), he has kept her a virgin so
that he will not be enchained by her and have to spend money
on her. Naturally his wife can take just so much of this. She
enters into a plot with one Armador, a sleight-of-hand artist, and
two others to get all of Hieronymus's money. Armador is introduced to Hieronymus as one of the world's greatest alchemists.
He promises to find the elixir of gold for Hieronymus and retires
to the cellar with his paramour, ostensibly to begin his experiments. Meanwhile, Hieronymus sits upstairs in his counting-
house planning, among other things, to buy the pope and the
Holy Trinity once he has all the money in the world. On one of
his trips up for air, Armador, pretending to be drunk, lets
Hieronymus take a black stone off him which he says grants
immortality to the wearer. Armador and his mistress escape after
murdering their two fellow conspirators and leave Hieronymus
with the bodies and a coffer full of counterfeit money. Arrested
and led out to torture and execution, Hieronymus remains
wrapped up in his grandiose self-delusion:

> I don't understand! What did you say? . . . The gallows?
> . . . The executioner? . . . (*He tears himself away*) It's
> enough to make one laugh! . . . (*He laughs*) Ho, ho! . . .
> You've been nicely tricked. I am the leader of the living.
> Bah! I'm every bit as good as the Emperor! . . . Me die?
> . . . I'll buy up Justice, ho . . . ho . . . ho! . . . Listen to
> me! . . . I'm the same as God. Yes! Don't you realize yet
> that I'm immortal? . . . (*He laughs at the top of his voice.*
> *They drag him out to the hooting of the crowd.*) [5]

La Balade du Grand Macabre is a thoroughly unbridled farce
that takes place in Ghelderode's Breughellande. Here the delu-

5. Michel de Ghelderode, *Théâtre* (Paris: Gallimard, 1950), I, p. 179.

sion of godhead is assumed by a strange, pilgrimlike figure calling himself Nekrotozar who thinks he is one of the archangels
sent down to earth to announce the imminent end of the world
—or at least of Breughellande. In Breughellande, or Brugelmonde as it is called in another play, the people have been
twisted body and soul by the workings of the Devil and are
taken up with the practice of one or another of the seven deadly
sins.

The play opens with an idyllic and passionate love scene
between two young lovers, the play's only innocents. They retire into an abandoned tomb to make love and are followed by
a hollow laugh and chattering voice coming from "the clouds
perhaps." The voice sardonically and gleefully predicts that the
lovers' bones "will be dispersed in the folds of the earth among
the rotting weeds and the clefts of the rocks. The passionate
gestures will be imprinted in the oozing slime." [6] The voice turns
out to be Nekrotozar's. He climbs down from the tree and pro-
claims that Breughellande will cease to exist at midnight. The
rest of the play is taken up with the exploits of Nekrotozar as
he goes around whipping everyone up into a frenzy with his
news until the night ends in a tremendous drunken orgy. He is
assisted in his efforts by Porprenaz, the town's chief drunkard,
and Videbolle, the henpecked state philosopher of Breughellande, whose job it is to reflect, a habit which the other citizens
are unable to contract, to declare (like Pangloss) that everything
is good and could not be better, and to make agreeable forecasts exclusively while giving agreeable explanations for any dis-
agreeable occurrences that may take place instead. The play
ends as Nekrotozar expires of an excess of drink and exertion,
and the lovers emerge from the tomb still totally wrapped up in
each other and completely oblivious of all that has happened.
They represent, presumably, the hope of better things for
Breughellande.

The fortunes of Brugelmonde, as it is called this time, are
continued in *D'un Diable qui prêcha Merveilles* (Of A Devil
Who Preached Wonders, written 1934). Here the sins com-

6. *Théâtre*, II, p. 32.

mitted in this northern Gomorrah are revealed in a series of
scenes in which all the leading citizens enter one after the other
and confess their failings to each other. The occasion for this
attack of communal breast-beating is not repentance but fear.
The town has just received word that news of its dissoluteness
has reached Rome and that a well-known hell-fire–and–brim-
stone preacher has been sent to clean the place up. And there is
certainly plenty of cleaning up to be done: the bishop uses the
poor-box money to finance his sybaritic banquets; the abbess is
pregnant by her confessor, a young Italian of great ingenuity at
thinking up new forms of erotica; the sheriff has embezzled the
town funds so his wife can finance her orgies; and other prominent citizens all display an equal reluctance to earn an honest
penny. Even the town's resident devil has grown neglectful of
his duties and is just reading a letter from the infernal regions
warning him that he will be turned into a hermit monk if he
doesn't get cracking and produce some really first-class sinners.
Capricant is in despair since he is old and no longer has any
taste for devil's work. But Fergerite, the local sorceress, advises
him to dress-up as the preacher and deliver the sermon in his
place while she sees to it that the real preacher is led astray. The
sermon is an enormous success since the devil simply advises
everyone to go on living in sin—with the Church's blessing. At
the end the devil and the preacher meet and go off to Rome
together, the preacher believing that the devil-monk is the only
just man he has met in Brugelmonde.

The tangible presence of death is always a very real concept
to Ghelderode and several of his plays contain scenes in which
either a personified Death is the protagonist or a character returns from the dead. *Le Cavalier Bizarre* has already been mentioned as a play in which Death is personified. *Mademoiselle
Jaïre* (written 1934) tells the story of a girl who dies and is resus-
citated by a sorcerer who is later crucified. The girl remains
alive only until the following spring, when a root-covered corpse
named Lazarus, who comes to visit her and whom she has
apparently known in the world beyond, bursts into flower. The
point of the play seems to be the paradox that death, even when
it takes the form of the mildew-and-damp-earth–covered putrefy-

ing flesh of Lazarus, is purer than life. Lazarus, for all of his repellent appearance, is embraced by Jaïre and speaks lyrically of the beauties of death that will be theirs when his flesh bears fruit and flower in the spring. In dying, in passing out of the world as Ghelderode sees it, one is translated from chaos to order, from impurity to purity, from the Devil to God.

Although Ghelderode's genuinely religious feelings may be somewhat obscured by his emphasis on the reverse side of the coin—the diabolic aspects of religion—in such works as *Fastes d'Enfer* (Chronicles of Hell, written 1929) and *D'un Diable qui prêcha Merveilles*, they are expressed most explicitly in *Marie La Misérable*. In this play Ghelderode is entirely on the side of the angels, although the diabolic element is by no means absent.[7] The play tells the story of Marie la Cluse, a saintly and very beautiful young recluse who lives in the church precincts and devotes herself to good works. A young nobleman, Eglon d'Arken, is overcome by lust for her; but when she rejects him with the proper amount of scorn, he accuses her of witchcraft and with the help of his deformed, dwarfish servant makes her appear guilty of theft. Marie is martyred and the true source of the machinations against her is revealed when the dwarf is killed and "revolting fumes, as if Hell were coming out of his carcass" rise up from his body.[8]

What happens when the powers of hell gain the upper hand over religion may be seen in Ghelderode's most notorious play, *Fastes d'Enfer*. This work caused a minor sensation when it was first produced by Jean-Louis Barrault in Paris in 1949—and no wonder. The main character is the Bishop of Lapideopolis, a titular see somewhere in Flanders. He is lying in state in an adjoining room, having just passed away to the great relief of every member of his staff. John of the Desert, as the bishop is called, is not even an ordained priest. Years before, he was washed up on the shore during a great plague, which was devastating the city. His appearance bearing a huge cross coincided with the end of the plague and he was elected bishop by acclamation, an act later confirmed by the Holy See, which knows

7. Cf. *supra*, pp. 99–100.
8. *Théâtre*, IV, p. 264.

a *fait accompli* when it sees one. As the priests, all of them grotesque, misshapen creatures, celebrate his passing, John suddenly appears in the doorway, apparently as alive as ever. It turns out he was unable to swallow the Host which he was given before dying and it is choking him. After an eerie battle with his successor and chief enemy, Simon Laquedeem, during which the room is wrecked as a tremendous thunderstorm crackles outside, he is finally able to spit out the Host and die. The priests, led by Laquedeem, celebrate his final passing by hopping about the room with their robes trussed up, gleefully breaking wind to express their relief.

Ghelderode turns the theme of the personification of Death into a hilarious farce in *La Farce des Ténébreux* (The Farce of the Shadows, written 1936). This play concerns Fernand d'Abcaude, a ridiculous fool worthy of rating with any of Ben Jonson's most extreme "humor" characters. D'Abcaude's pleasure is to imagine that he is dying of grief for his beloved Azurine. He spends all his time in darkness, starving himself and having his valet describe the extremely elaborate funeral procession he has planned for himself. He cannot wait to die so that the funeral oration he has written can be recited and the biography he has ghost written can be published. To disabuse Fernand of his wish to die in order to join Azurine in a mutually virginal eternity, his doctor hires an actress to play the fiancée's ghost. Failing this, the doctor plans to cure d'Abcaude by giving him a whale-oil enema. The ruse is effective, however, since the actress manages to persuade d'Abcaude that Azurine was not the virginal paragon he believed her to be but rather something little better than the town whore. After all sorts of misadventures in a brothel during a carnival, d'Abcaude finally loses his virginity and joy reigns.

All of the plays mentioned thus far are set in Ghelderode's home grounds—in the special world that he has created out of medieval Flanders and Brabant. Not all of his plays are placed in this setting, however. Some of them combine a Spanish setting with a Flemish setting, like *Escurial* (written 1927) and *Le Soleil se couche . . .* (The Sun Sets . . . , written 1933), which take place in Spain but constantly refer back to the characters' former lives in Flanders; or *L'Ecole des Bouffons* (The School for Buffoons, written 1937), which reverses the process. None of these plays is particularly interesting, although *L'Ecole des Bouffons* has first-class theatrical qualities. *Le Soleil se couche* . . . is a short play about the last days of the Emperor Charles V. *Escurial* views the famous Escurial as an old and dilapidated palace somewhere in Spain. The king, who appears to be in the last stages of febrile decay, is attended only by howling dogs, an executioner, a priest, and his Flemish jester. The play is purely and simply a mood piece—a study in decadence. It is unfortunate that this has been one of the few Ghelderode plays performed in English because it is one of his weakest works. *L'Ecole des Bouffons,* on the other hand, is one of Ghelderode's most successful exercises in grotesquerie. It is about a school of deformed dwarfs, which supplies jesters to the courts of Europe after having taught them that the secret of all buffoonery is cruelty.

Those of Ghelderode's plays which are completely out of his medieval Flemish world may be divided into two groups: those having a religious basis and those having a mythic basis.

Ghelderode is probably best-known to American audiences through his two specifically religious plays, *Barabbas* (written 1928) and *Les Femmes au Tombeau* (The Women at the Tomb, written 1928). *Barabbas* tells the story of the Passion and Crucifixion from the point of view of the robber who was released in Christ's place. Barabbas starts out as a defiant and unregenerate criminal reveling in his own toughness. He is to be crucified, but he promises the mob a good show when they come to see him nailed up. While he is in prison he meets Jesus, who never says a word and meekly accepts whatever abuse comes his way. Barabbas is greatly impressed by Jesus's behavior. He does not understand Christ's meekness, since it is entirely outside the bounds of his previous experience, and mistakes it for stoical courage, which he possesses to a high degree himself and therefore knows how to appreciate. When he is released in Jesus's place, not so much by the will of the people as by the cunning maneuvers of the high priest, he wanders aimlessly around the town, always stealthily followed by the

high priest's spies, who plan to kill him as soon as they have
an opportunity. Finally he comes to rest in an abandoned fair-
ground. Here he listens to a mysterious watcher describe the
agony of Jesus and gradually comes to think of himself as one
of Christ's followers. At the end he dies just after Jesus, stabbed
in the back by the clown:

> BARABBAS: Hey? (*He reels.*) They got me. In the
> back, eh? Pretty good work! (*He falls to his knees like an ox.*)
> No, no, they haven't got me yet. Got to do something first
> . . . (*He gets up painfully and cries, hoarsely:*) Hey there,
> beggars! Bear up! I'm coming. (*But he falls to his knees
> again.*) You'll make it all right without me. Yes, they've
> got me all right. Well, what of it? I was condemned to death
> anyway . . . It's all the same thing to me. I'm not scared
> anymore. And I'm bleeding. Hey! Jesus? I'm bleeding too.
> Sacrificed the same day. . . . (*He collapses and half raises
> himself again.*) But you, you had something to die for. Me,
> I'm dying for nothing. It's for you all the same . . . for you
> . . . Jesus. If you like . . . And if I could . . . I'd give you
> my   hand . . . and   see   you   smile . . . Jesus . . . My
> brother.[9]

Both *Barabbas* and *Les Femmes au Tombeau* are flawed as theatrical works by being too static. *Barabbas* consists principally
of the hero's comments—for the most part melodramatic, overwritten, and not particularly interesting—on the watcher's report of the doings on Calvary. Full of undramatic and awkward
devices, *Les Femmes au Tombeau*, in which a group of women
meet in a deserted house in Jerusalem to discuss the Crucifixion,
is simply a discussion play that lacks the brilliance of dialogue
and the intellectual acuity with which Shaw made the discussion
play a workable drama. Lacking action, both *Barabbas* and *Les
Femmes au Tombeau* are more like radio scripts than stage
works.

Ghelderode's mythic plays are all based on well-known and
frequently used literary myths. (By myth I mean a story, not

9. Michel de Ghelderode, *Théâtre* (Paris: Gallimard, 1957), V, pp.
172–73.

necessarily untrue, that has been used repeatedly in literature and has attained a conventional form so that it can be used by writers as a commonly understood point of reference.) He uses the Don Juan and Faust myths, which are almost obligatory for any dramatic author with a large body of work to his credit, the guileless-fool myth in *Pantagleize*, and the Judith myth in *Sire Halewyn*.

Both *Don Juan* (written 1928) and *La Mort du Docteur Faust* (The Death of Dr. Faust, written 1925) are written in a semipuppet play style with Ghelderode's penchant for the grotesque very much in evidence. In *La Mort du Docteur Faust* Ghelderode plays with a technique that has consistently fascinated him: the Pirandellian double-exposure technique. In addition to *La Mort du Docteur Faust* he has written two other plays specifically to exemplify this technique—*Trois Acteurs, un Drame* (Three Actors, One Drama, written 1926), a short, melodramatic, and clumsy play about three players trying to solve their real-life entanglements by incorporating them into the play they are acting, the only result being that the author shoots himself, presumably out of exasperation; and *Sortie de l'Acteur* (Exit the Actor, written 1930), an equally melodramatic and oversentimental play commemorating the death at the age of twenty-six of the Flemish actor, Renatus Verheyen, which ends in farce as the dead man escapes from his grave and is recaptured by angelic gendarmes who force him to skip up a golden ladder to Heaven.

La Mort du Docteur Faust, which Ghelderode has called his first important theatrical work (it was written in 1925 when he was twenty-seven), is about the transposition of the real, original Doctor Faust to a modern Flemish town where a carnival is in progress. He meets a modern girl named Marguerite, who fancies herself the Marguerite of the story, and the Devil, who is, of course, ubiquitous in every century. All three watch a performance of the Faust legend in a booth set up in a tavern and become inextricably mixed up with the actors playing their characters. The play is lively but diffuse and pointless, while the technique is based mainly on tricks.

Don Juan, which Ghelderode dedicated to Charlie Chaplin,

is probably his weakest play. He attempts to depict Don Juan
as an eternal figure with a heritage—the compulsion to make
love—handed down from generation to generation. The current
Don Juan realizes this when he meets a shriveled up little man
—"the little green man," Ghelderode calls him—who tells him
that he was the previous Don Juan and reveals that he, like all
Don Juans, has retired from the lists because he has been overcome by the ailments which inevitably result from indiscrimi-
nate dalliance.

A more appropriate play for Ghelderode to have dedicated
to Charlie Chaplin would have been *Pantagleize* (written 1929).
In this brilliant retelling of the saga of the guileless fool,
Ghelderode tells the story of Pantagleize, a harmless little man
who innocently trots around town on May Day telling everyone
what a lovely day it is. What he does not know is that the town
is seething with social unrest and that the innocuous remark he
has chosen to celebrate his joy in the beauty of the day is the
password for the beginning of a revolution. Pantagleize continues
to amble around the town throughout the day, totally unconscious of the strife he has started. Completely oblivious of danger,
he goes from one hair-raising situation to another until at the
end of the day he meets the fate of all innocents in a world
governed by the Devil—that of being massacred. As he dies, still
unaware of what is going on, he brings out for the last time the
innocent phrase, which remains innocent only in the minds of
those who have not lost their innocence: "What . . . a . . .
lovely . . . day!"

Ghelderode has recorded that the character of Pantagleize
was inspired by an anonymous inhabitant of the Rhineland
whom Ghelderode observed reading a book while walking across
a public square swept by heavy machine-gun fire during the
Spartacist revolt of 1919. In the middle of the square he stopped,
looked at the sky, opened an umbrella, and then went on his
way, still reading.[10] Ghelderode's profound pessimism can be
seen in the description of the character which the sight of the
oblivious reader inspired him to create:

10. Michel de Ghelderode, *Seven Plays,* translated by George Hauger
(New York: Hill & Wang, Inc., 1960), p. 147.

. . . a fellow like Pantagleize remains an archetype, an exemplary man, and a fine example who has nothing to do with that dangerous thing, intelligence, and a great deal to do with that saviour, instinct. He is human in an age when all is becoming dehumanized. He is the last poet, and the poet is he who believes in heavenly voices, in revelation, in our divine origin. He is the man who has kept the treasure of his childhood in his heart, and who passes through catastrophes in all artlessness. He is bound to Parsifal by purity, and to Don Quixote by courage and holy madness. And if he dies, it is because, particularly in our time, the Innocents must be slaughtered: that has been the law since the time of Jesus. Amen! [11]

Michel de Ghelderode has written several other short plays but none of them contains any significant additions to the main themes of his work. Ghelderode remains primarily the dramatist of his own personally created world of medieval Flanders, which is depicted not as a historical recreation but as a convenient microcosm in which he displays his moral view. It is a world governed by diabolic forces which warp its inhabitants into grotesque, clownish forms as they prance about ignoring the beauties of the world and allowing instead some obsession based on one of the seven deadly sins to corrode and finally damn them. Ghelderode's wildly farcical grotesqueries and unbridled vulgarity is really the expression of a deeply pessimistic but sincere and completely orthodox Christian religious feeling.

11. *Ibid.*, p. 148.

JEAN GENET
The Theater of Illusion and Disillusion

EVEN IF HIS plays were not particularly interesting in themselves, even if they were not important examples of a new dramatic technique, Jean Genet would have some of the fascination of a hunchback turned ballet dancer.

We have very little definite information about Genet's personal background before he began to write. He was abandoned soon after birth and grew up to be a delinquent and later a criminal. In 1943, when he was thirty-three years old, he began writing while serving a prison sentence for theft. In 1948, Genet, after starting to serve a life sentence as a habitual criminal, was granted a pardon by the President of France, who had been petitioned by some of the country's leading writers. Since then Genet seems to have lived peacefully.

Like all the modern avant-garde dramatists, Genet bases his plays on protest and paradox. His paradox is that there is no reality within society. Anyone who acts within the structure of society is literally unreal—nonexistent. What we call reality is only illusion piled on illusion. When all the layers of illusion are stripped away, what is left is emptiness. Another way of looking at Genet's vision of the world is as a diminishing spiral twisting concentrically down to nothingness. "Reality" to Genet is like Peer Gynt's onion. It would perhaps be correct to argue that this view was engendered in Genet by his peculiar role in the world as a person cast out from the "reality" of social living by his thievery and perversion, but the psychological reasons for his attitude toward the commonly accepted realities are not pertinent to a discussion of his views. The views are there and must be dealt with for themselves.

Genet demonstrates his views on the illusion of life by writing plays in which nothing is ever what it appears to be at first glance—or at second glance, for that matter. Jean-Paul Sartre has likened the working of Genet's mind to a whirligig spinning in an ever-increasing tempo.[1] Genet's thought processes are circular and they show us that at the ultimate core of things there is nothing: when Genet starts one of his "whirligig" thought processes, he is like a snake taking its tail into its mouth preparatory to swallowing ad infinitum.

Genet's first play, *The Maids* (Les Bonnes), was written for Louis Jouvet and produced by him at the Théâtre de l'Athénée in 1947.[2] There are only three characters in the play—the two maids and their mistress. Whenever the mistress goes out, the maids take over and play at mistress and maid themselves. Each maid takes a turn at dressing up in Madame's clothes and playing the part of the mistress, while the other serves her. In an effort to add more excitement to their little drama, the maids have denounced Madame's lover to the police with anonymous letters. When they hear that he has been released, they realize that they will be found out, and thus try to poison Madame. Their attempt fails, and instead the younger maid poisons herself, while the other plans to give herself up as her killer.

Here we see that Genet immediately starts the whirligig off with a gentle push by specifying that the three characters of the play be acted by boys.[3] The boys are to be dressed as women, but they must not act well lest the illusion take on the appearance of reality. To guard against this, Genet specifies that throughout the performance the stage must be flanked by large placards proclaiming the fact that the "actresses" are males. The second section of the paradox comes when we see that the maids are playacting at being mistress and maid. *They are not being themselves.* In fact, as we slowly and horrifyingly discover, they have no selves to be—except as illusions, they do not exist! At the same time the whirligig accelerates as we see that the actors

1. Jean-Paul Sartre, *Saint Genet: Comédien et Martyr* (Paris: Gallimard, 1952), p. 561.

2. Internal evidence seems to suggest that *Deathwatch* was written before *The Maids*, but the latter was both published and performed first. Furthermore, Sartre (*op. cit.*, p. 564) says that *Deathwatch* is Genet's second play.

3. Jouvet's production used women.

are playing women who are acting another role. When we have realized this, we are prepared to follow Genet's next step. The actor playing Solange is playing Solange the maid pretending to be Claire the maid, and the actor playing Claire is playing Claire the maid pretending to be the mistress. By this time the actors' whirligig is spinning merrily: the various shadowy figures on it have merged into each other and become indistinguishable except as fleeting blurs. None of the figures is solid enough to be real, but, on the other hand, they are all that there is. Sartre interprets the flickering individuality of the characters in a more sociopsychological manner when he asserts that the servants have no reality as individuals because when they are in the presence of their masters they have to act the part of the servant—obsequious or dignified, as the case may be; and when they are alone they are trying to ape their masters. Similarly, the masters have to act a part in the presence of their servants—they obviously cannot "be themselves" in front of them; and when they are alone they indulge in grandiosely romantic daydreams (like Madame's desire to follow her lover to Siberia or Devil's Island) engendered by their stagnant existence.[4] If one takes the masters as representative of the members of the social order and the servants as the social outcasts (the thieves, pimps, perverts, murderers—Genet's people), an interesting allegory can be developed. However, I am concerned here less with the sociological than with the philosophical and theatrical aspects of Genet's work. The climax of Genet's demonstration of nonbeing in being comes at the end of the play when Claire, purely as a gesture, commits suicide by drinking the poisoned tea which had been intended for Madame. Having failed to poison her mistress, Claire drinks the poison while pretending to be Madame again. She thus snuffs herself out while pretending to be someone whose individuality rests on equally flimsy foundations. Solange meanwhile steps out on the balcony and grandiosely declaims her own apotheosis as she imagines what will happen when she "confesses" to the murder of Claire. As the play ends, the

4. Sartre, *op. cit.*, p. 565.

whirligig slows down and stops; and we see that it is now empty.[5]

Deathwatch (Haute Surveillance), first produced in 1949, takes place in a prison cell. Here again Genet has created a triangular situation, with two of the convicts rivaling each other in their simultaneous love and hate for the third one. As in *The Maids*, there is a considerable element of latent homosexual attraction involved here. Again the play culminates in the violent death of one of the characters: Lefranc strangles the other "maid-convict," Maurice, in an effort to raise himself from a petty thief to a murderer like Green Eyes, the cell's "mistress-convict." The parallels between *The Maids* and *Deathwatch* are so close that the two plays might be called companion pieces.

The prison cell containing Maurice, Lefranc, and Green Eyes is as much a dead end as the overheated Empire room in Sartre's *No Exit*. The artificial hierarchical society that the three convicts have built up in their cell closely parallels the one set up by the maids in Madame's bedroom. Like Madame, Green Eyes, who occupies the place of honor in this society by virtue of being a murderer while the others are only petty criminals, keeps aloof from the play acting and quarreling of his two cellmates. Maurice and Lefranc parallel Claire and Solange. Like the two maids, the two convicts both hate (by way of envy) and love their superior and try to imitate him. Lefranc, who is older than Maurice as Solange is older than Claire, kills Maurice at the end, as Solange kills (though not in fact) Claire. *Deathwatch* is a little more rooted in reality than is *The Maids*: the whirligig is rotating, but only slowly. Green Eyes is really a murderer and Lefranc actually does kill Maurice. Genet seems to be saying that outside society, where primitive instincts untainted by the artificiality of civilization still prevail, there is more reality, more possibility of achieving the dignity of an existence.[6]

5. A detailed analysis of this play may be found in Oreste F. Pucciani, "Tragedy, Genet, and *The Maids*," *Tulane Drama Review*, VII (Spring, 1963), pp. 42–59.

6. Leonard C. Pronko, *Avant-Garde* (Berkeley, Cal.: University of California Press, 1962), p. 143, says that Genet uses the condemned man as a symbol of mankind because he remembers a lost paradise while making the best of it in a cell whose only issue is death.

Green Eyes *exists*—because he does not *try* to be anything. As he says, he is what he is in spite of himself. He did not seek his distinction as a murderer; he murdered in spite of himself, involuntarily, unintentionally: "I didn't want what happened to me to happen. It was all given to me. A gift from God or the devil, but something I didn't want." [7] Green Eyes is passive; he does not act: he reacts. He has achieved a precarious existence by becoming—or never rising above—a human version of Pavlov's dog. Just as the dog slavers when the bell is rung, so Genet's man murders when he is triggered into action by circumstances: "everything began to move. There was nothing more to be done. And so I just had to kill someone." [8] Genet seems to be arguing here—perhaps in his own justification—that the true criminal is simply being himself. He becomes a criminal by reacting to the stimuli of society. Maurice and Lefranc, however, are not content to be themselves: they are obsessed with the true social being's need of a hierarchy. Maurice, with his fawning, homosexual hero worship, and Lefranc, with his fierce, social climber's jealousy, admire and envy Green Eyes (and even more so Snowball, the prison's supercriminal). Their quarreling assumes a deadly seriousness that the conscious playacting of Claire and Solange never has, and at the end Lefranc actually does strangle Maurice with his bare hands. Now at last, he thinks, he is the equal of Green Eyes, who also strangled his victim with his bare hands. But Green Eyes quickly disillusions him. Lefranc has got nowhere because he was trying to ape someone else, and there is no reality in doing things in order to be like someone else.

When we come to *The Balcony* (Le Balcon, 1956), Genet's best-known play, we find the situation somewhat changed. It is like stepping off the plain into the forest. The whirligig that Sartre has suggested as the best image of Genet's works is spinning around madly once again. Genet is once more concentrating on his favorite paradox that appearance is all the reality there is. *The Balcony* is a sort of light-and-shadow optical-

7. Jean Genet, *The Maids and Deathwatch*, translated by Bernard Frechtman (New York: Grove Press, Inc., 1954), p. 161.
8. *Ibid.*, p. 131.

illusion puzzle in which the problem is to find the reality—if any.

"The Balcony" is the name of a fetishist whorehouse, called a "house of illusions" by its madam. Here insignificant little men come to play out in "reality" their grandiose fantasies. Each room in the house is fitted out like a changing stage set so that to suit the client it can be switched from the setting of one fantasy to another. The women of the house are chosen as much for their ability as actresses as for their ability as prostitutes. At the beginning of the play we see three of these fantasies being acted out. A gasman dressed in the robes of a bishop gives absolution to a scantily dressed penitent; another client plays a judge and extracts a "confession" of theft from his girl by alternately groveling at her feet and ordering his "executioner" to lash her; and finally a timid-looking, puny man dresses as a general and acts out his own hero's funeral à la the Duke of Wellington with the aid of a woman dressed as a horse. All these characters wear enormously padded shoulders and the Greek buskins to make them look bigger than life when they are playing their roles. The interesting thing about these scenes is that not only are the characters unreal (because they find it necessary to be someone else), not only are the figures that they pretend to be unreal (because they are the emanations of unreal minds), but Genet shows us that the figures that these emanations ape (the real bishops, judges, and generals that operate in our society) are unreal as well. This is the condemnation of the artificial structure of society by an outcast from society. Genet maintains that the system that judged and condemned him is dependent upon the free spirits outside it. The law is not an entity in itself (i.e., it is not "real"), since it depends for its existence upon the existence of "crime." Religion exists because "sin" exists. Hero figures exist because tribute is paid to them. The general in the third scene does not get a hero's funeral because he is a hero: he is a "hero" because the pomp and ceremony of the funeral transform him into a heroic symbol. The judge has power only when confronted with lawbreakers and backed up by the elemental savagery of the punishment ritual:

JUDGE: Look here: you've got to be a model thief if I'm to be a model judge. If you're a fake thief, I become a fake judge. . . . My executioner has hit hard . . . if he didn't hit how could I stop him from hitting? Therefore, he must strike so that I can intervene and demonstrate my authority. . . . My being a judge is an emanation of your being a thief. You need only refuse—but you'd better not!—need only refuse to be who you are—what you are, therefore who you are—for me to cease to be . . . to vanish, evaporated. Burst. Volatized. Denied. . . . But you won't refuse, will you? You won't refuse to be a thief? That would be wicked. It would be criminal. You'd deprive me of being! [9]

It is for this reason that the judge spends part of the scene crawling on the floor and licking the feet of the girl playing the thief. The bishop in the opening scene depends for his holiness only on being able to forgive sin, which is therefore primary.

The action of the play turns around a revolution going on outside in the streets of the city. The Chief of Police, who protects Mme. Irma's house of illusions, is in charge of stopping the rebels. He does this by persuading the three clients to assume their roles again and pretend to take the place of the men they pretended to be in their fantasies—the bishop, whose severed head is reportedly ornamenting the handle bars of a bicycle; the Attorney-General, who has died of fright; and the Generalissimo, who has gone mad. In this way the Chief of Police and the Court Envoy hope to delude the rebels into thinking that the heads of the state are still intact. With Mme. Irma, who is dressed as the Queen, the three step out on the balcony and show themselves to the populace. Later, after they have come back from a ride through the city in the state

9. Jean Genet, The Balcony, translated by Bernard Frechtman. Copyright © 1958 by Bernard Frechtman. (New York: Grove Press Inc., 1958), pp. 11–15.

carriage, the three impostors are still undetected. They are as completely changed from their former selves as if they had been transformed by plastic surgery; their sumptuous, glittering robes of office, shored up with tradition and imprinted as symbols in the popular consciousness by centuries of habituation, hide and protect them like the crenellated fortifications of a beleaguered city.[10] Not even those who know them well can see through the appearance to the reality, for in Genet appearance *is* reality: "Do you think we were recognized?" asks the judge; and the bishop answers, "No danger of that. You know whom I saw . . . with his fat, good-natured mug and pink cheeks . . . With his pimples and decayed teeth? and who threw himself on my hand . . . I thought to bite me, and I was about to pull away my fingers . . . to kiss my ring? Who? My fruit-and-vegetable man." [11] Actually, the carriage ride is without danger. The impostors are accepted by that time. They succeed as soon as they step onto the balcony, for the balcony is Genet's supreme symbol of illusion. In modern society the balcony is the place from which rulers greet the people. For Genet the ruler on the balcony is the figurehead that gathers into itself all the falsity inherent in the social system it represents. It is thus onto the balcony that Mme. Irma and her three clients step when they wish to embody the illusion of the state and onto the balcony that Solange steps in her final frenzy of deluded self-glorification. As soon as the three are no longer on the balcony or in the gilded carriage, the false figures lose their spurious dignity. To the cynical newspaper photographers who come to perpetuate their image they are just insignificant little men (although the photographers never suspect they are not dealing with the real dignitaries!). These men, accustomed to falsifying reality and feeding the masses with the pap of symbolism, are again only interested in illusion: "What I want is a

10. Pronko (*op. cit.*, p. 148) claims that the impostors do not like the reality of their roles. I believe rather that they become convinced of the reality of their pretense and like it.

11. Genet, *The Balcony*, p. 86. When reports pour into the rebel headquarters that the queen, the archbishop and the others have been captured, and one of the rebels asks what should be done, his leader dryly advises, "First undress them."

shot of *the* Judge. A good photographer is one who gives a *defi*nitive image." The bishop's photographer tells him, "Get set for prayer, because the world ought to be bombarded with the picture of a pious man. . . . Okay, facing both God and the camera. Hands together. Head up. Eyes down. That's the classical pose." [12] And then, for a picture of the bishop taking the Host, the photographer has the judge roll up his sleeve and place the general's monocle on the prelate's tongue.[13]

If everything inside Mme. Irma's house is unreal, then it would seem that the revolution, which is on the brink of destroying the government and with it the Balcony, would represent the opposite force—namely, reality. But the revolution is as unreal as the government. Starting out as an honest attempt to overthrow the symbol-ridden, illusionary government, it rapidly disintegrates because of the incurable yearning of the human race to be something other than itself. We see this in the contrast between the narcissistic vainglory of the young rebel Armand and the symbol worship of the revolutionary leaders in their use of the escaped whore, Chantal, as a Joan of Arc figure on the one hand, and the matter-of-fact clarity of Roger, the only true rebel, on the other. For people like Armand the serious protest of the revolution is just a joke. His participation is merely an opportunity for him to become the creatures of his daydreams. Like Claire and Solange, Armand never has any reality of his own because, being always engaged in aping someone else, he has no personality of his own:

> ARMAND (*gaily*): . . . it's better than being at the shop. (*He laughs as he looks at himself in the mirror; then, spreading his legs, he plants himself in the middle of the stage.*) Like on the enlistment posters for the Marines: the tanks roll between my legs! (*He strikes another pose.*) Taras

12. Genet, *The Balcony*, p. 89. The photographers' scene was unfortunately left out in Quintero's New York production.

13. Pronko (*op. cit.*, p. 149) says that the "true image, born of a false spectacle" demonstrated here is probably true of all ritual, whether theatrical or religious. Shaw touches on the same point in *St. Joan* when he has the Archbishop of Rheims say that a miracle is any act which induces belief.

Bulba! (*He laughs, takes out his revolver and aims at the bottles.*) Big Chief Buffalo! . . .

ROGER: If ever we had the misfortune of taking pleasure in shooting at men and bottles, it would be good-bye to the revolutionary spirit! As for a red-letter day, this is it! The Law Court's been burned to the ground. The churches have been looted. There are men who are going out to fight in judges' robes and surplices. It's a regular carnival. That ought to please you! [14]

Roger here sees the real purpose of the revolution (and it is Genet's real purpose too): destruction of society—burning the law courts, looting the churches, mocking the trappings of authority. The leaders of the revolution are just as bad as Armand in their way. They allow the revolt to congeal, as Mme. Irma aptly puts it in her epilogue speech. They set up Chantal as an heroic image for which the rebels can die since they will not fight to the death for *reasons*. The Chief of Police and the Court Envoy know this, which is why they are always serenely confident that the revolution will be put down and that it will happen again and again in the future, as it has happened again and again in the past:

THE ENVOY: . . . Chantal's image is circulating in the streets. A stylized image that resembles her and does not resemble her. She towers above the battles. At first, people were fighting against illustrious and illusory tyrants, then for freedom. Tomorrow they'll be ready to die for Chantal alone. [15]

We are now in a position to see what Genet is driving at in *The Balcony*. The play gives us a panoramic picture of society with its violence, oppression, injustice, vice, and falsity. With the exception of Roger (and he fades later, too) everyone in this microcosmos is unreal. They have all lost their own individuality through trying to be someone else. Some of them,

14. Genet, *The Balcony*, pp. 54–55.
15. *Ibid.*, p. 77.

like Mme. Irma, the cynical high priestess of falsity, and the Court Envoy, who manipulates everything like an unctuous Mephisto, seem never to have had any definite individuality of their own. They seem rather to be pieces of the very fabric of falsehood that have become animated.

In order to show us this *Weltanschauung*, Genet once more sets in motion the whirligig of his mind. The clients of the Balcony, all representative human beings, are stripped of layer after layer of unreality. Every part of them is the fabrication of some socially inspired fantasy. They are all hollow men, but after the various strata that seem to constitute their existence have been peeled off, it is seen that they have no husk as well as no core. The first client, for instance, is unreal to begin with because he needs a fantasy to feel real. So he comes to the Balcony to dress up as a bishop, pretend to give absolution, and thus attain a second level of unreality. The third level comes when he pretends the fantasy is real and convinces the populace; the fourth, when he becomes convinced that his imposture has been so successful that he now really *is* a bishop. When he gets to this point, he starts appointing priests and planning a basilica; the "judge" starts appointing magistrates and revising the legal code; and the "general" typically meanders around ineffectually, hoping someone will tell him what to do. In a sense, then, we have here a play within a play within a play within a play: the action is spinning perilously close to the center of the whirligig, where everything will disappear.

The individual characters are not the only things stratified by Genet here. The revolution has been put down, thanks to the impostors, and the Chief of Police is the new head of the state. As he meets with his "cabinet," he gives us Genet's view of the social structure:

> THE CHIEF OF POLICE: Well, gentlemen, above God are you, without whom God would be nothing. And above you shall be I, without whom . . .
>
> THE JUDGE: What about the people? The photographers?
>
> THE CHIEF OF POLICE: On their knees before the

people who are on their knees before God.[16]

Here we have an elaborate hierarchy: the photographers are the image-creators who cater to the people's desire to be deluded; the people create God, and God is sanctified by the functionaries of the social order. Above all is the hero symbol, the dictator, the arbiter of the social order, Genet's *bête noire* —in this case, the Chief of Police.

The Chief of Police is uneasy, however. Despite his success in crushing the revolution, he has still not attained the dignity of having an imitator. None of Mme. Irma's clients has yet had the idea of impersonating a chief of police. Bishops, judges, generals, corpses, kings, saints, crucified missionaries, even Christ in person—but no chief of police. The trouble is that people want to imitate the archetypal figures that are embedded in the collective unconscious; figures who, as the bishop complacently remarks, have the tradition of two thousand years behind them. A chief of police, the hated and despised power figure of the modern totalitarian state, is a mere parvenu in such company. Who would choose to embody a police chief when he could just as easily be a leper healed by the Virgin Mary or a policeman deflowering an archduchess? It gets so bad that the chief is reduced to entertaining the suggestion that he be personified in the form of an erect phallus as tall as himself. The Chief *is* finally imitated. Ironically, the new client is the Chief's greatest enemy—Roger, the rebel leader, who had abducted Chantal from the Balcony in the first place. He fell in love with her but lost her when she became the revolution's symbol ("In every revolution," says Mme. Irma, "there's the glorified whore who sings an anthem and is virginified."). When Chantal was killed and the rebellion suppressed, Roger, the only person in the whole mess who had any reality, lost the will to be himself: "Yes. Everything's washed up . . . and what's saddest of all is people's saying: 'the rebellion was wonderful!' . . . outside in what you call life, everything has crashed. No truth was possible." [17] So now he has come to submerge himself

16. *Ibid.*, p. 102.
17. *Ibid.*, pp. 111–14.

in the person of his archenemy. At the end of his fantasy he does something which is at the same time the ultimate gesture of hate against the abstraction he is personifying, the ultimate gesture of renunciation, and (because performed in a whore-house) the ultimate affirmation of falsity—he castrates himself. After this the Chief retires into his "tomb" in the House of Illusions. There he will wait two thousand years until he too will become an archetypal figure.[18] As he disappears, renewed machine-gun fire bursts out. "Who is it?" asks Mme. Irma, "Our side? . . . Or rebels? . . . Or? . . ." And the Court Envoy, enigmatic as ever, answers, "Someone dreaming, Madame . . ." Then the play ends as Mme. Irma turns out the lights and, stepping out of her role, addresses the audience:

> In a little while, I'll have to start all over again . . . put all the lights on again . . . dress up . . . (*A cock crows.*) Dress up . . . ah, the disguises! Distribute roles again . . . assume my own. . . . (*She stops in the middle of the stage, facing the audience.*) . . . Prepare yours . . . judges, generals, bish-ops, chamberlains, rebels who allow the revolt to congeal, I'm going to prepare my costumes and studios for tomorrow. . . . You must now go home, where everything—you can be quite sure—will be even falser than here.[19]

The whirligig grinds to a stop, and, as usual, there is nothing on it anymore.

The Blacks (Les Nègres, 1958) deals with the levels of unreality in the relations between whites and Negroes. Accord-ing to Genet, this lack of reality is inherent in the institution of colonialism. The artificial superiority of the whites leads to the usual subjective-objective dichotomy. The subjective reality of the Negroes can never be understood by the white man; all that exists for him is the objective reality he sees. But this ob-jective reality has been specially prepared by the Negro as a protective smoke screen: he shows the white man what the

18. Benjamin Nelson, "*The Balcony* and Parisian Existentialism," *Tulane Drama Review*, VII (Spring, 1963), p. 70, points out that Genet probably intends a reference to Franco's Valley of the Fallen here.

19. Genet, *The Balcony*, pp. 117–18.

white man expects to see. And thus we have the ludicrously unreal spectacle of the happy, primitive, inferior native blissfully gamboling about his jungle clearing and asking nothing better than to be "civilized" by missionaries and permitted to work on the plantations for nominal wages. In *The Blacks* Genet tries to make the Negro's real attitude clear to the whites. His play is written for Negro actors and white audiences. This relationship is essential to Genet's scheme. He will not permit white actors to perform the play,[20] and he insists that there be at least one white man or one symbol of a white man (the two are, after all, essentially the same in Genet's system) in the audience:

> . . . a white person, male or female, should be invited every evening. The organizer of the show should welcome him formally, dress him in ceremonial costume and lead him to his seat, preferably in the front row of the orchestra. The actors will play for him. A spotlight should be focused upon this symbolic white throughout the performance.
>
> But what if no white person accepted? Then let white masks be distributed to the black spectators as they enter the theater. And if the blacks refuse the masks, then let a dummy be used.[21]

The action of *The Blacks* is very simple. A group of Negroes enacts the ritual murder of a white woman. Another group of Negroes, wearing white masks and dressed in the trappings that give the whites their illusory authority, sits in judgment on them. Instead of being judged, however, the Negroes "kill" the "Whites." While the Negroes on stage are going through this mock catharsis, the real action of the play is transpiring offstage. A Negro traitor is condemned and shot, and at the end

20. Cf. the letter Genet wrote to Jerzy Lisowski, who had translated *The Blacks* into Polish, refusing him permission to produce the play in Poland on the ground that no Polish-speaking Negroes were available to act in it. (Jean Genet, "To a Would-be Producer," *Tulane Drama Review*, VII [Spring, 1963], pp. 80–81.)

21. Jean Genet, *The Blacks: A Clown Show*, translated by Bernard Frechtman (New York: Grove Press Inc., 1960), p. [11].

it becomes clear to the white audience that the whole play was merely an elaborate, conscious cover-up to disguise an incident in the war of the Negroes on the whites. When the white spectators leave, they realize at last that this war has been declared. Susan Taubes points out that *The Blacks* is not an ordinary play within a play, but a play within a situation: the confrontation of the dominating and the dominated in the only way that is still possible.[22] Direct communication between the two races is no longer possible: only the completely impersonal clown show can still bridge the gap. What happens when the war between the dominating and the dominated comes out into the open Genet shows us in his next play.

In *The Screens* (Les Paravents, published 1961) the Negroes are the Algerians and the whites are the French colonials. The main character is Saïd, the poorest and lowest of the Arabs. Saïd is the paradoxical hero par excellence. He is Genet's hero *because* he is unheroic. Saïd's poverty has put him outside society; and all his efforts are devoted to remaining outside. He marries the ugliest woman in the area, lives by stealing, not from his employers but from his fellow Arabs, and finally informs on his comrades. The contempt and ostracism he earns by this conduct are accepted cheerfully, even gleefully, by Saïd, for they testify to his devotion to himself and to his situation. Joseph McMahon points to some interesting parallels between the character of Saïd and Genet. The latter had lived for years outside society, its sworn enemy, accepting its opprobrium as a sign of his steadfastness to his ideal of individuality. Now, with the popular success of his plays, he runs the risk of being corroded by the approval of society:

> . . . he wants nothing to do with passing from the *enfant terrible* he was at the beginning of his literary career to the *enfant gâté* he seems to be becoming as the bourgeoisie, against whom he has organized his most acerbic attacks, assimilates his ideas, talks about them, and either accepts

22. Susan Taubes, "The White Mask Falls," *Tulane Drama Review*, VII (Spring, 1963), p. 87.

or rejects them. He wants no part of this because the very process by which he is spoiled is the process he has been attacking in all his later works: the presupposition that it is the bourgeoisie, the *decent* people, who rule ultimately on this earth and whose assent to any body of ideas is the modern world's imprimatur and canonization without which no man can be assured he has made his impact.[23]

In apotheosizing Saïd, Genet is in a way writing his own vindication. But there is more to the play than self-justification. Saïd's act of betrayal is also a vindication of the revolution because in rebelling against the masters' conception of him (as the Negroes are preparing to do in *The Blacks*), the rebel, if he is successful, becomes like his masters, for their conception of life is inherent in their position.[24] Thus the unwilling impostors in *The Balcony* immediately adopt the traditional attitudes of bishop, general, and judge as soon as they put on their trappings. Similarly, the planters, Sir Harold and Mr. Blankensee, in *The Screens* are perfectly aware of the fact that their authority resides in their appearance rather than in themselves. Hence Sir Harold's panic when he realizes that his huge mechanical pigskin glove no longer intimidates the natives as it used to do, and Mr. Blankensee's when he discovers the loss of the pads he wears around his midriff to give him an appearance of solid dignity: "A man of my age who doesn't have a belly and an ass hasn't much prestige. So one has to fake a little. . . . In the old days there were wigs." [25] Saïd's treachery is a recognition of the fact that the success of the revolution would mean the repetition of the same abominations as before. The rebels would simply become darker Sir Harolds and Mr. Blankensees. Saïd realizes that every man has to stand alone and not for a cause, even if standing alone means burying oneself in degradation and

23. Joseph H. McMahon, "Keeping Faith and Holding Firm," *Yale French Studies*, No. 29 (Spring–Summer, 1962), pp. 27–28.

24. Marc Pierret, "Genet's New Play: *The Screens*," *Tulane Drama Review*, VII (Spring, 1963), p. 95.

25. Jean Genet, *The Screens*, translated by Bernard Frechtman. Copyright © 1962 by Bernard Frechtman. (New York: Grove Press Inc., 1962), p. 73.

filth. The vocation of men is "to refuse the fate others impose on them and to deny the cultural conspiracy which maintains the illusion of their freedom." [26] The manner in which the revolution will be betrayed by itself is illustrated in this scene:

> THE SOLDIER (*severely*): You shouldn't talk that way any more. And to speak of a traitor the way you do is wrong. And what else? A thief, a bastard, a beggar . . .
>
> OMMU: Aha! . . . that was to be expected! Because you boys have now reached the stage of uniforms, discipline, jaunty marches and bare arms, parade and heroic death, while singing "Madelon" and the "Marsellaise" and martial beauty. . . .
>
> THE SOLDIER: Why not? There are other things than shit and filth. . . .
>
> OMMU: You lousy little stinker, you snotnose, go join the other side where there's stately beauty, you little snotnose! But maybe you've done it, you're joining them, and copying them excites you. To be their reflection is already to be one of them.[27]

Ommu, one of Genet's prophetic old beggar women, knows that man is eternally immersed in vileness and she knows "the consequent importance of remaining vile if one is to remain a faithful witness to one's situation." [28]

> OMMU: Do sins scare you? We've nothing else to live but sins, we've got to live them. I have nothing against God, but he can see that all he's left us is sins. And what's meant by going into mourning, gentlemen, if not to make oneself ugly? To cover oneself with crape, with ashes, with mud, with flies, with cow dung, to let one's beard grow, to let filth accumulate in the folds of the skin, to pluck out one's eyes, to scrape one's fingers, what's meant by going

26. Pierret, *op. cit.*, p. 97.
27. Genet, *The Screens*, pp. 134–35.
28. McMahon, *op. cit.*, p. 31.

into mourning, gentlemen? [29]

Beneath the empty trappings of social position all men are filth, and one must remain faithful to one's reality, which is filth. Genet plays an even more cynical variation on Burke's cynical aphorism when he maintains that defecation is a mighty leveler:

> THE SERGEANT: . . . when you squeeze, you get glassy-eyed, something clouds over . . . and . . . what is it that clouds over and blots out? The world? . . . The sky? . . . No. Your rank of sergeant, and that of captain! And all that goes with it: the uniform, the stripes, the decorations and the officers' school diploma when you've got one! . . . And what's left? Emptiness.[30]

In being true to his own filth Saïd becomes the lowest kind of criminal and at the same time a saint. For Genet the criminal and the saint are the same because both rebel against society.[31] Obedience to temporal power and subservience to social conventions are the worst crimes. Every other act, no matter how bestial, pales into moral insignificance by comparison. To say that crime is "immoral" or sexual perversion "bestial" is to make a value judgment based on social values. The pejorative value of such words as "immoral" and "bestial" is thus, in Genet's eyes, nil. Genet sees the act of betrayal as an act which requires courage and will power. It is also the most dishonorable of all acts in the eyes of society. In Genet's system it is therefore the most worthy of acts. To Genet, Judas's act of betrayal makes him more virtuous than Christ.[32] He would agree with the paradoxical conjecture of Nils Runeberg in J. L. Borges's short story, "Three Views of Judas," that Judas Iscariot and not Jesus Christ was God because in deliberately bringing upon himself the vituperation and hate of all Christians through the centuries Judas commits the greatest of all

29. Genet, The Screens, p. 133.
30. Ibid., p. 170.
31. Leonard Pronko, "Jean Genet's Les Paravents," L'Esprit Créateur, II (Winter, 1962), p. 182.
32. Ibid.

acts of self-abnegation.[33]

Genet's fascination with betrayal as the lowest crime is the result of a long and careful search for the perfect inversion of societal behavior. Throughout his early career as it is recorded in *Our Lady of the Flowers* and *The Thief's Journal* he was engaged in a painstaking and *conscious* pursuit of humiliation and contempt. In his first novel, *Our Lady of the Flowers*, he depicts Darling in the act of agreeing to stooge for the police—an earlier, microcosmic version of Saïd's betrayal:

> He liked selling out on people, for this dehumanized him. Dehumanizing myself is my own most fundamental tendency. On the first page of an evening paper he . . . saw the photograph of the ensign . . . who was shot for treason. And Darling said to himself:
> 'Old pal! Buddy!'
> He was thrilled by a prankishness that was born from within: 'I'm a double crosser.' . . . he walked down the Rue Dancourt, drunk with the hidden splendor (as of a treasure) of his abjection (for it really must intoxicate us if we are not to be killed by its intensity). . . .[34]

Similarly, Genet's homosexuality seems often when he speaks of it to be less the result of a psychological obsession (i.e., a natural impulse, which justifies itself) than of philosophical principle. Genet is trying desperately to defy society with the splendid panache of the Camusian hero defying death, but in so doing brands himself as just as much a creature of society as the whipped curs of convention he shows us in his plays. It is certainly true—and it is a trenchant insight into the falsity we blandly accept—that the bishop and the judge cannot exist without the sinner and that the sinner is therefore primary; but Genet's kind of sinner cannot exist without bishop and judge since his sins are based on a desire to exacerbate the bishop and

33. J. L. Borges, *Ficciones* (New York: Grove Press Inc., 1962), pp. 151–57.
34. Jean Genet, *Our Lady of the Flowers*, translated by Bernard Frechtman (New York: Grove Press, 1961), p. 92.

the judge and all that they represent. Genet seeking his abjection in theft and homosexuality and betrayal is no more real than the conventions that decree these activities abject. His ideal of the "natural criminal" who, like Green Eyes, didn't want what happened to him to happen, who murdered involuntarily, does not exist. Genet believes that "there is a mysterious and irremediable pattern of predestination in the universe . . . /that/ the revolver, the phial of poison, comes forward to meet the hand that will use it as ineluctably as the hand is advanced to grasp its opportunity." [35] This is, of course, pure nonsense; and Genet thus shows himself as much a dream weaver as the people he satirizes. Outside of the feeble-minded there are no criminals like Green Eyes. Genet needs, as do all criminals, society to press against. He is therefore dependent on society and in a very real sense an inextricable part of it. But the core of Genet's thought lies in his belief that there can be no reality within society. This should lead to an ethic of asocial behavior rather than to the ethic of extreme antisocial behavior it does in fact lead to.[36] A writer as skilled as Genet is not obvious and knows how to disguise the repellence of his ideas in the garb of an ingenious logical system. It becomes necessary under the circumstances to point out that Genet is a thinker whose means fascinate though his ends are wrong.

Much of the confusion that surrounds the plays of Genet and of his fellow avant-gardists can be traced to the influence of Artaud's belief that true drama had its roots among primitive, nonrational peoples. The drama as we know it reflects the artificial and hollow society in which we live. Real drama reflects only the basic human emotions as they were before they were covered up with artificial behavior. Artaud felt that drama should not appeal to the mind but to the emotions—and to such an extent that a process of communion takes place between

35. Richard N. Coe, The Vision of Jean Genet (New York: Grove Press, 1968), p. 229.
36. Coe (p. 23) asserts that the intensity of his feeling led Genet to deify sadistic traitors, such as the "brutal and unlovely teen-age thugs who worked for the Gestapo in France during the War," and to admire Hitler as the epitome of the antisocial creature.

actor and spectator in which both are roused to a high pitch of excitement. Artaud compared this condition to a man losing his reason under the influence of the plague. He also maintained that drama should show "cruelty," by which he meant it should give the impression that man is controlled from birth to death by blind and merciless forces. At the same time drama should be a defiance of these forces, no matter how ineffectual such defiance is doomed to be, and a protest against the encroachment of civilization upon man's naturally free spirit.

Genet conforms fairly closely to Artaud's specifications. The bias against contemporary society may be seen in his choice of scene. *The Maids* takes place in a wealthy household depicted with the utmost viciousness. *Deathwatch* and *The Balcony* take place in the two most antisocial milieus possible: the one in a prison, the other in a whorehouse. *The Blacks* and *The Screens* take place in savage settings where the actual conflict between the social and the antisocial forces is being fought. In all of the plays, moreover, we have the element of cruelty which Artaud claims as an essential ingredient of all true drama. In *The Balcony* this cruelty takes the form of the enacted sadomasochistic fantasies of the bishop, the judge, and the general. In *The Blacks* we see the reenactment of the ritual murder and the shooting of the jury. In *Deathwatch* Maurice is strangled on the stage; and in *The Maids* there is the attempted murder of Madame and the suicide of Claire. And, finally, in *The Screens* we have a constant stream of references to violence and scatology.

In all the plays the *intention* is to arouse the audience to an emotional frenzy in which they will instinctively reject the social structure disintegrating before their eyes on the stage and accept instead the atavistic emotions that Genet sends surging through them. This frenzy is analogous to Artaud's "plague," which sweeps through the audience like an epidemic and frees them from their socially impressed inhibitions, like a disease that leads to death inevitably will do. When Mme. Irma says of the rebellion, "Contagion? The rebellion is an epidemic. It has the same fatal and sacred character," we see that Genet uses the rebellion's ominous threat (emphasized by the intermittent machine-gun fire) as a device to whip up the audience's emotions and make the theater once more a ritual and a ceremony as it was in the theatre of Aeschylus and Sophocles and in the "theater" of the Orphic and Eleusinian mysteries and as it still is in the theater of the Orient. All this is straight out of the atavistic theater of savagery and irrationalism with which Antonin Artaud wanted to bring back drama to its original function of hypnotizing the audience into a frenzied communion with the action: to strike not at the brain but at the core of the human soul.

The German-Speaking Drama

THE CONTEMPORARY German-speaking drama differs from the French avant-garde drama in being more rational and more topical. It is influenced by Shaw and Brecht rather than by Jarry and Artaud. The themes of protest and paradox are still there, but speech is once again the medium of communication, although dramatic form continues to be broken down. The use of violence and cruelty continues, but it is now once more explicable and politically involved instead of cosmic and mysterious, as in the violence and cruelty of the "Savage God."

FRIEDRICH DÜRRENMATT
The Sardonic View

WHEN *The Visit* opened on Broadway on May 5, 1958, it was an instant success, and the name of Friedrich Dürrenmatt, known throughout Europe for some years, was suddenly brought to the attention of the American theater world. So profound an impression did this one play make that Dürrenmatt has shot up in the estimation of American theater people to a place on a level with Jean Anouilh as one of Europe's foremost current dramatic authors.

Dürrenmatt's plays can be characterized as fantasies from which lessons may be learned. The imputation of preaching frightens writers nowadays for some reason. They are convinced that they have no function other than to entertain. The pendulum, always erratic in the theater, has come full swing since the fervor of the turn-of-the-century social-propaganda play. Indeed, it seems to set Galileo's theory at defiance, for, instead of spending all its time in the journey from one end of its swing to the other, it spends all of it standing stock-still at one end and then flashing across to the other end in no time flat. Now we are at the nondidactic end again. Philosophy, Dürrenmatt insists, cannot be transmitted through drama. He feels that the theater exists solely as a medium for the creation of a special world—that the audience, in other words, comes to peep in at a new, wonderful, and strange world, a contrived set of circumstances in which fantastic things can happen quite as matter-of-factly as the spectators wistfully wish they might in real life. Beyond this Dürrenmatt refuses to go. He maintains that he does not care what lesson may be drawn from his plays, if any. Like T. S. Eliot, he is often enlightened as to the inner meaning of his works by reading the critics. His own attitude is simply that each person will choose from these created worlds whatever appears desirable or useful to him.

All of Dürrenmatt's created worlds seem to fasten upon and revolve (in a manner sometimes savage and bitter, sometimes impersonal and amused, sometimes ferociously jocular—but always detached and bitingly sardonic) around death. In Dürrenmatt's works death seems to be almost personified—a vague, grey shape leaning mockingly over the shoulders of his leading characters and edging them slyly on. Unlike Thornton Wilder, to whom death is only the last incident in life and who places the emphasis always on the process of living, Dürrenmatt sees life only as a long futility working up to an ultimate futility. Death is the culmination of life, but it is an anticlimactic and basically insignificant culmination. A process that culminates in an anticlimax can only be treated as a ridiculous joke. Hence the mordantly sardonic, lacerating note in Dürrenmatt's plays—"Man is ridiculous because he must die." Dürrenmatt's world is like a Punch and Judy show in which audience and puppeteer are part of the ridiculous antics.

They laugh at the futile wriggling of the puppets in their vain attempts to squeeze some consolatory meaning out of their tragedies; but the laughter is self-lacerating. Dürrenmatt's other principal theme is the effect of the possession of power on the human soul. His preoccupation with this theme may be summed up in Lord Acton's axiom, "Power tends to corrupt; absolute power corrupts absolutely." In all of his plays there is some figure unbalanced by the possession of power.

Dürrenmatt's best play is undoubtedly *The Visit*, originally titled *Der Besuch der alten Dame* (The Visit of the Old Lady). More than any other of his works it demonstrates his sardonic view of human behavior. *The Visit* takes place in Güllen, a seedy, run-down town somewhere in the German-speaking part of Europe. The inhabitants, most of them unemployed, spend their time sitting around talking wistfully of the former glories of the town. One group of four citizens, which acts as chorus to the action, spends its days lolling around the railroad station watching the trains roar by and reminiscing with vague bitterness about the days when all trains, even the crack trans-European expresses, used to stop regularly at Güllen. Now at last a ray of hope has penetrated the prevailing gloom: Güllen's most illustrious native is coming back for a visit. For Güllen is the home town of the world's richest woman, Claire Zachanassian, who left at an early age with the cloud of an unsavory affair over her and became a prostitute in Hamburg. There Zachanassian, the world's richest man, saw her and married her. Now he is dead and she owns everything—Armenian Oil, Western Railways, the North Broadcasting Co., and the Hong-kong red-light district. The townspeople hope to persuade her to pour some money into the town during her stay, and to this end they have appointed Alfred Ill, her former sweetheart, as her escort and charmer-in-chief with instructions to get at least a million. Alfred, we learn, was once a handsome young fellow who had a secret love affair with Claire. Now he is a run-down old man with a family, the keeper of the general store.

Mme. Zachanassian arrives with her entourage, which includes a butler, two blind eunuchs, a black panther, and an empty coffin. At first things go swimmingly: Ill, set on by the mayor and schoolmaster, who sniff around after the couple like a pair of unpractised but pathetically eager bloodhounds, takes Claire to all the places where they used to make love. He tries to recapture those days, but finds that every time he touches the old lady he touches ivory: she is made up mostly of artificial limbs. Nonetheless, he succeeds in eliciting a promise that she will give the town "millions."

Then, at the ceremonial banquet, comes the bombshell. Claire recounts how Ill refused to acknowledge his child and publicly proclaimed her a whore by means of bribed perjurers. She then offers to give the town a billion—half for the town and half to be equally divided among all the families—if in return they will give her justice:

> CLAIRE: I will give you a billion and I want justice in return.
> MAYOR: How am I to understand that, dear lady?
> CLAIRE: Just as I said it.
> MAYOR: But justice cannot be bought!
> CLAIRE: Everything can be bought.
> MAYOR: I still don't understand.
> CLAIRE: Come here, Boby.

The Butler comes forward and takes off his dark glasses.

> BUTLER: I don't know if any of you will still be able to recognize me.
> SCHOOLMASTER: Chief Judge Hofer.
> BUTLER: Correct. Chief Judge Hofer. Forty-five years ago I was chief judge of the Güllen Court. Later I became judge in the Court of Appeals at Kaffigen and remained there until Mme. Zachanassian offered to take me into her service as butler twenty-five years ago. I accepted. A somewhat peculiar career for an academic person, but the salary offered was so fantastic that . . .
> CLAIRE: Come to the point, Boby.
> BUTLER: As you have heard, Mme. Claire Zachanassian offers you a billion and wants justice in return for it. In other words, Mme. Claire Zachanassian offers you a billion if you undertake to correct the injustice done to Mme. Zachanassian in Güllen. Mr. Ill, if you please.

Ill gets up, pale, startled, amazed.

ILL: What do you want with me?

BUTLER: Come forward, Mr. Ill.

ILL: Certainly.

BUTLER: In 1910 I was Chief Judge in Güllen and sat on a paternity case. Claire Zachanassian, at that time Klara Wäscher, accused you, Mr. Ill, of being the father of her child. You contested the case, Mr. Ill, and produced two witnesses.

ILL: Old stories. I was young and didn't know what I was doing.

The two eunuchs are brought forward.

THE TWO: Here we are, here we are!

BUTLER: Do you recognize them, Mr. Ill?

Ill remains silent.

THE TWO: We're Koby and Loby, we're Koby and Loby.

ILL: I don't know them.

THE TWO: We've changed, we've changed.

BUTLER: Give your names.

THE FIRST: Jakob Hühnlein, Jakob Hühnlein.

THE SECOND: Ludwig Sparr, Ludwig Sparr.

BUTLER: Well, Mr. Ill?

ILL: I don't know anything about them.

BUTLER: Jakob Hühnlein and Ludwig Sparr, do you know Mr. Ill?

THE TWO: We are blind, we are blind.

BUTLER: Do you recognize his voice?

THE TWO: Recognize his voice, recognize his voice.

BUTLER: In 1910 I was the judge and you were the witnesses. What did you swear to the Court at Güllen?

THE TWO: That we slept with Klara, that we slept with Klara.

BUTLER: That is what you swore before the Court and before God. Did you swear the truth?

THE TWO: We swore falsely, we swore falsely.

BUTLER: Why, Jakob Hühnlein and Ludwig Sparr?

THE TWO: Ill bribed us, Ill bribed us.

BUTLER: With what?

THE TWO: With a bottle of gin, with a bottle of gin.

CLAIRE: Now tell what I did to you, Koby and Loby.

BUTLER: Tell.

THE TWO: The lady searched for us, the lady searched for us.

BUTLER: True. Claire Zachanassian had you searched for. Over the whole world. Jakob Hühnlein had gone to Canada and Ludwig Sparr to Australia. But she found you. What did she do with you then?

THE TWO: She gave us to Toby and Roby. She gave us to Toby and Roby.

BUTLER: And what did Toby and Roby do to you?

THE TWO: Blinded and castrated, blinded and castrated.

BUTLER: That is the story: a judge, a defendant, two false witnesses, a miscarriage of justice in 1910. Is it not so, Plaintiff?

CLAIRE: It is so.

ILL: Dead and buried long ago! Just a crazy old story.

BUTLER: What happened to the child, Plaintiff?

CLAIRE: It lived one year.

BUTLER: What happened to you?

CLAIRE: I became a whore.

BUTLER: Why?

CLAIRE: The decree of the Court made me one.

BUTLER: And now, Claire Zachanassian, you want justice?

CLAIRE: I can afford it. A billion for Güllen—if someone kills Alfred Ill.[1]

---

1. Friedrich Dürrenmatt, *Komödien I*. With permission of and copyright © 1958 by Peter Schifferli Verlags AG "Die Arche" (Zürich: Verlag der Arche, 1958), pp. 292–95.

This is a typical Dürrenmatt scene. Its structure may be compared to the piling on of straws until the camel's back breaks. Casually the evidence starts building up, dropping negligently, apologetically almost, on the imperceptibly, yet very really, increasing pile, until suddenly the whole innocent-and-insignificant-seeming mass is brought into focus by Claire's self-assured, deeply venomous remark, "One billion for Güllen—if someone kills Alfred Ill." It is like pulling a string that brings the whole structure tumbling down, jerking everyone, actors and audience, back to a startled and shocked attention. Dürrenmatt uses this enormously effective technique again and again. He uses it in the proposal scene of *Die Ehe des Herrn Mississippi* (The Marriage of Mr. Mississippi); in the scene of Archilochos' promotion in *Grieche sucht Griechin* (Greek Seeks Greek, a novel); in Odoacer's submission scene in *Romulus der Grosse* (Romulus the Great); and in the trial scene in *Die Panne* (The Breakdown, a novel adapted for the stage as The Deadly Game).

Things begin to move rapidly after the offer. The mayor at first indignantly turns it down in the name of humanity. Gradually, however, Ill's fellow citizens, starved of all luxury for so long, get deeper and deeper into debt as they buy things on credit in neighboring towns. Slowly their attitude toward Ill changes. They become more and more hostile as they "discover" the heinousness of his crime. Eventually Ill realizes that even his family wants him to die (his son has a new car and his wife a new fur coat—on credit); and, in a superbly ironic scene, a veritable tour de force of cynicism, he is sentenced to death while reporters from all over the world and TV and newsreel cameras look unsuspectingly on. The murder takes place immediately afterwards. Claire accepts the body for removal to the elaborate mausoleum she has constructed for it on the Isle of Capri. As she goes out, she calls the mayor, and, with a gesture of regal contemptuousness, drops the check at his feet. As the mayor stoops to retrieve the fluttering piece of paper— worth a billion, or a man's life, or the newly burdened conscience of the town—the curtain falls.

That is the story of a typical Dürrenmatt play. The two principal themes of death and the corruptive influence of power are already fully developed in *Es steht geschrieben* (It Is Written), performed in Zürich in 1947. In this, his first play, Dürrenmatt chose as his subject the Anabaptist blood bath in Münster under John of Leyden. The play deals with John's fanatical vanity, his gradual moral disintegration under the pressure of power, and the final "joke" of his horrible death as his broken body is thrown into the same dung cart in which he first arrived in Münster.

In *Romulus der Grosse* (Romulus the Great, 1949) the demonstration of futility assumes a more sophisticated character. The play is about the last days of the West Roman Empire. As in the play about John of Leyden, Dürrenmatt has taken a historical character and a historical series of events and altered them to suit his own purposes. Nothing could be more remote from the historical last Roman emperor than Dürrenmatt's Romulus. Dürrenmatt turns the end of the Roman Empire, under the child emperor Romulus Augustulus in 476, from an almost imperceptible death rattle, the inevitable last stifled sigh that follows centuries of inefficiency and corruption, to a sardonic commentary on idealism and self-sacrifice. The real Romulus reigned for less than a year (475–476) and was only about fourteen years old, but Dürrenmatt's emperor is an old man who has ruled for twenty years. Twenty years was a fantastically long time for a late Roman emperor to reign. Dürrenmatt's emperor manages it by not ruling. After becoming emperor by marrying the illegitimate daughter of the Emperor Valentinianus, he has spent the entire twenty years raising chickens in his country villa. Under his do-nothing policy the strength of the Roman Empire has been undermined and now German hordes led by Odoacer threaten to take Rome and exterminate the Imperium.

Dürrenmatt's Romulus poses as an urbane cynic with the mind of an eighteenth-century rationalist; but hidden beneath the worldly exterior is the moral fervor of a Puritan divine. Some idea of the type of person and ruler he is may be had from this conversation with his two chamberlains:

ROMULUS: . . . Fetch the Finance Minister.

ACHILLES: The Finance Minister has absconded, Your Majesty.

ROMULUS: Absconded???

PYRAMUS: With the State Treasury, O Emperor.

ROMULUS: But why? There wasn't anything in it.

ACHILLES: He hopes that his action will hide the fact that the country is bankrupt.

ROMULUS: An intelligent man. The best way to hide a big scandal is to start a small one. Let him be invested with the title, "Savior of his Country." [2]

As the play progresses, Romulus becomes more and more of a Shavian character (the whole play, in fact, might be straight out of the Shaw canon). He reveals to his wife that the sole reason he married her was to become emperor and thus fulfill the sentence he had passed on his country. For twenty years he has deliberately mismanaged and bankrupted the country. He has waited for twenty years to see the moment that is about to come: the fall of the Roman Empire to the Germans. With the implacability and steadfast purpose of a Catonian Roman he has pronounced his verdict and unflinchingly carried it out. Rome has failed; therefore Rome must die. He discloses all this in a conversation with his amazed wife, who for twenty years had thought him feeble-minded:

ROMULUS: . . . My political policy is to do nothing.

JULIA: You didn't have to become emperor to do that.

ROMULUS: Naturally enough my do-nothingness only made sense as long as I was emperor. To laze around as a private citizen is totally pointless.

JULIA: And to laze around as emperor endangers the state.

ROMULUS: Well, there you are!

JULIA: What do you mean by that?

ROMULUS: You have discovered the reason for my laziness.

JULIA: You can't possibly doubt the necessity of the state.

2. *Ibid.*, pp. 13–14.

ROMULUS: I don't doubt the necessity of the state:
I merely doubt the necessity of *our* state. It has become an
international empire and an institution which killed, plun-
dered, suppressed, and ravaged other peoples—until I came.

JULIA: I don't see why you had to become emperor
if that's the way you feel about the Roman Empire.

ROMULUS: The Roman Empire has existed for the
last few centuries only because it had an emperor. Consequently there was no other alternative for me than to become
emperor myself in order to be able to liquidate the Imperium.

JULIA: Either you are crazy or the world is.

ROMULUS: I have resigned myself to the latter
alternative.

JULIA: Then you only married me to destroy the
Roman Imperium.

ROMULUS: For no other reason.

JULIA: You have thought about nothing else besides Rome's downfall right from the beginning.

ROMULUS: About nothing else.

JULIA: You consciously sabotaged the safety of the
Imperium.

ROMULUS: Consciously.

JULIA: You've played the cynic and clown all the
time only so you could stab us in the back.

ROMULUS: You can put it that way too, if you·
like. . . .

JULIA: You are Rome's betrayer!

ROMULUS: No, I am Rome's judge.[3]

This view of the last Roman Emperor as a man who judges
Rome for its sins and deliberately destroys it is in itself a sufficiently novel and interesting reinterpretation of history to justify
a whole drama. But Dürrenmatt adds two more twists to his
plot. He is not interested in the decline and fall of the Roman
Empire; he *is* interested in the dissection of the rationalist-
moralist, Romulus.

3. *Ibid.,* pp. 57–58.

Romulus is not a power-crazy judge, dispassionately consigning Rome to the devil. He has only been able to justify his objective to himself all these years by promising himself that he will give his own life in expiation for his betrayal. The pure rationalist would have seen Rome's destruction was "necessary" and would have watched the consummation of his plans with considerable self-satisfaction; but the moralist has the martyr complex: he must find "justification" for the "necessity" in the sacrifice of his own life. Both types, Dürrenmatt is trying to tell us, are equally dangerous. They are guilty, among other things, of *hubris*. Like Hector in *Tiger at the Gates*, Romulus tries to halt the invincible phalanx of fate. Inevitably he fails.

The night before the Germans are due to arrive, Romulus' household leaves him after a farcical scene in which he discovers no less than nine potential assassins hidden in his bedroom. Only the sudden outcry announcing the imminent arrival of the Germans saves him. The next morning Romulus quietly awaits the German chieftain, Odoacer. Urbane as ever, faithful to his lifelong creed of "Face the world fearlessly, fearlessly do the right," he fully expects to be beheaded on the spot by the barbarians. Then, as in the banquet scene of *The Visit*, comes the surprise. Odoacer turns out to be a rationalist-moralist too. As urbane and cultivated as Romulus, instead of cutting his head off, he throws himself on his knees before the emperor. It turns out that Odoacer has conquered Italy for the specific purpose of abasing himself before the head of the Roman Empire and handing the German people over to him. He has realized that his nephew, Theodoric, is a true barbarian, a war-loving, savage machine (Dürrenmatt's intentional parallel to modern Prussianism is obvious) who will turn the Germans into a conquest-mad horde if he succeeds to the leadership. Theodoric has all the most dangerous symptoms: he doesn't like girls, drinks only water, sleeps on the hard floor, practices fighting daily, and does calisthenics in every spare moment; and the people love him. Odoacer sees only one solution: to conquer Rome and throw himself and his people under its humanizing influence. Like Romulus he has judged his people, and like Romulus he has misjudged them. Romulus becomes "Great" only at the end when, defeated in all his plans, he accepts the fate that is his. Instead of being the implacable judge, his role is to be a retired and superannuated emperor living out his life on a pension in a country villa while Odoacer governs. Both of them now know that they are only marking time during an interim, for as soon as he feels himself strong enough Theodoric will kill them both and the progress of history, which they have tried to impede, will resume.

In *Romulus the Great* we can clearly see the two themes that run through Dürrenmatt's work: the themes of death and power. Romulus is the type of the benevolent despot, and he is just as bad, Dürrenmatt tells us, as the more conventional type of despot. As soon as he gains absolute power, Romulus becomes, strictly speaking, insane. From the best and most reasonable motives he calmly proposes to destroy a nation. Despite his kindliness in his personal relations, with his family and the members of his household, despite his strong sense of personal justice, despite his genuinely felt humanitarian impulses, Romulus suffers from the disease of all morally fervid idealist reformers: he loses the human element when applying his theories. People in the mass are not individualized for Romulus, and so he consigns the people under his care to destruction. His proposed sacrifice of his own life becomes suddenly ridiculous when he comes face to face with the German chieftain. Nor, we then realize, would the sacrifice have been of any significance at all—certainly not as an expiation. The laughter of the gods seems to tinkle faintly through the conversation as the two old idealists, Romulus and Odoacer, sit discussing their situation amid the ruins of their grandiose plans.

In *Die Ehe des Herrn Mississippi* Dürrenmatt takes his two principal themes of death and power one step further. Again he is absorbed by the hideous results of absolute power in the hands of a single-minded idealist, only this time he extends the range of his subject by using symbolic characters in a symbolic setting. The death theme is also carried one step further—instead of being treated sardonically, it is treated with off-hand jocularity. Three of the four main characters are murdered in the last scene, but one of them has already been murdered in the first scene, so that we see the same murder twice—somewhat like seeing a movie trailer and then the movie itself. Furthermore, each of the corpses comes to life again immediately in order to explain the significance of his death to the audience.

The play, as Dürrenmatt tells us in his opening stage direction, is about the room in which it takes place. This room "stinks to high heaven" and represents the ordinary, everyday world in which the majority of people live. It is a room that has been depersonalized: a little of everything is to be seen in it. There are pieces of cheap bric-a-brac, Louis XVI mirrors, fin-de-siècle mirrors, Louis XIV chairs, a Louis XV buffet, Empire sofas, Spanish walls, Japanese vases, Meissner porcelain, and a Gothic grandfather clock. Russian elements, Dürrenmatt tells us, can be left out if the political situation makes such an omission desirable. In short, the room is an utter hodgepodge of styles— what the Germans call a Biedermeier room, which is the type of room most people would have if they had the money to buy the stuff. There are two windows in the rear wall, one giving a view of a Gothic cathedral and an apple tree, the other of a cypress and the ruins of an antique temple. The chief characters are similarly generalized through their names: Anastasia, Florestan Mississippi, Frederic Réné Saint-Claude, and Graf Bodo von Übelohe-Zabernsee.

Basically, the complicated plot concerns the reactions to each other of two fanatical ideal-pursuers, Saint-Claude and Mississippi, and one humanitarian, Count Bodo, as they revolve around their catalyst, Anastasia, the eternal *femme fatale*, the Whore of Babylon, as she is called at one point, the scabrous underside of *das ewig Weibliche*. The plot itself is pure melodrama. Dürrenmatt has created as banal a plot as possible in order to fix the audience's attention while he exposes the characters and philosophies of his protagonists. Anastasia poisons her husband and is blackmailed into marriage by Mississippi. At various times she takes Bodo, Saint-Claude, and Diego, the Minister of State, as lovers. In the end she tries to poison Saint-Claude, poisons her husband instead and is herself poisoned by him. Purely as a plot nothing could be more satisfactory. What lies behind this erotic blood bath is quite serious, however.

Like Romulus, Mississippi and Saint-Claude have single-mindedly fought to attain an abstract ideal and like him they have
ceased to be human beings and have become fanatical blinkered
automatons instead. Mississippi and Saint-Claude (names they
adopted when they began their careers) have grown up together
in the gutters of some great city. With the money they earned
as male prostitutes they opened a brothel. Both young men
made money and set out on the path determined for them by
the first books they read. In Mississippi's case the book was the
Bible, and he goes to Oxford to study law, obsessed with the
idea of restoring absolute justice to the world in the form of
the Mosaic law. In pursuit of this ideal he has already succeeded
in forcing through over 200 death sentences in his capacity as
state's attorney at the time the play opens. He is slowly changing the laws to return more and more of the offences listed in
the Mosaic law as punishable by death to the status of capital
crimes. By the end of the play he has over 350 death sentences
in 30 years as state's attorney to his credit. Saint-Claude, on the
other hand, read Marx: he has become a professional revolutionary, citizen of the Soviet Union, colonel in the Red Army,
honorary citizen of Rumania, member of the Polish parliament,
and member of the Cominform Politburo. None of these things
mean anything to him, however, since he cares no more for Communism than for capitalism. His hand, like Mississippi's, like
Romulus', like that of all determined ideal-pursuers, is against
everyone. Saint-Claude, at least, has the clear-sightedness to
recognize what has happened to him and Mississippi, although
he is now powerless to change himself: "We are the two last
great moralists of our times, and we have both gone under. You
behind a hangman's mask and I behind a Russian spy's." [4]

Mississippi and Saint-Claude meet again in the symbolic
room in Anastasia's house twenty years after they parted in the
brothel. The room is now Mississippi's as well as Anastasia's, for
he has been married to her for five years at this point. Five years

---

4. It is amusing to note parenthetically that Dürrenmatt told me he
deliberately gave Saint-Claude the kind of youth that most European Communists (many of whom were intellectuals of good family) wished they
might have had.

before, Anastasia had poisoned her husband when she discovered that he was having an affair with Mississippi's wife. Similarly, Mississippi had poisoned his wife—executed her in accordance with the Mosaic law, he calls it—when he discovered she was having an affair with Anastasia's husband. Then he forced Anastasia to marry him for purposes of mutual punishment and expiation. Their marriage was to be a hell for both so that their sins might be refined and purified. This Mississippi fondly believes to have happened: he himself has become inspired to the point of having succeeded in ramming through 150 death sentences in five years, and she has become known as the Angel of the Dungeons because of her solicitude for the men her husband has had condemned. Meanwhile Saint-Claude has entered the country illegally for the purpose of starting a revolution. He has decided to use his old friend as a target because the people hate him. Anastasia becomes Saint-Claude's mistress when she sees which way the wind is blowing. And when she sees that the government will not back Mississippi, thus knocking the heart out of Saint-Claude's little revolution, she becomes the chief minister's mistress. In the end Mississippi begins to suspect that she has been unfaithful and poisons her. At the same time he carelessly drinks another poisoned cup of coffee that Anastasia had prepared for Saint-Claude. All of this does Saint-Claude no good, for he is shot by the Communists for failing to put the revolution over. During the whole play the figure of Count Bodo von Überlohe-Zabernsee is present either in spirit or in person. Bodo is a direct contrast to Mississippi and Saint-Claude. A nobleman who has given away all his fortune in order to become a physician and open a clinic for the poor, he is the type of the good and useful idealist—the idealist who is interested in helping the individual and looks upon each individual as a separate human problem.

Mississippi, Saint-Claude, and Romulus deal in generalities: Mississippi feels that everyone must be bent to fit an arbitrary, abstract concept of justice; Saint-Claude feels that hunger and oppression must be eradicated by force; Romulus feels that Rome must die and lets the present citizens suffer for the sins of their ancestors. Bodo, on the other hand, deals in particulars:

he feels that sickness must be stamped out by giving each
sufferer complete medical care. Bodo's good work is ruined by
Mississippi's legal fanaticism. He is driven out of the country
because he has technically broken a law by giving Anastasia,
whom he loves, the poison to kill her husband under the impression that it was for her sick dog. He flees to Borneo, where he
opens a hospital but loses all his money and ruins his health.
The hospital is a dud too, since it cannot compete in effectiveness and popularity with the local witch doctors.

At the end of the play Dürrenmatt points his moral. Anastasia, Saint-Claude, and Mississippi have been killed and now
rise again and speak to the audience:

> ANASTASIA: A whore who meets her death without
> remorse.
> SAINT-CLAUDE: Yet whether we lie here in this ruin
> MISSISSIPPI: Or whether we die backed up against
> a white-washed wall, or on a pile of blazing faggots or bound
> upon a wheel, between Heaven and Earth
> SAINT-CLAUDE: Ever again we return, as always we
> have returned again
> MISSISSIPPI: Always in new disguises, always long-
> ing for ever-receding paradises
> SAINT-CLAUDE: Rejected by you now and again
> MISSISSIPPI: Nourished by your indifference
> SAINT-CLAUDE: Thirsting for your brotherhood
> MISSISSIPPI: We sweep over your cities . . . driv-
> ing the mill which grinds you down.[5]

This is followed by a vision of Bodo dressed as Don Quixote
tilting at a windmill: "the eternal comedy goes on . . . fed by
our helplessness."

In *Ein Engel kommt nach Babylon* (An Angel Comes to
Babylon, 1953) Dürrenmatt puts less emphasis on the two
themes that I have suggested underlie the plays discussed thus
far. The acidulously jocular view of death is still there in the
farcical key figure of the hangman, but the theme of the corrup-

5. Dürrenmatt, *op. cit.*, p. 167.

tive influence of power in the hands of a single-minded person is definitely relegated to a subordinate role. *Ein Engel kommt nach Babylon* is a rather unsuccessful attempt at a symbolic portrayal of human history in terms of individual character types. The play itself is fascinating because more than any other of Dürrenmatt's plays it takes place purely in a stage world. The trouble with it lies in the symbolism, which is suggestive but unclear and often even muddled, somewhat like the symbolism in a Bergman movie. All the chief characters are eternal types. Nebuchadnezzar and Nimrod and their ministers, as well as Akki the beggar, have lived since before the Flood. The other important characters are the angel and Kurrubi, a young girl recently personally produced by God out of the void.

The play is about the angel's mission to bring Kurrubi, who represents the quality of selfless love, to the lowest of men. The lowest of men, according to the angel's road map (a wonderful document that appears to combine the functions of a cosmic atlas, the *Encyclopaedia Britannica*, and the *Farmer's Almanac*), is Akki of Babylon, the last living beggar on earth. Unfortunately, King Nebuchadnezzar chooses this moment to disguise himself as a beggar in order to persuade Akki to give up begging and join the Babylonian civil service. Nebuchadnezzar has just become king again after serving for 900 years as King Nimrod's footstool and has decreed that begging must be abolished. All who disobey are to be hanged, but Akki has nonetheless remained obdurate; and so, in the best Haroun al-Raschid or "benevolent tyrant" tradition, Nebuchadnezzar has disguised himself as a beggar in order to bring Akki round. Akki and Nebuchadnezzar decide to hold a contest to see who is the better beggar, and of course Akki, the old pro, wins going away. This solves the angel's difficulty: obviously the loser in the contest is the lowest of men. Nebuchadnezzar's helplessness has meanwhile won Kurrubi's love. But in his rage at the fact that he has been given this gift of God as the lowest of mortals instead of as the highest, Nebuchadnezzar mistreats Kurrubi and gives her to Akki in exchange for Nimrod, whom Akki has won in the begging contest.

That is the basic situation out of which the rest of the play grows. Kurrubi becomes Akki's begging companion for ten days, and the whole town falls in love with her. The people insist that she marry the king, and she learns that the lowest of mortals and the highest are one—King Nebuchadnezzar is the beggar whom she loves. She refuses to marry Nebuchadnezzar unless he becomes a beggar again, but of course he cannot do this. Nor is anyone else willing to do it, despite the "love" they all profess for Kurrubi. In fact, when they see what Kurrubi's conditions are, the populace's "love" turns to hate and they demand her death. She is handed over to the hangman, but— Happy End!—the hangman is really Akki in disguise and they escape together into the desert.

Dürrenmatt is dealing with two parallel symbolic themes here: the impossibility of selfless love on earth and the ultimate triumph of the type of human being represented by Akki, the independent man. When she first appears, Kurrubi is only fifteen minutes away from having been formed by God—she is innocence and purity personified. Her first introduction to human ways, i.e., to evil, is when she sees the brutality of the soldiers who are in charge of Nimrod. The angel's explanation, "Be calm, my child. A simple accident only, which has no effect on the harmony of things," represents the viewpoint of the celestial powers, the viewpoint *sub specie aeternitatis*. Dürrenmatt's depiction of the angel is not specifically religious. The angel simply stands for the viewpoint of whatever superhuman powers the spectator may believe in; for those who do not believe, he can simply stand for the lack of understanding in a mindless cosmos. The angel's character throughout is that of a bumbling and absent-minded professor. An amusing example of this is the following passage, in which the angel tries to explain why Heaven is not concerned with kings:

ANGEL: I am an Angel of God.

NEBUCHADNEZZAR: What is your wish, Exalted One?

ANGEL: I have come to you from Heaven.

NEBUCHADNEZZAR: Why have you come? What do you want with a beggar of Nineveh? Go, Messenger of God, to Nebuchadnezzar the King. He alone is worthy to receive thee.

ANGEL: Kings, O Beggar Anaschamaschtaklaku, do not interest Heaven. The greater a man's lowliness, the greater his acceptability to Heaven.

NEBUCHADNEZZAR: (*amazed*) Why?

ANGEL: (*thinks*) No idea. (*thinks harder*) Actually it *is* rather peculiar. (*apologetically*) I'm not really an anthropologist. I'm more interested in the physical sciences. My specialty is suns. Principally red giant ones. My mission is to go to the lowest of men, but I have no means of knowing Heaven's reasons.[6]

Throughout the play the angel completely fails to grasp what is going on around him. It is all too insignificant, and besides he is busy collecting botanical specimens. His attitude is summed up in a remark he makes to Kurrubi near the beginning of the play. Kurrubi has been created to go among men and already has some of the human susceptibilities. When the angel tells her she is to go to the lowest of men, she answers that the lowest of men must surely be unhappy. The angel's answer is, "Whatever is created is good, and whatever is good is happy. In my extended travels throughout creation I have never seen the smallest atom of unhappiness." The evil that the angel is unable to see is the evil of human institutions, the means by which the power-possessors coerce the helpless majority. The accident of Kurrubi's falling in love with the disguised Nebuchadnezzar brings her directly into contact with the very apex of this pyramid of evil. Nebuchadnezzar and Nimrod, who alternately share the supreme power over their fellow human beings, represent the incessant historical seesawing of political power from one tyranny to another. However new the tyranny seems, Dürrenmatt is saying, it is really always the same: it is either Nimrod or Nebuchadnezzar. And the end result of this loveless tyranny (it cannot accept Kurrubi) will be the chaos embodied in the product of this system—the grinning idiot hopping back and forth in front of the throne whom both

6. *Ibid.*, p. 197.

Nebuchadnezzar and Nimrod acknowledge as their son and heir. As the opposing force to that of the two interchangeable kings and their political and theological ministers, Dürrenmatt has created the figure of Akki the Beggar. Dürrenmatt appears to be saying that only by disassociating completely from society and its laws—and thus becoming the lowest of the low from a worldly viewpoint—can one preserve independence and, consequently, dignity. Akki is far and away the most dignified character in the play. And he preserves his dignity by refusing to have anything to do with the things that might tend to associate him with those whom he despises: all the money and jewels that he accumulates each day by begging he throws into the Euphrates in the evening. The only thing he keeps is food—"The culinary art, properly cultivated, is the only facet of human endeavor about which nothing bad can be said." Dürrenmatt looks upon Akki and his kind as a sort of dike holding back the impatient floods of ignorance:

> AKKI: We are secret teachers, educators of the people. We go in rags for the sake of man's wretchedness; we obey no laws in order to celebrate freedom. We eat as greedily as wolves, and drink like sots in order to expose the terrible hunger and the burning thirst which is poverty. And the arches of the bridges under which we sleep we fill with the belongings of the vanished rich in order to show that all things come to the beggars in the fullness of time.[7]

Frank V—Oper einer Privatbank (Frank V—Opera of a Private Bank, 1959)—a rather ambitious title, for the work is really a satirical comedy with music (by Paul Burkhard)—was first produced at the Zürich Schauspielhaus in 1959. Frank V is the president of a private bank founded by his great-great-grandfather, Frank I. Even since its founding this bank has operated on two inflexible business principles: "Never make an honest deal" and "Never pay back any money." The play relates how, by sticking faithfully to these two maxims, which in years gone by had made the firm one of the richest and most power-

7. *Ibid.*, p. 196.

ful banking houses in Europe, Frank & Co. goes bankrupt. As the play opens, the firm is already in such a desperate position that Frank has to fake his death so that he can stick his life insurance into the business. The company is bombarded with one disaster after another. One of the biggest depositors withdraws his account, but, faithful to its second motto, the company sends out its most attractive teller to get the money back in a hotel room. Unfortunately she is thwarted by the vice squad. In another scene a new recruit is given an orientation lecture by Frank's wife, who, in the classical tradition of the female of the species being more deadly than the male, is the real brains behind the business. "You're murderers!" the horrified recruit exclaims when the full extent of the bank's operations is revealed to him. "No, no, not at all, my dear boy," Mrs. Frank says reprovingly, "Only business people in difficulties." The difficulties become more and more severe, and at the end *Frank V* fully measures up to Mrs. Frank's demands for a classic play. When the maid asks permission to watch *Richard III* Mrs. Frank grants it with the words, "a classical play. Doubtless there will be plenty of bodies." If the body count is any criterion, *Frank V* is at least as classical as *Richard III*. At the end the survivors sit around the safe, warily pointing submachine guns at each other. Dürrenmatt solves the mess by having Frank's children drive the crooks out and take over. Under Frank VI the firm of Frank & Co. becomes honest for the first time in its long history. The days of the robber barons are over—but not because the capitalistic private enterprise system has been cleaned up. Frank V and his tribe are outdated because their free-wheeling business anarchy is no longer exclusively their method of operation: everyone is doing it. Frank fails because he is behind the times. He has not learned to substitute the gloss of legality for the old-time strong-arm methods.

Dürrenmatt has also written several radio plays, of which only *Das Unternehmen der Wega* (Operation Wega, 1954) is significant for our discussion. In this play Dürrenmatt dramatizes the East-West conflict, which he believes is due mainly to willful bullheadedness on both sides. Fear and lack of understanding lead the "free" nations (in this play) into the most grotesque imaginable moral perversions. The *Wega* is a space ship on which the chief ministers of state of the Free United States of Europe and America travel to Venus in the year 2256 A.D. The use-honored and mischievous old saw that "war with Russia is inevitable" has at last come true, and the ministers are now on a mission to persuade the inhabitants of Venus to join their side. Venus has been used for years both by Russia and the West as a human garbage dump—it is a penal colony for habitual criminals and people whose politics happen to be incompatible with those of the place in which they lived on Earth. In the coming war the strategic position of Venus and its invisibility behind a permanent cloud bank will make its possession a decisive factor. The mission from the Free and United States is therefore under instructions to destroy Venus with cobalt bombs should the inhabitants prove intractable. If they prove tractable they are to be permitted to return to Earth once the war is won. However, the mission, under Sir Horace Wood, finds it rather difficult to negotiate. There is no government on Venus. The people live on small ships and are too busy fighting to survive to bother about government. Whoever is free at the moment designates himself as representative of the planet and speaks to the mission. Sir Horace finally locates Bonstetten, a former classmate of his at Oxford and Heidelberg, who was sent to Venus as commissar and deserted. Bonstetten tells Sir Horace that the people of Venus refuse to take sides in any war and that none of them wants to return to Earth. On Venus the weather consists of constant thunderstorms and constant hot rain; the ground is everlastingly being shifted by earthquakes; the sea is radioactive, and all sorts of strange monsters roam the planet; but no one wants to leave it. Bonstetten explains. On Venus men are at last free: they are too busy trying to stay alive to make laws. On Venus men have at last realized their ideals in practice: it is the only way to survive.

WOOD: What have you exchanged for the mildness of the earth? Steaming oceans. Burning continents, glowing red deserts. A raging sky. What knowledge has it given you?

BONSTETTEN: That Man is worth something and that his life is a boon.

WOOD: Ridiculous. We have known that on earth for a long time.

BONSTETTEN: Well? Do you live in accordance with this knowledge?

WOOD: And you?

BONSTETTEN: Venus forces us to. That is the difference. If we don't help each other here, we perish.[8]

Sir Horace tells Bonstetten that the *Wega* carries bombs, but that he will of course not order their use. He is amazed to hear that the Venusians had anticipated this. "After all, we too lived on Earth once" (Bonstetten explains). Nor does Bonstetten put any trust in Sir Horace's promise not to use the bombs. In a thoroughly cynical speech that is pure Dürrenmatt he tells his former friend just what will happen:

You will break your promise. Your mission is a failure. Now you still have pity for me, but once you get back to your ship your pity will fade and your mistrust will replace it. The Russians could come and make an agreement with us, you will think. You will of course know how impossible that is, that we will treat the Russians as we have treated you, but a little grain of fear that we could after all perhaps make a treaty with your enemies will remain in your mind. And because of this little grain of fear, because of the slight uncertainty in your heart, you will release the bombs. Even if it is senseless, even if they will hit innocent people—and so we will die.

And that is just what does happen. At first Sir Horace is horrified by what Bonstetten says:

WOOD: You are my friend, Bonstetten. I couldn't kill a friend.

8. Friedrich Dürrenmatt, *Das Unternehmen der Wega* in *Hörspielbuch 1955*. With permission of and copyright © 1955 by Peter Schifferli Verlags AG "Die Arche" (Frankfurt a. M.: Europäische Verlagsanstalt, 1955), p. 74.

BONSTETTEN: It is easy to kill when you don't see the victim and you won't see me die.

WOOD: You speak as if it were an easy thing to die!

BONSTETTEN: Everything that is necessary is easy. One only has to accept it. And the most necessary and most natural thing on this planet is death. It is with us always and everywhere. There is too much heat and too much radiation. The sea itself is radioactive. There are worms which burrow under our skin and into our entrails, bacteria which poison our blood, viruses which destroy our cells. The land is full of impassable swamps, seas of boiling oil and volcanoes, and ghastly monsters are everywhere. We do not fear your bombs because we live with death and have had to learn not to fear it.[9]

The play ends as Wood, who was, after all, quite sincere in his promise to Bonstetten, weakly gives the order for the bombing. And then in Sir Horace's last speech, Dürrenmatt adds his characteristic bitterly sardonic twist:

I'm fed up with everything. That Venus is horrible. They're all criminals there, after all. I'm sure Bonstetten wanted to make an alliance with the Russians. They were just putting on an act for us . . . Now the bombs have dropped and soon they'll drop on the earth. Thank goodness, I have a bomb-proof shelter as a public official. And what's more I'll have a vacation—Foreign Ministers always go on vacation during wartime. But I'll have to forget about fishing. I'll read the classics. T. S. Eliot preferably. He's the most soothing of them all. There's nothing unhealthier than exciting reading.[10]

The East-West conflict continues to obsess Dürrenmatt in his latest play, Die Physiker (The Physicists, 1961). If Dürrenmatt were as conscientiously didactic a playwright as Shaw, he would have called this play The Physicist's Dilemma. Dürrenmatt is mordant and sardonic where Shaw is genial and

9. Ibid., p. 77.
10. Ibid., p. 80.

optimistic, but the ethical problem of *The Doctor's Dilemma* and *Die Physiker* is essentially the same. Shaw examines the problem of the healer who has to step out of his accustomed purely medical realm of knowledge and make a moral decision about his profession. For the healer the problem is simply whom to heal when there is a shortage of medicine. His dilemma is that he cannot give enough. The physicist's dilemma, as Dürrenmatt sees it, is that he can give too much, and his problem is whether he should withhold his knowledge. Given the enormous inroads the physicists have made into areas of knowledge previously thought impenetrable, it is not inconceivable that at some time in the near future a key may be found that will enable men to understand all natural phenomena. Dürrenmatt postulates precisely this eventuality. A young physicist works out a formula for all possible discoveries. Horrified at the thought of what the politicians would do with his formula were he to publish it, he pretends to be mad and has himself shut up in a lunatic asylum. Only thus can he continue the mental exercises which are his life without at the same time endangering the future of humanity. Rather than be hailed as the greatest thinker of all times, he prefers to spend his life imprisoned and to die unknown. He has realized that absolute freedom of thought could be undesirable in a situation where all knowledge is possible and where all thinkers are at the mercy of political planners. He announces that King Solomon appears to him and, in an act of self-abnegation comparable to Romulus's, prepares to spend the rest of his life in a mental institution. When the play begins, Möbius has been in the sanatorium for twenty years. He has recently been joined by two other apparently insane physicists, one under the impression that he is Sir Isaac Newton, the other that he is Albert Einstein. They soon reveal themselves to be perfectly sane secret agents, Sir Isaac for the West, Professor Einstein for the East, bent on persuading Möbius to join their side. They are each famous physicists in their own right and have been able to gauge the tremendous potential broached in Möbius's doctoral dissertation. They have therefore been sent by their respective secret services to take him away. This turns out to be impossible, first of all because they have suddenly become ringed around by armed guards, secondly because Möbius has burned his papers and does not want to leave. The two secret agents realize that they are imprisoned forever, but they also realize, at last, that Möbius is right: their knowledge is too dangerous to be published. The Western physicist, who thought that the scientist's duty was to seek knowledge without caring what use might be made of it, and the Eastern physicist, who thought that the scientist's duty was to subject his knowledge to a political party, both realize the truth of the paradox that for thinkers freedom exists only in a lunatic asylum: "Only in the mental hospital can we still be free. Only in the mental hospital can we still think. Out there our thoughts are dynamite. . . . Either we remain in this lunatic asylum or the world becomes one. Either we extinguish ourselves in the memory of men or mankind itself is extinguished." [11] "Einstein" protests for a moment that they are caged like wild beasts, and Möbius calmly replies that they *are* wild beasts—"they must never unleash us on mankind again." Then, heroically, the three physicists resign themselves to their fate:

> NEWTON: Lunatic, yet wiser than before.
> EINSTEIN: Caged, yet freer than before.
> MÖBIUS: Physicists, yet guiltless.[12]

With the statement of the paradox that mankind can be saved only through the suppression of knowledge, the lesson of the play is complete. Dürrenmatt, however, has to insert his sardonic touch. Their heroic resolve to save humanity by suppressing their knowledge has made the three physicists technically guilty of *hubris*, for, as Möbius says, what has once been thought can never more be taken back again. They discover that the chief doctor and owner of the sanatorium, a grotesquely humpbacked old maid, is *really* mad and, acting on instructions from her own private vision of King Solomon, has stolen

11. Friedrich Dürrenmatt, *Die Physiker* (Zürich: Verlag der Arche, 1962), pp. 61–62.
12. *Ibid.*, p. 63.

Möbius's formulas. She tells the three physicists that their sacrifice has been in vain and that they will be imprisoned forever while she takes over the whole universe with Möbius's formula for attaining the key to all knowledge.

The Physicists is particularly interesting in a study of Dürrenmatt's dramatic technique because he has described in 21 points how he wrote it. The 21 points are, however, just as valid for any one of Dürrenmatt's other plays. They are:

1. My starting point is a story, not a thesis.
2. If a story is the starting point, it must be developed to its logical conclusion.
3. The logical conclusion of a story has been attained when events have taken their worst possible turn.
4. The worst possible turn of events cannot be foreseen. It occurs as a result of coincidence.
5. The dramatist's skill consists in the ability to bring coincidence into his plot with the most telling effect possible.
6. Human beings are the agents of a plot.
7. Coincidence in plot has to do with who meets whom by chance and where and when.
8. The more precisely men plan their actions, the more telling the effect when coincidence affects them.
9. Men who plan their actions precisely do so in order to attain a specific goal. Coincidence has the most adverse effect on them when as a result of it they attain a goal precisely opposite to the one they had planned: when they attain what they feared and had attempted with their planning to avoid (e.g., Oedipus).
10. Such a plot may be grotesque, but it is not incredible.
11. It is a paradox.
12. Dramatists can no more avoid paradoxes than logicians can.
13. Physicists can no more avoid paradoxes than logicians can.
14. A drama for physicists must consist of paradox.
15. It must not concern itself with the subject matter of

physics; only with its effect.

16. The subject matter of physics concerns physicists; its effect concerns everyone.
17. What affects everyone can only be solved by everyone.
18. Any attempt by any one person to solve a problem that concerns all must come to grief.
19. Reality appears in the paradox.
20. He who faces paradox faces reality.
21. The drama can persuade the spectator to take exception to reality, but it cannot force him to stand firm against it or to conquer it.[13]

Besides describing Dürrenmatt's method of constructing his plays, this sums up his philosophy as well. Everything happens by chance in Dürrenmatt's universe and the worst chance always comes up. This is not simple-minded mysticism: men unconsciously create chance, and the result is always the worst possible because man is psychologically corrupt and does not learn by experience. The chances that control our destiny are created by those in power, and human psychology is simply unable to bear up under the burden of power. To Dürrenmatt the only positive statement about human beings is Akki's remark in *An Angel Comes to Babylon*: "The culinary art, properly practised, is the only facet of human endeavor about which nothing bad can be said." Piling irony upon irony and paradox upon paradox, his plays show us that the worst men are the good men. The most dangerous man is the man filled with sincerely good intentions. To Dürrenmatt the most sinister expression is the benign smile and the amiably twinkling eye. For such an expression marks the *Weltverbesserer*, the man who thinks he knows what is best for others and insists on imposing it on them. Romulus, Möbius, Mississippi, and St. Claude, to take the most obvious examples, are good men, but their attempts to achieve progress are doomed. They can neither create a new and better human race by subjugating it

13. Friedrich Dürrenmatt, *Theaterschriften und Reden* (Zürich: Verlag die Arche, 1966), pp. 193–94.

to a foreign power, nor by clamping the lid on further knowledge, nor by punishing people by the "God-given" biblical standard, nor by making them all economically equal. All attempts to achieve progress end in disaster and become perverted in their aims because they involve aping God—who does not exist or is paring his fingernails or oiling his watch (or letting it rust?). Dürrenmatt has stated that in the world of today the only viable form of tragedy is comedy since only by being laughed at can the facts and conditions of life be faced. Conversely, the creation of a tragic plot would, by its very inadequacy in contrast to the conditions of reality, be a cause at best of laughter, at worst of boredom. In our time, the paradox comes full circle: the tragic is comic; the comic is tragic. Strictly speaking, of course, the true tragic form of our time should be the newsreel but the newsreel is not art because it is not invented. It has only a numbing effect because it tells us what we already know and only fulfils expectations. The newsreel is the animated hot dog and soup can: it is pop tragedy.

In *Der Meteor* (The Meteor, 1966) Dürrenmatt writes directly about death. He calls the play a comedy, though it is actually a ribald farce. Death, the end of traditional tragedy, becomes a theme for desperate farce in a world without faith. In Dürrenmatt's play a Nobel prize winning author comes back to die in the attic from which he started out. He has already been certified dead once at the nursing home where he has spent the last year being gradually dismembered internally by a famous surgeon. Having crawled out from beneath the funeral wreaths, he has come back to his beginnings to stage his own death. But do what he will he cannot die. Instead he seduces the wife of the painter currently living in the attic, is certified dead once again, crawls out from under the wreaths again, and, to pass away the time, watches the people around him die. The minister who comes to pray over him has a heart attack; his wife, a 19-year-old former call-girl, commits suicide; his mother-in-law dies while he is talking to her; the painter is accidentally killed by the landlord; and several other characters are ruined and have nothing further to live for. At the end the Nobel prize winner is serenaded by the Salvation Army, which looks upon him as resurrected, and cries despairingly, "Will I never be able to die?"

Dürrenmatt has expanded on his theory of tragedy and comedy in his latest play, a completely revised version of *Es steht geschrieben*. Now called *Die Wiedertäufer* (The Anabaptists, 1967), it follows the plot of the earlier version in the principal details. What Dürrenmatt has changed is the ending. In line with the principles he has developed in the intervening twenty years, he has changed the play from a tragedy to a comedy. In the earlier play John of Leyden shcwed up in Münster asleep on a dung cart and left it on that same cart after his execution. An acceptable enough exercise in the ironically macabre. In the new version John has become an unsuccessful strolling actor who turns cynically to preaching when the periods between engagements become too frequent. The new ending shows John handing Münster over to its plunderers while he himself demands and obtains a lifelong engagement in the Cardinal's private theatre. The purpose of this seemingly flippant ending is explained by Dürrenmatt in a closely reasoned afterword that is an expansion of the "Twenty-one points on *The Physicists*." Direct tragedy not being any longer possible, as already explained in *Theaterprobleme*,[14] the dramatist is faced with the fact that there are three kinds of comedy; and in order to create *Welttheater* which will show the pathos and irony of the human condition he must pick the right one.

Comedy can consist of character, of character plus situation, and of situation alone. The first kind is what Dürrenmatt calls "clown comedy." Here the humor derives from the clown figure itself—from his peculiar appearance, his foolish behavior, and his tendency to do ordinary things in an extraordinary manner. The second kind is the social comedy that Dürrenmatt traces in a straight line from the Greek New Comedy to con-

14. *Ibid.*, pp. 120ff.

temporary "boulevard" theatre. Here the humor derives from
the type characters—miser, would-be gentleman, etc.—and from
the situations in which they are placed. The third kind is
Welttheater comedy, where the situations are comic but the
characters, while essentially comic on a primary level because
they cannot cope with the situations, become tragic because
the situations defeat them.[15] To illustrate the manner in which
tragic themes can become *Welttheater* comedy, Dürrenmatt
gives as an example different ways of treating a realistically
tragic theme. Taking the story of Captain Scott's death in the
Antarctic on his way back from the South Pole in 1912, he
gives us a description of how the situation would be dramatized by Shakespeare, Brecht, Beckett, and by a *Welttheater*
comedy writer. Shakespeare would have based the tragedy on
a flaw in Scott's character—on a combination of the hero's
overriding ambition and the jealousies and betrayal of other
members of the expedition. Brecht would have attributed the
disaster to Scott's unfortunate upbringing in a capitalistic
society, which would have made him too snobbish to travel
in sleds pulled by dogs; his insistence on ponies would have
obliged him to skimp on the purchase of other supplies. With
Beckett we would have another version of *Endgame*: the
catastrophe would already have occurred, and Scott, encased
in a block of ice, would be lecturing his similarly encased com-
panions, unconscious of being heard by them. In the "comic"
version, however, Scott would not even get to start out on his
expedition; he would freeze to death as a result of being accidentally trapped in the refrigerator room of a butcher shop
while purchasing supplies.

We can now see the intent of Dürrenmatt's changed ending. To show Scott dying in the Antarctic blizzard or John of
Leyden broken on the wheel, as he was in *Es steht geschrieben*,
is to involve the audience in John's or Scott's fortunes. It is
to make tragic heroes of them and to make them primary and

15. Friedrich Dürrenmatt, *Die Wiedertäufer* (Zürich: Verlag die Arche,
1967), pp. 105–106.

the conditions in which they acted secondary. It is the function of the *Welttheater* writer to emphasize the conditions, however; to show that men are what they are because of the conditions that befall them. Man *reacts* to the events that act upon him. The real world is as closed and as arbitrary—and therefore as inexplicable—a system as the capriciously created world of the dramatist. John of Leyden walking out to join the Cardinal's theatrical troupe focusses our attention where it belongs: on Münster and on the victims who suffer because of the circumstances.

Throughout his works Dürrenmatt has a viewpoint that can best be described as sardonic. Dürrenmatt is a disillusioned analyst of the human character. Even the plays with political themes are ultimately about the human beings rather than the issues. Like Ionesco, like Beckett, like all the writers of the dramatic avant-garde in fact, Dürrenmatt feels deep down in himself that the problems of humanity are insoluble. And so he takes refuge from this knowledge in a mordantly sardonic portrayal of life. He himself remains detached. Romulus and Mississippi, Saint-Claude and Nebuchadnezzar, Frank V and Sir Horace Wood are viewed and dissected, laid out on slides and meticulously picked apart with scalpel and tweezers. Perhaps the only character in all of Dürrenmatt's works who is looked at with any kindness and compassion at all is Archilochos, the inoffensive little assistant bookkeeper who becomes head of the factory as a result of marrying the country's leading courtesan in the novel *Grieche sucht Griechin*.

Although Dürrenmatt derives his technique more from Thornton Wilder than from Antonin Artaud and the surrealists, he does resemble the authors of the current dramatic avant-garde in that his plays are dominated by the two qualities of protest and paradox. Dürrenmatt's two main themes are based on (i) the paradox that the power to do good corrupts the doer so that the goodness is negated and the power becomes purely evil; and (ii) the paradox that the omnipresence of death renders human acts trivial. What distinguishes Dürrenmatt from Beckett, who also feels that the events of life are basically meaningless, is that Beckett feels this to the point where he asserts that all events are flattened out and equally insignificant, whereas Dürrenmatt does recognize that events may have an immediate significance to those affected. It is here that the element of protest comes in: Dürrenmatt always implies that events must be resisted. Nothing is inevitable and determined in Dürrenmatt. The fact that things are insignificant from a cosmic viewpoint does not alter the fact that they are significant in the immediate present: it merely argues that they are finally insoluble and will always repeat themselves. The monomania of Mississippi and Saint-Claude, of Romulus and Nebuchadnezzar, and of the political leaders who lurk behind the action of several of the radio plays *must be resisted*. Dürrenmatt's protest, unlike that of the other current avant-garde writers, is not against the cosmos: it is against the world as it is and against the people who rule it.

MAX FRISCH
The Drama of Despair

MAX FRISCH was born in Zürich in 1911. Trained as an architect, he abandoned that profession for a writing career only after a long and painful struggle during which he actually forced himself to stop writing for a number of years. During the war, however, he was called to active service on the Swiss-German frontier when it was thought the Germans would invade. The Germans very wisely thought better of it, but the Swiss Army remained on guard anyway, and Frisch whiled away the long hours by keeping a diary, later published as *Blätter von dem Brotsack* (Leaves from the Knapsack). With that, Frisch's writing career was begun again and after his first successes (his plays are as popular in the German-speaking theater as Dürrenmatt's) he abandoned the practice of architecture altogether.

Frisch's plays, unlike those of Dürrenmatt, are not expressive of a particular *Weltanschauung*. This may result in somewhat naïve plays, such as *Santa Cruz* and *Als der Krieg zu Ende War* (When the War Was Over), but when Frisch is at his best, as he is in *Die Chinesische Mauer* (The Chinese Wall) [1] and *Biedermann und die Brandstifter* (Mr. Biedermann and the Arsonists),[2] there is no better dramatic author alive today.

The unevenness of Frisch's work can be attributed to the lack of any one guiding theme and to his own involvement in it. In this respect he differs from Dürrenmatt, who carefully detaches himself from the world he describes. Dürrenmatt's attitude is sardonic as he stands aside and shows us a world he considers absurd. He is like the manipulator of a puppet show who occasionally draws apart the curtain above the stage to reveal himself quizzically smiling and jiggling the strings play-

1. Max Frisch, *The Chinese Wall*, translated by James L. Rosenberg (New York: Hill & Wang, Inc., 1961).

2. Max Frisch, *The Firebugs*, translated by Mordecai Gorelik (New York: Hill & Wang, Inc., 1963).

fully with his fingers. At such moments (e.g., the opening and closing scenes of *Die Ehe des Herrn Mississippi,* the forest scenes in *The Visit,* the little monk's scenes in *Es steht geschrieben*) Dürrenmatt mocks his characters, the audience, and —necessarily—himself as well. The interest of Dürrenmatt's plays arises out of the *strength* of the dramatic conflicts in the various situations he creates—but the sardonic viewpoint is always primary and always the same. Frisch, on the other hand, writes plays about whatever happens to interest him at the moment, and as he is always passionately involved in the situations and characters he creates, the quality of his plays tends to fluctuate sharply. With Dürrenmatt we are always on the outside looking in: his theater is a peep show in which humanity is caricatured in order to prove a point. With Frisch we are on the inside, we are involved, we identify. Dürrenmatt leaves us with an acidulous, bitter, astringent taste; Frisch at his best rouses in us at least the terror part of the Aristotelian formula.

Although lacking a common, basic theme, Frisch's plays do have an idea that shows up in all of them: that men learn nothing from experience.

Frisch's plays can be divided into two categories: plays of the mass and plays of the individual. In other words, political polemics and analyses of individual but typical psychological attitudes. The only one of Frisch's plays that does not fall into either category is *Als der Krieg zu Ende War* (1949), in which a Russian colonel and the wife of a Nazi officer conduct a semaphor love affair (he cannot speak German, she cannot speak Russian) in the rubble of occupied Berlin. This is the only one of Frisch's plays that is a complete failure. He has written seven other plays, divided between the two categories.

PLAYS OF THE INDIVIDUAL

The psychological problem that fascinates Frisch is the inability of man to stand by himself, wholly independent of all other human beings. Man always strives to *be himself.* But, like Peer Gynt, he can do this only in his dreams. Man in search of himself is constantly either dreaming of running away to some idyllic paradise where he can live his own life away from all encumbrances and responsibilities, or he actually is running away. In either case he is invariably disillusioned, whether by awakening from the futile dream or by coming to the harsh reality of the wished-for paradise. "No man is an island . . .," Donne tells us, but most men spray their energies away trying to be one. Not surprisingly, Frisch connects this drive to be free with the everlasting battle of the sexes: the freedom for which men strive is equated with freedom from the bonds of marriage. In marriage the longing to be free, to do what one pleases, the longing for distant, delusive paradises, the longing, in short, to realize oneself, has to be curtailed. Money has to be earned through stultifying work, responsibilities have to be worried about, and children add fetters to tighten the mesh. Frisch caps his treatment of this theme with another play about that universal farcical-tragic hero, that Peer Gynt of the bedroom, Don Juan.

Santa Cruz (written 1944, published 1947), Frisch's first play, sets the freedom-and-marriage conflict in a fairy-tale milieu. A cavalry captain and his wife have lived together in his castle for seventeen years. During that time the regular, day-to-day, repetitive routine of married life has petrified their emotions so that they go through their days like mediocre actors condemned to play the same scenes for eternity to an ever-empty house. Seventeen years ago, just before their marriage, the couple were visited by a certain Pelegrin, who, although concrete enough (he is the real father of the wife's child), is a symbol for the longing to be free. Pelegrin had persuaded both the young man and the woman to come away with him to Hawaii, which here represents the elusive paradise where one can be free, independent, and true only to oneself. On the way to Hawaii, however,—at Santa Cruz—the two get married. The instinct to marry and multiply, to be safe, secure, and certain of the future triumphs. And now, after seventeen years, Pelegrin returns. His presence activates the old longings that have been lying dormant in the husband and wife during their whole marriage. The husband succumbs, leaves a farewell note, and goes off to make his own way at last. But in the wife the instinct for domesticity is stronger. She vanquishes Pelegrin in argument, whereupon Pelegrin dies and the husband returns. The symbolic circle is completed when we are made to realize that the spirit expressed by Pelegrin lives on in the daughter, who must go through the conflict between hearth and horizon in her turn.

Graf Öderland (Count Öderland, 1951) is technically and philosophically an advance from *Santa Cruz*. Here the problem is not so much freedom from the bonds of marital domesticity, but freedom from the monotonous routine imposed upon our lives by social position and profession. Technically the play is a precariously balanced tour de force, the whole action being an exposition of a megalomaniac dream that flits in a few seconds through a frustrated man's mind. The action takes place late at night in the study of a public prosecutor who is preparing a case against an obscure bank clerk. After fourteen years of unimpeachable probity and invariable punctuality, this clerk has suddenly grabbed a hatchet one evening and chopped up the first person he could find. To his consternation, the prosecutor realizes that the bank clerk has killed out of boredom and that he himself understands this state of mind very well. He understands that the man has reverted to an instinctual form of action in his attempt to break through the fetters imposed upon him by social convention, just as the Malayan natives do when they run amok. The prosecutor, too, has been becoming increasingly desperate under the pressures of his social and personal life (his wife is the defense attorney's mistress, but that can be forgiven Frisch as a permissible dramatic convenience). The more he thinks about the bank clerk's problem, the more absurd does his position of prosecutor seem to him; and as he broods about the crime, a similar explosion is triggered off in him. Since he is a more intellectual and a less elemental type than the bank clerk, however, the explosion is purely cerebral, though all the more violent in intensity.

In his dream the prosecutor runs away to a forest where he meets a young girl. He crosses the border with her, killing three frontier guards with a hatchet on the way. The hatchet becomes a sort of reassuring amulet for him, and he always carries it with him in a briefcase so that he can touch it and feel free whenever he wants to. His goal is the Isle of Santorin in the Aegean Sea, a place where one is completely free to be oneself. Santorin fulfills the same function in this play that Hawaii does in *Santa Cruz*; but just as the husband and wife in *Santa Cruz* never get to Hawaii, so the prosecutor, who has by now adopted the title of Count Öderland, never gets to Santorin. Instead he somehow gets sidetracked (like Pierre of Sartre's *Les Jeux sont faits*) and we next see him as the leader of a nihilistic underground movement operating in the sewers of the city in which the Count was formerly public prosecutor. The emblem of this movement is the hatchet, the symbol of freedom and independence and self-realization, but the movement has become a strictly militaristic organization composed of social outcasts (escaped convicts, misfits and malcontents, etc.) trying to overthrow the established order. In other words, there is no escape. The invisible walls that hem us in are not solely composed of social pressure: they are inherent in the psyche of the human animal. Madness is the only way out. Count Öderland finds himself the head of a complete miniature society even more rigid than the one from which he fled. Monotony led him to seek freedom, but the search for freedom only leads to another form of organization based on authority and submission and thus back to monotony. Frisch brings his round dance of irony and paradox full circle when he has Count Öderland overthrow the government and then installs him in the house he once occupied as public prosecutor. He has achieved his wildest dreams. He is the head of the state and has supreme power. He can order anyone to do anything: he is free—theoretically. But he is actually as enmeshed as ever. The triumphant dream turns into a frenzied horror of frustration—as it must. The Count finds his wife and her lover in the house. He shoots them, but the pistol shots have no effect. In a final gesture of defeat and ultimate frustration, he throws himself out of the window. The dream has ended.

Throughout his dream Count Öderland is accompanied by a young girl who changes identity several times, but always remains exactly like the prosecutor's maid. Similarly, the various enemies that the Count meets all have the face of Dr. Hahn, his wife's lover. These various roles are all played by the same person. Over and over, no matter how far he seems to get away from his old self, he encounters the same people:

> How do we know each other? Every now and again it seems to me—how shall I put it?—that there are only three or four faces one meets in one's lifetime in the final analysis. Even if one goes from one end of the earth to the other there is always a girl . . . and there is always a policeman who has to know one's name and where one wants to go, and everywhere there are fences to prevent one's going where one wants to go . . .[3]

At the end he realizes that everything is useless:

> Life is an illusion—I'm slowly beginning to realize that. Repetition, that's all it is. Repetition—that's the curse, that's the barrier, and no hatchet is any use against it even if one succeeds in bursting through the walls. Repetition! till one wakes up at the point of death and it's as if nothing had been at all, absolutely nothing, nothing but desires which flared up and glowed and were snuffed out. Desire for joy and for happiness. And error, anxiety, darkness; . . .[4]

It is useless to protest, useless to run amok, useless to do anything except to think as little as possible and get along as best one can.

With *Graf Öderland* Frisch produced a play which crystallizes the two most important themes of the contemporary drama, isolation and protest. One of the chief themes of the older drama was the achievement of perfect communion through romantic love. The contemporary drama deals mainly with the impossibility of communion, with the eternal mutual isolation of human beings. Frisch forces us to consider the problem of resigning ourselves to bear a world where we realize no communion is possible—ever. Unlike the playwrights who

---

3. Max Frisch, *Graf Öderland* (Frankfurt a. M.: Suhrkamp Verlag, 1951), pp. 35–36.
4. *Ibid.*, p. 125.

stick strictly to Antonin Artaud's dictum of protest in drama, Frisch does not confine himself merely to protest per se. He shows us that protest, too, is useless. The condition of freedom turns out to be just as stifling as the condition of social bondage. Artaud's protest is more in the nature of a communal release mechanism: actors and audiences are emotionally purged by their cry of defiance so that they can go back to build up their tensions once more. Frisch carries the process a step further to true tragedy, for he shows us that the protest is futile.

In his last play dealing with the individual, Frisch takes up that perennial dramatic hero Don Juan. Again Frisch's theme is the urge to be free. He uses the Don Juan theme because Don Juan is the perfect embodiment of a man striving to be independent and resisting domesticity. Don Juan (up to now) has never had to run amok to release his tensions because he has always been free. As the seducer par excellence he has always been a social outsider since the cardinal sin against society is flagrant violation of sexual mores. Don Juan has remained totally himself by seducing 1003 women instead of only one.

Frisch's theory, already expressed in *Santa Cruz* and *Graf Öderland,* is that man cannot be free. He is always either bound to domestic responsibility, like the husband in *Santa Cruz,* or he finds that freedom is no better than bondage, like Count Öderland. Don Juan, according to Frisch, is the personification of the youthful conceit that a man can realize himself completely alone. Frisch wants to show that such an attitude is at variance with reality. Don Juan never grows up. He retains the immature delusions of youth.

In Frisch's play Don Juan is not so much a ladies' man as a mathematician (the full title of the play is *Don Juan, or The Love of Geometry,* 1953). His seductions are purely accidental. He hopes to become free by immersing himself in the pure knowledge of mathematics. When we first see him, Don Juan is about to get married. He says "No" when he should say "Yes" at the altar and flees. On the way he seduces his best friend's fiancée and his intended mother-in-law, kills his intended father-in-law (the future stone statue) and callously helps his own father to a fatal heart attack. His own fiancée, whom he had seduced in the park on the night before the wedding without knowing who she was, drowns herself; and Don Juan's reputation is made. His whole purpose in all this has been to get rid of everything that might stop his complete absorption in the study of geometry. But Don Juan is never to achieve the freedom he believes resides in the exclusive exercise of pure reason. Women succumb to his reputation as a seducer. It is not that Don Juan is particularly attractive to women or that he makes any special effort to captivate them; it is simply that his initial escapade (committed in order to rid himself of women once and for all) has had the effect of making it de rigueur for every woman to succumb to him. To meet Don Juan and not to go to bed with him would have been a disgrace too deep for any woman's reputation to bear. And thus Don Juan, who is so indifferent to sex as to play chess when he is dragged along to a whorehouse, becomes history's foremost sexual hero.

Frisch's punishment for Don Juan's *hubris* is pure ironic farce. Since a Don Juan play without the Stone Guest is unthinkable, Frisch includes it; but since he is also writing for a hypermodern audience, he treats it as a deliberate hoax of Don Juan's. Twelve years and 1003 women after the beginning of his career Don Juan is bankrupt and fed up. He gets the idea of inviting several women and the Bishop of Cordoba to a last dinner, dressing up the madam of the local whorehouse as the Commandant's ghost, and then jumping through a trap door to "hell." To the bishop he proposes that in return for thus giving the Church a legend, he be permitted to spend the rest of his life studying geometry in a monastery. The latter part of the plan backfires when the "bishop" turns out to be one of the many husbands Don Juan has cuckolded. Despite the false bishop's denunciations, however, everyone else is taken in by the transparent hoax, and the Don Juan legend is completed. Don Juan still has no money, and he cannot get any more since he officially no longer exists. He winds up as the husband of a former prostitute who is now the widow of a nobleman, and the play ends as she informs the Don that he is about to become a father. It is the final indignity. The man who wished to stand alone is given poetic justice for his presumption in challenging the gods, as he does at the end of the first part of the play when the drowned body of his fiancée is laid at his feet: "Do not expect me to cross myself and do not hope to see me weep. Bury the poor thing. And stay out of my way. I no longer have any fear. We'll see now which of us, Heaven or I, makes a fool of the other!" [5] It is Don Juan who turns out the fool, for—and this is man's tragedy, Don Juan's and Count Öderland's, the cavalry captain's and everyone's—no man can stand alone. Protest is futile. We see the light but our psychology binds us: that is Frisch's paradox in his plays of the individual.

In his latest play, *Biografie* (Biography, 1967), Frisch continues his thesis that human beings are bound by the circumstances of their psychological make-up and cannot change their lives even if they have the knowledge and the power to do so. In *Biografie*, as in his novels, most notably *Stiller*, and in the film scenario *Zürich-Transit*, Frisch is fascinated with the problem of re-living one's life. What would one do if one were thought to be dead and were free to start one's life over again? Would one live it differently or would one start out on a new trail that would soon turn out to be a duplicate of the old one? In *Biografie* one of the characters is a Narrator who carries a book in which the protagonist's whole life is set down and offers him an opportunity to start it anew at any point. The protagonist insists that if he had his life to live over again with foreknowledge of what was to happen, he could improve it. But the changes he makes after repeated false starts are trivial and impulsive changes that, if anything, make his life worse than before. Once again, Frisch says, instinctual feelings conquer reason: the human being is the triumph of obsession over mind.

PLAYS OF THE MASS

If the paradox of the plays of the individual leads us to

5. Max Frisch, *Don Juan oder Die Liebe zur Geometrie* (Frankfurt a. M.: Suhrkamp Verlag, 1957), p. 79.

resignation, the paradox of the plays of the mass forces us to despair. It is the paradox (by no means put forward for the first time here) that man does not learn by experience. No matter what happens to him, man is still the same blind fool at the end as at the beginning. The presence of this idea makes Frisch's dramas despairing pleas, somewhat like the sermons of a dressed and basted missionary to the cannibals. The four plays in this group are *Nun singen sie wieder* (And Now They Sing Once More), *Die Chinesische Mauer, Biedermann und die Brandstifter,* and *Andorra.*

Nun singen sie wieder (published 1946) is Frisch's play about the war. It deals with a group of hostages shot by the Germans. The spirits of these hostages meet in a sort of limbo where they exist in communal brotherhood and sing. The only really interesting aspect of the play is Frisch's analysis of the two German officers in charge of the shooting. The two are old schoolmates and one of them is the son of their teacher. The latter cannot stand the consciousness of his guilt, deserts, goes back home, and hangs himself. His father, on seeing this, makes some treasonable remark and is sentenced to be shot. The other officer, his son's former colleague and the best student he ever had, is put in charge of the old schoolmaster's execution.

Frisch deals with what was perhaps the most horrifying aspect of the Nazi regime in this play: the schizophrenia of the German intellectual. How was it possible for persons like Herbert, the former star pupil, persons who were familiar with the culture of their own and other countries, to become moral monstrosities? Herbert gives his old schoolmaster an answer just before he orders him shot. It is an inadequate answer, as all such answers must be, and certainly not a true one, but Frisch is not trying to give an answer here but to fix a portion of the guilt. That portion falls—and quite rightly—on the harmless and well-meaning old schoolmaster whom Herbert accuses of prevaricating when his students asked him for the truth. When his students saw that the schoolmaster was too cowardly to stand up for the truth, they lost faith in it and decided to dedicate themselves to destroying it as a false god—to destroy it in the name of a better and purer god whom they could respect. Thus the worship of Race and Nation replaced the worship of Truth and Ethics.

Neither the warped and self-indulgent philosophy of the officer nor the cowardly one of the schoolmaster will survive, Frisch implies. What will survive is the spirit represented in the tranquilly singing dead, the direct and indirect victims, respectively, of the two doomed philosophies.

Die Chinesische Mauer (1946; revised 1955) is one of the most brilliant plays of the modern theater. Frisch was stimulated to write it by the explosion of the atomic bomb over Hiroshima and Nagasaki. Frisch makes no use of the usual grotesque sensationalism. What he is horrified by is the fact that with atomic power one man can destroy the human race for a personal whim. He disposes of the argument that the release of atomic power is a blessing since no one is going to start a war knowing that it will inevitably destroy his own side as well as the enemy. Man is controlled by impulse and does not pause to ponder the results of actions triggered by his rancid gastric juices or the water on his brain or his irritation at his parlor-maid's frigidity. Above all, man does not learn by experience, *he does not improve*—and we have many figures in our history who were restrained in the extravagance of their megalomania only by the limitations of the instruments and methods at their disposal. *Die Chinesische Mauer* is a brilliant play, but also a cosmically despairing one.

In order to give the play a universal quality, Frisch has chosen to create a *Welttheater* encompassing all areas of the world and all ages of humanity. The scene is medieval China just before the building of the Great Wall. The Emperor of China, Hwang Ti, serves as Frisch's universal symbol of political tyranny. He is the ever-successful conqueror who is never quite sure of the loyalty of his people. He has just subjugated the last of the "barbarians" (i.e., enemies, in the semantics of tyranny) and now proposes to keep his people busy by building a great wall which will make his empire safe forever. Only one thing worries him: there is a certain Min Ko among his subjects who makes up defamatory jingles about him. These jingles are sung along the banks of the Yangtze-Kiang and in the yellow mud and slimy manure of the Hangkow rice paddies no matter how industriously the Imperial Secret Service lays about it with thumbscrew, bastinado, and Mongolian bamboo wheel. The action of the play takes place at a party Hwang Ti gives to celebrate his victory. Among the guests—besides the expected Oriental contingent—we find such figures of history and human imagination as Romeo and Juliet, Philip of Spain, Pontius Pilate, Napoleon, Brutus, Don Juan, Cleopatra, Christopher Columbus, and L'Inconnue de la Seine. Binding all these together is the narrator, an anonymous Man of Today. Dressed in an ordinary business suit, he is the focal point for the audience, bringing the colorful and diverse crowd within the range of their own experiences.

There are two parts to the plot. One is the Man of Today's relationship—*our* relationship—to the historic figures; the other is the Emperor's search for Min Ko the dissenter and its effect on the Man of Today. The historic figures are divided into two groups. There are the actual historic figures—Brutus, Columbus, Philip of Spain, Cleopatra, Napoleon, Pontius Pilate—who represent the mistakes from which Man will not learn, for they keep coming again and again; and then there are those figures which are the products of the human mind—Romeo and Juliet, Don Juan, etc. These, as well as L'Inconnue de la Seine, who represents the great anonymous mass of past humanity, are in danger of being destroyed by the Philips and Napoleons and Hwang Tis and their present-day counterparts, whom we know well enough. The Man of Today circulates among them, vainly sounding his warning:

> I am worried, yes. We can no longer stand the adventure of absolute monarchy, Excellency, nowhere ever again on this earth; the risk is too great. Whoever sits on a throne today holds the human race in his hand, their whole history, starting with Moses or Buddha, including the Acropolis, the Temple of Maia, Gothic cathedrals, including all of Western philosophy, Spanish and French painting, German music, Shakespeare and his youthful pair: Romeo and Juliet. And included in it all, our children and our children's chil-

dren. A slight whim on the part of the man on the throne, a nervous breakdown, a touch of neurosis, a flame struck by his madness, a moment of impatience on account of indigestion—and the jig is up! Everything! A cloud of yellow or brown ashes boiling up toward the heavens in the shape of a mushroom, a dirty cauliflower—and the rest is silence—radioactive silence.[6]

None of the characters listens to him. All they want to do is come back and do the same things all over again. Napoleon wants to go on conquering, Philip of Spain wants to continue the Inquisition, Brutus wants to go on fighting for ideals, Columbus still wants to discover new lands, and Cleopatra still wants to "inspire great men." The figures these characters represent are still with us, and they have learned nothing. The same abominations are blandly committed again and again. Frisch's Man of Today makes one last frantic appeal:

> . . . All of you, my lords, all of you, you must not return. It is too dangerous. Your victories, your kingdoms, your thrones by divine right, your crusades hither and thither, they just don't make sense any more. We want to live. Your way of making history—we can't put up with it any longer. It would be the end, a chain reaction of madness—[7]

The appeal is choked in the omnipresent trivialities of social behavior, the demands of which muffle so much that is vitally important, as waiters come on and drown out the appeal with cocktails.

The second part of the plot deals with resistance to political tyranny, represented in Hwang Ti. The Emperor takes as his jester the Man of Today, whom Frisch uses as a representative of the intellectual class, and orders him to defend a dumb peasant who is accused of being the subversive Voice of the

6. Max Frisch, *The Chinese Wall*, translated by James L. Rosenberg. Copyright © by James L. Rosenberg (New York: Hill & Wang, Inc., 1961), p. 28.

7. *Ibid.*, p. 37.

People. The Man of Today knows perfectly well that the peasant boy cannot possibly be Min Ko, the Voice of the People, because he cannot speak at all. But the Man of Today suffers from the universal disease of intellectuals: he is powerless against brute force. He suppresses his instincts and even works actively for what he knows to be wrong (except in those very rare cases where the intellectual is also a man of exceptional physical courage). In those cases he is crushed for his principles —and what good does that do? Frisch's typical intellectual is too rational and too cynical about himself to make even the semblance of a protest: "How could I doubt, Your Majesty: have I not seen your naked dagger? . . . I want to live." And so he stands aside, making no protest as the mute peasant boy is handed over to the Imperial torturer. Mee Lan, the daughter of Hwang Ti, who represents love and idealism in Frisch's symbolic system, has fallen in love with the intellectual, but she shies away in horror at his passiveness, for like all idealists she is irrational and not cynical. The intellectual explains his moral impasse to her:

> MEE LAN: You knew he was mute.
>
> THE MAN OF TODAY: Yes.
>
> MEE LAN: And you are going to permit this mute boy to be tortured—you, who know everything?
>
> THE MAN OF TODAY: Permit?
>
> MEE LAN: You shrug your shoulders. And that's all! Shrug the shoulders, light another cigarette—while they torture a mute to force him to scream; and you, who can speak, stand there and keep silent—and that's all!
>
> THE MAN OF TODAY: What can I do?
>
> MEE LAN: You with your learning! Time and space are one; how comforting! Destruction of the world by heat, how exciting! And the speed of light is unsurpassable; how interesting! Energy equals mass times the speed of light.
>
> . . . .
>
> THE MAN OF TODAY: What can I do? He will be tortured. I know. As thousands before him have been. First the thumbscrew, then the nailed whip, then the business with

the block and pulleys (which tear the tendons so that he will never again be able to lift his arms), then the white-hot wire, then the bone-breakers, repeated as often as necessary —all that, I know, has been going on right up to today. And whether we cry or laugh, whether we dance, sleep, read— there is probably not a single hour that goes by today in which some man somewhere is not being tortured, flayed, martyred, disgraced, murdered. But has any intellectual ever been able to forestall destiny simply because he foresaw it? We can write books and make speeches, even angry speeches: "Why this can no longer go on!" And yet it goes on. Precisely so. Great and learned persons arise and call to mankind: "The cobalt bomb, which you are now producing, will be the end of you!"—and people go on making the cobalt bomb.[8]

The explanation is, of course, true; and Frisch's irony reaches a crescendo of derisive barking. The play ends as the intellectual and the idealist, the powerless and the despised, look at each other helplessly, as surely bound fast by their natures in this world as if they were locked in iron fetters.

Frisch tells us right at the beginning that this is a play without a solution. No one learns anything, and everything goes on as before. Only this time there is a possibility that the repetition of the same old imbecilities will result in the self-extinction of the human race. The play is therefore in the strictest sense a *farce*; and Frisch has thus described it. It is a warning, a warning that has to be made even though it is foredoomed to be ignored. Great Walls can no longer be thrown up to hold off the inevitable. The play takes place now, "in an era when the building of Chinese Walls has become . . . a farce." [9] Man's mind has become lopsided: its scientific development has completely outstripped its humanistic development. It no longer has the power to give a moral synthesis to its newly uncovered facets. Consequently it has lapsed into a narcotic complacency,

8. *Ibid.*, pp. 96–97.
9. *Ibid.*, p. 23.

fatalistically accepting everything that happens or lazily juggling things around a bit until they seem less menacing. It is this modern mental habit born, probably, of a multishock-induced numbness that Frisch is crying out against when he has Hwang Ti step out of his part and address the audience in the most important speech of the play:

> HWANG TI: I know well enough what you're thinking, you out there. But I laugh at your hopes. You're thinking, this very evening you will see me hurled from this throne, for the play must have an ending and a moral, and when I am dethroned then you can complacently return home and drink your beer and nibble on a cracker. That's what you would like. You with your dramaturgy! I laugh. Go out and buy your evening newspaper, you out there, and on the first page you will find my name. For I do not intend to be dethroned. I don't believe in dramaturgy. I just sit on my throne with my hydrogen bomb ready to hand and smile as I watch you peacefully going home . . .[10]

Frisch's best play is *Biedermann und die Brandstifter* (Mr. Biedermann and the Arsonists, 1958). This is a carefully worked out political allegory about the rise of totalitarian governments. Frisch's thesis is that the final coup d'etat by which totalitarian governments come to power is purely incidental: by the time that final act happens, the disaster is ineluctable. The coup is the culminating point of a long series of small incidents, each of which seems unimportant, yet any one of which could have been prevented. Had it been prevented, the whole structure would have toppled. Frisch's play is a warning—again. But, like *Die Chinesische Mauer*, it is a despairing warning: Frisch knows that what has happened many times before will inevitably happen again. Human nature, he believes, is static: Man is no more developed now than when he was scratching his

---

10. *Ibid.*, p. 65. The last sentence of this quotation does not appear in the Rosenberg version. It is my own translation from the German edition (Max Frisch, *Die Chinesische Mauer* [Frankfurt a. M.: Suhrkamp Verlag, 1955], p. 75).

pithecanthropic armpits. His only advances have been in technical knowledge, which his nature has led him to use for deleterious purposes. It is the belief that men cannot learn (at the end Biedermann, in hell, wonders whether he is damned) that differentiates Frisch's play from Bertholt Brecht's *Der Aufhaltsame Aufstieg des Arturo Ui*. Brecht's play is a point-to-point allegory of the rise of Hitler told in terms of a Chicago gangster. His thesis is that at any one of a number of points Arturo Ui could and should have been stopped. Frisch's play is a point-to-point allegory of the rise to power of any totalitarian system, but his thesis is that although the gangsters could and should have been stopped at any one of a number of points, the nature of Biedermann (*homo ordinarius-Jedermann*) incapacitates him. Biedermann is cowardly and guilt-ridden and incapable of learning that the exposure of his own failings would be a lesser evil than the wholesale disaster his reticence helps to promote.

Structurally the most interesting aspect of the play is Frisch's use of a chorus of fire fighters who hang about the peripheries of the scenery and occasionally come forward to sound Cassandra-like warnings in verse. They represent the unused power that can destroy the arsonists. Their constant refrain is that they are always ready to come but cannot do so until they are called. The tiers of watchful firemen all round the action provide a timeless setting for the contemporary story of the Biedermanns and their foolishness.

On its primary level the story is simple. Biedermann is a typical businessman, owner of a very successful hair-lotion manufacturing concern. Like all very successful businessmen (Biedermann is a millionaire), he has accumulated his money by ruthless methods, keeping just this side of the border of legality, though not of morality. His hair lotion is a fake—his customers might just as well bathe their bald heads in their own urine, he tells his wife. In addition he has just fired his oldest and most faithful employee, the inventor of the process by which the hair lotion is made. The employee kills himself. These two facts leave our businessman without a moral leg to stand on when he tries to face down the frankly immoral arsonists. "Every citizen above a certain income," says one of the arsonists, "is, strictly speaking, legally punishable."

Biedermann knows exactly what to expect from the arsonists. Their method of operation is always the same. One of them pretends to be homeless and asks for a night's lodging, and the next day the house is a heap of ashes. Just as Biedermann is meditating on the newspaper reports of the latest fire, an enormous man practically forces his way into his house, and, always behaving with an excessive cordiality that occasionally switches to an Uriah Heep-like obsequiousness, installs himself in the attic. Gradually Biedermann sees the arrangements for his own destruction being completed. First another arsonist is smuggled into the attic. Then barrels of gasoline are dragged up. Biedermann makes a feeble attempt to assert himself and threatens to call the police; but just then the police do arrive— with the news of the unjustly discharged employee's suicide. Ensnared in his own guilt, Biedermann feels himself helpless. The arsonists are completely established now, and Biedermann knows it. He decides to make friends with them, to ingratiate himself with them in the hope that they will relent. Surely they will not burn his house if they see he is on their side, if they see what a fine fellow he really is! The arsonists have dropped all pretense now. They tell Biedermann they are going to burn his house. Biedermann affects to take this as a joke and invites them to dinner. At the end of the dinner, fire sirens are heard. "A good thing it isn't us," Biedermann piously murmurs as the engines rush by. The arsonists tell him it's only a ruse of theirs, though: they always have a false alarm sounded in a remote part of town when they are about to do a job. They plan to fire several other houses in the vicinity, they tell Biedermann. With luck and a favorable wind the fire should carry to the tanks of the municipal gasworks. As they leave, they ask Biedermann for a box of matches. Completely defeated, he hands them the instruments of his own destruction.

The allegory and lesson of the main part of the play are quite plain. Frisch is giving his audience both a historically correct parable and a warning. The arsonists represent the insidious forces of totalitarianism, first worming their way into

bourgeois society, then, once they have gained the foothold of
tentative or apprehensive acceptance, asserting themselves, and
finally engulfing and destroying their victims. It is an example
of two classic clichés—of giving an inch and having an ell taken
and of having the hand that fed, bitten. The lesson is don't
give an inch and don't feed. The manner in which the two
arsonists gain a foothold in the Biedermann household is precisely the manner in which the Nazis gained a foothold in
Weimar Germany. It is the usual pattern for internal revolutionaries in the initial stages of their campaign. Their task is
made all the easier by the moral helplessness and cowardice of
the bourgeoisie, which should be a solid, resilient, antagonistic
mass against which the arsonists should be as helpless as fire in
an asbestos-lined vacuum, but which instead is as soft as mildew
and as porous as a termite-infested log. This is no farfetched
analogy. Frisch makes his allegorical intention clear with the
name he chooses for his representative bourgeois. Biedermann
in German has the same connotation as Babbitt in English.
Gottlieb Biedermann: Godlove Babbitt. The Babbitts and the
Biedermanns are helpless against the forces of arson and destruction because they are themselves guilty. When Willi says
to his fellow arsonist that everyone above a certain income is,
strictly speaking, punishable, he may be exaggerating a little.
What is true, Frisch tells us, is that everyone above a certain
income has a guilty conscience and is thus ready to compromise.
"If I report them to the police," reasons Biedermann, "I'll
make enemies of them. What's the good of that? One match
and our house goes up in flames. What's the good of that?" In
this state of mind it is no wonder that Biedermann actually
helps the arsonists to destroy him. Like a condemned man trying to ingratiate himself with the hangman by greasing the
rope, he holds the fuse so Willi can measure off the requisite
length. Then he goes and salves his conscience by contributing
money to the fire department. Of course, after contributing the
money he has to go and compromise with his enemies in order,
as he thinks, to be able to make more money: "I don't know if
Gottlieb is always right," sighs his wife, "He's gone through
this before—Of course they're hoodlums, he tells me, but if I

antagonize them, then I may as well pour our hair lotion down the drain. And no sooner had he joined the Party—" What happens when he joins the Party we can see for ourselves.

In the epilogue, which was unfortunately omitted from the New York production, but which is as essential to the play as is Shaw's epilogue to *St. Joan*, Frisch shows us Biedermann and his wife after the disaster. They have been burned to a crisp and are in hell, of course—although they can't bring themselves to believe it. "Why shouldn't we be in Heaven?" Biedermann says, "Everyone we know is in Heaven, even my lawyer. For the last time—this must be Heaven. What else? We have to be in Heaven. People like us haven't *done* anything!" [11] They are finally informed by a long-tailed monkey who bears a peculiar resemblance to a friend of the arsonists that they really are in hell. They are going to escape the fires, however, because hell is about to go on strike. Satan and Beelzebub are fed up with getting only puny, insignificant sinners like "Babbitts and intellectuals, pickpockets, adulterers, ladies' maids who stole their mistresses' nylons, and draft dodgers." All the really big sinners have been pardoned: "Whoever goes around in uniform, or wore one when he killed, or promises to wear one whenever he kills or orders killings, is saved." This is the news that the Devil (who, by the way, is none other than Willi the arsonist) has just brought back from heaven. Disguised as a bishop, Willi has tried to find God in order to arbitrate the dispute, but he has been unsuccessful. Heaven, he says, is not what it was the last time he was up there:

> I very much doubt what I saw was really Heaven. They said it was, but I doubt it. . . . They wear medals there and all the loudspeakers have got clouds of incense coming out of them. I saw a whole Milky Way of medals—enough to make the Devil feel sick. All my clients were there, all my mass murderers with the angels cruising around their bald spots. Everyone greets everyone else and rolls around drinking

11. Max Frisch, *Biedermann und die Brandstifter* (Frankfurt a. M.: Suhrkamp Verlag, 1958), p. 134.

hallelujah and whispering of remission of sins. The saints are noticeably quiet, since they're made out of wood or stone, and the princes of the Church (I circulated among the princes of the Church in order to find out where God is) are quiet too, even though they're not made of wood or stone. . . . I disguised myself, and those in power up there were so busy forgiving themselves they didn't recognize me —they let me bless them.[12]

Things being as they are, the Devil decides to bank the fires of hell and go back to earth to try and drum up some more business. Once again he and Beelzebub change back to the costumes in which we first saw them at the beginning of the play, and off they go to earth to burn down once more the cities which the Biedermanns have built up again. At the end, Biedermann and his wife are left alone on the stage. Organ music swells up, they fall on their knees, and "Do you think we're saved?" the wife asks. And Biedermann, having, as always, learned nothing, still self-righteously convinced of his innocence, answers, "—I think so . . ."

Frisch's latest play, *Andorra* (1961), is an examination of anti-Semitism. Andorra is a tiny republic with no native Jews.[13] It borders on a violently anti-Semitic, militaristic state that has systematically wiped out all its Jews and is now threatening to invade Andorra. Twenty years previously Andorra's schoolmaster had fathered an illegitimate child in the neighboring country of the Blacks. Too cowardly to admit that the baby was his (since this would have hurt his social position in Andorra), the schoolmaster gave out that the child was Jewish and that he had rescued it from a Black pogrom. Andri, as he is called, has therefore grown up as the schoolmaster's foster son. The Andorrans, although they have never known any Jews, know all the anti-Semitic clichés and attribute them to Andri.

---

12. *Ibid.*, pp. 156–57.
13. Frisch states in a prefatory note to the play that the name "Andorra" has nothing to do with the real country of that name, nor with any other specific country. (Max Frisch, *Andorra* [Frankfurt a. M.: Suhrkamp Verlag, 1961], p. [4].)

They are not overtly prejudiced against him at first—not until the militantly anti-Jewish Blacks threaten to invade. Their attitude is that they are trying to be friendly to Andri but that he is forever rebuffing their good intentions with his "Jewish" oversensitiveness. The irony of it all, of course, is that Andri is not a Jew at all. But by the time he discovers this, his hate against those who have made him suffer because of his supposed Jewishness is so great that he refuses to cease being one.

Frisch's main purpose is an analysis of the anti-Semite's hypocrisy. Interspersed between the scenes are little speeches given by the various characters, in which they explain their actions as if on a witness stand years later. They have, of course, learned nothing. They are totally unrepentant, and their one purpose is to emphasize that it wasn't *their* fault. Through each of their speeches runs the refrain, "We didn't know he wasn't a Jew," so that they unconsciously assert their guilt as they imply that their actions would have been excusable if Andri really had been a Jew. Lest this may sound strangely specious to English or American ears, let it be said here that Frisch is not inventing or even exaggerating anything for his polemic purposes. A speech such as the following by the Andorran physician can be heard in private conversation today in any German-speaking city:

I should like to express myself briefly, though much that is being said today needs correction. It's always easy to say afterwards how one should have acted—quite apart from the fact that, as far as I'm concerned, I really don't see why I should have acted otherwise than I did. What, after all, did we do? Absolutely nothing. I was the town physician, and I still am today. I don't remember any more what I was supposed to have said in those days. That's the way I am—I say what I think, in the good old Andorran fashion. . . . I admit that we were all mistaken, which is something which can only be regretted. How often do I have to say it? I'm not in favor of such horrible things—I never was. . . . All I can say is that it wasn't my fault, quite apart from the fact that his bearing (unfortunately it cannot be denied) became more and more (let us be frank) somehow Jewish, although, to be sure, the young man may well have been an Andorran like the rest of us. . . . Let us not forget that those were troubled times. As far as I'm concerned, I never took part in any of those unpleasant acts, nor did I ever encourage anyone else to. . . . To be sure, it was a tragic affair. It's not my fault that it happened. I think I speak for everyone when I say once again that we can only regret the course of events—back then.[14]

Despite Frisch's refusal to link his play with specific events, one cannot help noticing the strong parallel between Germany's Anschluss with Austria and the Blacks' bloodless conquest of Andorra. Many of the speeches put into the Andorran townspeople's mouths read like parodies of Viennese talk. If the leading citizens can speak like this after the event—and they do—then there is ample reason to look upon *Andorra* as Frisch's most complete expression of despair in the potential of human nature.[15]

In the plays here discussed, particularly the last three, Frisch reveals himself as a traditionalist. The trend in the contemporary drama—and this includes also Frisch's countryman and rival, Friedrich Dürrenmatt—is to treat characters impersonally. With the principal "experimental dramatists" (Beckett, Ionesco, Adamov, etc.) this impersonal treatment is motivated by the conviction that in modern society individuality has been castrated. These writers see modern man as a sort of blind, groping creature playing a perpetual game of blindman's buff. Dürrenmatt treats modern man in the same way, but he assumes the Olympian position. He is an aged and very wise lecturer indulgently explaining the foibles of mankind. Frisch is none of these things. He is a human being like everyone else. It is a status that he never forgets and never rejects. He is *involved*. His characters are human beings, and we understand

14. Frisch, *Andorra*, pp. 101–102.
15. Frisch's specific instructions in the text that all overt reference to past events (through the design of the uniforms, for example) should be avoided implies that he is writing about a possible future.

them through recognition, through a sort of intuitive Bergsonian identification. They are not the bloodless specimens split open on the dissecting table that Dürrenmatt and the experimentalists provide for us. Frisch's characters are fully rounded psychological beings. His themes—the psychological impossibility of human self-sufficiency and the inability of men to learn by experience—are presented in a personal manner, sometimes to the extent of becoming personal pleas. Frisch's two best plays, *Die Chinesische Mauer* and *Biedermann und die Brandstifter*, are consciously foredoomed pleas for a better world. The irony implicit in them no longer sounds like the scornful laughter of the gods we hear in Dürrenmatt; it sounds like the self-reproaching wailing of the damned.

FRITZ HOCHWALDER
The Drama within the Self

Fritz Hochwälder was born in Vienna in 1911. Like so many other prominent theater people in Germany and Austria, he fled to Switzerland when the Nazis came to power. It was in Switzerland that Hochwälder wrote his first important play. *Das Heilige Experiment* (The Holy Experiment, 1943) was written while Hochwälder was on leave of absence from the labor camp in which he and many other political refugees had been interned by the Swiss. The play was first performed in Biel, Switzerland, in 1943, and was subsequently played at the Burgtheater in Hochwälder's native Vienna, as well as in Germany, France, Holland, Sweden, Finland, Norway, Argentina, Brazil, and Greece. After the phenomenal run of over 400 performances at the Theatre de l'Athénée in Paris, the play opened on Broadway in September, 1953, and closed after seven performances. The American failure was probably caused by two principal factors: Hochwälder's plays are distinctly more suitable for an off-Broadway audience than for a Broadway one, and the version used was an adaptation by Eva Le Gallienne of the French adaptation and was thus twice removed from Hochwälder's original text.[1] At any rate, a Broadway failure is no reason for discounting a serious playwright.

Fritz Hochwälder's dramas deal with conflict within the human mind. All drama is conflict of one sort or another, but the drama of conflict within one human mind is the oldest and purest form of drama. With the introduction of the second actor by Aeschylus it became possible to present the drama of conflict between *two* human minds. In the modern theater (which means roughly since the first World War) we have seen further refinements of this in the drama of conflict between a human mind and an idea and even in the conflict of two or more ideas.

1. The Le Gallienne version was performed under the title, *The Strong Are Lonely*. The authorized American translation is by the present writer under the title *The Holy Experiment*.

Of the trio of writers who have made the most significant contribution to the contemporary German-speaking theater, Fritz Hochwälder is the only one who has concentrated on the most basic form of drama. The other two, Frisch and Dürrenmatt, have branched out for the most part into the drama of personified ideas.

A dramatist ideally raises a conflict in the mind of the protagonist and lets us see him grow to an awareness of it. The purest drama is condensed into that moment in which the character, for the first time, sees himself as he is, when he becomes conscious of the difference between the illusion he has lived and the reality he should have lived. It is the moment of self-realization for the character and for the audience watching him. It is the horror of looking into a kaleidoscope and suddenly seeing the randomly scattered crystals fall into a rigidly ordered array of graduated prisms. This horrifying destruction of illusion and rearrangement of personal values is the basis of Fritz Hochwälder's drama.

Hochwälder's most representative play, *Das Heilige Experiment*, deals with the expulsion of the Jesuits from Paraguay in 1767. The Jesuits had established what amounted in effect to a sovereign state within the Spanish-held territory of Paraguay. This state acknowledged the sovereignty of the king of Spain, but maintained its own army in order to keep out the Spanish colonists, who simply wished to enslave the Indians. The Jesuit state in Paraguay was, in fact, a true communist state, with all sharing equally in the benefits and profits of the community as a whole.

The creation of a Utopian state in the midst of a non-Utopian one inevitably creates an intolerable economic situation. The inhabitants of the Utopian communal state obviously produce goods better and more economically than the inhabitants of the non-Utopian competitive society. The latter become jealous and start intriguing to have the Utopians declared immoral, dishonest, illegal—whatever you please. In Hochwälder's play the Spanish settlers have secretly transmitted slanders about the Jesuit state to the Spanish crown. The king of Spain perceives that these slanders, if accepted at face value, will enable him to confiscate the rich territory of the Jesuits. He therefore accepts them, draws up the edict dissolving the Jesuit state, and *then* sends out a commission to "investigate" the accusations. The commission is to hear both sides, but it already has the king's signed sentence in its possession. In other words, the investigation, like all investigations in which the investigator is one of the interested parties, is to be a deliberate farce. It is at this point—with the arrival of the commission—that Hochwälder's play begins.

The head of the commission, Don Pedro de Miura, is an old friend of Alfonso Fernandez, the Jesuit Father Provincial. He is determined to conduct a completely fair and impartial investigation for the show of the thing and also in order to satisfy himself personally of the truth or falsity of the accusations. He knows, of course, that the sentence is already passed, but he wishes to satisfy himself of its justice. The investigation quickly brings out the obvious fact that the accusations are *untrue*; that, in fact, they are slanders invented by the Spanish colonists who envy the Jesuits their rich harvests and devoted laborers. Nevertheless, though he privately acknowledges to the Father Provincial that the charges are untrue, Don Pedro has to carry out the sentence. He pronounces the Jesuit state dissolved. Father Alfonso's answer is to arrest him: he and his fellow Jesuits have decided to fight to maintain their Kingdom of God on earth. All this time an elderly, dapper little Italian traveler has been watching the proceedings with a genteel air of disinterest. This Signor Querini, as he calls himself, now tells Father Alfonso that he is the emissary of the general of the Jesuit Order. He orders Father Alfonso to release the king's commissioner and obey his demands. The reason that he gives is that the Jesuits of Paraguay have committed a sin in founding a state based literally on the teachings of Christ. The miseries and injustices of this world are no concern of theirs, he asserts, since the task of the Jesuits is to prepare people for the world to come. The Jesuits should side with the cruel, the unjust, and the powerful in the hope of converting them to virtue and charity. What is behind all this, of course, is the same thing that is behind the Spanish colonists' hatred of the Jesuit state: economics. Querini says that hundreds of thousands of Indian souls and lives must be sacrificed because otherwise the hatred of political forces in Europe might injure the order. Despite the obvious cynicism of this attitude, Father Alfonso is forced to obey the rules of the order. He hands his written surrender to Don Pedro and commands the reluctant fathers under his charge to obey. With the exception of Father Oros, the military commander of the Jesuit state, they, like their Father Provincial, are too numbed at this point to do anything but mechanically obey in accordance with the vow of obedience they have taken. Father Oros alone renounces his vow. He is the only one to perceive that a vow of obedience, however fearsome the threats of damnation with which it is enjoined, is invalidated the moment it exacts an immorality. Despite the Father Provincial's orders, fighting breaks out— whose fault this is is not made clear—and he is himself wounded while trying to stop it. In his fury he tears the map of Jesuit Paraguay from the wall and curses his work.

And now comes Hochwälder's psychological turning point. As Father Alfonso lies dying of his wound and as he watches Don Pedro sign the death warrants of Father Oros and a number of Indian hostages, he realizes he was wrong—wrong to obey his vow, wrong not to do what he felt to be right. At the same time he realizes that to meet violence with violence, to defend the right with blood, is also wrong. Nothing is solved:

> FATHER ALFONSO: . . . Should we place ourselves on the side of force?—Never! Should we serve the mighty of the world?—Never! Should we surrender everything without resisting?—Never! Should we renounce the Kingdom of God on Earth? Never . . . Oh—I hear the rebellious voice in my breast saying, Never! Never! Never! I listened to it —but my mouth spoke otherwise. I told my voice it was right—but to my men I said . . . "I command you! Listen to me! I am the Provincial! I command—obey me!"—and I myself obeyed! Obeyed—obeyed—the rebellious voice in my heart . . . First I cursed, in anger and in the blindness of my pain, this state—as the wound bit into my flesh, I

destroyed it with my own hands—I destroyed this work
. . . and thus I leave this world still ruled everywhere by
oppression—slavery—and everything was in vain . . .
whispers . . . the voice . . .[2]

At the time of critical decision life becomes an impasse, Hochwälder is saying. Father Alfonso realizes at the moment of
death that everything he had ever believed in and lived by was
wrong. He has wavered between two courses of action, both
wrong; and there were no other alternatives. Devoutly religious
all his life, he is faced at the moment of death with the knowledge that religion has no solution to the problem of life. Hochwälder's play is the tragedy of moral frustration.

In *Der Flüchtling* (The Fugitive), written in 1945, Hochwälder treats a psychological problem that has always puzzled
and horrified thinking men all over the world. It is the problem
of the apparent schizophrenic nature of the world's monsters.
We all know the stories, which the tabloids gleefully serve up
to us whenever they have the opportunity, about insanely
vicious murderers or child-rapists or animal-torturers who are
found upon investigation to have a happy family, admiring
neighbors, doting parents, and an unctuously approving superior
at the office. Jack the Ripper was very probably a staid and
highly respected member of Lincoln's Inn Fields. This Dr.
Jekyll and Mr. Hyde duality in human nature is the subject of
Hochwälder's play.

Der Flüchtling takes place in what seems to be the southwest corner of Germany, near the French and Swiss borders.
There are only three characters: the fugitive, the border guard,
and the guard's wife. The fugitive is trying to get across the
border to a neutral country, and the wife feels herself obligated
to help him when he stumbles exhausted into her house. The
border guard is the real protagonist, however. It is his duty to
catch the fugitive and hand him over to the secret police. He
knows quite well they will torture him and kill him, but that,
of course, is none of his business. In the border guard, Hoch-

2. Fritz Hochwälder, *Das Heilige Experiment* (Basel, Switzerland:
Kurt Reiss Theaterverlag, 1946), p. 88.

wälder gives us a picture of the people who formed the backbone of the Nazi regime. These are the petty officials who are able to compartmentalize their lives and live as upright burghers in one part and as inhuman monsters in the other. We have always had this type festering among us: the public executioner used to wipe the honest sweat off his brow, roll down his sleeves, and go home to play with his children after a hard day with the thumbscrews and the rack. Such people do not lack moral sense; they merely have the faculty of transferring their guilt. *They* are not responsible, *they* have not given the order. Hochwälder's border guard is a perfect example of this type. At home he is a model husband, deeply and sincerely in love with his wife; on duty he is an automaton, ready to do anything that he is ordered to do. His moral sense is not dead: he realizes what he is doing, but he rationalizes everything by convincing himself that he is doing it for his wife's sake. To preserve his wife's peace of mind he would do anything—and besides, he does it because he is ordered to do it, and therefore he is not morally responsible. The old argument.

When the guard learns that his wife is hiding the fugitive, he is horrified. Their whole happiness is jeopardized. What should he do? Pretend to help the fugitive to escape and then shoot him in the back as soon as he is outside the house— obviously! Death will be instantaneous, the fugitive need never know anything, and the happy home life will be preserved: the perfect plan. There is just one hitch: the wife, who has been sheltered from reality up to now, refuses to yield to expediency when she is at last faced with a real moral problem of her own. Leaving her husband contemptuously, she barricades herself in the bedroom with the fugitive. Later she falls asleep and the fugitive comes down and offers to try and cross the border alone before she wakes up. The guard, appreciating the decency of the proposal, offers the fugitive his hand. It is scornfully rejected:

GUARD: What have I done that you won't . . .
FUGITIVE: You've got a clear conscience, haven't you? Innocent as a newborn babe! Wouldn't hurt a fly!

Waters the flowers in his garden every evening, feeds his
rabbits, and thanks God he lives in peace. The whole country's shot to pieces and dried up, but that doesn't bother
him—oh no, he just sits at home and thinks the hell with
those outside!—And watch out, anyone who dares disturb
his sacred peace! Then he becomes a beast and doesn't ask
whose fault it is. At one stroke the good-humored fellow
becomes a devil and quickly draws up a list of his fellow
citizens to denounce and murder—murder! at the first opportunity.

GUARD: No! That's not true! I just thought . . .

FUGITIVE: Innocence in person! He just thought!
Doesn't care what happens all around him, doesn't care
that bloody gangsters are setting the world on fire. None of
his business if they round up free men and send them into
slavery! He just obeys orders! But whose orders he obeys—
that he doesn't care to know and whoever tells him the
truth is his enemy, for if he listened maybe he'd find out
he was a gangster himself and not even as much as a hair's-
breadth better than his masters. . . . And still he just
wants to live in peace. At any price! [3]

As he realizes why no decent man can shake his hand, the
events of his life suddenly rearrange themselves in the guard's
mind and drop into their proper places. He looks down the
long corridor of his past, as it were, and it is like looking into
the abyss itself. He helps the fugitive to escape with his wife,
and then calls out the news of his treachery to the approaching
militia. They answer with a shot, and he falls dead across the
threshold that he had ruined his life to protect.

As might be expected from a writer whose political disagree-
ments with the Nazis had forced him to flee his native country,
the rise of the German despotism continued to fascinate Hochwälder. A conscientious artist feels the compulsion to explain
to himself what is wrong with the world; and it is in responding to his explanation or in denying it that his audience either

3. Fritz Hochwälder, *Der Flüchtling* (Elgg, Switzerland: Volksverlag
Elgg, 1954), p. 56.

learns more about the world or becomes convinced that it is impossible to learn anything—which is a solution of sorts too, as the writers of the theatre of the absurd have demonstrated. In *Der Flüchtling* Hochwälder explored the effect of a totalitarian state on an average individual mind; in *Esther* he wrote a complete allegory of the rise of the Nazi mentality in terms of the Biblical story of Esther, Mordecai, and Haman.

The story of Esther is, of course, tailor-made for the project. The plans of Haman and Hitler are so similar that Hochwälder hardly has to stretch any facts to create his allegory: he merely has, for the most part, to transpose names and transfer situations from one milieu to another. Hochwälder does, however, make certain significant changes in the character and career of Haman to make him correspond more closely to Hitler. Instead of being a nobleman elevated by the king, Hochwälder has Haman start out as a servant in Mordecai's household. Later he is thrown into the king's prison and, while confined there, hears of and joins a secret organization which seeks to improve the state (which is in the midst of a profound economic depression) by violent means. Haman contrives to make himself leader of the organization, which up to now has been little more than a society of discontented talkers, by impressing upon it the need for action. It is his idea that the Jews would make ideal scapegoats and he soon makes himself a powerful demagogue among the discontented lower classes of the city. He comes to power when the nobles persuade the king to call him in, although they thoroughly disapprove of him. Both the nobles and the king look upon the elevation of Haman to supreme power as a measure of temporary expediency, but of course it is Haman-Hitler who is master of the expediency device. Pleading expediency, he obtains the king's consent to the extermination of the Jews and is only foiled when Esther finally intervenes. The parallels are so obvious that they hardly need to be pointed out: the only thing wrong with Hochwälder's allegory, in fact, is that in 1940, when he wrote it, the execution of Haman was unfortunately only a piece of self-indulgent wishful thinking on his part.

The characteristic Hochwälder touch of inner revelation

comes at the very end in *Esther*. Unlike the Biblical heroine, Hochwälder's has not been particularly anxious to save her people. Mordecai's lesson of concealment has been so well driven into her that she no longer considers herself a Jewess and feels disinclined to concern herself in any political affair. In the Biblical story Esther obtains the king's favor and the privilege of having any wish granted. She simply accuses Haman of treachery, and that is that. Haman is taken out and hanged; Mordecai is made the chief minister; and the Jews are granted the privilege of using the time set aside for their own extermination to slaughter their enemies. Hochwälder's Esther does not have so simple a task, nor could Hochwälder, writing in 1940, present so sanguine an ending. Esther traps Haman with an elaborate plot that reveals he had been planning to overthrow the king. But even so the Jews' troubles are not over. The king recognizes that the country does need a scapegoat and that the Jews are the obvious choices for the position. He will not, of course, exterminate them, he assures Esther, but merely persecute them a little whenever the people need to have their attention diverted from official corruption and inefficiency. To show that he is not really prejudiced against Jews, he will marry Esther (she has been his concubine up to now) provided she keeps her origin a secret, and he will ennoble Mordecai. The latter tears up his charter of nobility and tells the king he will not be singled out but will share the fate of his people. As Esther quietly watches the scene, she experiences the typical Hochwälderian inner revulsion and announces that she gives up her chance for the throne to go with Mordecai. Until such time as justice reigns in the world and her people are judged on an equal basis with other peoples, she can do nothing—nor has she any right to save herself alone.

In *Der Flüchtling* and in *Esther*, more than in any other of his plays, we can see Hochwälder's use of the flash of moral enlightenment as a dramatic and didactic device. One decisive key event occurs that changes a man's whole life by rearranging the perspective of his memories. What could be more dramatic than this moment of inner realization? The same "moment of truth" appears in most of Hochwälder's other plays.

In *Donadieu* (published 1953), for example, the problem is the rejection of revenge. Again a complete reversal of a man's purpose in life is involved. The action takes place during the Catholic-Huguenot conflicts in France. Donadieu is the leader of a self-contained Huguenot community in southern France where fugitives from all over the country are welcomed. Donadieu's one passion in life is revenge. During his absence from the garrison several years previously, his wife was brutally murdered and the rest of the villagers burnt alive in the church by a group of Catholic banditti. Since then, Donadieu has lived in suspended animation, so to speak, until the moment when he will have the murderer in his power. But when one of two travelers wearing the king's uniform is recognized as the leader of the murderers, Donadieu is unable to do anything, for the murderer is entrusted with the king's declaration of indulgence for the Huguenots. If he takes his revenge, Donadieu prevents the Huguenots from obtaining their rights. He refrains. Again the psychological enlightenment that Hochwälder shows us is complete. Donadieu does not refrain merely because the circumstances make it expedient: he refrains because he has realized the futility of his desire for revenge. Like the border guard and like the Father Provincial, he has been granted a moment in which the whole course of his life has become visible to him; and his life, like theirs, has been—as it must be—totally changed by it. Even when the man who has killed his wife deliberately taunts him, hoping to provoke a fight and thus invalidate the declaration of indulgence, Donadieu remains firm. Even though those who had previously urged him to forego the luxury of his revenge now urge him to silence the vicious taunts, Donadieu maintains his claim. And so the general cause is saved—through Donadieu's moment of self-revelation.

Similarly, in *Meier Helmbrecht* (published 1956), Hochwälder tells the story of a medieval landowner whose son becomes a bloodthirsty robber who pillages the countryside until he is finally caught himself. The point of the play comes in the third act, when Helmbrecht is tried by a jury of his peers on the smoking ruins of his farmhouse. Slowly he is made to realize that his protestations of innocence are willful self-delusion and that

he too is responsible for his son's crimes. What his son has become Helmbrecht's neglect and indulgence made him: the sins
of the children must be visited upon the fathers. Hochwälder
unfortunately gives his play a rather weak ending by reconciling
Helmbrecht with his now crippled and blinded son as he starts
to rebuild his house.

Since most of Hochwälder's plays were written during or
immediately after the war, it is only natural that he should be
so taken up by this question of the placing of guilt. In *Meier
Helmbrecht* he argues that the fathers are responsible for the
children. In *Der Flüchtling* he argues that a man is responsible
for his own integrity—that the plea that he is only a cog in the
machine is valueless. The plea that "orders are orders" and one
has no choice but to follow them was, of course, one that became almost an automatic, rhythmic refrain after the war, when
every German chanted it like a daily prayer. Hochwälder deals
with the justice of this plea on the part of the older generation
in *Meier Helmbrecht,* on the part of the man in the street in
Der Flüchtling, and in *Der Öffentliche Anklager* (The Public
Prosecutor, published 1954), a melodrama about the French
Revolution, he deals with the leaders of the people—the politicians, officials, and generals. Like these people, Fouquier-Tinville, the cold-blooded public prosecutor who engineered the
Reign of Terror, pleads that he is a servant of the state and
that it is his duty to obey orders:

> Here we only obey our orders. No blame attached to us,
> we can serve all parties with a clear conscience. We fol-
> low whoever is in power. Keep that in mind, . . .
>
> . . . .
>
> Reactions? I am not concerned with politics. I obey the law
> and carry out such orders as may come to me. I don't ques-
> tion whether they are good or bad.
>
> . . . .
>
> I was merely employing the means I was given—carrying
> out my orders. That is why I feel I can reject any personal
> responsibility.[4]

4. Fritz Hochwälder, *The Public Prosecutor,* translated by Kitty Black
in J. C. Trewin, ed., *Plays of the Year* (London: Elek Books, 1958), pp.
334, 337, 361.

Nobody is enlightened in this play. Fouquier-Tinville satisfactorily falls into the trap he has been tricked into setting for himself and that is that. He fully deserves his end, for Hochwälder makes it clear that his explanations are consciously specious and that his actions are dictated by cynical opportunism and an insane thirst for power.

Hochwälder has written three other plays that are outside the main philosophical stream of his work. They are *Hotel du Commerce* (published 1954), an adaptation of Guy de Maupassant's "Boule de Suif," *Der Unschuldige* (The Innocent Man, published 1958), a melodrama about the deceptiveness of circumstantial evidence, which he wrote as a bravura piece for Attila Hörbiger of the Vienna Burgtheater, and *Donnerstag* (Thursday), an extremely confused and clumsily constructed modern morality play written for the Salzburg Festival.

Some may quarrel with Hochwälder's theory of psychology. Man, they will say, is not transformed, except in the rarest of rare cases, into a completely different psychological being by one occurrence. Few men are that sensitive. In fact, it is probably nearer to the actual human truth to say that man never learns by experience, that he is irredeemably set in childhood upon a labyrinthine and enclosed psychological path. But Hochwälder's view of human nature is nonetheless the most dramatic possible. The luxury of precise psychology must be left to the novelist, who has the space and the structural flexibility to indulge in whatever he will. The dramatist is bound by the exigencies of the stage. He must depict the events of the world at their highest intensity, regardless of whether or not they would happen precisely thus in real life.

Beginning with *Donnerstag* (Thursday, 1959), written for the Salzburg Festival, Hochwälder enters on a new phase of his career. While he continues to make the psychological balance of the protagonist—what I have called the drama within the self—his chief concern, he no longer concentrates on setting up a situation in which a single moment encapsulates the protagonist's whole psychological experience and reverses it. In *Donnerstag*, subtitled "a medieval morality play," and in *1003*

(1964), which Hochwälder considers to be a sequel to it,[5] he deals with the spiritual emptiness of modern man. In *Donnerstag*, which uses the Everyman legend as its source, Hochwälder depicts a man who has achieved everything as far as material matters are concerned but feels a nagging sense of insufficiency and incompleteness. Hochwälder's Everyman is N. M. Pomfrit, an enormously successful architect who has designed every kind of building imaginable. As a symbol of the spiritual sterility of man in modern society the figure of the successful architect could hardly be improved upon since prominence in that profession can be attained only by a single-minded devotion to the principle of functionalism. The seven lamps of architecture have never even been lit for Pomfrit: his life, like his buildings, is without inspiration. His search for faith, hope and love is shown as a struggle between the orthodox virtues of the Everyman legend and modern materialism. The diabolic side of the struggle is represented here with incisive appropriateness by a huge industrial concern headed by a Chief Engineer (the Devil) which offers faith, hope and love in the form of our mass media-induced dreams of perfection: magically appearing electronic appliances, "freedom" through space travel and other modern versions of alchemy, and animated nubile cover-girls. Poor Pomfrit strives pitifully to find the truth and become free, but is, of course, doomed from the start because of his conditioning.[6] In *1003* (the title refers to the number of Don Juan's Spanish seductions) Hochwälder continues the theme of sterility as he shows a playwright attempting to write about modern man conversing with the character he has created and realizing that this "character" is only an aspect of his own personality. Both these plays are experimental in form and suffer from Hochwälder's reliance

5. Fritz Hochwälder, "Über mein Theater," *Wort in der Zeit*, XII, iii (1966), p. 62.

6. For an excellent analysis of this play, cf. Herbert Knust, "Moderne Variationen des Jedermann-Spiels," in Sheema Z. Buehne, James L. Hodge, and Lucille B. Pinto, eds., *Helen Adolf Festschrift* (New York: Ungar, 1968), pp. 309–41.

on the monologue as a substitute for plot.

In his two latest and best plays Hochwälder returns to the conventional plot structure at which he excels. *Der Himbeerpflücker* (The Raspberry Picker, 1964) takes place in a remote village in the Austrian Alps. Twenty-five years earlier the village had been prosperously located next to a thriving concentration camp. Now the place is run-down and dull, somewhat like Dürrenmatt's Güllen, and the inhabitants nostalgically bemoan the golden days that are gone when the smartly-uniformed and well-paid guards from the camp made the village a place worth living and doing business in. One man in particular they remember: a sharpshooting enthusiast who used to order the inmates to gather raspberries from a clump of bushes in a little hollow next to the camp and then amuse himself and the fawning villagers by picking them off with his high-powered, telescopic-lens rifle. The "raspberry picker," as he was known, escaped, leaving a hoard of gold with the innkeeper. The play concerns the reactions of the villagers to their erroneous conviction that the "raspberry picker"—actually a small-time jewel thief and con man who faints at the thought of blood—has returned. All their hero-worship of the man revives, and their only concern is saving the murderer from retribution. Hochwälder achieves superb ironic effect when he shows the reaction to the news that the Nazi mass-murderer is actually a half-Jewish confidence man. No one dreams that he has done any wrong, of course: the whole affair is put down as another instructive lesson in diabolic Jewish underhandedness. This play is one of the most scathing indictments—not least because it is hilariously funny—of the survival of Nazism in Austria.

Der Befehl (*The Command*, 1965), an equally powerful play,[7] repeats this theme in an urban setting. A Chief Inspector in the Vienna police is given the assignment of discovering the murderer of a Dutch resistance leader's child during the war. The inspector, who has been suffering from amnesia, discovers

7. Translated by Robin Hirsch in *Modern International Drama*, Vol. IV, No. 1 (1970).

that he is himself the criminal he has been ordered to pursue. He is killed when he deliberately exposes himself to a cornered criminal's fire, and his assistant tells the father of the girl, now a prominent Dutch official, that the murderer is anyone he might see by looking out of his hotel window.

With his two latest plays Hochwälder has made the most successful attempt to date to analyze the mentality of the people who supported Nazism—a far more subtly psychological view than the better-known but more simplistic one of Rolf Hochhuth.

The New English Dramatists
The Experimentalists

THE DRAMATIC avant-garde movement has flourished in
England like aspidistra in the Gobi desert. The old cliché about
the hidebound Englishman is nowhere so true as in art. This is
not to say that the Englishman is incapable of holding revolutionary ideas. Slow as the English nation as a whole has always
been to change and adapt, individual Englishmen have tradi-
tionally burst forth with visionary religious ideas or radical
political ones that have made the most independent thinkers of
other nations blench. These revolutionary ideas, however, have
always appeared *sub rosa*, so to speak. As Shaw pointed out, the
English seem to associate art with "immorality," i.e., socially
rebellious conduct, and too often regard the practicing artist in
somewhat the same light as a paroled felon: they await with
bated breath the appearance of any overt aberration from the
norm. Then they pounce—or, rather, they blandly disregard.
The effect is the same: the artist is crushed. It is not surprising,
therefore, that the English artist shies away from experimentation with the techniques of his craft. There are always plenty
of new *ideas* floating around the back streets of Hampstead and
Chelsea, but there are hardly ever any new *forms*. The play of
traditional construction with realistic dialogue is still the form
British authors seem instinctively to turn to. For the most part
the young British dramatists appear to be unaware of the avant-
garde movement of Beckett, Ionesco, Genet, and Adamov in
France; Martin Esslin quite correctly includes only Harold

Pinter and N. F. Simpson in his survey of the theatre of the absurd. Failure to adhere to the principles of the avant-garde drama is, of course, not in itself a crime. The drama of protest—the only kind of worthwhile and serious drama—can be incorporated just as well (*vide* Shaw) within the framework of the conventional play form.

The rapturous ecstasy with which the English critics have received the "new British drama" represented by Harold Pinter, John Osborne, Bernard Kops, Arnold Wesker, John Mortimer, Shelagh Delaney, N. F. Simpson, Doris Lessing, Nigel Dennis, Brendan Behan, and John Arden would seem to indicate that the English theater has undergone its greatest renaissance since the days of Elizabeth I. Unhappily, this is not the case. The English critics have apparently been overcome by the sudden flood of competently written dramas produced in the latter part of the nineteen-fifties. Their critical faculties dulled by this unexpected eruption, they have been pontificating about the regeneration of the English theater and the rebirth of intellectual responsibility in the English drama. To critics fed for so long on the post-Pinerotic pap of the West End drama, the plays of the new English dramatists necessarily seem masterpieces. Unfortunately, one is forced to suspect that much of this enthusiasm is attributable to thankfulness for boredom relieved and for national sensitivities assuaged.

HAROLD PINTER
The Comedy of Allusiveness

HAROLD PINTER has an extremely acute sense of stage situations—a perception of what will "go" on stage. In all of his plays, static and incomprehensible though they may often seem, Pinter demonstrates a truly extraordinary ear for the speech patterns of ordinary people, as well as a highly developed ability to create interest and suspense by means of a series of momentarily sustained conflicts. The dialogue in Pinter's plays fascinates by its very monotony and repetitiousness because the audience *recognizes* it—they have heard this sort of talk before. Ionesco does the same thing with ordinary speech patterns in *The Bald Soprano,* but whereas he deliberately extends the monotony and repetitiousness until they become caricature, Pinter knows where to stop: precisely where real-life speech patterns stop. Pinter uses human dialogue as a verbal sparring match in which the participants feint and parry with words to avoid involvement with each other. His characters are not strapped tight within separate cocoons, as Adamov's and Ionesco's are: they remain convinced, just as ordinary people do in reality, that they *can* touch each other with the verbal jabs they flick out, but they live in terror of the moment when they will hit their mark.[1]

Pinter himself has indicated that his purpose is to observe what happens to people.[2] In order to do this, he usually chooses as his central image a room—any ordinary room where people live—to serve as a microcosm of the world. In the room people feel safe. Outside are only alien forces; inside there is warmth and light. It is a womb in which people can feel secure. The conflict in Pinter's plays occurs when one of the outside forces penetrates into the room and disrupts the security of its occupants. Pinter's role is that of dispassionate observer, and much of the apparent difficulty of his plays stems from the fact that he writes them as if he were eavesdropping on his characters and recording their often pointless stream of consciousness. He has described the genesis of three of his most important plays as coming from a simple curiosity as to what could happen to two people in a room: "*The Room* came after going into a room with one person standing and one sitting. *The Birthday Party* after going into a room with two persons sitting. *The Caretaker* after looking into a room with two persons standing." [3]

1. Bernard Dukore, "The Theatre of Harold Pinter," *Tulane Drama Review*, VI (March, 1962), p. 48.

2. Martin Esslin, *The Theatre of the Absurd* (Garden City, N. Y.: Doubleday & Company, Inc., 1961), p. 199.

3. Harold Pinter, "Writing for Myself," *Twentieth Century*, CLXIX (February, 1961), p. 174.

The Room (1957), Pinter's first play, is a simple story about two people living in a tiny globe of light set in an immense and menacing void of darkness. People venture out into the dark occasionally, but only fearfully and unwillingly. People come in from the dark occasionally, but only to bring danger to the people in the light. The room is inhabited by an elderly couple. The man has to go out and the woman is left alone. We learn that she never goes out and that she does not even know how the house she lives in is laid out. Furthermore, the landlord, who has lived there for years and years, does not know either. When the woman goes to put out the garbage, she finds a young couple standing at the door. Coming as they do from the mysterious, nebulous outer regions, their sudden appearance has a distinctly eerie effect, which is intensified when they inform the woman that they have been wandering all over the house for a long time without finding any light except that in the room. They are looking for living quarters, they tell the woman, and while groping around the pitch-black basement they heard a disembodied voice politely telling them that No. 7 was to let. The woman tells them that they are in No. 7 but that she intends to stay. She ushers them out, but her sense of security has been shattered: the outer forces are beginning to encroach on her. Then the landlord comes in and tells her that a mysterious stranger has been waiting for days to see her. He has been patiently lying in the damp basement waiting for her husband to go out. The woman is unwilling to see anyone, but the landlord insists and brings in an old blind Negro. The Negro seems to know her, although she frantically denies knowing him. Her name is Rose but he calls her Sal, apparently a childhood name, for she seems to recognize it, and tells her he has a message from her father asking her to come home. The husband returns and speaks for the first time. When he has finished boasting about how fearlessly he drove his van along the dark, icy roads, he sees the Negro, kicks him out of his chair, and beats him unconscious (possibly he kills him). Rose suddenly screams that she is blind, and the curtain falls.

The Room shows all the defects of a first play by a young author, but it also shows the germs of Pinter's very consider-

able technical skill. As a mood piece—the mood being horror
—the play is excellent—almost a subdued Grand Guignol piece.
Unfortunately, Pinter has spoiled the play by succumbing to
the temptation to put in some juvenile symbolism. With the
entry of the blind Negro, whatever he represents, the play disintegrates. The Negro may symbolize death, the woman's past,
or some hidden guilt complex—probably the latter, since she
is struck blind when her husband beats the Negro. But there
is no hint as to what his function really is nor as to why the
husband beats him so savagely. He is simply an emissary from
the outside who has succeeded in breaking into the circle of
light. As a result, the womb is broken, and the dwellers are
cast out from the light into the darkness.

The Dumb Waiter (1957–1960), another one-act play about
a room, is far more successful. Here we have a pure Grand
Guignol play. Two men are staying in a miserably furnished
room that does not even (horrors!) have proper facilities for
making tea. The men chat about football teams and various
items in the newspaper. As they talk, Pinter very skillfully makes
us gradually aware that the two men are hired killers under
the orders of a mysterious, hierarchical organization, which
sends them around the country murdering people. All their
time is spent in various rooms to which they are sent awaiting
their next assignment. Like Rose in The Room, they feel
secure in their haven, although, knowing they will have to go
out soon, they are made extremely jumpy by any signs of intrusion from the outside. Pinter creates a really remarkable effect
of suspense by simply having footsteps approach the door. An
envelope is then shoved under the door and the footsteps fade
away. The gunmen put their revolvers away and breathe easily
again. Some more casual talk ensues, and then suddenly a
dumbwaiter, hitherto unnoticed by the two men, starts operating at the rear of the room. The two "torpedoes," Ben and
Gus, find a waiter's order slip on it. They decide that there
must be a restaurant above and that they are in what used to
be the kitchen. (In England the kitchens of restaurants are
usually below the dining room and communication between
the two is maintained by means of a dumbwaiter.) Frantically

Ben and Gus search their pockets for food and send whatever scraps they have. The dumbwaiter comes down again and again bearing orders for progressively more and more exotic food. Pinter plays with this excursion into pure absurdity for all it is worth, since he uses it to lead into the contrast with his "shock-of-horror" climax. Gus goes into the next room (out of the safe world in Pinter's system) and Ben receives some instructions through the dumbwaiter's speaking tube. When Gus comes back he is stripped down to his shirt and his gun is gone. As the curtain falls we realize that Ben has been ordered to kill his partner.

In Pinter's full-length play, *The Birthday Party* (1958), we catch more than ever the quality of allusiveness that seems to pervade all of his works. I am not, obviously, implying that Pinter is a plagiarist. His works simply tend to remind one of other works in an allusive manner—in a manner, that is to say, as if Pinter had been unconsciously influenced by something he had read. There would be nothing wrong with this, of course, even if the influence were markedly direct: a writer should be judged not by the originality of his plots but by his treatment of them. And Pinter's treatment of his plots is for the most part masterly. What I mean by Pinter's allusiveness is that reading *The Room* reminds one of Beckett—specifically, of the atmosphere of a Beckett play. Similarly, reading *The Dumb Waiter* makes one think that Pinter has remembered a distant Grand Guignol play. *The Birthday Party* irresistibly reminds one of Hemingway's "The Killers."

The Birthday Party is about the death of Stanley Weber, a small-time piano player who had apparently once offended some extremely powerful forces. He has been hiding out in a seedy rooming house in a seaside resort town, thinking himself safe from pursuit. He does not seem to know in what way precisely he has offended his pursuers. All he knows is that his promising career as a piano player was ruined when his second concert was called off without warning. His description of this incident in his life reads like a paranoid's nightmare:

STANLEY: Played the piano? I've played the piano all over the world. All over the country. (*Pause.*) I once

gave a concert . . . Yes. It was a good one, too. They were
all there that night. Every single one of them. It was a
great success. Yes. A concert. At Lower Edmonton. . . .
I had a unique touch. Absolutely unique. They came up
to me. They came up to me and said they were grateful.
Champagne we had that night, the lot. . . . My father
nearly came down to hear me. Well, I dropped him a card
anyway. But I don't think he could make it. No, I—I lost
the address, that was it. . . . Yes. Lower Edmonton. Then
after that, you know what they did? They carved me up.
Carved me up. It was all arranged, it was all worked out.
My next concert. Somewhere else it was. In winter. I went
down there to play. Then, when I got there, the hall was
closed, the place was shuttered up, not even a caretaker.
They'd locked it up. . . . A fast one. They pulled a fast
one. I'd like to know who was responsible for that. . . . All
right, Jack, I can take a tip. They want me to crawl down
on my bended knees. Well I can take a tip . . . any day
of the week.[4]

Soon after, two ordinary-looking men, an Irishman and a Jew,
rent rooms in the house. It soon becomes apparent that their
job is the same as Gus and Ben's in The Dumb Waiter—they
have been sent by some mysterious, high-up power to kill
Stanley.

Pinter's handling of the scenes in which McCann and
Goldberg appear is masterful. The two killers become more
and more sinister, and the horror of the situation accumulates
as the audience contrasts its knowledge of the two men's real
function with their behavior. Goldberg, the leader of the two
killers, is portrayed alternately as a stock East End Jew, replete
with nostalgic memories of his Mamma's gefilte fish and sen-
tentious maxims about familial togetherness, and as a cold-
blooded hoodlum who has killed dozens of people. He talks
about his eminence as a murderer with the same complacent
pride that a bright young executive might talk of his rise from

4. Harold Pinter, The Birthday Party and The Room (New York:
Grove Press, 1961), pp. 23–24.

an office-boy's job; and he steadies the less-experienced Mc-Cann's nerves in the manner of a football coach reassuring a third-string halfback before his first big game. They organize a birthday party for Stanley although the latter keeps insisting that it is not his birthday. However, it makes no difference what Stanley says. As soon as he learns that one of the visitors is named Goldberg, he seems to know he is doomed, and from that point on he acts like an ox being led to slaughter. During the party, in which he is an unwilling participant, Stanley breaks down and goes berserk. On the next day he comes down from his room dressed in formal funeral clothes. He seems to have no will of his own anymore; and he is in fact nothing but a walking corpse by this time. Goldberg and McCann take him away in a big, black, hearselike car with a large ("There's just room . . . for the right amount.") trunk.

The Birthday Party is Pinter's best play, and in it he has made his closest approach to the French avant-garde school. Both the first-act–curtain scene where Stanley marches round the room frenziedly beating on a toy drum and the second-act–curtain scene in which Stanley goes berserk during a game of blindman's buff and tries to strangle one woman and rape another would have been highly approved of by Antonin Artaud.[5]

Pinter again uses his "room" theme here, but this time he uses it far more effectively than in the two previous plays. In *The Room* and *The Dumb Waiter* the enclosed space was a safe place in a vaguely defined void. Characters ventured out of the room occasionally—when they had to—but never seemed really to know what the outside was like. It was as if only the room *really* existed—a snug refuge in a sea of impersonal hostility, like an igloo on an ice floe. In *The Birthday Party* there is nothing sinister or undefined about the outside world, and

5. This approximation of Artaud's ideas appears to be fortuitous. Pinter has specifically rejected the suggestion that he has a preconceived plan or idea before writing a play. His dramas grow out of an imaginative development of characters in a situation (Esslin, *op. cit.*, p. 205). Pinter, in other words, claims, like Shaw, that his plays are not planned in advance, but grow naturally as he writes them, as if he were recording the conversation and actions of characters performing in his mind.

the room is a refuge only for Stanley. Stanley, we learn, never leaves the house. He is conscious of guilt, and the area outside the house seems sinister only to him because it is from there that retribution will come. It does not matter that the retribution is unjust or that he has convinced himself it is unjust. Justice does not enter into the matter. The victim's viewpoint is not important. Stanley might be anyone, and he might not have done anything in particular. He has simply perceived his own helplessness, has recognized the illusory solidity of the bulwarks every person builds around himself. The anesthetic of existence as a social being has worn off for Stanley and he is thus exposed to the vengeful and implacable "forces" that govern human existence. On one level Goldberg and McCann are certainly emissaries of the hostile, unknowable power that takes the place of God in the avant-garde drama's philosophical view of the human condition.[6] But they are also at the same time ordinary, common-or-garden killers on the temporal level of the play's action. It is the contrast made by their macabre casualness and their victim's conscious helplessness that gives the play its ironic force. Stanley's "birthday party" is really his death, and when he comes down the next day in striped trousers, black jacket, white collar, and bowler hat, it is as if he had already been laid out in his coffin. Like two particularly unctuous funeral directors, Goldberg and McCann lead Stanley, who is now moving with the robotlike gestures of a somnambulist, out to the big black car; and he disappears forever from the sight of his friends, who notice nothing wrong. They will simply go on living and forget. Like Stanley they have amounted to nothing in life, but unlike him they do not know it. Stanley knew and therefore had to pay the penalty: he is dissolved and washed away, like the victims of Peer Gynt's button-molder.

In his other full-length play and first big success, *The Caretaker* (1960), Pinter leaves the macabre and savage humor that

6. Dukore, *op. cit.*, p. 52. Dukore sees Goldberg and McCann as being the agents of society come to pour Stanley into the collective mold. I do not myself feel that Pinter's meaning in this play can be narrowed down so specifically, though Dukore makes out a plausible case for his view by citing Goldberg's constant use of clichés.

characterized his previous plays and takes us to a Beckett-like static drama about three men who are waiting for something that will never come. Again the characters are encased in a room that represents safety. This time the room is a huge, cluttered one on the top floor of a large house, the rest of which is shut up. The house belongs to Mick and is being taken care of by his older brother Aston, who lives in the room. Aston brings Davies, an old tramp whom he has rescued from being beaten up, into the room. Davies turns out to be one of those belligerently self-assertive personalities who feel that everything is theirs by right. As soon as Aston offers to put him up in the room until he can get himself straightened out, Davies starts acting as if the room were his. Gradually he seems to get the idea that he is doing Aston a favor and that Aston's insistence on keeping the room as it has always been is a personal affront to him. Despite Davies's constant nagging dissatisfaction, Aston continues to be kind to him and offers him the job of caretaker while he redecorates the house. He even reveals that he once received electric-shock treatments in a mental institution. Davies cannot resist playing the two brothers off against each other, first trying to persuade Mick (who also offers him the job of caretaker) that his brother is still insane and ought to be put back in the institution; and then, when Mick finds him out, trying to wheedle himself back into Aston's good graces. All that Davies succeeds in doing with his troublemaking is, paradoxically, to bring the brothers closer to each other. At the end Davies is left pleading tearfully and vainly with Aston for another opportunity to "belong."

Like all plays of the avant-garde, *The Caretaker* is open to several interpretations. On the surface it is about two brothers who have drifted away from each other and are now brought closer together again by their contact with a tramp that one of them has taken in. But it is also, like all the plays discussed up to this point, the story of the room in which it takes place. The room is cluttered, dirty, and draughty. The roof leaks, the gas is disconnected, and the sanitary facilities are of the most primitive; but to the three people in the play it represents a haven in which they can hide from the world. To Davies, the homeless old tramp, it comes to be a place where he can settle down at last; and, insofar as the play is a tragedy, it is the tragedy of his failure to qualify for a place in this contracted, modern-world paradise because of his inability to curb his natural maliciousness. To Aston it is a refuge from the world with which he was unable to cope. As long as he remains in the room and keeps his mind strictly on the needs of the house which he is supposed to be decorating, he is safe from the lunatic asylum and the electric-shock treatments. His existence is a careful and deliberate attempt to keep his mind off the things with which he cannot cope by absorbing himself in the precise, step-by-step performance of routine actions. Throughout the play he calms himself by fiddling with an electric plug he is trying to repair, somewhat in the manner of Hemingway's Nick in "Big Two-Hearted River" going through the routine of fishing to keep his mind off less pleasant things. To Mick, the younger brother, the room is a haven in reserve. He does not live in it, but keeps it as a place to fall back on. The bed Davies sleeps on is his, and his antagonism to Davies when he first meets him and later when he chases him round the dark room with the vacuum cleaner is based on his fear of being dispossessed. All three men—Aston, Mick, and Davies —are waiting for something that the audience realizes will never happen. Like the two tramps in *Waiting for Godot*, they are marking time through life, buoying themselves up with the hope of an unattainable ideal. Davies's one thought in life is to get down to Sidcup and recover the papers that will prove his identity. Aston's one thought in life is to build the shed in the garden, the symbol of his recovered sanity. And Mick dreams of someday turning the run-down old house into a nightmarishly tasteless parody of a millionaire's penthouse apartment with teal-blue, copper, and parchment linoleum squares, oatmeal tweed armchairs, and mahogany and rosewood bedroom furniture. None of these things will ever happen, but they will go on thinking about them; and in thinking about them they will obtain the illusion of having a purpose in life.[7]

Harold Pinter has also written a number of minor plays for radio and television. These include A *Slight Ache*, A *Night Out*, *The Dwarfs*, *The Collection*, and *The Lover*.

A *Night Out* (1960), is a slight, though well-written, reversion to the conventional play form. The allusiveness here is to Sidney Howard's *The Silver Cord* as Pinter tells the story of a young man helplessly shackled to a self-pitying, domineering mother. He has one outburst of defiance as he threatens to hit his mother with an alarm clock and rushes out of the house. He allows himself to be picked up by a prostitute and at last it looks as if the cord is to be snapped. But all he is capable of doing is a repeat of the scene with his mother. His rage is merely transferred to the prostitute and he threatens her with the alarm clock and says to her all the things he has never dared to say to his mother. Then he goes home and resumes his "little boy" role. In its way this play is a small masterpiece. The only trouble is that ever since Freud popularized it, the mother-fixation theme has become commonplace in literature and consequently no longer carries the shock value it still ought to have.

In A *Slight Ache* (1959) and *The Dwarfs* (1906), both radio plays, Pinter has gone to the extreme limits of possible experimentation with breakdown of form. These plays are formless even for radio, where, of course, a much looser form is possible in the first place. Both plays are concerned with the elusiveness of identity, a favorite theme of the modern avant-garde drama. In A *Slight Ache* a self-satisfied writer of philosophi-

---

7. *The Caretaker* has been interpreted in a number of different ways, all of which suffer from being too specific. Bernard Dukore (*op. cit.*, p. 50) sees Aston as the one-time social rebel rendered impotent by society through the symbolic brain operation. Ruby Cohn (*Tulane Drama Review*, VI [March, 1962], pp. 55–68) suggests that Mick and Aston represent the System, which crushes Davies. They tantalize him with faint hope in order to crush him all the more completely at the end. J. R. Taylor sees the whole play as an elaborate plot by Mick to get rid of Davies with Aston's unconscious consent so that he can continue rehabilitating his brother (Taylor, *Anger and After* [London: Methuen & Co., Ltd., 1962], pp. 246–47). To Esslin (*op. cit.*, p. 211) Davies's expulsion takes on "the cosmic proportion of Adam's expulsion from Paradise."

cal essays talks to a mysterious old matchseller who has been standing outside his cottage for weeks without selling anything. The matchseller makes no response to the writer, and gradually the latter's self-confidence breaks down as he goes on talking. At the end he has been so reduced by the long monologue in which he has inadvertently demonstrated his own emptiness that his wife hands him the tray of matches and goes off with the silent old man.

The Dwarfs is more complicated. Here there are three characters, Len, Pete, and Mark, who fade in and out and seem at some points to merge with each other. Pinter is talking here mainly in some personal nightmarish symbols about the sinister army of dwarfs which has invaded the world and is insidiously ruining it. There are also vague suggestions that Len is a Christ figure ("They make no hole in my side. They make a hole in my side.") and equally vague suggestions that Mark is a papal symbol. Mark has a particular key, he is of Latin origin, he has a ring, he bets on the "treble chance," and so forth. Pinter keeps everything deliberately vague and allusive, and it is impossible to get anything definite out of the play at all.

In The Collection (1961) and The Lover (1963), both originally written for television, Pinter has turned to a rather enigmatic drawing-room comedy style. His television plays give the impression of perfect familiarity and straightforwardness, but they leave the spectators asking themselves, "What on earth was he really talking about?" There is little possibility that The Collection and The Lover will be successful television plays in the United States, where the audiences demand not only a schoolmasterish clarity but also an ostentatiously gleaming sexual purity culminating in a "moral" ending unexceptionable to even the most rabidly sensitive of the indigenous Puritan groups. In Britain, however, the home audience seems to be made of sterner stuff, for they were able to accept even The Birthday Party: "While viewers were clearly exasperated by the lack of the cheap and obvious motivation to which they were used in their daily fare, they were also visibly intrigued. For days one could hear people in buses and canteens eagerly discussing the play as a maddening but deeply disturbing experience." [8] In the United States, unhappily, there would only be exasperation at the lack of obvious motivation.

Although *The Collection* would be impractical for American television, it has been produced successfully on the off-Broadway stage. Both this play and *The Lover* are concerned in a milder and much less agonized way, with the same problem that obsesses Genet: "What is a person's reality?" To Genet human beings are composed of layer upon layer of illusion draped around a nonexistent core; to Pinter human beings are simply inscrutable, to themselves as well as to others. They may be emptiness surrounded by illusion, but they may also, without knowing it, possess a solid center of reality. The point is that they do not know and are too frightened to find out. It is in *The Collection* and *The Lover* that the image of Pinter's dialogue being like a verbal sparring match in which the participants are always just barely keeping out of each other's reach becomes really pertinent. Even more so is the comment which Pinter wrote for the program of *The Room* and *The Dumb Waiter* when they were performed at the Royal Court Theatre:

> The desire for verification is understandable but cannot always be satisfied. There are no hard distinctions between what is true and what is false. The thing is not necessarily either true or false; it can be both true and false. The assumption that to verify what has happened and what is happening presents few problems I take to be inaccurate. A character on the stage who can present no convincing argument or information as to his past experience, his present behaviour or his aspirations, nor give a comprehensive analysis of his motives, is as legitimate and as worthy of attention as one who, alarmingly, can do all these things. The more acute the experience the less articulate its expression. [9]

8. Esslin, *op. cit.*, p. 207.
9. Quoted in Esslin, *op. cit.*, p. 206.

This is precisely the case in *The Collection*, which is about four people, each emotionally affecting all the others, yet none ever succeeding in actually touching one of them and making sense to him. The plot revolves around the question whether or not two of the characters slept together while attending a dress designers' convention in the north of England. The wife comes home and for no discernible reason (is she trying to reach him?) gives her husband a circumstantial and highly spiced account of how she spent a night in bed with someone else. The husband (his name is Horne, interestingly enough) visits his rival and taxes him with his wife's story. The rival denies everything at first, but then, when Horne's urbanely casual manner changes to a thinly veiled menace, corroborates the wife's story, even going so far as to add a juicy detail or two of his own. Horne goes home to brood and be urbanely casual with his wife, and the audience sits back with a sigh of contentment as it recognizes the unfolding of another familiar "eternal triangle" drama. But with Pinter the sides of the triangle obstinately refuse to fit together. It appears that Bill, the rival, is being kept by Harry Kane, an older man, who naturally does not care to have his domestic arrangements spoiled by his protégé's philanderings, hypothetical or otherwise. Harry goes to see the wife and gets her to admit she made the whole thing up. Confronted with this evidence, Bill switches his story again and agrees that nothing happened. Horne goes home and appeals to his wife for confirmation of the new story. The curtain falls as she looks at him enigmatically.

The Lover is specifically written with television-production techniques in mind and would require considerable rewriting for transfer to the stage. This has now been done. As it stands, in its original form, it is one of the most brilliant plays to appear in the English language since the end of the war. The opening scene shows a stuffy businessman leaving his suburban home to go to the city and politely inquiring whether his wife plans to entertain her lover that day. The wife replies that she does and asks him to come home late. Then she transforms herself into a seductive siren and awaits her lover. The bell rings and she goes to answer the door. It is her husband. In the second act we see that these two are in the habit of playing out a series of interlocking semisadistic fantasy scenes which all culminate in an aggressive entrapment of one partner by the other. The allusiveness here is to Genet's *The Balcony*, but although the sexual fantasies remind one of the three opening scenes of that play, Pinter's purpose is not the same as Genet's. Genet's characters indulged in their sadistic fantasies to give themselves the illusion of being someone, whereas Pinter's indulge in them in order to achieve sexual potency. They can achieve physical communication only through an elaborate bypassing of emotional communication. The sterility, both physical and emotional of this typical modern couple is so great that they can come close to each other only in a fantasy world. During the play the husband tries to break out of this vicious circle where illusion equals sexual potency equals mutual understanding equals illusion, but the wife is too far gone and frantically appeals to him to continue the game. In the end he yields, and they drift off into their fantasy life again. *The Lover* is Pinter's bitterest, most cogent, and most expertly written statement of his belief that the tragedy of people today is their "deliberate evasion of communication." [10]

The evasion of communication is carried to its ultimate point in *The Homecoming* (1965), which resembles nothing so much as a gathering of like magnetic poles circling round each other and always repelling each other just at the edge of communication. Set in a large, seedy house in North London, the play shows the effect on his family of the unexpected return of the eldest son, a professor of philosophy at an American university, together with his wife. With his glossy academic patina, Teddy hardly seems to fit into his coarse family circle anymore. He has been away for six years, having married Ruth, a local girl and, as it turns out, former prostitute, just before leaving. The family is completely unaware of the marriage,

10. Statement of Pinter in an interview with Kenneth Tynan, quoted in Esslin, *op. cit.*, p. 207.

which has produced three boys back in America. During the course of the play Ruth is persuaded to abandon Teddy and throw in her lot with the family while he returns to America and the children. To pay her way she agrees to return to prostitution and to service the family in her spare time. Teddy, totally unmoved by all this, leaves.

A plot as strange as this is inexplicable in itself. In the attempt to find a specific meaning one finds oneself making elaborate analyses to no end. An easy way out of the dilemma would be to dismiss the play as wilful nonsense or as a hoax by Pinter, who really *was* writing plays as the result of walking into rooms [11] and is now turning the tables on critics who have insisted on saddling him with hidden meanings. Easy ways out, however, are out of style. And while it is not at all clear, there is definitely a mythic sub-text running through this play. More than in Pinter's previous plays, the dialogue and plot in *The Homecoming* are a protective topsoil covering the fertile ground beneath.

Richard Schechner's remark that the play is "a probe of the dark male attitudes toward the 'mother-whore' and the equally compelling female desire to play this double role," [12] seems to me a provocative suggestion that is definitely on the right track. Schechner also suggests that Teddy, very much a man of this family despite his superficial differences, has deliberately brought Ruth back "to be devoured" by the family, which she then enslaves herself.[13] Teddy's attitude towards the loss of his wife, which I do not believe he intended, could be explained better, though, as an exaggerated exercise in disassociation from emotion, a practical application of his philosophy, such as it is: "It's a way of being able to look at the world. It's a question of how far you can operate on things and not in things." [14] Teddy is the only one to verbalize this disassociation from emotion, but I believe that this, together with the

11. Cf. *supra*, p. 225.
12. Richard Schechner, "Puzzling Pinter," *TDR*, XI, ii (1966), p. 183.
13. *Ibid.*
14. Harold Pinter, *The Homecoming* (New York: Grove Press, 1966), p. 61.

bisexuality of virtually all the characters (which is the reason for the disassociation of personality), is the key to the sense of the play. Perhaps the best image for the action of the play would be a magnetic ballet in which all the characters circle each other with their like (or repelling) poles toward each other. The two poles that each character possesses are the male and female poles of his nature. Only Sam, who neither repels nor attracts but is uncharged, does not have this double nature, for he has never grown to the point at which natures split (i.e., pubescence). The others, including the dead matriarch Jessie, all have bisexual natures, the female/mother pole representing real dominance and the male/child pole representing spurious dominance. Jessie and Ruth are essentially the same, the latter replacing the deceased mother, without whom the household under the feeble aegis of Max's female pole has been sputtering along lamely. When she first appears Ruth *seems* to be diffident and unsure of herself but is actually extending her strongest pole, the feminine mother-whore, which attracts the infantile males who think *they* are seducing *her*. At the end Ruth, like Jessie before her, is the Queen Bee surrounded by her adoring drones. She has become the head of the household in effect, has assumed the trappings of temporal leadership, characteristic of the male side of nature, and, in being pampered and protected by the others, reverts instinctively to the semi-infantile male side of her nature. She remains fully feminine at the same time and thus completely in control since she now has both poles at her call in the magnetic dance. Max, as already noted, has been wavering between the two sides of his nature since his wife's death (he cooks and uses effeminate expressions alternately with being the domineering father); with Ruth's coming he is released and can revert to the infantile male role. At the end he crawls babbling to Ruth, who will, of course, repel him. Ruth's desertion leaves Teddy, who has displayed the gloss of masterful maleness all through the play, free to swing to the female pole of his nature as he returns to America to mother his three children. Lenny and Joey show this split to a slightly less obvious extent. Both of them display strong, masterful natures, Lenny as the swaggering man-of-the-world, Joey as the muscular destroyer; and both of them are captured and attracted by Ruth's stronger female pole, revolving in orbit around her at the end. Like Schnitzler, Pinter has written a profound, Freud-inspired play about the round-dance of sex; but whereas in Schnitzler the pattern is that of a neat circle, in Pinter it is that of randomly dancing atoms whose sexual charges occasionally lead them into temporary molecular clusters.

In July, 1969, Pinter produced two minor plays, *Landscape* and *Silence,* which seem to indicate a new direction in his work. Both of these plays are in the style of Tardieu's *La Sonate,*[15] although the direct influence is obviously the later Beckett. In *Landscape* a man and a woman, apparently husband and wife, sit in the kitchen of a large country house of which they are the caretakers talking, but not to each other. Each follows his own thoughts, the speeches interweaving and counterpointing each other. The man speaks to the woman about the things he did yesterday and today, but she does not hear. The woman speaks, but not to her husband, nor does he hear her. Her mind is fixed on nostalgic reminiscences of the past, in which she takes refuge from the sordid present and from growing old. *Silence* is a considerably looser combination of three voices—one woman and the two men with whom she is involved. In these two short plays Pinter seems to be approaching a static type of drama of the kind toward which Beckett has been working. They are not, however, in any way slavish imitations of Beckett but logical developments of his own work. Never a dramatist of ideas, Pinter is inevitably, though I think unfortunately, coming round to a drama of psychological isolation.

Harold Pinter has established himself as the most promising of England's young playwrights. Without a doubt he has far and away the most original mind (with the possible exception of N. F. Simpson) of any of the new English dramatists,

15. Cf. *supra,* p. 108.

and (again with the exception of Simpson) he is the only one of them who is unafraid to experiment with new dramatic forms and techniques.

N. F. SIMPSON
Parallel to Logic

AMONG THE MORE remarkable results of the current so-called "renaissance" in the English drama has been the work of N. F. Simpson, a London schoolteacher. His four important plays are A Resounding Tinkle, The Hole, One Way Pendulum, and The Cresta Run.[1] Like Alfred Jarry and his descendants, the 'Pataphysicians, Simpson has created a parallel reality that runs alongside our reality and clowns at it. Simpson's way of showing up what he considers the ridiculousness of the world is to create a special world in which reality is satirized by being placed in a new context. His plays, like 'Pataphysics, are a perversion of logic—the impossible carried out in accordance with the laws by which the possible exists.

Someone once said that comedy was the most serious art form. The avant-garde drama is rapidly demonstrating that farce is the most serious of all art forms. The appreciation of farce requires a highly developed sense of the ridiculous and an ability to cut the mind loose from prosaic literalness. These are, unfortunately, rare qualities, so that instead of receiving the wholehearted laughter he deserves, Simpson has all too frequently been the victim of humorlessly obtuse analyses such as John Russell Taylor's. Taylor sees Simpson only as a repetitive prankster whose absurdity "rapidly loses its charms in a life-and-death struggle with the law of diminishing returns."[2] As a contrast to this view, Martin Esslin finds that Simpson *is* a serious artist—"a more powerful social critic than any of the social realists"—whose work culminates in One Way Pendulum with its picture of "a society that has become absurd because

---

1. Simpson has also written a one-act play called The Form. This is a Pinter-type play on shifting identities and not characteristic of Simpson's work.
2. John Russell Taylor, Anger and After (London: Methuen & Co., Ltd., 1962), p. 64.

routine and tradition have turned human beings into Pavlovian automata." [3]

Simpson's first play, A Resounding Tinkle (1957), seems to be an exercise in formlessness and free association which he uses as a vehicle for taking jabs at various aspects of social behavior. Like Ionesco, Simpson favors the average middle-class home as a setting. He gets his humorous and satiric effects by turning the natural events of this setting topsy-turvy. In A Resounding Tinkle, for example, we are in the living room of the Paradock home. Two comedians come in and entertain the Paradocks with a vaudeville skit that has nothing to do with the rest of the play. Then they sit down and get drunk on a purple-colored liquid which is supposed to be nectar and discuss ways of making the audience laugh. There is a great deal of this sort of self-conscious intrusion into the play on Simpson's part—a great deal too much, in fact. A character designated as the author's mouthpiece comes on and discusses the play in a long lecture to the audience, and later a "technician" delivers an oration on the "laughter index" of the audience. Finally Simpson puts a crowd of critics on the stage to deliver their judgments on the play. All of this self-conscious fiddling only tends to detract from the real humor of the play, which lies in such inspired idiocies as the Paradock family's dilemma over an elephant they have purchased, which turns out to be too big for their house. They exchange it for an equally dissatisfied neighbor's python, which is so small it fits into a pencil box.

The only point in the play at which Simpson can be said to be really serious is in his satire on the ritual of religious services. Like Beckett, Simpson takes as the cardinal point of his Weltanschauung the paradox that human thought is useless. Man can know nothing, and his attempts to understand the universe and create a coherent place for himself in it, which have resulted in the elaborately and finely spun opacity of the mental network we call religious ritual, are consequently

3. Esslin, op. cit., p. 224.

nothing but convoluted cerebrations continually twisting round on themselves. This is the central theme which both Beckett and Simpson demonstrate in their plays. The difference between the two, apart from the obvious stylistic one, is in their attitude toward it. Beckett's despair is hidden under a sardonic objectivity and a deliberate choice of laconic and allusive speech patterns. Simpson's attitude, on the other hand, is one of hair-clutching hilarity. To him the world is not so much depressing as ridiculous—and therefore to be laughed at. The paradox renders the world so ridiculous to Simpson that he can express his feelings only in the "beyond realm" of nonsense. He becomes serious only infrequently, whereas Beckett does precisely the opposite: he lights the prevailing gloom with occasional flashes of ribald vaudeville humor.

When Simpson does get serious it is some time before the audience realizes it. The seriousness emerges slowly from the torrent of nonsense, most of which is extremely funny but hardly germane either to the philosophy or to the plot of the play. In A Resounding Tinkle, for example, Mr. and Mrs. Paradock and the two comedians sit down and "have a read" with their afternoon coffee (in the Paradock household it is customary to take a book with one's coffee) when the radio suddenly starts blaring out a divine service. Nobody listens except the First Comedian, who chants the responses under his breath:

> PRAYER: Let us sing because round things roll:
> RESPONSE: And rejoice that it might have been otherwise.
> PRAYER: Let us praise God for woodlice, and for buildings sixty-nine feet three inches high:
> RESPONSE: For Adam Smith's Wealth of Nations published in 1776:
> PRAYER: For the fifth key from the left on the lower manual of the organ of the Church of the Ascension in the Piazza Vittorio Emmanuele II in the town of Castelfidardo in Italy:
> RESPONSE: And for gnats.

PRAYER: How flat are our trays:

RESPONSE: Our sewers how underground and how rat-infested altogether.

. . . .

PRAYER: Let us give thanks for air hostesses and such as sit examinations, for the Bessemer process and for canticles, that all who live in France may be called Frenchmen and that nothing may be called useful that has no purpose.

RESPONSE: Amen.

. . . .

PRAYER: Let us throw back our heads and laugh at reality:

RESPONSE: Which is an illusion caused by mescalin deficiency.

PRAYER: At sanity:

RESPONSE: Which is an illusion caused by alcohol deficiency.

PRAYER: At knowledge which is an illusion caused by certain biochemical changes in the human brain structure during the course of human evolution, which had it followed another course would have produced other biochemical changes in the human brain structure, by reason of which knowledge as we now experience it would have been beyond the reach of our wildest imaginings; and by reason of which, what is now beyond the reach of our wildest imaginings would have been familiar and commonplace. Let us laugh at these things. Let us laugh at thought:

RESPONSE: Which is a phenomenon like any other.

PRAYER: At illusion:

RESPONSE: Which is an illusion, which is a phenomenon like any other.[4]

The same sort of thing occurs in *The Hole* (1957). This one-act play takes place around an open hole in the street.

4. Thomas Maschler, ed., *New English Dramatists 2*. With permission of and copyright © by N. F. Simpson. (Middlesex, England: Penguin Books, 1960), pp. 99–100.

Various people come in and look down into the hole. Each sees there some different aspect of life or each sees some different aspect of the same thing. At the side of the hole sits a queer huddled-up figure, the Visionary, who claims he is forming a one-man queue to see the unveiling of a stained-glass window in the cathedral which he sees in the hole. The other men—Endo, Cerebro, and Soma—represent a more active side of life: they keep seeing games being played in the hole. Dominoes, boxing, badminton, and darts follow each other in rapid succession and are in turn chased away by cards, chess, tennis, high jumping, pool, dice, wrestling, tug of war, and golf. This scene is merely another extension of the "inability to think" theme. Endo, Cerebro, and Soma are always looking for evidence of which game is being played but are never able to make up their minds for long since as soon as they have decided on something, some other bit of evidence floats into view and they are up in the air again. The point is that the human mind is not even capable of grasping *empiric* evidence reliably.

There are three main satiric points in the play. The first of these comes when the watchers catch sight of a tennis game in the hole and start calling the score in unison, standing as though for the National Anthem. Later on Simpson brings in an even more effective jab at religious ritual than the one in *A Resounding Tinkle* when the watchers see a lot of fish in the hole and decide that there must be three different tanks down there—three tanks in one or one tank in three, they can't decide which. Then they stand at attention and recite in unison:

> I believe in one aquarium which was and is and shall be; in which shall be comprehended the sprat and the Black Widow; in it the sole and the carp shall swim together, the swordtail and the water-flea; with the gudgeon shall float the mackerel, with the roach the guppy; duckweed shall be there, and foaming moss; neither shall the water at seventy-five degrees Fahrenheit be at variance with the water at forty degrees Fahrenheit, or eschew it. And the

freshwater shall be salt and the saltwater fresh, and no distinction shall be made between them, for all are of one aquarium and there is no other aquarium, but this.[5]

Finally they spot a prisoner pacing his cell in the hole, and here Simpson satirizes the tendency of people to rationalize everything in accordance with convention. To the mass of people, represented here by Endo, Soma, and Cerebro, ethics are relative and depend on the currently accepted prescription:

> SOMA: He has done wrong, and he has chosen to do it illegally.
> CEREBRO: It is the duty of every one of us to avoid those crimes we know to have been blacklisted.
> SOMA: To act otherwise is evil. More than that, it is a breach of the law.[6]

The scene in the prison cell gradually changes to another one in which a particularly brutal ritual murder appears to be taking place. The watchers are horrified, but, being ordinary people, their reaction to horrors is to run around shouting slogans and appeals for someone else to do something, thus salving their own consciences. The play ends with another satiric jab at religion as Soma delivers a mock sermon about an electric junction box with three cables, and possibly a fourth, running out of it. The junction box, which has appeared in the hole, takes the place of the mysteries of religious faith:

> For each time we draw near to the cavity and together peer down into the depths, we are not only giving expression by that act to the unquenchable curiosity that is in us, but we are at the same time reaffirming the truth of the eternal and inscrutable paradox—that it is upon this cavity that we build our faith.[7]

The Hole is undoubtedly Simpson's most trenchantly satiric play. Always maintaining his lofty objective attitude, he ridi-

5. N. F. Simpson, *The Hole* (London: Samuel French, 1958), p. 20.
6. *Ibid.*, p. 23.
7. *Ibid.*, p. 40.

cules the accepted forms of belief and behavior in the manner of a man who feels he ought to cry but cannot stop laughing. Simpson's feeling about the world is somewhat like the one about America expressed by H. L. Mencken when he said that a man would have to have a petrified diaphragm not to laugh himself to sleep every night. This attitude comes out even more strongly in Simpson's most successful play, *One Way Pendulum* (1959). If we are to look for any influence in this play it must be in the work of Alfred Jarry and his cult of 'Pataphysics. As in 'Pataphysics, we have here a deliberate transference of events to a track that runs parallel to conventional logic. 'Pataphysics is the "science of imaginary solutions," a way of protesting against the evils of the world by making fun of the thought processes which created them. This is done by making use of those thought processes to attain utterly ridiculous results. In other words, a new and fantastic world is built up by a strict adherence to a rigid logical system. This method is best described in nontechnical terms by Simpson himself in his dust-jacket note to *One Way Pendulum*. It is, he says, "a gravely serious attempt to make nonsense out of everything, including nonsense. It hopes thereby to arrive from time to time at a kind of sense, but the journey is what really matters. There is a serious side to the play, for those who nevertheless want it but it is right underneath, just above the sump and difficult to get at. . . . It is best left alone . . . it has . . . appeal for those who want . . . a play in which to find whatever it is they are looking for. They will be able to come back to it again and again to see whether what they are looking for has turned up yet or not."

In *One Way Pendulum*, as in all the works of the 'Pataphysicians, a vague aura of discomfort seeps through the curtain of hilarity: when the spectators' laughter is at its peak, it suddenly turns hollow. As in *A Resounding Tinkle*, the setting in *One Way Pendulum* is a banal, middle-class home in which everything seems to be just slightly slanted away from the ordinarily used main track of life. Mr. Groomkirby, the head of the house, "earns his living" by setting up a row of parking meters behind the house and then standing next to

each one for an hour a day so that the sixpence he has put into
it will not be wasted. At the end of the week he empties the
meters and collects the money. The reason he always stands
a full hour next to each meter is that he is afraid he might
lose his own patronage if he feels overcharged. Despite this
rather bizarre method of making money, the Groomkirby
household seems to live fairly comfortably—so much so, indeed, that Mrs. Groomkirby frequently has to hire an enormously fat woman, a professional eater, to come in and eat up
the leftovers. Sylvia, the Groomkirbys' daughter, is fairly normal (comparatively speaking), her only real peculiarity being
a feeling that her arms are too short and a consequent desire to
be turned into an ape. Far and away the most offbeat member
of the family is young Kirby Groomkirby. Kirby lives by logic
alone. Having read Pavlov, he can now do nothing unless he
hears a bell rung first. His one obsession in life is to wear
black, but, being a very logical fellow, he feels he can only wear
black as a sign of mourning for someone he knows. He has
therefore so far approached no less than forty-three strangers,
told them a joke in order to establish acquaintanceship, and
then hit them on the head with a crowbar. He has grown
tired of this, however, because his sense of honor requires him
to think up a new joke for each victim, which can get to be a
bit of a strain, and has now embarked upon his grand project
to keep him legitimately i.e., logically, in mourning for the rest
of his life. He has collected five-hundred "speak-your-weight"
machines—weighing machines, common in England, which
not only show the person's weight but also announce it by
means of an internal recording device—and is teaching them
to sing the Hallelujah Chorus from Handel's *Messiah*. His
intention is to take them all to the North Pole, where he
hopes that the enormous crowds of people who will collect to
hear the machines will be so overcome with amazement that
they will jump up and down to relieve their feelings and thus
cause the earth's axis to shift. This should bring the British
Isles into the polar zone and cause a sufficient number of
people to freeze to death to keep Kirby in mourning for the
rest of his natural life. The details of this diabolical plot come

out at Kirby's trial, which takes place in the Groomkirby living room. Mr. Groomkirby, an amateur of the law, has bought a scale model of the Old Bailey Criminal Court and set it up. As soon as he plugs it in, a judge and other officers of the court appear and proceed to trial. Kirby is found guilty but is let off by the judge for the rather bizarre reason that putting him away would deprive the state of the opportunity of punishing him for any future crimes that he might commit if let go free.

In *The Cresta Run* (1965) Simpson turns his attention to the British Secret Service, which he portrays as inspired bumbling carried to its ultimate extreme. Like *The Hole, The Cresta Run* is a seriously intended and thoroughly acerbic satire as well as an exercise in farcical logic. The plot concerns Sir Francis Harker, head of the British Secret Service, who suffers from "Bolgerhausen's multiple allegiance syndrome"—in other words, from an irresistible urge to betray state secrets. During the play an attack of the dread Bolgerhausen syndrome leads Sir Francis to call on Leonard Fawcett, a mild-mannered and mousy man, and reveal to him the details of a Russian plot to corner all the caviare in England. The British counter-plan set up to thwart this threat has been cut up into sixteen pieces by Sir Francis, each piece contained in a little capsule. Sir Francis asks Fawcett to hide one of these capsules in the hollow ballcock of his lavatory cistern and explains to him how it will eventually be recovered:

> The precise location of this capsule, as of the other fifteen, will be known to only five men. No one of these five is known to the other four. Their first knowledge of one another's identity will be when they meet for the first time under the floorboards of a typical suburban house somewhere in Greater London. . . . To which they will have gone—ostensibly as pest control officers—to inspect the joists for death watch beetle. Now. Each of the five will have brought with him part of a telephone handset . . . These parts, when assembled under the floorboards, will provide the equipment necessary for making an ordinary telephone

call. . . . They will then stage a mock fight. Under the floorboards. All but one will get knocked unconscious, and this one will promptly dial the secret number assigned to him and ask for Bob. This will be the signal to the operator to block all other incoming calls for thirty-five seconds. Among the calls so blocked will be one from a special agent in West Hartlepool, who will have been dialling continuously every ten seconds for six weeks prior to this moment. . . . Now, when he finds his call blocked, he will act quickly, in accordance with sealed instructions which he will have had secreted on his person since the previous October. What these sealed instructions are, I cannot of course divulge . . .[8]

The whole project is almost driven out of Sir Francis's mind altogether by the discovery that the Russians have landed sixteen ostriches equipped with telescopic monocles on the East Coast. Despite this deliberately frivolous nonsense, there is an easily discernible vein of contemptuous commentary on bureaucratic stupidity running through the play, which is far closer to the seriousness of *The Hole* than to the light-hearted juggling of logic for its own sake in *A Resounding Tinkle* and *One Way Pendulum*.

N. F. Simpson's plays are perfect examples of the drama of protest and paradox that sprang directly out of Jarry's *Ubu roi*. Although clearly influenced also by Ionesco, he is of all the current avant-garde dramatists—French or English—perhaps the closest in spirit to Jarry himself.

8. N. F. Simpson, *The Cresta Run* (New York: Grove Press, 1966), pp. 13–14.

The New English Dramatists
The Traditionalists

WITH PINTER and Simpson we come to the end of the experimentalists in the current English drama. The other writers in the English dramatic regeneration are entirely traditional in their technique. The form of any of Wesker's or Kops's or Osborne's plays in no way differs from the form employed by any of the prewar playwrights: it is a direct descendant of the nineteenth century well-made play. This may not seem to be a drawback at first. Form in the drama is, after all, not of primary importance. In drama, content is all-important. If the content of the drama is interesting, then the form of the drama, as long as it is not so disorganized as to interfere with comprehension of the plot, is comparatively unimportant. The form of the drama can, however, increase the scope of the content. A well-made play is confined to the drama of individual relationships and conflicts, whereas the drama of indefinite form (the avant-garde drama, for example) can take the whole cosmos as its field of action. Within their necessarily limited field of endeavor, however, the new dramatists of the traditionalist group do present fresh viewpoints. The new English drama, whether traditional in form and subject or whether imitative of the avant-garde, is a drama of rebellion. Like the French avant-gardists, the English writers are uniformly iconoclastic. Their purpose is protest against things as they are, and their method usually hinges on a central sardonic paradox. They are dramatists without illusions (with the exception of Kops and Wesker): they have looked conditions full in the face and have not flinched from what they have seen. This honesty and courage distinguishes the new English dramatists and differentiates them from their predecessors.

JOHN OSBORNE
"Angry Young Man"?

THE "NEW MOVEMENT" in the British drama actually began officially on the night of May 8, 1956, when John Osborne's Look Back in Anger opened at the Royal Court Theatre in London. The reviews in the daily newspapers the next day were in general cautiously favorable.[1] But it was not until Kenneth Tynan's review came out the following Sunday that the "movement" was properly launched. Tynan climaxed his panegyric by saying, "I agree that Look Back in Anger is likely to remain a minority taste. What matters, however, is the size of the minority. I estimate it at roughly 6,733,000, which is the number of people in this country between the ages of twenty and thirty. And this figure will doubtless be swelled by refugees from other age-groups who are curious to know precisely what the contemporary young pup is thinking and feeling. I doubt I could love anyone who did not wish to see Look Back in Anger. It is the best young play of its decade."[2] This will strike most people as pretentious, self-publicizing gush rather than criticism, but it had its effect. Overnight, Osborne, previously an obscure provincial actor, became famous; and sundry despairing young playwrights who had been furtively scribbling away in seedy rooming houses on the Earl's Court Road, in Hampstead, Hackney, Poplar, Whitechapel, and Newington Butts suddenly took heart and set to with renewed industry. They were fortunate. John Osborne's timing was

1. The full story of the reviews, with excerpts, is very well told in Taylor, op. cit., pp. 31–32.
2. The Observer, May 13, 1956, p. 11.

precisely right. A few years earlier or a few years later *Look Back in Anger* might well have been passed off by the critics as callow breast-beating, but in 1956 the critics and the public were ready for something new. The sincerity of the Osborne play must have come as a tremendous relief after the seemingly endless stream of elephantiasis-afflicted plots trying to be fey that characterized the efforts of the fashionable West End dramatists. There was also the factor of the international success of Arthur Miller and Tennessee Williams. At last someone had appeared who could challenge the Americans' position as representatives of the English-speaking drama. Chauvinism stirred in the critics as they watched *Look Back in Anger*; and the angry-young-man movement was born. Now, one play doth not a movement make; hence the renewed scraping of pens in Earl's Court and Hackney. The new English playwrights got their chance because English national pride was aroused by the success of Osborne's first play.

Look Back in Anger was a rallying point. It came to represent the dissatisfaction with society reflected in the novels of such young writers as John Wain, Kingsley Amis, and John Braine. Jimmy Porter, its rancorous protagonist, was thought to symbolize the fury of the young postwar generation that felt itself betrayed, sold out, and irrevocably ruined by its elders.[3] The older generation had made a thorough mess of things, and there was nothing the new generation could do except withdraw (Jimmy Porter, an educated and cultured university graduate, supports himself by peddling candy in the streets) and indulge in the perverse and vicarious pleasure of nursing its resentment. Society is so rotten that there is no longer any point in attempting to be useful. It is not that Jimmy is *content* to stagnate. He just feels that he has no chance. His withdrawal is not one of choice. He does not even permit himself the consolation of gloating over conditions with the cynical hindsight of superiority. He simply feels

3. Taylor (*op. cit.*, pp. 40–45) recognizes that *Look Back in Anger* is basically a well-made, domestic-psychological drama, but he spoils his analysis by desperately trying to twist it into an angry-young-man play with the aid of isolated passages taken out of context.

himself to be unjustly crushed down with no visible hope of ever getting up again. He reminds one of a fighter who has been knocked down, and, instead of getting up again, just lies there spitting insults at his opponent and grinning with sardonic masochism whenever the latter kicks him in the ribs.

But is this what Osborne really intended when he wrote the play? Or has it been read into it by eager critics who have been searching for a symbol of a new postwar "lost generation" to rival Hemingway's creation of Jake Barnes as a personification of post-World War I disillusionment? Is Jimmy's defeatism a symbol of the numb quiescence of post-World War II youth, as Jake's castration was of the sterile euphoria of post-World War I youth?

John Osborne must have been the most surprised man in England when he suddenly found himself placed at the head of the angry-young-man movement.[4] He had written a carefully and intelligently worked out dramatic study of a psychotic marriage relationship and was hailed instead as the creator of a revolutionary literary movement. Certainly Jimmy Porter makes a good many cutting remarks about contemporary society, but he only makes them as a result of his own peculiar personality problems. There is absolutely no indication in the play that Osborne ever intended Jimmy's remarks to be taken as a general condemnation of society. Jimmy is an extremely unusual young man and anything but representative of the young men of our time. Osborne has not put his diatribes against society in his mouth in order to orate in the manner of a Hyde Park soap-box messiah. Instead, Jimmy's rantings are always the natural outgrowth of his psychotic state: they are a defense mechanism he uses to hurt his wife, whom he suspects of being imperfectly devoted to him, and to avoid facing up to the problem of his own helpless character. Granted that a representative of the generation which reached adulthood in the early fifties would execrate his elders (what generation

4. Osborne himself characterized Look Back in Anger as "a formal, rather old-fashioned play," and said that he did not dare "pick up a copy of Look Back nowadays. It embarrasses me." (John Osborne, "That Awful Museum," Twentieth Century, CLXIX [February, 1961], p. 216).

this side of early Victorianism has not?), his anger could hardly be embodied in Jimmy's rantings if any justice is to be done to him. He has a right to rant and he has a right to be heard; he has a right even to throw up his hands in disgust and retire, whether it be into a Zen or a beatnick euphoria or simply into a flabby, unthinking, irresponsible lassitude. But Jimmy's tirades are not representative of any attitude. Osborne has given Jimmy a certain facility in composing biting remarks, but there is no real sense, no mature criticism in those remarks. Examined closely, Jimmy Porter's self-conscious orations are the·veritablest sophomoric piffle.

Look Back in Anger was strenuously fiddled up into an epoch-making play by the London critics. It is nothing of the sort; but, on the other hand, it is by no means a worthless play either. Osborne has created an excellent, minutely accurate dissection of a perverse marriage in the style of Strindberg. Look Back in Anger irresistibly recalls the Swedish author's Dance of Death. Jimmy Porter's problem is not the vicious injustice and hypocrisy of the social order: it is his suppressed awareness of the insoluble psychological paradox caused by his desperate, overriding need to possess a woman's complete, unquestioning love and his simultaneous constitutional inability to get along with anyone. His outbursts are the overflow of his bitterness whenever his wife fails to measure up to the standards of devotion that he expects of her at the same time that he knows them to be impossible. Jimmy's biting sarcasms are in a sense really directed inwardly against himself in the manner of the guilt-ridden Dostoyevskian hero who tortures himself by torturing others. His real purpose, as he deliberately tries to destroy his wife's love for him because it is not the love he had envisioned, is self-laceration. Jimmy is the sort of man who needs, but is too proud to demand, absolute devotion. He needs it all the more from Alison because she comes from the sort of upper-class family which he, as a good socialist, despises as useless and effete and which at the same time he envies and resents because he knows that it looks down on him. In order to possess her he has had to marry her and submit to the conventionality that he hates. His dilemma is perfectly presented in Alison's description of his reaction to her virginity: "afterwards, he actually taunted me with my virginity. He was quite angry about it, as if I had deceived him in some strange way. He seemed to think that an untouched woman would defile him." [5] By being a virgin she is pulling him into the vortex of social convention. She is what she is *expected* to be in *her* circle. But Jimmy cannot show pleasure because that would be the conventional reaction, though if his wife were not virginal he would have to resent it as evidence of her fickleness. What he really wants, as Alison explains to her friend, Helena (who becomes Jimmy's mistress when Alison leaves him), is "something quite different from us. What it is exactly I don't know—a kind of cross between a mother and a Greek courtesan, a henchwoman, a mixture of Cleopatra and Boswell." [6] Jimmy's tragedy is simply that he will never find this ideal, and he knows it. He will spend the rest of his life bathed in self-pity, yammering impotently at the misfortunes he himself has created.

Osborne's second play, *The Entertainer* (1957), was a clumsily constructed hodgepodge about a talentless vaudeville actor with the morals and feelings of a toad. It is chiefly interesting as a first fumbling attempt at the Brechtian episodic method which Osborne used later in *Luther*.

Epitaph for George Dillon (1958) was actually Osborne's first play, written in collaboration with Anthony Creighton, but it was not produced until the success of *Look Back in Anger* had established Osborne's name as "safe." It deals with a lazy and basically untalented young man who is trying to become a playwright with a minimum of effort. Unable to get anyone interested in his laborious attempts at serious drama, he sells out to a producer of honky-tonk road shows, and then submerges himself completely in the bourgeois milieu that he despises by marrying the brainless daughter of the family that has been supporting him. Dillon is a heartless chiseler, but his

5. John Osborne, *Look Back in Anger* (New York: Bantam Books, 1959), p. 28.
6. *Ibid.*, p. 113.

fall is the fall of the artist who finds the inertia of society too much for him and just gives up.

Another interpretation that could be applied to the play is that it is about the fragility of artistic integrity. Dillon starts out by attempting to be a serious playwright. He tries to gain time and comfort by sponging off an ordinary, middle-class family. He amuses himself by playing the part of the great and enigmatic artist for their benefit and sniggering to himself whenever their backs are turned. But sooner or later his bluff has to be called, and he has to sell out to the honky-tonk promoter to save the image he has manufactured. Someone once said— it was Hemingway, I think—that an artist's integrity is like a woman's virginity: once lost it can never be regained. Dillon illustrates the truth of this perfectly. Once he has compromised himself he *has* to sell out and do hack work. Thus when the family swallows him up at the end, it seems natural and inevitable to us. The power of inner resistance can only be maintained by constant use, Osborne and Creighton are saying; George Dillon bends once and is lost.

By the time *Look Back in Anger* and *The Entertainer* were produced, Osborne had been hailed as the angry young man so much that he had actually become one. If there is a prototype of the angry-young-man play, *The World of Paul Slickey* is it. Written as a musical, it failed when first produced. And no wonder. There is so much direct criticism of society (castigation would perhaps be a better word) in it that just about everyone must have been made uncomfortable. When criticizing social institutions on the stage it is advisable to use the gentle touch if one wishes to have a successful show. People will accept the offhand slaps of a witty mind because if they can laugh at the object of the satire they can feel superior to it: nobody consciously identifies himself with ridiculousness. But even if they will allow themselves to be slapped under the illusion that someone else is being slapped, they will not allow themselves to be openly and directly attacked. Osborne is no George Dillon. He does not compromise. He does not slip unobtrusively under his opponent's guard: he beats it down with a two-fisted attack. He is an angry young man, not a contemptuous one. *The World of Paul Slickey* is pure spit and vomit thrown directly into the teeth of the audience. Commercially it has been Osborne's least successful play; artistically it is his best. Inability to compromise may be disastrous from a diplomatic viewpoint, but art is not diplomacy: it is truth.

In his dedication Osborne leaves no doubt as to his intentions:

> No one has ever dedicated a string quartet to a donkey although books have been dedicated to critics. I dedicate this play to the liars and self-deceivers; to those who daily deal out treachery; to those who handle their professions as instruments of debasement; to those who, for a salary cheque and less, successfully betray my country; and those who will do it for no inducement at all. In this bleak time, when such men have never had it so good, this entertainment is dedicated to their boredom, their incomprehension, their distaste. It would be a sad error to raise a smile from them. A donkey with ears that could listen would no longer be a donkey; but the day may come when he is left behind because the other animals have learned to hear.[7]

During the play Osborne lashes out indiscriminately at, among other things, the cold war, the arms race, parliamentary double talk, scandalmongers, debased public taste, vindictive legal punishment (a character sings a song advocating a return to beheading because hanging is too crude), income-tax evasion by the rich, popular songs, and the prostitution act (get them off the streets: see no evil, hear no evil, speak no evil—just do it!). All these criticisms are embodied in the songs scattered throughout the work. The framework of the plot is directed against love as practiced in the modern world, which Osborne sees as merely passionless lust.

It is a pity that the intensity and frankness of the anger in *The World of Paul Slickey* will always prevent its being popu-

7. John Osborne, *The World of Paul Slickey* (London: Faber & Faber, Ltd., 1959), p. [5].

lar, for it is a good play. In it Osborne finally becomes the angry young man.

In *A Subject of Scandal and Concern* (1960) and *Luther* (1961), Osborne continues to be the angry young man, but he seems to have absorbed the lesson of *The World of Paul Slickey*. In these two plays Osborne attacks the establishment indirectly instead of leaving his glove in its face. Both plays concern historical characters, and Osborne leaves the implication very clear for us that "it could happen again."

Despite the fact that the play is about a trial that took place in 1842, the very title, *A Subject of Scandal and Concern*, indicates Osborne's sense of the immediacy and urgency of the problem. This short television play is about the trial of George Jacob Holyoake, who was the last person tried for the "crime" of blasphemy in England. Holyoake's offense consisted in stating publicly that he did not believe in God and that the amount of money spent on religion was criminally large in view of the fact that a great many people were living in a poverty which could be substantially relieved by the diversion of church funds to charitable purposes. Curiously enough, although George Holyoake was the last person actually to be imprisoned in England for the "crime" of blasphemy, it would still be dangerous from a social and professional standpoint, if not from a legal one, for a man in a responsible public position (Holyoake was a teacher) openly to proclaim his atheism. That, of course, is the point over which Osborne is exercised. He gets it across by having a modern lawyer serve as narrator to the play. He treats the action patronizingly, as befits a modern lawyer talking about an archaic legal problem, but at the end of the play it becomes evident that the lawyer, who has been sitting in a prison interview room, is about to represent a client in a case similar to Holyoake's.

Luther presents a more difficult problem. Written in an imitation of Brecht's epic style, it presents a series of historically accurate episodes from Luther's career. Osborne takes Luther from the time he is admitted into the Augustinian Order in 1506 to his declining years, when he is living with his wife and child in the now abandoned convent in which he celebrated his first mass. At the beginning of each scene a knight carrying a banner appears and "Briefly barks the time and place of the scene following at the audience." [8]

Osborne's main purpose in *Luther* is to continue in a less offensive way the angry young man literature expected of him. *The World of Paul Slickey* was unpalatable because an audience likes to identify with at least one of the characters in a play—but the world of Paul Slickey was inhabited by uniformly despicable characters. The only angry young man in that play was outside it—John Osborne in person, dribbling black bile and trying to spatter the audience with it. In *Luther*, however, the angry young man is the hero, and the audience can easily identify with this hero—a universally respected religious reformer dead over three hundred years.

There is no harm at all in identifying with such a man and in feeling indignation with him at society. It is easy to feel rebellious and indignant when society is represented by such as John Tetzel. We all notice that Tetzel is nothing but a Madison Avenue or Tottenham Court Road huckster, but the effort to transpose him is too much. He remains a sixteenth century figure—painless and harmless. In short, *Luther* is the sort of thing that might and should have been written during the second World War if England had been occupied by the Nazis. Anouilh's *Antigone* would not have been acclaimed as a very effective play if it had been produced in 1961 either. It must be said in Osborne's defense, however, that when he did write a completely honest play—*The World of Paul Slickey*—the public reacted as if their seats were fitted with slowly emerging spikes.

As long as Osborne sticks to his point, emasculated as it necessarily is by the transposition of time and place and by the inevitable intrusion of purely religious considerations, he does well. The scene in which Tetzel gives his sales oration is first-class writing and first-class drama. But this scene and one other are the only ones in which Osborne is able to make a point. The other scene is the one showing Luther's dispute

8. John Osborne, *Luther* (New York: Criterion Books, Inc., 1961), p. 11.

with Johan von Eck at the Diet of Worms, in which Eck makes the now all too familiar plea that we must stick together and that anyone who thinks differently or questions the status quo is an enemy since he gives the real enemy the impression that there is dissension and, consequently, dissatisfaction. Besides this there is nothing but pretentious, overblown rhetoric— Osborne simply lacks a poetic style—and sloppy symbolism. Osborne's repeated references to Luther's constipation may lead the spectator to believe that he attributes the rise of the Reformation to the constant exacerbation of Luther's mind and spirit by the stubborn flabbiness of his lower intestine— a theory which I would be the last to reject. Who knows what world-shaking events are really ultimately traceable to some great man's irritation with the chambermaid's lack of complacency or with the inordinate activity of the fleas in his wig? Osborne's theory is surely a valid one—but what is one to do with an author who can write lines like these: "I'm like a ripe stool in the world's straining anus, and at any moment we're about to let each other go"? [9]

After *Luther*, Osborne wrote two short plays, *The Blood of the Bambergs* and *Under Plain Cover*, produced together at the Royal Court Theater in July, 1962, under the collective title of *Plays for England*. They reveal only too clearly what one is to do with him—leave him unproduced. That these two plays were accepted by a professional management is in itself incredible, and is a disturbing indication of how far the directors of the Royal Court have become bemused by the mirage of the "movement" which they initiated and nursed along. *The Blood of the Bambergs* is so unbelievably bad, so monumentally inept, that it would have earned its author instant and deserved expulsion from any competently taught amateur playwriting class. *Under Plain Cover* illustrates the fact that Shaw's remark about the net result of the English stage censorship being to let through embarrassingly tasteless exhibitions while it bars serious discussions of sexual relationships is as true now as it was in the eighteen-nineties.

9. *Ibid.*, p. 55.

The genesis of these two plays is not difficult to reconstruct. What happened, probably, is that Osborne, feeling that it was time to write a new play, started casting about for fresh things to be angry at. He decided to be angry at (i) the phoniness and extravagances of royalty, and (ii) the prejudicial attitude which the bourgeoisie adopts toward people who amuse themselves with some of the gamier practices described by Krafft-Ebing.

The Blood of the Bambergs seems to have been vaguely·inspired by the Anthony Armstrong-Jones–Princess Margaret wedding. At any rate, it involves the wedding of a photographer with royalty. The real bridegroom has been killed in a car crash while speeding to the ceremony. The preparations have been so elaborate and costly that the organizers do not dare call it off. They explain that the government will inevitably fall if the ceremony is not held and cast desperately about for a solution to their difficulty. They are about to give up in despair when (surprise! surprise!) they find, fast asleep in the deserted cathedral, an Australian photographer who is really an illegitimate son of the Prince of Bamberg and the dead prince's double. The rest of the play is merely a witless farrago of disorganized scenes, none of them germane to anything in real life.

The critics did not have anything good to say about *The Blood of the Bambergs*, but they were kinder to *Under Plain Cover*. Kenneth Tynan was the most enthusiastic, as usual. He found that "Mr. Osborne's courage is doubly flabbergasting: not only does he state the facts about a sadomasochistic *ménage*, he also refrains from condemning it." He goes on to say that "perhaps the most audacious statement ever made on the English stage" is that "an anal-sadistic relationship need not preclude love." [10]

The second of the *Plays for England* is about a young married couple whose pleasure it is to dress up in various costumes and act out sadomasochistic sexual fantasies. Between charades they indulge themselves in lengthy and incredibly boring fetishistic discussions of female underwear. After a bit, a newspaper reporter ambles on and informs us that, unbeknownst to them,

10. *The Observer*, July 22, 1962, p. 20.

Tim and Jenny are really brother and sister. Parted as little children, they met and fell in love as grownups (by a coincidence no more or less contrived than the convenient discovery of a bastard Bamberg snoozing in the cathedral), married, had two children, and lived happily with their fetishes and their charades. Tim and Jenny are parted, and Jenny marries someone else. She then runs away and returns to Tim. For seven years they live together in their old house, never once going out and presumably parading happily around in their underwear. Then the reporter appears again, and gives us what is presumably Osborne's message: "To Timothy and Jenny I leave this message. You can't escape the world. Even if you want to, it won't let you. Come out then, I say. Show yourselves. Be brave. Be courageous. Fear not. Fear not." [11] Osborne seems to be suggesting here that sexual perverts should flaunt their abnormalities publicly—or at least that they should be permitted to do as they please. But the problem, surely, is that they find it necessary to do it. The immaturity of Osborne's thought processes can be seen by comparing *Under Plain Cover* to Pinter's *The Lover*, which deals with very much the same theme. Pinter's treatment is sophisticated, accurate, witty, and meaningful; Osborne's is jejune and tasteless. Instead of being a protest, *Under Plain Cover* is only the cheaply sensational story it purports to be protesting against.

It is doubtful that anything significant can be expected from John Osborne after *Plays for England*. He has become a victim of his own critical success. Left alone, he might have developed into a modestly talented writer of competently constructed, slightly acidulous hack plays. The strong streak of trite sentimentality which marred *Look Back in Anger* would undoubtedly have taken over had Osborne not been promoted into the figurehead of a new "movement," and he would have peacefully joined the ranks of the television and provincial repertory company playwrights. Osborne is now committed to being angry; but he got all his anger off his chest in *The World of Paul Slickey*. In *Luther* he tackled a subject far beyond his

11. John Osborne, *Plays for England* (London: Faber & Faber, Ltd., 1963), pp. 135–36.

intellectual powers. The result was ludicrous rather than en-lightening. In *Plays for England* he is preaching—and making no more sense than if he were fulminating from a real pulpit.

In the seven years since *Plays for England* was produced in 1962 Osborne has come out with five more plays, and the pre-diction made in the previous paragraph has been amply borne out. He has remained the darling of the newspaper reviewers, particularly in England, where they continue to display a touching gratitude to him for pulling the English theatre out of the Coward-Rattigan vortex. Essays on Osborne by serious dramatic critics have dropped off sharply in the past few years, however; and it is these critics who will determine whether Osborne is a writer or a curiosity of theatrical history.

Osborne started out in *Look Back in Anger*, as I have sug-gested, as a writer of psychological analysis with vaguely Strind-bergian roots. As the result of some extraordinarily cynical criti-cal puffing led by Kenneth Tynan with most of the London reviewers bobbing along in his wake, Osborne became the pro-totype of the "angry young man" and found himself under the rather embarrassing necessity of developing anger to order. His efforts in this direction culminated in the painfully strained "anger" of *Plays for England*, where the triviality of feeling is matched only by its artificiality. I do not intend to imply by all this that Osborne is a hypocrite: his anger can be quite legitimate and valid, as he has demonstrated in *The World of Paul Slickey* and in some of his essays; but he is not a suf-ficiently skilled or inventive playwright to be able to dramatize his anger effectively, and because of the pressures on him he has been forced to fiddle up a good deal of spurious "anger."

With *Inadmissible Evidence* (1964) Osborne entered on a new phase of his career. Or perhaps it would be more accurate to say that he was returning, now that success had enabled him to indulge himself, to his original purpose of writing plays of psychological analysis. Unfortunately, his strength as a drama-tist had been in his anger, however forced; and even more unfortunately his psychological insights have turned out to be confined to the Jimmy Porter type of character. Jimmy Porter angry turns into Jimmy Porter petulant in *Inadmissible Evidence*. Bill Maitland is Jimmy Porter grown older, a definitive failure. The candy stall has not been a success and is about to fold: the customers are dieting and the helpers are all deserting to work in the chocolate factory. Maitland is Jimmy left all alone in his attic, sobbing and moaning self-pityingly. The only essential difference is that Maitland is a lawyer, which gives Osborne the opportunity to create the conceit that his hero is trying himself. Maitland is, however, the most unbelievable lawyer in all literature, displaying about as much knowledge of the law as Jimmy does of selling candy. The play is virtually a monologue, a fact that reminds one that Osborne's principal weakness as a dramatist is an inability to write dialogue. Unlike Jimmy's monologues, which, although they are almost uninterrupted inanity, are at least live and occasionally even amusing, Maitland's are dreary and without thrust, lamenting the decline and fall of an eminently dreary being.

In *A Patriot for Me* (1965) Osborne wrote another panoramic historical drama along the lines of *Luther*. This time he deals with a high-ranking officer in the pre-World War I Austro-Hungarian Secret Service who is blackmailed into betraying secrets to the Russians because of his homosexuality. Osborne portrays the genesis and gradual take-over of Redl's homosexual emotions rather well, but when all is said and done the play leaves one with a rather empty feeling. Like Peter Shaffer's *The Royal Hunt of the Sun*, the play resembles a huge, brightly-colored balloon covered with sparkling, tinselly ornaments: all outline and no substance. Redl, like most dedicated army careerists, is a basically uninteresting man, devoid of personality; his sexual foible, like most sexual foibles, is more absorbing when described in case history form than when dramatized; and the pre-World War I Austro-Hungarian setting has so many operetta associations that it is impossible to take anything that happens in it seriously. It is this setting that is the most troublesome aspect of the play. If Osborne intended to castigate our outmoded horror of homosexuality and the dangers it poses to national security or even if he merely intended a study of the psychological suffering of a homosexual in a heterosexual society, it would have been immeasurably more effective in a contemporary setting. One is led to suspect under the circumstances that the operetta setting was chosen purely for theatrical reasons: to give an opportunity for the climactic ball scene, in which a large segment of Viennese society shows up in drag and indulges in a lot of "daring" conversation and coy flirting.

A *Patriot for Me* was written when the Lord Chamberlain's censorship was still in effect, and the published version of the play includes an appendix listing his Reader's demands. The last incumbent of the office seems to have been an altogether worthy successor to the tradition of Redfern and Smyth-Piggott, expressing pious horror at the use of words like "clap" and "crabs." The required cuts were not made, and the play was produced with the time-honored fiction of calling the theatre a private club. In a way one can lament the passing of the stage censorship in England, for with it went the only absolutely nondiscriminatory clubs in existence.

Osborne's next play, an adaptation of Lope de Vega's *La Fianza satisfecha*, was produced in 1966, although it had been commissioned in 1963 by Kenneth Tynan in his capacity as literary manager of the National Theatre. Osborne in his preface says that Lope's play "was in three acts, had an absurd plot, some ridiculous characters, and some very heavy humor." [12] Osborne's play, A *Bond Honoured*, is in two acts,[13] has an absurd plot, some ridiculous characters, and some very heavy humor. The play concerns a young man who harbors an incestuous passion (which he consummates) for his sister. In Osborne's version she is his half-sister *and* daughter, being the result of his rape of his mother. Unhappily, as one reads Leonido's egoistic monologues, the edge is taken off the bizarre action by the suspicion that Leonido is none other than our old friend Jimmy Porter in Renaissance costume. Lope's defiant

12. John Osborne, A *Bond Honoured* (London: Faber & Faber, Ltd., 1966), p. [9].
13. Osborne states in his preface that his version is in one act; it is, however, in two.

character has become a whining, pleading brat whose toughness is all a façade over his infantile incestuous desire.

Of both *Time Present* and *The Hotel in Amsterdam* (1968), Osborne's latest plays, I can only say that they are the most meaningless and utterly boring plays I have ever encountered. The former is the story of two women, one an actress, the other a Member of Parliament, who are living together so as to console each other since they have just finished unfortunate affairs. Pamela, the actress, is the daughter of a famous actor of the old school who is dying in a nearby hospital. She is shown as being full of resentments and antagonisms, mainly against her half-sister, who is going with a bearded young man whom Pamela refers to as "Dave the Rave." Pamela's lengthy speeches are perhaps the worst attempt in current literature to capture the "with-it" expressions of the young, a fact which ceases to surprise when we perceive that Pamela is not a creature of current times at all but is, in fact, vintage '56, being none other than our old friend Jimmy Porter again, this time in a skirt. Towards the end of the play the actress and the M.P. go their separate ways again, the former to an abortionist, the latter to a lover. Absolutely nothing has happened.

Absolutely nothing happens in *The Hotel in Amsterdam* either. Here three couples show up in a hotel in Amsterdam for the weekend and engage in interminable discussions of brands of Scotch, Dutch tipping practices, the sights of Amsterdam, and their own cleverness at escaping from their employer, a big-shot movie producer with a mother-hen complex. At the end we hear that the producer has killed himself, presumably in chagrin over his employees' escapade. The only adequate criticism of these two plays is the one Shaw made on seeing Sydney Grundy's *Slaves of the Ring* in 1894: "It is not a work of art at all: it is a mere contrivance for filling a theatre bill, and not, I am bound to say, a very apt contrivance at that." [14]

14. George Bernard Shaw, *Our Theatre in the Nineties* (London: Constable & Co., Ltd., 1948), I, 1.

ARNOLD WESKER
"Awake and Sing" in Whitechapel

SOME TWENTY odd years ago Clifford Odets wrote
Awake and Sing, a play about Jewish family life in the Bronx.
The play had a success in its day, though it was never very
good, and then faded out. A production of *Awake and Sing*
in the United States nowadays would be as anachronistic as
a May Day parade down Fifth Avenue. Not so in England.
Inspired by the hopeful, before-the-fact announcements of the
critics that England is experiencing a dramatic renaissance under the second Elizabeth to rival the one under the first, Arnold
Wesker has written a trilogy that does for the Jews of London's
East End what *Awake and Sing* did for the Jews of the Bronx.

Wesker's trilogy is an extremely curious piece of work.
Partly, I suspect, because Wesker is the first English playwright
to announce anything as impressive as a trilogy of connected
plays, and partly because Wesker himself has done a great deal
of self-conscious talking about the "seriousness" of his art, it
has had a distinct *succès d'estime* in England. The English
look upon the Wesker trilogy as their answer to *Mourning
Becomes Electra:* Englishmen can write epics about crumbling
families too. Wesker, then, was extremely shrewd when he
announced that he intended to write a trilogy. He was shrewd
because (i) the series of plays is not a trilogy (the second play,
Roots, is, strictly speaking, not connected to the other two
plays at all); (ii) it assured the production of the last two plays
once the first was produced; and (iii) the designation of
"trilogy" gave the work an appearance of profundity, just as
Galsworthy had given *his* scenes eavesdropped from family
life an appearance of profundity 52 years earlier by calling them
a "saga." Just how shrewd he was we can see from J. R. Taylor's
remark that "he has already been hailed as 'the most promising
and exciting young dramatist to come into the English theatre
since the end of the war,' and the eventual performance of
all three Wesker Trilogy plays in sequence at the Royal Court
in 1960 found the critics almost without exception ready to

bring out their most unequivocally enthusiastic adjectives, and hail the work as an unparalleled achievement." [1]

The trilogy is often called the "Chicken Soup trilogy" after the name of the first play, *Chicken Soup with Barley*. The other two plays are *Roots* and *I'm Talking About Jerusalem*, and the whole trilogy concerns the fortunes of a family of London East End Jews from 1936 to 1959. Actually only the first and third plays deal with the family. *Roots* is about an entirely different family, a family of Norfolk farmhands which is indirectly affected by a member of the Jewish family.

The stories of the plays are briefly told and are, in fact, comparatively unimportant. The real substance of the plays is in the quips and in the little pathetic vignettes scattered here and there throughout them. It takes no great perception to see that Wesker's literary forebears were the play doctors of the Yiddish popular theater.

Chicken Soup with Barley (1958) is the story of the Kahn family. The family consists—naturally—of a strong mother; a weak father; a beautiful, sweet, and innocent young daughter of the biblical Ruth variety; and a brilliant, confused son whose portrayal is so blatantly autobiographical as to be positively embarrassing. In drawing Ronnie Kahn, the hero of the trilogy, Wesker seems to have compiled a catalog of all the clichés of adolescent behavior.

The whole trilogy is essentially the story of Ronnie's growing pains. In *Chicken Soup with Barley* Wesker shows us Ronnie's exposure as a child to the spirit of militant Communism prevalent among most East End Jews of the nineteen-thirties. Wesker portrays this Communism as purely nonideological, a reaction against the economic injustices of depression slum life rather than a rationally held belief. As Ronnie grows up, his character is formed by his fear, on the one hand, of becoming a failure like his weak-willed father, and, on the other, by his rebellion against his strong-willed, domineering mother. At the end of the play Ronnie, now twenty-five years old, comes back from Paris, where he has been working as a cook (just as

1. Taylor, *op. cit.*, p. 143.

Wesker himself did) and tells his mother that he has lost his faith in life and doesn't care about anything anymore. His confession is accompanied by much breaking of the voice, turning of head to wall, and impotent clutching of air. The literary style of the play as a whole might be described as Yiddish lachrymose.

Roots (1959) is about a young girl's visit to her family back on the farm. Beatie Bryant has been away for three years, and now she has come back to the lonely flatlands of Norfolk where the men of her family have been farm laborers for generations, full of news about the man she hopes to marry. She has been working as a waitress in a café and has met and fallen in love with a fellow worker, a self-educated "intellectual." Throughout the play she tries to prepare her family for Ronnie's visit. He never appears, but he is the play's invisible protagonist. Practically everything Beatie says is a quotation from Ronnie— "Ronnie say . . ." and "Ronnie do it this way . . ."—until we almost feel that Ronnie is some sort of dybbuk speaking through Beatie. None of the other members of the family can understand this sort of talk. To them life is working on the land, cooking, eating, sleeping, drinking, and meekly accepting whatever happens. Reading is the daily tabloid. Recreation is popular music and movies. Talking is gossip. Into this atmosphere Beatie comes with her discussions of politics and moral problems, her classical music, her abstract painting, her books —and her quotations from Ronnie. For two weeks she pesters and reproaches her mother for her Philistinism and tries to change her with arguments from the fountainhead. But her mother remains unaffected. At the end of the two weeks Ronnie himself is supposed to arrive, and the family gather nervously around, creaking uncomfortably in their best clothes, to do him honor. Instead of Ronnie, however, a letter from him arrives. In it he tells Beatie that their relationship has been a failure: for three years she has fought him, refused to listen to him, made fun of his beliefs. She has refused to listen to his kind of music, refused to read his kind of books, refused to discuss his kind of politics, and derided his intellectual conversation and that of his friends. He has tried, he tells her, to devote all his energies to making at least one human being better; and his experience with her has convinced him that it cannot be done. Beatie is shattered, and her mother, who is the type that likes to exalt her ignorance into a virtue, crows triumphantly that "the apple doesn't fall far from the tree."

Beatie's reaction to the letter is the turning point of the play. Up to this it has appeared to be chiefly a cheap satire on "pseudointellectualism," with Beatie's ridiculous aping of Ronnie's attitudes and her Norfolk Ma Kettle mother's cornball common-sense deflations. In short, television-level drama. After her initial shock has worn off, Beatie turns on her complacent, self-satisfied family, who are openly pleased at her collapse, and starts tongue-lashing them. At first, tearfully and angrily stammering, she bravely swallows her pride and prefaces her accusations with the customary "Ronnie say . . ." Gradually during the long scene she gains confidence, forgets herself, forgets Ronnie finally, becomes carried away. She says the same things Ronnie has always said, but for the first time she says them in her own words because for the first time she herself really believes them. For three years she has lived with Ronnie and fought him and derided him exactly as her mother has fought and derided her, but now at last she believes. Her family and she were wrong; Ronnie, the intellectual whose quoted clichés have been ridiculed throughout the play, was right. The curtain falls on Beatie jubilantly shouting, "It can be done, Ronnie . . ."

With this last scene Wesker alters the whole meaning of his play, or, rather, gives it a meaning. What had seemed to be a reassuring pat on the back for the fools and Philistines becomes a bold vindication of the intellectual's Weltanschauung, made all the stronger by the sudden turnabout. The painstaking realism of the first part of the play, the precise transcription of the obvious, repetitive, cliché-ridden conversation, almost as if Wesker had been prowling around with a tape recorder under his coat, turns out to be a condemnation rather than a glorification. The only really serious objection that one can make against the play is that Wesker has put the commonly heard clichés of pseudointellectuals into Ronnie's mouth instead of something really sensible.

The less said about the final play in the Chicken Soup trilogy the better. *I'm Talking About Jerusalem* (1960) is an unmitigated disaster. Once again Wesker is trying to treat a theme of social significance in terms of his Jewish working-class family and once again he is unable to do anything except write Yiddish theater clichés. In *Chicken Soup with Barley* Wesker had tried to show the East End Jew's involvement in the Communist movement of the nineteen-thirties as a largely instinctive antifascist reaction. In *I'm Talking About Jerusalem* Dave Simmonds, Ronnie Kahn's brother-in-law, who had gone to fight for the Spanish Loyalists in *Chicken Soup with Barley*, tries to practice a sort of William Morris-type socialism in the Norfolk fields. Disillusioned by his experiences in Spain and in World War II, Dave decides that mass movements will never build Jerusalem (i.e., the ideal state of life on earth): only individual action will build individual Jerusalems. He and his wife decide to retire into the isolation of the Norfolk fens and live off the land, doing everything for themselves, relying on no one. Ronnie is still the hero since Wesker tells everything from his point of view—in other words, what we see is not so much Dave's experience in living but rather how Dave's experience affects Ronnie.

Dave's attempt to put socialism into action on an individual basis fails, as one English critic admiringly puts it, not only because of "the debased values of a hostile society debauched by materialism and its by-product cynicism," but also because of "inherent weakness" in Dave's own character.[2] This is perfectly true: the only thing wrong with it as a critical statement is that it is written admiringly. Wesker is obviously trying to write a play about individual socialism in action. Such a play can be significant only if it deals with the reasons why individual socialism is impossible today. Wesker's play fails to achieve significance because it deals mainly with one man's psychology. This is not to say that character drawing is unim-

2. Robert Muller in Arnold Wesker, *I'm Talking About Jerusalem* (Middlesex, England: Penguin Books, 1960), p. 7.

portant. Of course the characters must be well-rounded, motivated people and not puppets on strings labeled "social forces."
But the characters themselves must not cause the failure of
this experiment. It *is* important to put individual socialism into
practice today because of the "debased values of a hostile society, debauched by materialism and its by-product cynicism."
To show, as Wesker does, that individual socialism is impossible because the person who practices it is congenitally stupid
is defeating his own purpose. Wesker's main concern, however,
is to show the effect of Dave's failure on the awkward, mawkish
adolescent, Ronnie. Ronnie, according to Wesker, grows up a
little more. At the end of the play he bursts into tears for the
umpteenth time in the two plays of the trilogy in which he
appears and then, affirming, I suppose, that Dave's failure is
really in some mysterious sense a triumph, he yells, "We must
be bloody mad to cry." On this sophomoric note the play and
the trilogy closes.

The extent to which Wesker's reputation in England has
been built up on the strength of the Chicken Soup trilogy is
absolutely extraordinary. Wesker is regarded as the theater's
leading creative thinker and even his most naïve outbursts are
received with the sort of respect one imagines the more gullible
among the ancient Greeks reserved for the latest bulletins from
Delphi. Since the success of the trilogy, Wesker's earliest play,
The Kitchen, has been produced, published, and made into a
film. It has been received with the reverence usually accorded
to the juvenilia of the masters.[3] *The Kitchen* is based on
Wesker's experience as an apprentice pastrycook in Paris and
Norwich. Naturally there is a Jewish pastrycook with an all-
embracing love of humanity in the play—a sort of Whit-
manesque figure constantly gazing into eggyolks to see the halo
round his head. Wesker himself has explained what he was
trying to do in the play in these words: "The world might have
been a stage for Shakespeare, but to me it is a kitchen: where

3. Lawrence Kitchin, for example, calls it "a compressionist masterpiece." (Lawrence Kitchin, "Backwards and Forwards," *Twentieth Century*, CLXIX [February, 1961], p. 170).

people come and go and cannot stay long enough to understand each other, and friendships, loves, and enmities are forgotten as quickly as they are made." [4] Two things are notable about this remark: the willy-nilly dragging in of Shakespeare as a point of reference in order to show that the "New English Drama" represents a renaissance analogous to that of Elizabethan times; and the blissfully unconscious bathos of the comparison. From *Welttheater* to *Küche*. From a panorama of humanity to burnt crêpes suzettes, sausages and eggs, and fried flounder.

The Kitchen (1959) is what the French might describe as a *tranche de veau* drama. We see the kitchen of a large restaurant with the cooks standing round a huge circle of ovens performing their various specialties. The hero is the boiled-fish cook, a lunatic German who is having an affair with a married waitress. There is also an Irish fish-frier who keeps lamenting his fate in a rich brogue, an Italian pastrycook, the aforementioned Jewish pastrycook, another German cook, and a number of Cypriot chefs. The play consists largely of a series of vignettes between various chefs and waitresses. As might be expected, these vignettes deal with the usual stock situations of melodrama. There is the situation of the hero-cook and his waitress girl friend, who is pregnant by him but is reluctant to get rid of her well-to-do husband. There is the waitress who sprays plates of boiling Brown Windsor soup all over the place as she faints from the results of an attempted abortion; and of course there is the plain, elderly waitress who calls the German cook a dirty Boche when he annoys her.

What Wesker is trying to get across in this play is the lack of mutual understanding and affection between people—even between people who are constantly thrown closely together, such as the workers in the kitchen. Each person stands at his particular station around the huge stove, absorbed in his own visions and totally unable to understand his neighbor. This is essentially the same theme that we find in Arthur Miller's *A Memory of Two Mondays*, in which the young hero realizes

4. Thomas Maschler, ed., *New English Dramatists* 2, p. 7.

at the end that the people with whom he has worked in the automotive parts warehouse have not really been aware of his existence: they have just been going through the motions to keep the illusion of communication they need so much. It is instructive to compare Miller's method of getting his point across, for it gives us a capsule contrast between a mature playwright and a juvenile one. Miller's method is objective and demonstrative—he shows you what is happening and lets you observe it and learn from it; Wesker's method is subjective and explanatory: he beats the audience over the head with his moral and carefully holds the magnifying glass over his bleeding heart for us.

In 1961 Wesker published an article in which he reviewed his past work and made some predictions about his future. He concluded the article by saying, "I am becoming more conscious of style, and I bet the rest of my plays are no bloody good." [5] Wesker has proved himself to be a very on-and-off sort of prophet in the event: his next play, *Chips with Everything*, showed absolutely no increasing consciousness of style.

Chips with Everything opened at the Royal Court Theatre, London, on April 27, 1962. The scene is a Royal Air Force basic training camp, in which a group of new recruits has just arrived. The group, like the cooks in *The Kitchen*, is a variously assorted one, including the inevitable Jew, the Cockney, the Northern industrial slum boy, the Scotsman, and, most important of all for Wesker's purposes, the upper-class boy in rebellion against society. For *Chips with Everything* is not about the cruelty and stupidity of the military basic training routine, but about the ever-looming British class conflict.

Arnold Wesker has never been able to rid himself of the deep-seated inferiority complex he seems to have developed as a result of being born into the working classes. He appears to be unaware of the fact that, long before he was born, Shaw's *Pygmalion* demonstrated that the so-called English class distinctions are pure, meaningless illusion, nor has he troubled to

5. Arnold Wesker, "Art Is Not Enough," *Twentieth Century*, CLXIX (February, 1961), p. 192.

open his eyes to the fact that in modern England even these illusions have ceased to exist any more. In present-day England class distinctions have disappeared for all practical intents and purposes. It is no longer necessary even to change one's accent in order to get ahead. But to Wesker, class distinctions have not yet become the occasion for derisive laughter they now are for all normal Englishmen. He is still angry at the injustice of it all. Furthermore, he does not show his anger by spitting venom at what he dislikes, as Osborne's Paul Slickey does: his method is to whine, to hold his bleeding heart up to us and tell us how much it hurts. What Wesker does in this latest instalment of his saga of English *Klassenschmerz* is to show how "Pip" Thompson, the son of a banker and former general, who rebels against his background by enlisting in the ranks and refusing to become an officer, is broken by the "system." Thompson at first stirs up his fellow recruits against the officers and makes his stand when he refuses to participate in bayonet practice. The climactic scene of the play comes when Thompson is brought back to the bayonet range and charges the dummy, screaming maniacally. The breaking down is accomplished by a junior officer, who informs Thompson that the upper classes are invincible, that they see right through him, and that no act of rebellion he could ever think up could make the slightest dent in their self-assurance. Thompson thereupon gives up, charges the dummy, and becomes an officer. There are two good scenes in the play (the revolt in the recreation hut and the theft from the coal dump), but they depend for their effect exclusively on pantomime. Whenever a character has to talk, the writing becomes embarrassingly gauche. The most level-headed of the British reviewers was, predictably, the anonymous one in the *Times Literary Supplement*:

> . . . the play is a neat polemical exercise derived from the basic (highly arguable) assumption that service life is a microcosm of civil life, the class struggle and so on, and using all the resources of the theatre to bludgeon the point home . . . one becomes uncomfortably conscious that for a good political cartoon a clear grasp of the real facts is re-

quired before they can be adapted to the particular require-
ments at hand. There are parts of *Chips with Everything*
which are so blatantly far from the truth—any sort of truth
—that the spectator rebels, and once the theatrical spell is
off him there may not be very much left.[6]

It is instructive to compare this with the remarks of the jour-
nalistic reviewers, who, for the most part, went into an ecstasy
of cringing abasement before the light of Wesker's "genius." [7]

In his desperate attempt to produce a working-class literature that would imitate the real life of ordinary people, Wesker
has paradoxically been able to produce only a caricature of real
life based on all the century-old literary stock situations. He has
achieved precisely the opposite of what he wished to achieve.
His drama is no more representative of the real life of the working classes than Mr. Crummles's was. Crummles and his type
of company puffed out pipe dreams for the working classes so
that they could temporarily forget the misery of their reality.
Wesker puffs out pipe dreams for our contemporary, unctuously self-conscious "socially aware" intellectuals, who like to
see visions of a working class that is as hairy-chested as they
would like to be and as sensitive and introspective as they like
to think of themselves as being.

Like Osborne, Wesker is a playwright who continues to be
graced with critical attention only because his first few plays
were so puffed-up that he became a "leading" playwright whose

6. *Times Literary Supplement,* August 10, 1962, p. 606.
7. Harold Hobson in *Sunday Times,* May 6, 1962, p. 41: "*Chips
With Everything* is the first anti-Establishment entertainment of which
the Establishment need be afraid. It is this because it is a magnificent play,
exceedingly funny, yet of complete tragic seriousness, informed with a
passion which, despite its intensity, is always under control; and because
it attacks the Establishment, not in some crumbling outpost which any
intelligent Tory would be glad to abandon, but in the centre of its
strength and the heart of its goodness. As no other play of its kind has
done, it rises to the height and grandeur of its argument and purpose."
Or Bernard Levin in *Daily Express,* May 6, 1962, p. 27: "It is shot through
with Mr. Wesker's anger and compassion, throbbing with love and life,
rocking with laughter. For sheer exhilaration, for the feeling it generates
that it is good to be alive on the same planet as the author, it is his best
play yet."

every utterance deserved to be solemnly scrutinized. In his two most recent plays Wesker continues to demonstrate that he possesses a mind paralyzed by a goggle-eyed idealism that has failed to develop since he formulated it in elementary school.

In *Their Very Own and Golden City* [8] Wesker writes about his vision of a social utopia. His hero is an architect who wants to build six new co-operatively owned cities for 100,000 inhabitants each. These cities would be designed so that people could live in them and realize their full potential as human beings. The industries would be owned and managed by the workers, and theatres and other cultural institutions would be at the centre with banks and municipal buildings shoved off to the side somewhere. During the eight years or so that it will take to build these cities there would be public discussion meetings every week so that the investors could control the design and progress of the city. While this play has better writing in it than any of Wesker's other plays—less of the coltish mawkishness that is the hallmark of his style—its vaporous idealism vitiates any point that he is trying to make. There will be no golden cities that are anybody's very own—ever. They will remain the property of business combines in a capitalistic society, of the bureaucratic power elite in a collectivist one. The "little man," for whom Wesker's heart aches with the sentimental fervor of a social worker looking down on orphaned waifs, will continue to play the role of the duped victim that Ionesco gives him in his far more realistic "radiant" city.[9]

In *The Four Seasons* Wesker attempts to write a two-character poetico-symbolic drama of love. A man and a woman—the man, appropriately enough, an academic authority on the Romantic poets—come to an empty house and live there for a year. Both are recovering from unhappy love affairs, and their own affair mirrors the simple allegory of the seasons: dormant when they arrive in winter, it grows in the spring, climaxes in the summer, and peters out in predictable niggling bitterness

---

8. This play was written before *The Four Seasons*, although it was not performed until 1966, one year after the later play.

9. Cf. *supra*, p. 72.

in the autumn. A writer with some feeling for language could conceivably make something theatrically viable out of this theme, but Wesker has his two lovers talk to each other like little children sedulously repeating the formulas they have been taught in their deportment classes. There are few things more embarrassing than a congenitally prosaic person trying to be poetic; and Wesker complacently presenting childish platitudes as profundities in a language the elevation of which is reminiscent of schoolboy, literary magazine style makes us squirm with embarrassment. In the climactic scene, called "the miracle" by Wesker, the man actually makes a "Hungarian apple strudel" on stage. Actors learn to fence, Wesker tells us, so "why not to cook?" [10] The scene leaves one wondering why Wesker ever left the pastry cooking profession: he has as much feeling for language as a suet pudding.

10. Michael Billington, ed., *New English Dramatists* 9 (Harmondsworth, Middlesex: Penguin Books, 1966), p. 191. There is, at least, a historical precedent for the cooking scene. While acting in *Cramond Brig* early in his career, Henry Irving had to learn how to cook a sheep's head on stage (Lawrence Irving, *Henry Irving* [London: Faber & Faber, 1951], p. 229).

BERNARD KOPS
The Jew as "Everyman"

ACCORDING TO THE Bible, Judaism is a patriarchal religion; and indeed Jewish families always dutifully pay lip service to the father as the nominal head of the household. His position in the household, however, is somewhat like that of the President of France under the Third Republic: his function is mainly to find a new wife when the old one dies. The real power in the Jewish family resides with the mother, and young men like Bernard Kops and Arnold Wesker, who have been brought up in traditional Jewish families, usually grow up with what is best described as an unwhelped Oedipus complex: runny-nosed mama's boys looking up worshipfully at the all-encompassing Mother Earth figure. A few trips to those Yiddish theaters still remaining will convince anyone of this. The mothers are always large-bosomed, domineering figures and the fathers hollow-chested, runty little men skipping along behind their wives like coracles towed in the wakes of galleons. Watching Yiddish drama one wonders how the children were ever begot.

If Arnold Wesker demonstrates the disastrous consequences to the potential playwright of being formed in a traditional Jewish household, Bernard Kops demonstrates his possible salvation. This salvation lies in humor: if you can laugh at your heritage, you can transcend it.

This is precisely what has happened to Bernard Kops, another one of the promising young sparks of the "New English Dramatists" movement. Kops's work, like Wesker's, has been entirely determined by his Jewish heritage. So far he has published three plays: *The Hamlet of Stepney Green*, *The Dream of Peter Mann*, and *Enter Solly Gold*. Of these the second is an unfortunate attempt at writing a Jewish folk play in expressionistic style, while the other two are simple Jewish folk plays set in contemporary London but modeled on the type of Jewish folk literature written by Sholom Aleichem or Isaac Babel.

The Hamlet of Stepney Green and *Enter Solly Gold* are opposite sides of the same coin. In the former, Kops takes himself seriously and fails; in the latter, he does not take himself seriously and succeeds. It is as simple as that, and the lesson for the Jewish playwright is inescapable. The Jew is apt to be extremely emotional and to have a sharp, self-critical sense of humor. Extreme emotion is dangerous on the stage at the best of times. It is successful only when it is entirely impersonal and objective, as in Shakespeare and in the Greek drama. The Jewish form of emotion, as portrayed by Kops, is, however, strictly of the breast-beating, *mea culpa* type, sung solo with wailing-wall chorus obbligato; and this makes for embarrassed rather than sympathetic audiences. Another drawback to Kops's serious plays is that serious plays require some sort of philosophical orientation. When a man writes a serious play he has to take a definite position with respect to his view of reality. Now, Kops, though a first-class humorist, is anything but a thinker. He feels that the world is really a wonderful place and that everything would be all right if people would only jiggle around flapping their arms and smiling through. To Kops reality is one long, manic vaudeville act.

The Hamlet of Stepney Green (1958) transposes Shakespeare's hero to Stepney Green, one of the seedier districts of Jewish East London. Hamlet becomes David Levy, a young and rather feeble-minded good-for-nothing who wants to be a crooner instead of following in his father's footsteps as a pushcart peddler:

> DAVID: I want to be a crooner—I want to be a king —to be looked at—to be looked up to. I want people to nudge each other as they pass and say 'Look! there goes David Levy—the most famous—fabulous crooner in the world.' I want to hear my voice blaring from the record shops as I whizz by in my Jaguar—I want to switch on the radio—any time—and any day and hear my voice on records.
>
> . . . .
>
> I'd stun them—I'd be the greatest thing—don't ya see— I want to make people happy—I'VE GOT TO MAKE

them listen—they'd love me.[1]

Hamlet's father becomes Sam Levy, Whitechapel's leading pickled-herring peddler. Sam has a habit of moving his bed into the back garden and announcing his death. One day he really does die out there, and David, thinking his father's last words accuse his mother of poisoning him, becomes even more cracked than before. The rest of the play concerns David's relations with his father's ghost who comes back to try and straighten him out—a fairly hopeless task. At the end of the play everything is resolved as David decides to become a singing herring peddler, and the ghost fades away announcing the moral of the play:

> Make the most of your youth—because youth is a wreath of roses—make the most of your life—because life is a holiday from the dark—make the most of the world—because it is YOUR WORLD—because the world is a wedding—so— Let the wedding continue—.[2]

In *The Dream of Peter Mann* (1960) the hero has become a clothes peddler who dreams the world is coming to an end. He meets a tramp who persuades him to steal his mother's money and come away with him. While he is trying to get the money out of the safe, the safe falls on his head and he has the dream that is the main part of the play. In the dream Peter Mann—the name indicates that Peter is an Everyman symbol —comes back after twelve years of digging for uranium to find that everyone in his local pushcart market is also digging. He rallies them and persuades them all to go to work for him. In the next scene of the dream he has organized shroud factories all over the world. The shrouds are to be a protection against the Bomb, which duly explodes after Kops has let off a great many obvious, clumsily put reasons why it shouldn't. When Peter finds himself alone in the world, he wakes up, marries (of course), and bounds off into the middle distance spouting the following:

1. E. Martin Browne, ed., *New English Dramatists* (Middlesex, England: Penguin Books, 1959), pp. 108–109.
2. *Ibid.*, p. 170.

Don't you see—you can always make money, but you can't always make merry. You're saving up for nothing, going nowhere, hoarding nothing, losing—everything—What will YOU bid for LIFE? Here it is. A kiss in the dark. The one and only—all shapes and sizes—lovely, lousy, terrible, terrific. Magnificent! Ridiculous! But it's the only one we've got. A great opportunity never to be repeated—a unique bargain—going—going—so make the most of it before it's gone! [3]

When we come to *Enter Solly Gold* (published 1961) it is quite a different story. The plot is basically the same, but the approach is different. Once again we have the talkative, picaresque Jewish rogue, but this time that is all he is. Solly Gold has no notion of being a world-betterer. He spouts no juvenile pronunciamentos on how to live or on what to do about the bomb: he simply has fun. Solly's one idea in life is that getting a job is the ultimate horror. He starts out by confiscating some chickens by posing as a chicken inspector. Then he dresses up as a rabbi and peddles his chickens from door to door by announcing that it is the Rabbinical Chicken Sunday of the American Reform Orthodox Proxy Rabbi's Association. Finally he succeeds in convincing a harried millionaire that he (the millionaire) is the Messiah—or will be when Solly Gold has taken all his money. At the end, of course, poetic justice is served with Solly losing everything. The curtain falls as he picks cigarette butts out of the gutter and contemplates further grandiose confidence plans.

The contrast between Kops's first two plays and *Enter Solly Gold* is amazing. It seems hardly possible that the first two exercises in sophomoric philosophy were written by the same man who wrote the gay and witty *Enter Solly Gold*. And yet Kops seems to have committed the unforgivable crime in the eyes of the English critics by writing *Enter Solly Gold*. He is no longer part of the upsurge of the British drama. He is guilty of not being serious, which puts him on the level of Terence Rattigan (though Rattigan has of late been hailed, with breath-bereaving

3. Bernard Kops, *The Dream of Peter Mann* (Middlesex, England: Penguin Books, 1960), pp. 85–86.

insouciance, as a convert to the New English Dramatists because of *Ross*, his "study" of T. E. Lawrence). The latest round up of "new dramatists" (in *Twentieth Century*, February, 1961) does not even mention Kops. It seems he will not merit the favor of the English critics until he returns to the schoolboy solemnities of his two earlier plays. As Mervyn Johns says admiringly in his preface to *The Dream of Peter Mann*, the New English Dramatists had the effect of someone playing a guitar in a cathedral.[4] That appears to be the idea of daring and originality held by the English critics who are fostering the new movement.

4. *Ibid.*, p. 9.

DORIS LESSING
The Angry Young Cocoon

WITH DORIS LESSING, a British colonial writer who is known primarily as a novelist, the angry-young-man school of the New English Dramatists takes a new turn. More objective and realistic than Osborne, Miss Lessing shows contemporary society as it is rather than as she interprets it. In the angry-young-man drama the angry young man is always the author, who shows his irritation either by purposely exaggerating some aspects of society for satiric effect or by putting ranting, soap-box denunciations into the mouth of his hero. This is all very well, but it is purely subjective and gives us one man's view of society only. The fact is—and it must be painfully obvious to anyone who takes the trouble to keep his eyes open—that although there may be some angry young authors in contemporary society, there are no angry young men. The angry young man is a mythical creation born in the minds of some writers—novelists for the most part—who use it to criticize the complacency and inequity of society. What society is actually composed of is young men who are the very opposite of angry. Or, rather, if they are angry at all, they are angry at those who would force them to be involved in the problem of society and therefore angry at it. The real representative of the younger generation is the angry anti-angry young man—the angry young cocoon.

Such a young man is the hero of Doris Lessing's *Each His Own Wilderness* (1958). Tony Bolton is twenty-two and the typical post-World War II young man. He has just come home from his two year stretch in the army, which he has served willingly and unthinkingly, and indeed, rather enjoyed: "Rather nice, the army—being told what to do, everything in its place, everything tidy . . ."[1] His one thought now is to settle down, to have a home and security. Politics does not interest him, and he has successfully anesthetized himself to the potentially

1. E. Martin Browne, ed., *op. cit.*, p. 15.

mortal dangers of the international situation. In fact, modern young man—and Miss Lessing has observed him with amazing accuracy—has paradoxically reverted to the ideal of midnineteenth-century woman—all he wants is *Kinder, Kirche, und Küche*. Tony's clash is with his mother, who belongs to the generation which grew up in the social turbulence of the nineteen-thirties, when there really *were* angry young men. Myra Bolton is a totally unregenerate survivor of those times. Her whole life still revolves around social issues, and she spends all her time organizing committees to warn people against the Bomb and making plans to chain herself to the railings of the House of Commons in order to make her protest more effective. She is, in fact, a sort of female Lord Russell. The only effect all this has on her son is to make him squirm with embarrassment at the lack of social dignity implied in such actions. Tony, a representative of the younger generation, is a perfect prig. His only anger is directed against those who would draw him out of his cocoon of safe conventionality. His mother's carefree Bohemianism and humanitarian idealism mean nothing to him. All he wants to do is settle down placidly in his house and be left alone to live his life in a tight circle of security. The climax of the play comes when he learns that his mother has sold the house so that he can have money to travel around and enjoy himself. Mother and son realize that, coming from different generations, they come from different worlds: they will never understand each other. He is furious that his carefully woven cocoon has been broken, and she, paradoxically, is the one who wants to go out into the world to seek more adventure:

> I'm nearly 50—and it's true there's nothing much to show for it. Except that I've never been afraid to take chances and make mistakes. I've never wanted security and safety and the walls of respectability—you damned little petty-bourgeois. My God, the irony of it—that *we* should have given birth to a generation of little office-boys and clerks and . . . little people who count their pensions before

they're out of school . . . little petty-bourgeois.[2]

To which the younger generation's only reply is,

> . . . listen—never in the whole history of the world have
> people made a battle-cry out of being ordinary. Never. Sup-
> posing we all said to the politicians—we refuse to be heroic.
> We refuse to be brave. We are bored with all the noble
> gestures—what then . . . Leave us alone, we'll say. Leave
> us alone to live. Just leave us alone . . .[3]

2. *Ibid.*, p. 94.
3. *Ibid.*, p. 95.

SHELAGH DELANEY
The Drama of Alienated Youth

IN MAY, 1958, the Theatre Royal in Stratford, East London, which, under Joan Littlewood's direction, had become the leading experimental theater in England, produced a new play by a nineteen-year-old girl. The play was Shelagh Delaney's *A Taste of Honey* and it was an immediate success, so much so, indeed, that it was later moved to a West End theater and produced on Broadway soon thereafter. According to the story circulated at the time, Shelagh Delaney had been working as an usher in a theater and had become so fed up with the gritless pap being dribbled at the audiences that she decided to sit down and do better herself. Sit down and do better is precisely what she did when she turned out *A Taste of Honey*. To put criticism of *A Taste of Honey* on its most elementary level, there is at least nothing in the play that resembles what Helen, one of its characters, complains of in the modern drama: "The cinema," says Helen, "has become more and more like the theater, it's all mauling and muttering, can't hear what they're saying half the time and when you do it's not worth listening to." [1] Miss Delaney is talking about the general incompetence of most present-day actors and the equally widespread unimportance of contemporary plays here, and she has taken particular care to avoid any suspicion of this sort of thing in her first play.

A *Taste of Honey*, like so many other good modern plays, sees the human condition as one of loneliness. In choosing this theme—or rather, in having it chosen for her, since an artist is *compelled* by his view of society—Shelagh Delaney tacks herself on to the avant-garde movement of Beckett, Ionesco, Genet, and Adamov, all of whom use the feeling of alienation from the world and from its other inhabitants as their leading theme.

Miss Delaney's method of demonstrating the impossibility

1. Shelagh Delaney, *A Taste of Honey* (London: Methuen & Co., Ltd., 1962), p. 27.

of communication without at the same time "mauling and muttering so that you can't hear what they're saying half the time" is the direct-address technique. The two leading characters of A *Taste of Honey*, Helen and her daughter Jo, address their opinions about each other directly to the audience so that as far as the latter are concerned the barriers between people are broken down. Essentially the device is the old nineteenth-century technique of taking "asides" to the audience, brought up to date by rapid-fire delivery and constant, almost imperceptible, switching back and forth from the actor to the audience. The result is very effective direct dramatic irony, with the two characters remaining strangers to each other while the audience is privy to their real thoughts.[2]

Shelagh Delaney resembles the current avant-garde writers as far as theme is concerned, but she differs in technique. Her plays are not "theatre of the absurd," in which a segment of life is taken out of its context and exaggerated or distorted until the action itself becomes a wryly satiric commentary on reality. The Delaney plays are pure realism, slices taken directly from the life of the industrial North of England milieu in which the author was born and raised.

In A *Taste of Honey* Miss Delaney tells the story of a mother and daughter who never really come into contact with each other. The mother, who is described as a "semi-whore," earns just enough from her occasional encounters with men to keep them going. During the course of the play, one of her admirers, a man ten years younger than she, inexplicably marries her and she cheerfully abandons her daughter. The latter consoles herself with a brief affair with a passing Negro sailor and is nursed through her pregnancy by a young homosexual. Just before the birth of the child the mother comes back, chases the homosexual out, and takes over her daughter's problems herself. One gets the idea that nothing is solved and that the two will reach the same impasse as before.

The Lion in Love, so far Shelagh Delaney's only other play,

2. J. R. Taylor (*op. cit.*, p. 114) says that this device was one of Joan Littlewood's contributions.

was first produced in September, 1960, at the Belgrade Theatre, Coventry, and later moved to London. This play has even less of a definite plot than A *Taste of Honey*. It is simply a series of episodes in the life of an extremely unconventional family living in a semibombed out house in the North of England. Miss Delaney's implicit theme of revolt consists in the unexpected and unorthodox events within the framework of conventional family drama. The Fresko family is constantly on the verge of breaking up. Members come and go with gypsylike irregularity. The mother is constantly being locked up for drunk and disorderly conduct. The father is constantly thinking of running away with a fellow peddler from the street market where he "works." The daughter elopes with a casual pick up (although Miss Delaney is youthfully romantic enough to imply that this one will work out); and the whole raffish establishment is watched over by the grandfather, a lawless, Rabelaisian type who is full of the old vigor yet.

It is too soon yet to see how Miss Delaney will develop. Her greatest gift is her ability to write live, snappy stage dialogue; her greatest drawback is her inability to get a coherent plot together. Her future will depend on her ability to combine her considerable native talent and the cheerful iconoclasm that marks her first two plays to produce something with a definite meaning instead of only the hint of a meaning.

JOHN MORTIMER
The Apotheosis of Failure

The plays are . . . intended as comedy, comedy being, to my mind, the only thing worth writing in this despairing age, provided the comedy is truly on the side of the lonely, the neglected, the unsuccessful, and plays its part in the war against established rules and against the imposing of an arbitrary code of behaviour upon individual and unpredictable human beings.

There may, for all I know, be great and funny plays to be written about successful lawyers, brilliant criminals, wise schoolmasters, or families where the children can grow up without silence and without regret. There are many plays that show that the law is always majestic or that family life is simple and easy to endure. Speaking for myself I am not on the side of such plays and a writer of comedy must choose his side with particular care. He cannot afford to aim at the defenceless, nor can he, like the more serious writer, treat any character with contempt.[1]

With this statement John Mortimer puts himself firmly on the side of the drama of protest. Like most of the current English writers, however, his protest is a severely limited one. It is not a cosmic, nihilistic protest, as in the French avant-garde drama, but a protest against the oppressiveness of society's rules. It is a protest, furthermore, that has its feet firmly and distinctly planted within the society it protests against. Mortimer is not only against—he is also *for*. He is for those who have been unable to cope with society: for the failures, the flotsam, the drifting scum of society; for the rejects and the defeated; for the hopeless and the numb; and for those who have chosen to conceal their hopelessness even from themselves in a desperate pretence. John Mortimer's plays are the glorification of the failure.

1. John Mortimer, *Three Plays* (London: Methuen & Co., Ltd., 1958), pp. 10–11.

A failure is hardly a heroic figure. Mortimer's failures receive their stature by analogy: they are the antitheses of the organization men. The efficient compromisers are the villains of Mortimer's plays, even though they do not appear in them personally. They are condemned by contrast. Mortimer has no use for the survival-of-the-fittest doctrine, since, as he sees it, the terms of the survival are dictated by those who know they will triumph under those terms, the sum of which constitutes the society we live in.

Although he began his writing career as a novelist, Mortimer's talent definitely does not lie in the direction of the longer stage forms. *The Wrong Side of the Park* (1960) is interesting only as the representative of a type of play much favored by the young English writers. It is a rather clumsily told story of an incipiently schizophrenic housewife in suburban London who is saved on the brink of lunacy by her husband's sudden awakening from the torpor into which his job as a civil servant has sunk him. The interesting thing about this play is its exemplification of a syndrome that appears to afflict most of the current young English playwrights. The syndrome is the writer's need to exorcise his personal drab middle-class background by producing a work in which his origins are denigrated and ripped apart. In Mortimer's play, as well as in Osborne's *Epitaph for George Dillon*, Bolt's *Flowering Cherry*, and Shaffer's *Five Finger Exercise*, we see the writer serving his apprenticeship with a play about family life in suburban, semi-detached houses where restless adolescent children rebel against their parents, usually a weak-willed and ineffectual husband married to a stronger but unpleasantly neurotic wife. N. F. Simpson's A *Resounding Tinkle* shows the same thing in a rather slanted way, as do Shelagh Delaney's *The Lion in Love* and Arnold Wesker's *Chicken Soup with Barley* in a somewhat different social milieu.

The real value and originality of Mortimer's drama lies in his one-act plays. Like Jean Tardieu in France, Mortimer seems to have made the one-act form peculiarly his own. It is here that his failures come into their own—here that they become successes at last by alienating themselves completely from the society that has trodden them down through decreeing terms they have found impossible to honor.

The most successful of Mortimer's one-act plays, and the best-known in the United States because of their presentation on television here, are *The Dock Brief* and *What Shall We Tell Caroline?* Both of these plays take place in Mortimer's world of the misfits and failures. It may be possible, Mortimer tells us, to write plays about "successful lawyers . . . wise schoolmasters, or families where the children can grow up without silence and without regret." But such plays are not John Mortimer's cup of tea. *The Dock Brief* and *What Shall We Tell Caroline?* are about unsuccessful lawyers, blundering schoolmasters, and families where the children grow up in silence and regret. The lawyer in *The Dock Brief* is a pathetic figure who has gone gray waiting for a "dock brief" (charity case) to show up. Now, at sixty-three years of age, he has finally been chosen to try his first case. It is a murder case, and he has no doubt at all that it will make him famous. Already he sees visions of himself on the bench, his chambers besieged by befurred and bejeweled society people, his name in the headlines as the most famous barrister in London. He spends most of the time allotted to him for interviewing his client in acting out his pipe dreams of success with the result that when the time comes to go to trial he is totally unprepared. The case is hopeless, anyway. In the second scene we learn that the lawyer has failed again. Instead of the brilliant two or three day address to the jury which was going to move strong men to tears and cause women to faint, he said nothing. No words would come; and so he just sat down again and gave up. His client is convicted, of course, but is immediately afterwards pardoned on the grounds that the incompetence of his lawyer rendered the trial an unfair one. Momentarily depressed, the lawyer cheers up again at the thought that his client, with whom he has become quite friendly, may need some little legal advice in the future. As the curtain falls, both men happily dance out of the cell whistling a gay tune. After a brief excursion into the cruel world of reality for which he is simply unfitted, Morgenhall, the lawyer, scampers back into the dream world where he fiddles away his existence with his crossword puzzles and his dreams of glory. His address to the jury fails for the same reason as his attempt to propose to the woman he loved failed:

> MORGENHALL: . . . It was the moment when I should have spoken, the obvious moment. Then, something overcame me, it wasn't shyness or fear then, but a tremendous exhaustion. I was tired out by the long wait, and when the opportunity came—all I could think of was sleep.
>
> FOWLE: It's a relief. . . .
>
> MORGENHALL: To go home alone. To undress, clean your teeth, knock out your pipe, not to bother with failure or success.
>
> FOWLE: So yesterday . . .
>
> MORGENHALL: I had lived through that moment so many times. It happened every day in my mind, daydreaming on buses, or in the doctor's surgery. When it came, I was tired of it. The exhaustion came over me. I wanted it to be all over. I wanted to be alone in my room, in the darkness, with a soft pillow round my ears. . . . So I failed.[2]

He simply does not have the stamina to make his way in the everyday world; and Mortimer's sympathy is entirely with him and with his kind.

In *What Shall We Tell Caroline?* the debonair pretender becomes a faded London roué who has been an assistant master at a small boys' boarding school on the bleak Norfolk coast for eighteen years. For eighteen years he has kept his spirits up by reminiscing about his days as a gay young blade on the Earl's Court Road. Accompanying himself on a banjo as he tells stories of lurid escapades that probably never happened, he brings a little light into the drab life of the school. It cheers things up, as he says, when "the results of the squash rackets competition and the state of the weather and the suspicion

2. *Ibid.*, p. 50.

about who pinched the nail brush off the chain in the down-stairs loo have been powerless to quicken the pulse." [3] The one thing wrong with the household is that Caroline, the headmaster's daughter, has not spoken to anyone for a long time. At the end of the play she finds her voice again and announces that she is going to London. But the play is really about the aging roué who has been hiding out from the reality he constantly talks about and dreams about for eighteen years.

Mortimer's other plays, *I Spy*, *Call Me a Liar*, *Lunch Hour*, *David and Broccoli*, *Collect Your Hand Baggage*, and *Two Stars for Comfort* are all similar efforts. All of them deal with people who are unable to cope with the world and who seek refuge in their illusions. Mortimer's sympathy is entirely with these characters, for he feels that their rejection of the conditions of society—their mute rebellion as it might be called—is justified. To function in society and be a success is commendable only if we accept the conditions set up by society as correct. This there is no reason to do. The laws of society are purely arbitrary, and there is nothing wrong, Mortimer feels, in receding into an individual world of one's own. Mortimer's view of people is one of personal sympathy, much like Brendan Behan's: "I respect kindness to human beings first of all, and kindness to animals. I don't respect the law; I have a total irreverence for anything connected with society except that which makes the roads safer, the beer stronger, the food cheaper, and old men and old women warmer in the winter, and happier in the summer." [4]

3. *Ibid.*, p. 105.
4. Quoted in program of *The Hostage* production at Wyndham's Theatre, London, 1959.

BRENDAN BEHAN
The Irish Primitive

LACK OF respect for the law and total irreverence for anything connected with society are even more pronounced in Behan than in Mortimer. Mortimer, indeed, might be described as a genteel and refined Behan. Where Mortimer shows us gentle characters who have been too weak to cope with life or who have politely declined to have anything to do with it as it is lived in modern society, Behan shows us rough-and-ready types who have kicked society in the teeth.

Brendan Behan is a primitive author in the best sense—instinctive, untutored, uninfluenced. The two plays by which he is known—*The Quare Fellow* and *The Hostage*—both show this primitivism even in their published forms, which have been considerably reworked by Joan Littlewood. Brendan Behan, it should be noted, is emphatically not a member of the New English Dramatists movement. His first play, *The Quare Fellow* (1945), was written well before Osborne's breakthrough with *Look Back in Anger*, and his second, *The Hostage* (1957), is related neither in theme nor in style to the angry-young-man syndrome. For Brendan Behan was most definitely not an angry young man, though he has far more reason to be one than any of the writers dubbed with that title by the critics. Behan spent nine of his forty years in some kind of penal institution. Every minute of those nine years' imprisonment was an injustice, since Behan was no criminal but a nationalist who had been caught acting in a manner considered rebellious by people whom he considered usurpers of his country's sovereignty. Instead of making him "angry," all this served to do was to make him an ever-bubbling wellspring of elemental good cheer. The main thing that strikes one about Behan's work is the compassion and understanding that he has for both sides of any conflict—for jailed and jailers in *The Quare Fellow*, for English and Irish in *The Hostage*. The only type of person that Behan cannot stomach is the person who tries to impose his authority and swell his dignity in the name of some abstract ideal, which, Behan implies, is not really sincerely held but manufactured to justify the person's behavior. Behan's villains are thus the mealy-mouthed, hypocritical prison visitor Holy Healey in *The Quare Fellow* and the puritanical, self-important I.R.A. leader, whose behavior ironically apes that of the British upper-class officers, in *The Hostage*.

Brendan Behan began playwriting more or less accidentally. After his release from prison in the late nineteen-forties, he worked as a painter for a bit and then began writing a column for the *Irish Press*. In his spare time he wrote a radio script originally entitled *The Twisting of Another Rope*. This was rejected by Radio Eireann and by the Abbey Theatre, and finally came to the attention of Alan Simpson, the producer, director, founder, and owner of the Pike Theatre, a tiny house he had built himself in a Dublin back-street garage. Simpson helped Behan rewrite the play, gave it its new title of *The Quare Fellow*, and put on its first performance anywhere, at the Pike Theatre in 1954.[1] The published text of *The Quare Fellow* is a later version, rearranged with the help of Joan Littlewood.[2] According to Simpson, this is an inferior version since it tends to mix up the characters of Donnelly and Regan, two of the warders.[3]

The Quare Fellow is a highly specialized slice-of-life play —nothing more or less than that. It is a play that becomes powerful and interesting through its situation, which is that of life in a cell block on the eve of an execution. The events leading up to an execution are perhaps the easiest of all possible theatrical situations to ruin through tastelessness, mawkishness, and misplaced social fervor. Behan avoids all the traps, most notably the one involving the condemned man's appearance. The "quare fellow" (prison slang for a condemned man) never does appear, and all we see is the reaction his fate has

1. Alan Simpson, *Beckett and Behan and a Theatre in Dublin* (London: Routledge & Kegan Paul Ltd., 1962), pp. 39–41.

2. Brendan Behan, *The Quare Fellow* (London: Methuen & Co., Ltd., 1961).

3. Alan Simpson, *op. cit.*, pp. 44–45.

on his fellow prisoners. Behan makes his play a success by
rigidly avoiding any hint of sentimentality and by displaying
an equal feeling of sympathy and understanding for the prisoners and the guards, both trapped victims of an invisible system that is beyond their power to comprehend.

Behan's other important play is *The Hostage*.[4] This was
originally written and performed in Gaelic, having been commissioned by Gael Linn, an organization devoted to the revival
of the Irish language. As *An Gáill* it was first performed in
Dublin in 1957. After being translated, it was reworked with
the help of Joan Littlewood and directed by her at the Theatre
Royal, Stratford, in 1958. Alan Simpson remarks very justly
that it was this play, Miss Littlewood's most successful author-
director collaboration, that helped bring about the widespread
acceptance of her type of dramatic production.[5] Simpson
gives this the rather vague name of "dramatized social realism,"
but actually it is a form of exuberant, perpetual-motion communication between audience and actor. *The Hostage*, with its
constant stops and starts, its songs and dances, its jokes and
vaudeville routines, is the perfect vehicle for this kind of production. The fact that *The Hostage* has a plot and a purpose
is almost obscured under the blanket of sheer nonsense covering the whole action. This "nonsense," however, is itself an
integral part of the action since it serves to imply that it is
nonsensical to take seriously the problem that the plot deals
with. The situation that Behan deals with in *The Hostage* is
at one and the same time deadly serious and ridiculous. An
eighteen-year-old I.R.A. member—a boy far too young to have
had any personal experience or knowledge of the Irish Rebellion—is to be hanged by the British in Belfast for terrorist
activities. The British thus compound the idiocy of the boy's
misguided and anachronistic terrorism by another idiocy; which
is then further compounded by the fanatical, self-conceited
I.R.A., who capture a young British soldier and announce they

4. He also wrote *The Big House*, a radio play recently adapted for
the stage by Alan Simpson, as well as two radio sketches, *The New House*
and *The Garden Party*.
5. Alan Simpson, *op. cit.*, p. 28.

will shoot him in retaliation for their member's execution. The action takes place in a Dublin whorehouse on the night before the execution. The British hostage has been brought here for safekeeping since a whorehouse is the last place the police would associate with the I.R.A. The head of the house is a real veteran of the Irish Rebellion. He is roused into a positive ecstasy of withering contempt by the posturings of the strutting young I.R.A. officer and absolutely refuses to take the matter seriously. One of the weird inmates of the house finally betrays the place to the police, and the hostage is inadvertently killed in the ensuing raid. But Behan immediately has him spring up and lead the cast in a mocking song that sums up the whole "devil take it" attitude of the play: "The bells of hell/Go ting-a-ling-a-ling,/For you but not for me,/Oh death where is thy sting-a-ling-a-ling?/Or grave thy victory?" [6]

In *The Quare Fellow* and *The Hostage* Brendan Behan wrote two of the best plays of the contemporary English theater. They are completely original and owe nothing to anyone. His untimely death has deprived the English theater of one of its few promising writers.

6. Brendan Behan, *The Hostage* (London: Methuen & Co., Ltd., 1962), p. 108.

NIGEL DENNIS
The Return of Intellectual Satire

FOR A man born as long ago as 1912 Nigel Dennis's literary output has been unusually small—two novels and three plays.[1] As a rule, the cliché that lack of quantity indicates high quality does not hold true in literature: a writer who says little usually has little to say. That, however, is not the case with Nigel Dennis. His work seems to be small in bulk for much the same reason that the end product of a refining process is small in bulk: what remains after all the distillations is the pure, ultimate essence of the substance.

Perhaps the reason for Dennis's excellence is that he is an unabashedly intellectual dramatist. At the same time his plays are vastly entertaining and first-rate theater. They do not, however, resemble the average Broadway or West End play. They are not, like commercial dramas, built around a situation into which some references to serious problems have been injected. Dennis's plays, like Shaw's, are built around a serious moral or intellectual problem, and the situation of the play grows out of the problem (that is to say, it is created solely for the purpose of theatrically illustrating the problem).

The problems that Dennis chooses to discuss in *Cards of Identity* and *The Making of Moo* are nothing less than the two basic problems with which the mind of man is confronted; namely, religion and psychology: his relationship to the universe and his relationship to himself. The two plays are preceded by a long and brilliantly written essay that further strengthens Dennis's right to be looked upon as a worthy, direct-line descendant of Shaw.

The two plays are philosophically related, as Dennis emphasizes in his preface, although they deal with totally different situations. *The Making of Moo* is subtitled "A History of Religion in Three Acts." It is Dennis's expression of his athe-

1. Dennis's third play, *August for the People*, is a farce about the British aristocracy's vested interest in democracy. It cannot compare with his first two plays.

istic beliefs. Despite his nonbelief, he is not particularly opposed to religion *per se*. Dennis is an extreme individualist, and as such he feels understandably irritated by the attempt of believers to whittle him down into their image. One might get the idea that Dennis suffers from a paranoid complex about religion. Not so! He simply wants to be let alone to do as he pleases. He does not want to bother anyone, and he expects the same treatment in return. He does not want to be bothered by proselytizing busybodies or by prescriptive pronunciamentos on morals and mores from a dogmatic Olympus. He contends that the sickness lies rather with those who cannot be content to find peace for themselves and insist on enjoining the "joys" of their "peace" on everyone else, forcibly if necessary. Furthermore, Dennis feels that all evangelical zeal is based on a huge, mushrooming chain reaction of swindle since all religions originate in one man's idea and his need to fortify it with fellow believers (known as disciples). In short, Dennis's views of the beginnings of religion can be summed up in the well-worn saying, "Religion began when the first knave met the first fool." *The Making of Moo* is about the origin of a religion—the religion of Moo. The implication is that all religions begin and develop like the religion of Moo.

Moo is the name of a new god created by an English civil engineer to replace Ega, an old god whom he has inadvertently "killed." It seems that Ega was a river god who was suffocated when the engineer (Frederick Compton by name) built a dam across the African stream he inhabited or haunted or permeated. Compton's British sense of the white man's burden and all that sort of thing is deeply disturbed when he hears of this, especially as the crime rate seems to be going up sharply now that Ega is no longer around to punish wrongdoers. He determines to whip up another god for the natives before he leaves. Moo, named after the lowing of the cows which infest Compton's front lawn, is the result. Moo starts out as a purely rational, personified code of ethics which Compton is going to work out for the benefit and improvement of the natives—a sort of mathematically systematized Taoism. But then Compton's wife and secretary join in. She wants to write the Bible of Moo, and the secretary, an amateur musician, wants to write the liturgy of Moo. Pretty soon Compton himself gets carried away with all this emotionalism, and the first act ends as he harangues his butler on the subject of Moo in the manner of St. Paul to the Corinthians.

In the second act we see the Moo religion two years later. The Comptons and their secretary have remained in Africa as "prophets"; their butler has been appointed pope. Moo is now in the primitive state of religion: barbaric ceremonies, human sacrifices, prophecies direct from the horse's mouth, rampant emotionalism, and so on. No trace of Moo's proposed rationalism remains. The religion is now based exclusively on emotion, revelation, and atavism. This is what happens to all religions, Dennis tells us in his preface. The theologians create something Invisible and Intangible, and consequently Inexplicable. Something Inexplicable can either be rejected out of hand as ridiculous or it can be accepted on blind faith. The latter is usually the case, since people have a psychological need to cling to something. Since it is Inexplicable and, therefore, believed in blindly, the theologians—the impresarios of the show—can manipulate it at will without danger of being scoffed at. Thus the religion, in order to survive, pronounces such dogmas as "Love Moo—and you will never think again" or "And Moo has said: 'In my arms there is no room for reason, and where there is no room for reason there is no room for doubt, and where there is no room for doubt there is room for Moo only.'" [2] Persons who point out flaws in the religion at this point are usually accused of heresy and eliminated at an auto-da-fé, a ceremony designed to make new men out of the onlookers while it makes no men out of the participants. This edifying ritual, which took the form of burning alive among the European Christians and heart gouging among the Aztecs, is here represented by the beheading of Fairbrother and his clerk. This stage gradually leads into the religion's solidified form.

2. Nigel Dennis, *Two Plays and a Preface* (New York: Vanguard Press, 1958), p. 194.

In the third act, which takes place many, many years later, Compton is a senile patriarch, and the Church of Moo is so well-established that businessmen are donating funds to it and scientists are "discovering" in carbon deposits evidence of its existence millions of years ago. Barbarities are no longer practised; everything is staid and respectable; and religion is transacted over teacups instead of buckets of blood. In short, the Moovian religion at this stage is similar to the Church of England today, or, as Dennis puts it in his preface, "Protestantism retains its barbarities only in verbal form: worshippers still sing 'There is a fountain filled with blood' and even ask to be washed in it; but by now the blood has ceased to register as such and would create sheer disgust were it not regarded simply as a colourful word in a fanciful jug." [3] At the end of the play Compton's son, a Moovian priest, goes off into the wilderness to seek the "original purity" of the religion, and the allegory thus comes full circle.

The Making of Moo is essentially an attack on universalized absolutism—there would be nothing wrong with Moovianism (or with any other religion), according to Dennis, if its devotees did not insist that its truth is absolute. For if it is absolute it follows that nothing else is right and, therefore, everyone should believe in it. And that is where the individualist stands up and begs to be excused: " 'Everything absolute belongs to pathology,' says Nietzsche—which does not mean that no one may give tongue to an absolute if he pleases, only that its pathology should not be enjoined on others. The intellectual may, if he please, make God in his own image: we rebel only when we are made in it as well." [4]

The intellectual with the established *idée fixe* is unhappily concerned with our social life as well as with our transcendental life. The religious fanatic's counterpart is the social brainwasher, the planner who wants to mold individual psyches to conform to his preconceived blueprints. The Moovian prophets, who want to control our lives by forcing their religious

3. *Ibid.*, p. 12.
4. *Ibid.*, p. 21.

"beliefs" on us, are supplemented in modern society by the Identity Club members, who wish to impose their personal dogma of social behavior on us.

Cards of Identity illustrates Dennis's thesis that modern psychology, with its emphasis on making people "adjust" to the society around them, is stifling individualism. For Dennis personal conspicuousness is not a sign of mental aberration, and his play is a protest against the pressing-iron technique of modern psychiatry. The process of psychoanalysis is analogous to the process of religious conversion: the Fisher for souls and the Fisher for minds are essentially one and the same. Man, according to the modern political brainwashers and psychoanalysts, must submerge his identity if he is to be "saved": "only when he swallows his pride can he be hooked to safety by the Great Fisherman. Once this has happened, his life and identity become utterly changed. Packed in a tin with other decapitated fish, his broken loneliness disappears; he is now a segment of the One Truth." [5]

The way the psychoanalysts accomplish this is by playing on the patient's inner life, on his memories, Dennis tells us. A man is made what he is by the experiences he has undergone. These experiences are all in the past and consequently exist only in the man's memory of them. It follows that if a man's memory of things is changed, the things themselves are actually changed; and the man's personality becomes reformed in accordance with the new set of experiences he now remembers. Thus, if a man can be made to "remember" things that never really happened (through suggestion, hypnosis, persuasion, terror, etc.) and if his personality is contingent upon his memory of his past experiences, then a man can be molded into any desired psychic shape. He becomes a piece of wet clay on a potter's wheel.

Cards of Identity is about a club, the Identity Club, whose members occupy themselves with changing other people's personalities. Three members, posing as husband, wife, and son, have taken over a country estate. They proceed to "make

5. *Ibid.*, p. 40.

over" various people of the neighborhood. The doctor becomes a gardener, his nurse becomes a mental patient, another local character becomes the butler, complete with memories of alcoholism and crime in his younger days. At the annual meeting of the Identity Club the three conspirators plan to do away with the president, who is senile, and replace him with their leader. After an abortive attempt to poison the president, which results in the death of the founder's daughter, they incite another member to shoot him. After this the club clears out, and, its influence removed, the victims slowly come back to their senses.

That is all there is to the plot. The interest lies in Dennis's thesis that the Identity Club is comparable to all modern organizations dedicated to the standardization of personality, e.g., psychiatrists and psychoanalysts, totalitarian political parties, absolutist religious sects, and similar groups. Dennis is strictly for the individual's right of self-determination. If we *must* have a religion then he is for the worship of the fourth-century divine, Pelagius, the opponent of St. Augustine, who is Dennis's *bête noire*. The main tenet of Pelagianism is that man has complete freedom of the will—no matter what his past may have been he has the ability at any given moment in his life to make a decision for good or evil. He must, therefore, accept full moral responsibility for each and every one of his acts. If he does this, he is safe. The Identity Club and the Moovians can only gain control of those who think they are not responsible for what they do—of those who feel they are determined by factors outside themselves.

In Nigel Dennis the English-speaking intellectual drama has found a new representative. *Cards of Identity* and *The Making of Moo* are superbly written plays with an innate and instinctive sense of the theater. They, together with the brilliantly witty preface (so witty in spots that the brilliance outsparkles the clarity) constitute the best that the British drama has produced since the death of Shaw.

JOHN ARDEN
Idealism and Promise

WHILE John Arden lacks the brilliance of Nigel Dennis, he too is primarily an intellectual dramatist (i.e., one who starts with an idea rather than with a situation). He tends to plod where Dennis sparkles, but he has a far better sense of play construction, stage situation, and character. Arden's strength lies in his ability to create dramatic atmosphere, to build up a believable stage world. Of all the playwrights writing in England today, with the possible exception of Pinter, Arden stands the best chance of surviving beyond the current vogue.

Arden's first important play was *Serjeant Musgrave's Dance* (1959). This is still considered his best work by the British critics, most of whom feel that he has not fulfilled the promise he showed in that play. *Serjeant Musgrave's Dance* is a pacifist play intended by Arden to show the injustice and barbarity of imperialism.

He tells the story of four deserters from Queen Victoria's army. Led by Serjeant Musgrave, they come to a snow-bound mining town in the North of England, carrying with them a skeleton and a small arsenal of guns and ammunition. The skeleton (not the least important "character" in the play since Arden rather tastelessly gives it a love scene to "play") used to be covered with the flesh of Billy Hicks, a home-town boy who ended up with a knife in his back in one of the remoter spots of the ever-sunlit Empire. Five natives were gunned down to expiate the crime. All of the soldiers thereupon experienced a revulsion at the barbarity of their calling and have come to convince the townspeople of the evils of killing. Musgrave, however, turns out to be an insane religious fanatic who claims that he lives by absolute logic—"logic" in this case consisting of five eyes for an eye, for he proposes to kill twenty-five leading townspeople in expiation for the five natives. This proposal is received with the scorn it deserves, and the situation is saved as loyal dragoons come trotting up in the nick of time over the snow-topped slag heaps, à la the Relief of Lucknow.

What Arden is *trying* to do in *Serjeant Musgrave's Dance* is to show how fanaticism can turn even excellent intentions such as Musgrave's into abominations. Musgrave believes himself to be the direct instrument of God's vengeance. Instead of being a study of the tragic paradox of militant pacifism, the play becomes simply a clumsily written case study of a lunatic.

A year before he made his reputation with *Serjeant Musgrave's Dance*, Arden had had *Live Like Pigs* produced at the Royal Court. In this play he gives a hint of his real talent. Like Bernard Kops, Arden founders every time he tries to deal seriously with significant themes; unlike Kops, he has not yet discovered that his real talent is for writing pure farce. Insofar as *Live Like Pigs* is pure farce it is an excellent play of its kind; but Arden ruins it by trying to turn it into a sociological commentary. In his introduction to the play, Arden says that he intended the play to be "a study in differing ways of life brought sharply into conflict and both losing their own particular virtues under the stress of intolerance and misunderstanding." [1] In order to do this, Arden sets his play in a low-cost municipal housing project. One of the houses has been given to a raffish and unwashed family that had been living in an abandoned tram on the outskirts of town and supporting itself by petty thieving and prostitution. Naturally, as soon as they move in, the house is turned into an incredibly filthy shambles. The "conflict" comes when the Sawneys are thrown against their new neighbors, a typical lower-class bourgeois ménage. This is a situation rich in comic possibilities and even of a certain amount of serious-minded satire, since it shows up, by implication, the hidebound muddle-headedness of municipal bureaucracy. Unfortunately, Arden is not content with so simple and unambitious an object. He tries instead to instill some sort of "tragic" quality into his play by telling us in his preface that the Sawneys are really fine old English stock whose behavior is due to the impasse between their traditional "free"

1. Thomas Maschler, ed., *New English Dramatists 3* (Middlesex, England: Penguin Books, 1961), p. 95.

way of life and the modern regularized one to which the neighbors are accustomed:

> The Sawneys are an anachronism. They are the direct descendants of the "sturdy beggars" of the sixteenth century, and the apparent chaos of their lives becomes an ordered pattern when seen in terms of a wild empty countryside and a nomadic existence. Put out of their fields by enclosing landlords, they found such an existence possible for four hundred years. Today, quite simply, there are too many buildings in Britain, and there is just no room for nomads. The family in this play fails to understand this, and becomes educated in what is known as the "hard way," but which might also be called the "inefficient way." [2]

The trouble with this kind of thinking is that it has nothing to do with reality. If there are people in England today who act as the Sawneys do, it is not because the building boom has left no room for nomads, but because they are criminal types of low mentality and primitive living standards who do not deserve sympathy but rather require coercion. To look upon people who wallow in verminous filth, disturb their neighbors with earsplitting noise, destroy their houses with wanton vandalism, and live off thievery and prostitution, as wide-eyed, innocent children of nature who deserve commiseration because the building boom has dispossessed them from their idyllic life among the flower-bedecked hedgerows is the merest muzzy-headed romanticism.

The Happy Haven, produced at the Royal Court Theatre in September, 1960, received a far less enthusiastic critical reception than his previous plays, although it deserved a better one. The Happy Haven is an old folks' home run by an obsessed young scientist who thinks he is on the track of the Fountain of Youth. Out of the bubbling, rainbow-hued fluids in his chromium-plated retorts and alembics he hopes to concoct something that will make old people young again. Dr. Copperthwaite is endowed with all the irresponsible, self-centered

2. *Ibid.*

callousness so common among scientific researchers, whose goal is all too often fame and fortune at any cost. The old people, who have all been failures in their lives, find out about Dr. Copperthwaite's plan and, full of resentment at being used as guinea pigs, steal the solution and jab it into the doctor. The play thus ends as the scientist, hoist with his own petard, is transformed into a squalling baby and wheeled out. Arden has hit upon an excellent dramatic idea here, but the eccentricities of his style mar it as a stage piece. Most of the comment on *The Happy Haven* has centered on Arden's use of masks, which most of the characters wear. These masks are actually unimportant and are in no way integrated into the play, which could be just as effective, if not more so, without them.

In *The Workhouse Donkey* (1963), magnificently produced at the Chichester Festival, Arden has at last solved his problems. In it he has found his niche as a dramatic author. *The Workhouse Donkey* is a superbly comic farce about municipal corruption in a North of England industrial town. Both the Conservatives and the Laborites are depicted as unmitigated scoundrels (although the Laborites are amiable ones), and the only honest man is the neutral Police Commissioner, the "man who stands alone." Roguery triumphs in the end, of course. In *The Workhouse Donkey*, also, Arden has hit upon the correct way to integrate his songs and dances into the action: he makes no pretense at suspension of disbelief and has the whole play written half at the audience in the manner of vaudeville skits.

Little needs to be said about Arden's subsequent major plays. *Left-Handed Liberty* (1965) was commissioned by the City of London to celebrate the 750th anniversary of the Magna Carta. Arden has put together a thoughtful and well-written chronicle play that disseminates none of the usual illusions about the Magna Carta being the basis of all subsequent English liberty. Instead, he shows the events immediately following the signing of the Charter, emphasizing the fact that the principles enunciated were merely paid lip-service; and that the whole incident of the Charter was one of many ploys in the Machiavellian game of bluff and power politics played between

King John and his barons.

Armstrong's Last Goodnight (1965), subtitled "An Exercise in Diplomacy," continues Arden's fascination with the game of power politics. This time he shows how the machinations of Sir David Lindsay, poet and politician, led to the hanging of the Border freebooter Johnny Armstrong of Gilnockie in 1530. Arden claims to have been influenced in this play by Conor Cruise O'Brien's *To Katanga and Back*.[3] While I am grateful that this remark has led me to a perusal of Mr. O'Brien's brilliant book, I fail to see the similarity of moral problems of which Arden speaks. In any case, it is unnecessary to seek such a connection. The play is perfectly capable of standing by itself as an example of psychological analysis on stage in the beautifully worked out contrast between the cynicism and callous Machiavellian duplicity of Lindsay on the one hand and the oddly attractive child-like vanity and primitive brutishness of Armstrong on the other.

On the evidence of the plays he has written so far, there can be little doubt that John Arden is potentially the best of the dramatists that were given their opportunity as a result of Osborne's mole-hill. Only Harold Pinter can rival him in consistency of production and level of quality, although his plays are virtually in a different genre.

3. John Arden, *Armstrong's Last Goodnight* (London: Methuen & Co., 1965), p. 8.

Hope Deferred

The New American Drama

EVER SINCE the now almost historic first production of *Look Back in Anger* in 1956 the English drama critics have been beating their drums for a renaissance of the English drama. They have succeeded in creating a hypnotic atmosphere in which their readers could be made to believe that the plays being produced by Osborne, Wesker, Kops, et al. were really significant. The persistent rhythm of their verbal tom-toms convinced almost everyone that there was something called the angry-young-man movement, which had crystallized out of the infinite aridity of the drawing-room desert over which Terence Rattigan hovered like a too frequently descending sandstorm. This movement was later expanded into the more inclusive—and, indeed, as it has turned out, catch-all—New English Dramatists movement. American playgoers have a right to be puzzled as to why this English drama movement has not been paralleled in their own country. The fact is that there have been plenty of new American dramas, most of them every bit as interesting as their English counterparts. The lack of a "movement" in the United States is due to the much greater difficulty of getting a play produced in the commercial theater and to the stubborn refusal of the New York drama critics to get together and form a cheering section for the American drama.[1]

1. John Mason Brown, one of the leading American theater critics, in writing an article on the state of the current theater, recognized that

The American writers whose plays have been successful and interesting enough to provide the kind of counterbalance to the Tennessee Williams type of drama that the New English Dramatists have provided to the Terence Rattigan type of drama are Edward Albee, Jack Richardson, Jack Gelber, and Arthur Kopit. With one exception, to be considered later, these writers have shown more promise than achievement so far, but the promise is definitely there.

"Within the last ten years . . . a generation has appeared, writing in a different manner, with a different purpose, from a different view of man in a melodramatically altered world. This new generation has by no means taken over the whole of the theatre. It is as yet mainly a force on the fringes. How long its vogue will last and how abiding its influence will be, no one can say. But its coming was needed and its impact has been healthy." But his list of the best plays produced on the American stage in recent years does not include any of Richardson's works and finally boils down to *J.B.*, *Becket*, and *A Man for All Seasons* (John Mason Brown, "What's Right with the Theatre," *Saturday Review*, May 11, 1963, pp. 19–21). .

EDWARD ALBEE

IN THE unlikely event that anything like a "movement" of young American dramatists will ever get off the ground, the world premiere of Edward Albee's *The Zoo Story* will undoubtedly be commemorated as its starting point. Characteristically enough, this world premiere did not take place in the United States, where the critics seldom hail anything new in the arts until they have had the green light from across the Atlantic. In this case the green light came all the way from West Germany, where *The Zoo Story* was first produced in Berlin on September 28, 1959. The story of how *The Zoo Story* was first produced in Germany and subsequently became a success in New York after having previously been rejected right and left over here is extremely instructive for those trying to understand the fantastic world of the New York theater with its Alice-in-Wonderland economics, according to which the producers and theater-owners rake in all the money (and pay the featherbedding stagehands, house managers, and public relations men with it) while the actors and authors, unless the play is exceptionally "successful," starve. Naturally enough, if the sole purpose of theatrical productions is the personal enrichment of the producer and the theater-owner, new plays such as *The Zoo Story* have not the faintest chance of being put on unless they come with some built-in guarantee of success such as a European reputation. That is exactly what happened to Albee's play. After being passed around New York for a bit, it was sent to Europe by a friend of the author, and there it was finally produced. When it came back, it came with critical acclaim behind it and labels reading "avant-garde," "philosophy of the absurd," and "disciple of Beckett" plastered all over it. It was thus safe to produce and duly opened at the Provincetown Playhouse in New York on January 14, 1960, being obediently accorded enthusiastic reviews by critics who almost certainly didn't understand a word of it but who had done their homework on the European press notices and the academic pronouncements.

The Zoo Story is both an extremely simple and an extremely mystifying play. It is mystifying *because* it is so simple. Like Ionesco, who is clearly his literary progenitor, Albee is not *saying* anything with his play, which is nothing but an excessively fantastic slice-of-life pastiche: he is exemplifying or demonstrating a theme. That theme is the enormous and usually insuperable difficulty that human beings find in communicating with each other. More precisely, it is about the maddening effect that the enforced loneliness of the human condition has on the person who is cursed (for in our society it undoubtedly *is* a curse) with an infinite capacity for love.

There are only two characters in the play, which is essentially a monologue. A rather seedy, down-and-out young man approaches a somewhat older, pillar-of-society type sitting on a bench in a remote section of Central Park on a sunny Sunday afternoon. The man on the bench is middle-aged, well-to-do, respectable. He has a good position, a happy family, a comfortable home life. The desperation that Albee feels the human condition must engender in a sensitive man does not touch him. Not because he is a naturally insensitive being—he isn't. He is a cultured, well-read man, perfectly aware of all the things that are bothering his companion; but he is aware of them only in the abstract. Because he is walled-in by the protective barricades of society, they do not disturb him. Our social order, as Albee sees it, is a set of devices that protect the individual from the realities of the human condition. As a respectable member of society (family man; business executive; registered voter; college graduate; civic, social, and fraternal club member) Peter is granted immunity from the discomforts and anxieties of real human emotion. Man in society need no longer recognize that he is really naked and afraid, that he is really a helpless mote drifting in a hostile void governed by the elemental forces of the "Savage God." Albee sees society, in other words, as a sort of Chinese Wall protecting those within from the barbarian hordes outside. Occasionally, though, one of the inhabitants of this artificial enclosure inadvertently strays too near the line and is overcome by an intruder. This is what Albee shows us happening to Peter on his peaceful bench in Central Park. Jerry is an outsider—rootless and aimless, he is the absolute antithesis of Peter. Nothing protects him and, consequently, he feels the full agony of knowing the world as it *really* is (as do, for example, Beckett's two tramps or Adamov's cripples or any number of other characters from the current French avant-garde theater). He meets Peter and tries to make him understand. He fails, of course, and finally, in utter despair, tries to achieve a sort of communication through enmity by baiting Peter into a fight.[1] In the end, Jerry immolates himself by running onto his own knife, which Peter is holding out to ward him off, and thus finally forces a sort of human relationship between them by creating a perverse blood brotherhood.

The Zoo Story is not only remarkable as a young writer's first play: it is remarkable by any standards for the spareness of its construction and the daring of its conception. It takes a man who has in him at least the germs of a master writer to bring off as fantastic a situation as the one in which the schizoid Jerry suddenly switches personalities, picks a fight with his companion, and then impales himself on his own knife. Albee manages to make this entirely believable and—what is even more important—entirely understandable once the initial shock has worn off.

Between *The Zoo Story* and his next significant play, *The American Dream*, Albee wrote two more short plays, *The Sandbox* and *The Death of Bessie Smith*. Both plays were written in 1959, and, like *The Zoo Story*, *The Death of Bessie Smith* was first produced in Berlin. Neither of these plays is worth much comment. *The Sandbox* is a skillful piece of writing in the current avant-garde vein, but it is essentially merely a preliminary sketch for *The American Dream*, several of whose characters it duplicates. *The Death of Bessie Smith* is Albee's impressionistic recreation of the circumstances surrounding the death of the famous Negro blues singer who died in an automobile accident in Memphis, Tennessee, in 1937. The

1. Bertolt Brecht used the same device as early as 1922 when he wrote *Im Dickicht der Städte*.

main character (Bessie Smith herself does not appear) is the admissions nurse at one of the hospitals that refused to treat Miss Smith because she was a Negro. Through her Albee tries to probe the mentality of a typical Southern white woman. He tries to show that the viciousness of such a person's resentment against the Negro is the result of a series of constant frustrations. His attempt, unfortunately, fails. The nurse is an entirely incredible character as portrayed, and the whole play collapses with her. Albee plans the entire action around the nurse, and the death of the Negro blues singer is treated only as something that accidentally impinges upon her life. James Baldwin very acutely points out that the trouble with the play is that it is bloodless: there is nothing in it to "illuminate the contrast between the wonderfully reckless life and terrible death of Bessie Smith and the whited sepulchre in which the nurse is writhing." [2] This ties in with Henry Goodman's perceptive remark that Albee's enmity to the false values of society seems to be more a case of personal revulsion than of social conscience.[3]

In *The American Dream*, his most important play to date, Albee has picked an ideal subject and title with which to start a movement. As he notes in his preface, several critics have taken sharp exception to the play on the grounds that it is negative in approach, that it tends to denigrate its subject, and that it is "nihilist, immoral, and defeatist" in content.[4] All these things are undoubtedly true. But what did the critics expect? A play that *celebrates* the American dream would be utterly pointless, would, indeed, strictly speaking, be precisely what the critics called Albee's play. It would be nihilist, immoral, and defeatist because it would be perpetuating a lie. The "American Dream," the principle of freedom and individuality for which the country was founded has, as any clear-thinking

---

2. James Baldwin, "Theatre: The Negro In and Out," in John A. Williams, ed., *The Angry Black* (New York: Lancer Books [1962]), p. 21.

3. Henry Goodman, "The New Dramatists, 4: Edward Albee," *Drama Survey*, II (Spring, 1962), pp. 72–79.

4. Edward Albee, *The American Dream* (New York: Coward-McCann, Inc., 1961), p. 7.

and courageous person cannot hesitate to admit, become thoroughly corrupted by precisely the things Albee is attacking in his play: by misplaced hero worship; by values based exclusively on the crassest commercialism; by flabby, unthinking complacency; and by brutal destruction of human emotions. To *celebrate* the "American Dream," even supposing there were anything left to celebrate, would be utterly useless. What would be the point of flattering an audience and sending them away with hands folded in self-congratulatory complacency on their comfortably rounded stomachs? This is a function performed efficiently enough by our annual open-air, massed-voice, historico-patriotic pageants, most of which are staged, significantly enough, in the South. The function of the drama is not to celebrate what is good but to protest against what is bad. Progress can come about only through criticism.

Albee's technique in *The American Dream* is caricature. He takes the traditional elements of the American dream—the happy family, the efficient go-getter, the idealistic hero—and shows them in the grotesquely distorted form that he feels they have assumed. The happy family becomes an emasculated money supplier dominated by an emotionally sterile, nagging wife; the efficient go-getter becomes a sexless female machine; the idealistic hero becomes a handsome, empty-headed, hollow shell of a man with the outlook and philosophy of a professional pimp. Interestingly enough, as the critics might have known had they been the competent drama scholars they should be instead of the ill-educated journalists casually kicked onto the drama desk by their editors that they are, Albee is by no means the first man to treat the American dream theme in this way. Back in 1933 George O'Neil, who might well have become one of America's greatest dramatists had he not died early, wrote a play called *American Dream* which deals with the degeneration of the American ideal using even more "nihilism, immorality, and defeatism" than Albee's play. O'Neil used the panoramic method, showing the moral disintegration of one American family through several generations, while Albee shows us a caricatured version of the end product; but the general idea is the same. It would be instructive to be able to see parallel productions of the O'Neil and Albee plays.

Albee sets his little parable in his conception of a typical slice of *Suburbia Americana*. Mommy and Daddy sit opposite each other in their foam-rubber and fumed-oak living room, the former babbling vacuous inanities, the latter keeping himself just conscious enough to register what she is saying. The scene is irresistibly reminiscent of Ionesco's *The Bald Soprano*, in which Mrs. Smith sits and mumbles the English equivalents of Mommy's inanities. Here, as in *The Bald Soprano* and *The Zoo Story*, we see the impossibility of communication even in the closest of relationships. The parallel between the two plays is carried further when Mrs. Barker comes in. She has been sent for, but she does not know why; nor do Mommy and Daddy know why they have sent for her, although they have both been eagerly awaiting her. Like Mr. and Mrs. Martin in *The Bald Soprano*, who have to go through a long chain of inductive reasoning to find out that they were married to each other (but only possibly, since the maid points out a fatal flaw in their reasoning immediately afterwards), Mrs. Barker has to probe around interminably. She is, however, so entangled in all the commitments she has made in her capacity of "professional woman," that she is totally unable to find out what she is supposed to be there for. It takes Grandma, Mommy's somewhat jaundiced eighty-six-year-old parent, to set her straight finally. Grandma is easily Albee's most memorable character; his play, indeed, stands or falls on her, for nothing is easier than for the actress playing her to make her cute and precious. The danger is that the actress will play the tough-talking, wisecracking Grandma for laughs. This would be tempting and easy to do but ruinous for the play since Grandma is its only admirable character. Grandma is an anachronism: she represents the solid pioneer stock out of which the American Dream might have come had it not been corrupted instead. Grandma reveals to Mrs. Barker that she is there in her capacity of fieldworker for an adoption agency. Twenty years before, it seems, Mrs. Barker had provided Mommy and Daddy with a baby that had turned out to be a disappointment. To discourage its disobedience, Mommy found it necessary to gouge its eyes out, cut its hands off and its tongue out, and emasculate it. Finally it died and now Mommy and Daddy want either their money back or a new and more satisfactory baby. At this point a caricature of the traditional "All-American boy" enters—big, muscular, handsome in a glossy, Hollywood-studio way, utterly brainless, and ready to do anything—*anything* (the emphasis is his)—for money. He was not always like this, though; and he can still grope around in the dim recesses of his mind for memories of a time when he had an identical twin brother (who represents his potentialities for good) from whom he was separated a long time ago. Since the separation he has been steadily going downhill until now he is totally unable to feel anything: "I cannot touch another person and feel love. . . . I have no emotions. I have been drained, torn asunder . . . disemboweled. I have now only my person . . . my body, my face. . . . And it will always be thus." [5] The young man's story touches the old woman deeply, for it rouses the stirrings of a distant racial memory she had thought long dead. Grandma is not merely an exceptionally spry eighty-six-year-old; she is Albee's conception of the Great American Earth Mother who recognizes deep within herself the memory of the original dream that the founding of the New World gave to the human race. She, the pioneer stock, remembers the real dream: "I don't know you from somewhere, but I knew . . . once . . . someone very much like you . . . or, very much as perhaps you were . . . Someone . . . to be more precise . . . who might have turned out to be very much like you might have turned out to be." [6] But it is too late for that now, so Grandma conceives the idea of persuading Mrs. Barker to give the young man to Mommy and Daddy as their new son. Grandma leaves at the end of the play, and Mommy and Daddy enthusiastically accept the flawed, maculate image of the dream that they deserve. Few plays have shown up the sterility of the society in which they were written so uncompromisingly and savagely as this play of

5. *Ibid.*, pp. 78–79.
6. *Ibid.*, p. 79.

Albee's. As James Baldwin points out, it is hardly a "dream" anymore: "Its vision of the antiseptic passivity of American life, and the resulting death of the masculine sensibility makes it more closely resemble a nightmare." [7]

Albee's next play, *Who's Afraid of Virginia Woolf?*, was his first full-length effort. It is unhappily considerably more than full-length since it lasts well over three hours. Although the play could be tightened (it has at least one hour of purely excess dialogue), the process would merely result in making meaninglessness more playable. After the promise of *The American Dream*, *Who's Afraid of Virginia Woolf?* is a disappointment. It was perhaps too much to hope that Albee would produce something as significant as *The American Dream* for his first Broadway effort; too much to hope that the production of *Who's Afraid of Virginia Woolf?* would mark the entrenchment and acceptance of the off-beat, paradoxical, enigmatic plays of Albee, Richardson, Kopit, and Weinstein that constituted the off-Broadway seed of the putative new American drama. In *Who's Afraid of Virginia Woolf?* Albee has succeeded merely in producing a long piece of intellectualized *kitsch*.

There are only four characters in Albee's play, which takes place in a small New England college. The scene is the living room of a history professor who has been married for over twenty years to the daughter of the college's president. Theirs appears to be a marriage based by now almost exclusively on a sort of vaguely good-humored bickering which flares out every so often into open savagery. Their bickering is automatic and off-hand, with the touch of professionalism brought by years of practice. His main gambit is her drinking and the fact that she is six years older than he is; hers is his spinelessness and his failure to rise in academic circles despite his connections as the president's son-in-law. Just now they are returning at 2:00 A.M. from a party at the president's house and are preparing to receive a late visit from a young biology professor and his wife. The rest of the play is taken up with George and

7. Baldwin, *loc. cit.*

Martha's constant hacking away at each other while the biologist and his wife watch and are slowly and unwillingly dragged into the vortex of their hosts' affairs.

During the play Martha repeatedly humiliates George in front of the guests, even going so far as to try to seduce the young biology professor. George gets even at the end by announcing that a telegram has arrived saying their son, who is supposed to return home for his twenty-first birthday celebration the next day, has been killed in an automobile accident. This reduces Martha to a state of sniveling hysteria; and we learn that the son we have been hearing about all through the play is purely imaginary—an illusion George and Martha have maintained between themselves. Martha, in telling the guests about him, has violated the compact she has had with George never to mention the imaginary son to anyone else, so he revenges himself by publicly, i.e., irrevocably, destroying the comforting little teddy-bear secret they have been hugging together for so long. At the end the guests leave, and George and Martha are left to rearrange their perspectives and pick up the pieces.

It might be as well to pause here and examine this play in the light of Albee's subsequent development. Everyone recognized a distinctly promising theatrical talent in *The Zoo Story* and *The American Dream*. At the same time it was obvious that these two plays were directly derived from the French avant-garde drama. Excellent imitations though they were, they were still imitations. Literary reputations are based on a writer's ability to state and develop a theme, not on his ability to improvise on someone else's theme. Thus it was that when *Who's Afraid of Virginia Woolf?*—and subsequently *Tiny Alice* and *A Delicate Balance*—appeared, it was hailed by the majority of the critics (Robert Brustein, Tom Driver, and Richard Schechner were honorable exceptions) as the advent of Albee's own distinctive style. The fact is, however, that Albee is as derivative in his later plays as in his earlier ones. The difference is that he has moved from the honesty of Ionesco to the shrewdly calculated, box-office oriented claptrap of Tennessee Williams. *Who's Afraid of Virginia Woolf?* belongs squarely in the Williams school of transom-peeping drama, where the whole effect is based on a concrete realization of the habitual gossip column peruser's wildest fantasies. Such a play, of course, while it may well become a commercial success, is not necessarily one that will be taken seriously by critics and scholars. For that, intellectual profundity is essential; and since the amorphous boundaries between appearance and reality constitute the *stoff* of one of our more vexing critical problems, the *appearance* of profundity is as a rule quite enough. There are two ways in which this appearance can be brought about. One is the imposition on the play of the expectation of profundity based on the playwright's past performances. Thus the critics were psychologically prepared to find profundity in *Who's Afraid of Virginia Woolf?* when it came out because they had found it in *The Zoo Story* and *The American Dream*. The most extraordinary significance can be read into the flattest drawing room comedies and into soap operas exuding essence-of-banality given the *a priori* assumption that significance of some sort must be there. The other way in which the appearance of profundity can be created is by spraying symbols around. As a result of all this we are afflicted with a flood of mildly ingenious interpretations of *Who's Afraid of Virginia Woolf?* showing that it is really a parable of the decline and fall of Western society or of the moral bankruptcy of the intelligentsia. Alternatively, we may be told that the play is about the achievement of mutual honesty through the purgation of illusion or about the conflict between humanitarianism and soulless science. Such interpretations are based on the fact that the protagonists are called George and Martha (as in the first First Family—the contrast between the two families shows how far we have degenerated), that the setting is called New Carthage (the new is as effete as the old and must also be destroyed), that George reads the Catholic burial service over his imaginary son, or that George and Nick (whom one critic, in an inspired crescendo of idiocy, identified with Nikita Khrushchev) [8] represent the struggle be-

8. In all fairness I should say that Albee himself has blessed this interpretation by admitting he had this identification in mind. Cf. Michael E. Rutenberg, *Edward Albee: Playwright in Protest* (New York: Drama Book Shop, 1969), p. 232.

tween science and humanities because one is a historian (who has never done anything) and the other is a biologist (who has not done anything yet). Actually, the arguments between George and Nick about their respective specialties would impress even a bunch of sophomore engineering or business administration students as dull and obvious. To anyone reading the play without previous assumptions it should rapidly become clear that these allusions were put in by Albee precisely so that they might be picked up by unwary critics.

One other point needs to be made about *Who's Afraid of Virginia Woolf?* and that is the persistent rumor that the play was originally written for four men. Albee has specifically denied this,[9] although "The more sophisticated interpreters simply step over Albee's denials and assume that the play, whoever it was written for, is really about a homosexual marriage."[10] Not being very sophisticated in these matters, I assume nothing of the sort. Given a considerable adjustment of acting style, the play might possibly be viable in homosexual terms (persistent reports of such productions that are actually supposed to have taken place would seem to confirm this), but I see no reason to add public mendacity to the list of Mr. Albee's sins, nor do I see any reason for not taking the play at face value. It is that value that is in question—and it would certainly not be enhanced by being inverted.

Tiny Alice (1964) has aroused more controversy and criticism than any other Albee play. The five characters are a lawyer known as "Lawyer," a butler named Butler, a Cardinal who keeps cardinals (birds), Miss Alice, who lives in a castle containing a replica of itself which contains a replica of herself and so on (possibly) *ad infinitum*, and Julian, the only one who does not have his own *doppelgänger*. Miss Alice, the richest woman in the world (one is reminded of Claire Zachanassian, a far more meaningful and dramatic "richest woman in the world"), undertakes to pay the Catholic Church (why *Catholic* Church? So the Cardinal can have his cardinals, of course!) an enormous

9. *Ibid.*, p. 255 and Gerald Weales, *The Jumping-Off Place* (New York: Macmillan Co., 1969), p. 42.

10. Weales, p. 42.

sum of money provided the transaction is handled by Julian, the Cardinal's lay secretary. It soon becomes evident that Lawyer, Butler, Miss Alice and, later, the Cardinal are all conspiring to sacrifice Julian to Tiny Alice, the occupant of the miniature castle-within-the-castle. They do this by first having Miss Alice seduce and marry him and then shooting him so that he dies leaning on the replica of the castle in a crucified position.

At first sight this is an extremely complex play, but Albee himself assures us that "the play is quite clear." [11] I think Albee means this remark quite literally, and I think he is right. In the sense that meaninglessness is inevitably clear, the play *is* clear. *Tiny Alice* is a veritable alphabet soup of symbols, like Tennessee Williams' *Camino Real*. The symbols are thrown in at random so that each critic can pick them out and form his own pattern. All that is required to render such a play significant is a group of docile, symbol-hunting, jig-saw puzzle enthusiasts. Given Miss Alice (symbol of wealth), the Cardinal (symbol of religion), Julian (symbol of lost faith), the martyrdom, the Chinese box puzzle of the castles-within-castles, and the perverse sexuality, one can come up with almost anything—except coherence. The key to the whole matter almost certainly lies in the sexual aspects of the play's plot, the central event being the seduction of Julian, a seduction which is initiated in extremely ambiguous terms as he kneels before Miss Alice's open robe, under which she is presumably naked, and buries his face in her sex—or thereabouts. This is the only apparently heterosexual act in a play that is shot through with blatant homosexual references, but while I am prepared to accept Martha and Honey as having been intended as females all along, I cannot but think that Miss Alice was originally a man. The homosexual aspects of the play are further reinforced when we learn that "tiny alice" is homosexual jargon for the male anus.[12] This is something that Albee either did or did not know when he wrote the play.[13] If he did not know it, then its use as the

11. Edward Albee, *Tiny Alice* (New York: Pocket Books, 1966), author's note preceding p. 1.

12. Weales, pp. 43–44. I have also heard this from other sources.

13. He denies having known it. Cf. Rutenberg, p. 254.

title of a play already full of homosexual references is an extraordinarily unfortunate coincidence. If he did know it, then the play is a truly outrageous piece of effrontery concocted with the utmost cynicism.

A *Delicate Balance* (1966) is a much simpler play than *Tiny Alice*. It takes place in the comfortable home of a well-to-do suburban couple. The husband is an amiable ditherer, the wife a rather severe woman, clearly the power in the house, who toys with the idea that she is going insane. There is also the wife's sister, a drunkard who provides comic relief with predictable wisecracks on the passing scene, and the daughter, just home after her fourth unsuccessful marriage. The action concerns the attitude of the family to their invasion by another couple, their best friends, who move in on them after being seized with nameless terror while sitting quietly at home. The couple finally leaves, after sensibly deciding that they cannot impose on their friends anymore since they themselves would certainly not put up with such behavior. Harry and Edna, the unwelcome visitors pursued by a nameless terror, are plainly refugees from a Boris Vian or an Ionesco play. What ruins Albee's play is his failure to make Harry and Edna credible. We are told that they are fleeing a nameless dread, but we see no signs of it in them. They are exactly like the family they invade: solid and realistic. Their link to the world of the absurd is too far-fetched. Because of their ordinariness we cannot believe that something outside ordinary experience has happened to them. This mixing of styles has been Albee's principal fault in his later plays. One cannot suspend one's disbelief sufficiently to accept Tobias and his family and friends or George and Martha as people living in a special world of their own where things outside ordinary experience are likely to happen.

In his latest play, variously called *Box-Mao-Box* or *Box and Quotations from Chairman Mao Tse-tung* (1968), Albee departs entirely from conventional theatrical form and experiments with "the application of universal form to dramatic structure." [14] Again, as with *Tiny Alice*, Albee informs us that these

14. Edward Albee, *Box and Quotations from Chairman Mao Tse-tung* (New York: Atheneum Press, 1969), p. ix.

two plays are "quite simple" and "can be apprehended without much difficulty." [15] Again, as with *Tiny Alice*, Albee is quite right—and for much the same reason.

Box and *Quotations from Chairman Mao Tse-tung* are interrelated plays in the sense that *Quotations* is sandwiched between sections of *Box* and that lines from *Box* are inserted throughout *Quotations*. *Box* is so called because the set is a box opening out towards the audience. There are no characters, only a disembodied voice coming out of the public address system and intended to represent the voice of the box itself. The words spoken by the voice are somewhat incoherent. The gist of the monologue seems to be a lament for better days and for the demise of artistry or craftsmanship as well as an excoriation of man's cruelty. The box, one critic informs us, is "the symbolic coffin from which emanate the last surviving thoughts of a decimated civilization." [16] At this point in our consideration of the play it might be as well to give credit where credit is due by pausing to take off our hats and bowing thrice in the direction of Samuel Beckett. The state of stasis on stage toward which Beckett has been painfully working for so long from *Waiting for Godot* to *Play* is here achieved all at once by Albee. The effect is as spurious as Beckett's work is sincere and motivated with its gradual, even reluctant, edging toward immobility. Perhaps the difference is that Beckett has been shrinking the dimensions of his stage world in a linear manner rather than in the sudden McLuhanesque manner of Albee.[17] The content of the speech emanating from the box is, furthermore,

15. *Ibid.*
16. Rutenberg, p. 204.
17. Rutenberg (p. 206) makes a good deal of the influence of McLuhan's babble on *Box-Mao-Box*. He is probably right about the influence, though wrong in supposing that the influence is beneficial. Most ·people who have been impressed by McLuhan have made the mistake of not stopping at a consideration of his brilliant insight that linear, sequential information and the logical thought processes that produce it are in danger of being eliminated by our electronic environment. Instead, they have followed him in approving this disaster and celebrating the necessarily mindless take-over of fragmentary, non-sequential and therefore chaotic so-called thought processes.

a watered-down, vulgarized version of Lucky's speech in *Waiting for Godot*. The theme of the decline and death of civilization is counterpointed through *Quotations*, which is itself an exercise in dramatic counterpoint as three characters pursue entirely disparate verbal melodies while a fourth remains mute. *Quotations* takes place on the mock deck of an ocean liner contained within the box. Albee takes care to warn us against specific interpretations of his play, saying that we must get rid of the notion of conscious symbolism and "begin to understand the use of the unconscious"—that's where *Box* and *Quotations* are, he tells us, and they must not be "pigeonholed, examined, and specified." [18] Despite these protestations of unconscious motivation, one cannot help noticing that here we are on an ocean liner contained within the box from which the voice lamenting the death of civilization has spoken. On the ship we have Mao Tse-tung interminably spouting platitudes from his little red book; a garrulous lady who is as obviously American as Mao is not (she and Mao are, of course, unaware of each other's utterances); a mute Man of God into whose tired ears the garrulous lady is pouring her complaints about her inability to communicate with her daughter and about her altogether accurate suspicion that the world is passing her by and she is about to die; and a shabby-looking old lady who does nothing but recite a doggerel poem about being put in the poorhouse by her ungrateful children. The political allegory here is so obvious that one would be hard put to it to let one's unconscious come into full play, as Albee would have us do. Mao chanting his optimistic and self-righteous formulas is the East, the garrulous lady babbling her doubts and guilts to the mute minister (the helpless Church that we still worship) is the West about to experience its final *Untergang*, and the indomitable little old lady is Albee's nostalgic reminiscence of Grandma in *The American Dream*—what the West would be like if it had not gone soft. The ocean liner is adrift ("outward bound"?) and contained within the doom box. Clear as all this is in the telling, it is not at all so in the play, which, being plotless,

18. Rutenberg, p. 247.

remains incomprehensible on its own terms and undramatic despite all appeals to McLuhan's theories of simultaneous perception.

JACK RICHARDSON

OF THE TWO young American dramatists who have shown the greatest promise of future achievement, Edward Albee has perhaps the more imagination and originality, while Jack Richardson has definitely the more powerful intellect. If Albee has learned his lesson from Ionesco, Richardson has as clearly been influenced by Shaw. The three remarkable plays Richardson has written so far are distinguished by the excellence of their construction, the clarity of their style, and the powerful intellect they display. Although Richardson resembles most other modern dramatic authors in that the subject matter of his plays is based on paradox, he is definitely not a member of the avant-garde as far as style is concerned. His closest affinity with living dramatists is with Dürrenmatt and Frisch. He has the same sardonic view of the world, the same precision of technique, the same effect of intellectual stimulation. The first impression that a careful reading of Richardson's plays gives one is that here at last is a playwright with brains, an intellectual who, like Shaw and Dürrenmatt and Frisch, has the ability to get a didactic message across and be entertaining at the same time. He resembles Dürrenmatt more than Frisch or Shaw perhaps in that he has a detached rather than an involved attitude towards humanity. He is interested and observant rather than evangelistic.

The use of the ancient Greek dramatic legends has been fairly common in the modern theater, but rarely, if ever, has one of the Greek legends been transposed so brilliantly as in Jack Richardson's *The Prodigal*. Using the *Oresteia* legend as a framework, Richardson has written a parable about man's enforced subservience to the demands of society. In Richardson the philosophy of determinism is placed on a purely temporal level: there is nothing to prevent man doing as he pleases except the laws and conventions of society, but these bind him as effectively as the vague cosmic forces of the metaphysicians.

The Prodigal opened at the Downtown Theatre, a small off-Broadway house, on February 11, 1960. It received a moderately good press and had a moderately good run. Later on it achieved a sort of consolatory *succès d'estime*, being produced in a few of the higher-class summer-stock theaters and in some college theaters. But the fact that nobody thought *The Prodigal* fit for a full-scale Broadway production, that it remains an unknown quantity to the vast majority of theater-goers, and that the name of Jack Richardson is still as obscure after the production of his first play as before speaks ill for any hopes that we can have for a new movement of young American dramatists to parallel the enthusiastically accepted new movement in the English drama. For *The Prodigal* is not merely a solid, well-written play, as sophisticated in content as it is precisely constructed in form: it is undoubtedly the most brilliantly written new American play to come out since the end of World War II.

In Richardson's retelling of the Orestes legend, Orestes becomes a modern "angry young man" who wishes to dissociate himself completely from the duties society requires of him. He has neither patriotism nor family feeling and looks upon Agamemnon and Aegisthus with equal contempt. His mother's betrayal of his father and her liaison with Aegisthus merely inspire him with cynical amusement. His one care in life is not to become "involved": in a world he considers mad he intends to remain detached and sane. The play shows how Orestes is forced to abandon this sensible and entirely admirable position. The two forces that work upon him and inexorably squeeze him into acquiescence are the opposing views of Agamemnon and Aegisthus. The latter, in an extremely skillful portrait, is shown at the beginning as a combination of eighteenth-century rationalist and Italian Renaissance Machiavellian politician. During Agamemnon's absence he has introduced a new state religion which clearly resembles Protestant fundamentalism in its emphasis on simple faith and the equality of each man's offering in the sight of the gods. Aegisthus' simple verses (he writes all the hymns and prayers for the new religion) reassure the people that their lives are valuable and worthwhile, and that tilling the soil and herding sheep are occupations as worthy and virtuous in the eyes of the gods as

performing heroic deeds in battle. Later on, once he has got
rid of Agamemnon and has become secure in his power,
Aegisthus of course becomes unbalanced and, in accordance
with Lord Acton's dictum about the corrupting influence of
power, starts hanging everyone who opposes him.

Agamemnon, on the other hand, is totally unable to see
that his life-long emulation and pursuit of the heroic ideal has
been useless and mischievous. Unable to persuade his son to
join him in opposing Aegisthus, he deliberately goads the latter
into killing him so that Orestes's hand will be forced. And
forced it is. Although Orestes is sent on a long journey by
Aegisthus, he can get no peace. He has no interest in either
Agamemnon or Aegisthus and certainly has no wish ever to
rule. His one wish is to settle down peacefully somewhere and
be forgotten. But his destiny—not the destiny the gods have
mapped out for him, as in the ancient Greek plays, but the
destiny required of him by the conventions of society—pursues
him relentlessly. Even his cynical friend, Pylades, deserts him:
he does not want to have his social reputation besmirched by
being associated in the public mind with a man who will not
avenge his father. Even the peasant girl whom Orestes had
hoped to marry and settle down with in obscurity so that he
could "cultivate his garden" is forced to desert him by family
pressure:

> Yes, I loved her—both for herself and what she offered me.
> I was to have children, I was to tell them stories with happy
> endings, and to make love with gentleness. I wanted to stay
> within our small garden and watch conception, birth, decay,
> and death, and to give myself to the same process.[1]

Finally Orestes realizes that he is too weak to struggle any
further—as anyone but the most superhumanly single-minded
and self-righteous person would be—and succumbs. He will go
back, kill Aegisthus and Clytemnestra, assume his rightful place
on the Argive throne and become involved in the affairs of the

1. Jack Richardson, *The Prodigal* (New York: E. P. Dutton & Co.,
Inc., 1960), p. 107.

world:

> The world demands that we inherit the pretensions of our
> fathers, that we go on killing in the name of ancient illu-
> sions about ourselves, that we assume the right to punish,
> order, and invent philosophies to make our worst moments
> seem inspired. Who am I to contradict all this any longer?
> I will return to Argos. I belong to no other place.[2]

Jack Richardson continues his commentary on man's entrapment by social forces in his second play, *Gallows Humor. Gallows Humor* is actually two separate but interrelated one-act
plays, one dealing with the condemned and one with the executioner. Richardson's thesis here is that a large number of people
have become so deindividualized by the routine of their social
existences, so unthinkingly obedient to the prescribed routine,
so "automated," in fact, that it has become difficult to distinguish the quick from the dead. Many people are just walking
dead—meekly going through the motions until the day they
finally stop breathing and keel over, officially dead. The two
plays are preceded by a prologue speech delivered by the
"Death" character from the old morality plays. He explains
that he has not been permitted to appear in the play and has
been relegated to the prologue because he has lost his touch.
The living and the nonliving are no longer as precisely differ-
entiated as they used to be, and Death consequently has become rather confused:

> . . . in the last years, I seem both to have expanded and
> blurred my activities without knowing it. The grave's dimen-
> sions suddenly have grown to include those who have not
> yet achieved the once necessary technicality of ceasing to
> breathe. It appears I now infiltrate those still bounding to
> music, still kissing their wives, still wiggling their forefingers
> in the air to emphasize those final truths by which they think
> their lives are lived. But are they, after all, living? [3]

2. *Ibid.*, p. 109.

3. Jack Richardson, *Gallows Humor* (New York: E. P. Dutton &
Co., Inc., 1961), pp. 14–15.

The two playlets which make up *Gallows Humor* illustrate this theme. In Part One a condemned man with just a little over an hour to live is visited in his cell by a prostitute, compliments of the State. It is the State's charitable idea that the condemned should mount the gallows with sprightly step and gleaming eye so as to confute the opponents of capital punishment. Walter, the condemned man, has other ideas, however. He is, in every sense of the word but the technical one, dead already and understandably he does not want to be revivified at this point. He is quite happy, indeed. In prison his life has once again taken on the ordered tranquillity that it had before he broke out and became a murderer. Except for one brief period he has lived his life in a substitute womb of business, social, and family life in which everything was prescribed, even the number of times to make love (four times a month, only with his wife and always in bed). Now he is looking forward to his actual physical death as if he were a stray bit of protoplasm instinctively straining to be remerged with the mother mass. The prostitute's presence disturbs him since it reminds him of the one terrible period of his life, which began with his losing a cut-and-dried court case because his client developed hiccups, continued with a round of Bohemian parties and extramarital affairs, and culminated when he administered forty-one strokes of a golf club to his wife's head. The prostitute wins out, of course, and Walter goes to the gallows paradoxically more alive than the hangman, who forms the subject of Part Two of Richardson's play. The hangman really is dead in effect, because he is never able to break out of the grooves prescribed for his particular existence. During the play he makes a couple of feeble attempts to break out of the routine, first by trying to persuade the warden to let him wear a medieval executioner's black hood at hangings so that he can have more "individuality," and then by threatening to leave his wife after he catches her kissing the warden. This last attempt is really pathetic. The executioner tells his wife he plans to go to the tropics, where nothing is hard-and-fast and everything shimmers in the heat. After he has recuperated there, he plans to go to work again as a free-lance executioner, strangling the living dead

—all those whose days are precise copies of each other and whose lives are regulated by rules they unquestioningly obey. But he has waited too long: he cannot even open the kitchen door to go out, although it opens quite easily when the time comes for him to go out to work. Nor can he strangle his wife: although he strains as hard as he can, his muscles refuse to do the work. He goes out to hang Walter, but he is less alive than his victim.

Gallows Humor failed when it was first produced off-Broadway in 1961. Perhaps it is too intellectual and objective to appeal to the mass and at the same time not so obviously cynical as *The American Dream* to appeal to the few. Whatever its commercial success, however, it confirms the impression made by *The Prodigal* that Jack Richardson is America's best young playwright.

One of the most intriguing aspects of the 1962–1963 theatrical season was to have been the first Broadway productions of plays by America's two most promising young playwrights, Edward Albee and Jack Richardson. Albee got his entry in first and scored a major hit with his chronicle of sexual perversity in an upper-class American home. Richardson's play, *Lorenzo*, folded quietly after four performances. Once again the New York drama critics displayed their total incompetence and irresponsibility as they wildly applauded Albee's cunningly calculated combination of Behrman's finesse with Williams' perversity while shouting down Richardson's sophisticated and beautifully written *Lorenzo*. Unlike Albee, Richardson makes no compromises in his first Broadway work. He has refrained from pandering to the mass audience of Broadway, as Albee has done with his pretentious, supposedly authentic picture of the private life of the degenerate American intellectual. Eschewing Albee's "drama through the keyhole" technique, Richardson has written a work on a universal theme.

Written with Richardson's usual mastery of language, *Lorenzo* is about a group of strolling players caught in one of the frequent factional skirmishes between the city-states of Renaissance Italy. Lorenzo's company is by no means a good one —it is irresistibly reminiscent of Mr. Vincent Crummles's—

but, goaded by the single-minded devotion of its leader, it is a dedicated one. It plays anything anywhere, and it always honors its contracts. Lorenzo adheres fanatically to the old theater adage that the only excuse for not going on is personal death —and even then an effort should be made. To him reality is what happens on the stage, and, as far as he is concerned, nothing else matters. The play shows what happens when reality as it really is obtrudes into his comfortable, make-believe world. His son goes off to fight, his daughter runs off to become the mistress of the ruthless mercenary general who represents the harshness of life as it is, and his best actor is killed defending her. Goaded at last out of his protective shell of illusion, Lorenzo challenges the general, and, in attempting to match his flashy stage sword play with the soldier's efficient professionalism, is easily killed. Lorenzo's son comes back from the battle, sated with reality by what he has seen of it, and gathers the decimated company together. He urges them on in his father's old manner: they will fulfill their engagement in Padua after all. The force of illusion has triumphed over reality; and perhaps, reality being what it is, it is better so in Richardson's view.

The unjust failure of *Lorenzo* had an unfortunate effect on Richardson since it led him to produce *Xmas in Las Vegas* (1965), whose failure on Broadway was considerably more justified. Possibly the lesson of Richardson's unhappy Broadway career is that there are some writers who are just natural off-Broadway playwrights. Richardson, with his fine ear for style and his mordant wit, is certainly one of these. *Xmas in Las Vegas* is about a man who brings his family to Las Vegas every Christmas in the hope of breaking the bank at Mr. Olympus's blackjack emporium. This year, he swears, will be the last time; if he does not make it this year, he will retire to the boredom and defeat of respectability. For a moment he thinks he has the world in the palm of his hand when he picks up a widow from New Rochelle who knows nothing about gambling but seems to be unable to lose. She starts to lose, of course, just as she is on the verge of bringing Ed Wellspot to the conquest of Olympus. At the end, Wellspot, true to his promise, throws his hand in. He toys with the idea of shooting himself, but is dissuaded by his wife, who, in the play's closing line, asks, "Edward, won't going back to Boston accomplish the same thing?" Gerald Weales rightly points out that this is not a "satisfactory" ending and that Richardson has therefore not sold out to the brutal artistry-dulling exigencies of Broadway.[4] On the other hand, he has not created a sensible play either. If giving up and going back to Boston and a mind-deadening life as business executive is defeat, then success in gambling is victory. The idea that a man is only really alive and aware when he is gambling is apparently something Richardson really believes. So, at least, one would suspect from a purportedly confessional article called "Grace through Gambling" that he published in the April, 1967, issue of *Esquire* in which he described gambling as his salvation from an overpowering feeling of Sartrean *nausée*. This does not strike me as a particularly sensible attitude (though, to be sure, I have no better solution to the *nausée* of everyday life), since I would be willing to bet that the roulette wheel will soon enough bring Richardson back, in the eternal circle, to the *nausée* in intensified form. One cannot blame Richardson, however, if he feels *nausée* and no longer takes the writer's traditional remedy of compulsive work because he has remained so unappreciated. There is no place for his brand of civilized writing on the American commercial stage, and if he chooses to seek solace from the Pascalian condition in the casinos of Macao and Baden-Baden, who can blame him?

4. Gerald Weales, *The Jumping Off Place* (New York: Macmillan Co., 1969), pp. 70–72.

ARTHUR KOPIT

ASIDE FROM Albee and Richardson the future looks rather bleak for the "new American drama." The only other playwrights produced so far who show any signs that they might some day produce significant drama are Arnold Weinstein and Arthur Kopit. Both these writers are represented so far by only one play. Weinstein's play is *Red Eye of Love*, a clumsily overwritten parable that tries to show America in terms of a skyscraper meat market with one floor for each state. Nevertheless, it is obvious that once Weinstein is able to curb his exuberant bad taste, his genuine talent for satire and wry humor will enable him to write significant plays. Kopit has made a greater public impression than Weinstein because of his long-run hit, *Oh Dad, Poor Dad, Mamma's Hung You in the Closet and I'm Feelin' So Sad*. It can be safely said, without in any way detracting from the play's real qualities, that a good part of Kopit's success, particularly as far as getting the play produced in the first place was concerned, is due to his bold and shrewd composition of the title. Some of Kopit's other titles, as yet unproduced on the professional stage, such as *On the Runway of Life You Never Know What's Coming Off Next* and *Sing to Me through Open Windows* might lead people to believe that his chief talent lies in title writing, but that would be a serious mistake. Like most modern playwrights —like most modern thinkers of any kind—Kopit has a distinct tendency to view the rotting underside of life from below. There is nothing particularly new about this—Kopit's contribution lies in the wry imagination he brings to his description of life as he sees it:

> Life is a lie, my sweet. Not words but Life itself. Life in all its ugliness. It builds green trees that tease your eyes and draw you under them. Then when you're there in the shade and you breathe in and say, "Oh God, how beautiful," that's when the bird on the branch lets go his droppings and hits you on the head. Life, my sweet, beware. It isn't

what it seems. I've seen what it can do.[1]

In a way it would be quite unfair to form any judgment of
Kopit's abilities as a playwright and thinker on his one produced play. *Oh Dad, Poor Dad . . .* is essentially a huge practical joke. Kopit has written a brilliant satiric take-off on the
conventions of the avant-garde drama, and most of the play's
popularity undoubtedly stems from the fact that it is wildly
funny without being at the same time even vaguely disturbing.
Passages like the one quoted above, while they certainly express a probably seriously held view of life, are easily accessible
to the most uncomplicated senses of humor while losing none
of their savor for more sophisticated ones. Kopit's method of
playwriting consists chiefly of creating fantastic characters, placing them in fantastic situations, and giving them either *non
sequiturs* or facilely suave pessimistic comments to utter. Thus
we have Madame Rosepettle, who is both fabulously rich and
fabulously eccentric, traveling around Latin America measur-
ing yachts and protecting her son from life. She has just arrived
in Havana, where she finds Commodore Roseabove's yacht, the
biggest of them all. She captivates the Commodore and then
tells him the story of her life, which is mainly that she married
the ugliest man she could find and then had him stuffed when
he died. He is now hanging in her bedroom closet, and she
slyly invites the Commodore to take a peek. The latter, understandably, crawls out of her overpowering presence, all thoughts
of romance gone. Besides leading on admirers and then dis-
couraging them in this unique manner, Mme. Rosepettle also
amuses herself by walking along the beach at night, kicking
sand into lovers' faces. Her main interest, however, is to keep
her son away from life. He is never permitted out of the hotel
room lest he be contaminated, and his one attempt to break
out ends in disaster as he strangles a young girl who is trying
to seduce him on his mother's bed. He then buries her under
a small mountain of stamps, rare coins, and books, leaving his

1. Arthur Kopit, *Oh Dad, Poor Dad, Mamma's Hung You in the
Closet and I'm Feelin' So Sad* (New York: Hill & Wang, Inc., 1960),
p. 44.

father's body, which had fallen out of the closet during the tussle with the girl, lying on the floor. The play ends as Mme. Rosepettle returns from one of her nocturnal beach rambles and discovers the mess:

> *Robinson!* I went to lie down and I stepped on your father! I lay down and I lay on some girl. Robinson, there is a woman on my bed and I do believe she's stopped breathing. What is more, you've buried her under your fabulous collection of stamps, coins, and books. I ask you, Robinson. As a mother to a son I ask you. *What is the meaning of this?* [2]

On this somewhat vaudevillian-joke curtain line the play unexpectedly ends. We can hope much from Kopit on the basis of the little we have received.

2. *Ibid.*, p. 89.

JACK GELBER

THE RELUCTANCE of the American drama critics to get together, wind their red, white, and blue mufflers around their necks and raise their beer steins in a toast to a new American dramatists movement has now been remedied by Kenneth Tynan who was the ringleader in the creation of the angry-young-man myth when *Look Back in Anger* came out. In his preface to the published edition of Jack Gelber's *The Connection*, Tynan hails it as "the most exciting new American play that off-Broadway has produced since the war." [1] He goes on to say that the play "explores a frightening territory with clear, unprejudiced eyes and a gift for words that makes its vision ours." [2] The "frightening territory" that Gelber explores is that of drug addiction in its more unpleasant forms—that is to say, as practised by mental degenerates, congenital morons, and the inevitable jazz musicians. This is a territory which, I fear, no gift for words can make intelligible to an outsider—and if there is a contemporary dramatist who is more incoherent and has less sense of the precise nuances of words and of the niceties of verbal rhythms than Mr. Gelber, we can only give thanks that he remains unproduced. Furthermore, Gelber does not look at the problem of drug addiction with "clear, unprejudiced eyes"—he looks at it with a strong bias in favor of the addict.

The Connection has no plot. A group of drug addicts sit around waiting for their "connection" or drug supplier. While they wait they chat aimlessly, boringly, and stupidly. Gelber's purpose in all this is to try and convince us that these people are not actors playing addicts, but real addicts. This is, of course, a project that is doomed from the start since even the most gullible member of any given audience will know that he is watching actors and not addicts. Recalling a distant and in-

1. Jack Gelber, *The Connection* (New York: Grove Press, Inc., 1960), p. 11.
2. *Ibid.*

correct reading of Pirandello, Gelber begins by having two actors playing the producer and the author come on stage (from the audience, naturally) to announce that we are about to see a play improvised by real addicts. In a way this constitutes a technical tour de force: right away Gelber has actors playing addicts who are improvising a play about addicts—who are in other words, playing actors who are playing addicts. A play within a play within a play within a play right off the bat. This is impressive, certainly, but hardly the way to write a play; and definitely not a basis for hope of a new American drama movement which would drag our theater away from the Williams-Inge axis of pseudopsychological drama. Gelber's attempt to achieve verisimilitude with the pretense of an immediately organized improvisation fails because of his fundamental ignorance of the true function of the theater. The theater is an illusion, and there is no way to get around that. The use of an improvisational technique, which is necessarily self-conscious on the part of the actors (it is possible to improvise but not to *pretend* to improvise, which is what the actors in Gelber's *The Connection* and *The Apple* are doing), a self-consciousness that is accentuated by Gelber's insistence that the actors in *The Apple* use their real names, is merely embarrassing and ultimately offensive. In *The Connection* the actors have fictitious names but the director's real name and the name of the theater is mentioned. Gelber does not realize that all theater is a cooperative effort in which the audience has a very definite part. The audience's contribution to the theatrical experience is suspension of its disbelief. Mr. Gelber, who totally fails to recognize this, spends most of his time trying to coax the audience into suspending its disbelief, never realizing that the audience automatically does this as soon as it enters the theater. Consequently, Gelber attempts an exercise in absolute realism, which in the theater is merely a contradiction in terms, by having actors play addicts who are putting on an amateur and naturally clumsy imitation of themselves; the point being that when they seem to forget to act the audience will accept them as real junkies. If this is not Gelber's aim, then there is no sense to the play's introduction, which is only silly pretense to people who know what goes on in a theater. And with all this fake rigmarole, what has Gelber to say about drug addiction? [3] Nothing. Presumably his transcript of junkie talk and his picture of junkie life are accurate, since he claims he has lived among these people. But what of it? Gelber presents us with an apparent slice of life, but he has nothing to say about it. His purpose is probably to make us *understand* these people and to sympathize with them. The actual effect is precisely the opposite.

Gelber's other play to date, *The Apple*, is, if possible, totally without meaning. The play, if it can be called that, takes place in a coffee shop, but Gelber works very hard at trying to convince the audience that the theater *is* the coffee shop by having a drunken patron of the shop circulate among the playgoers in the lobby before the performance and by spending most of the time in having his actors discuss what they are going to improvise that evening. Since they can never make up their minds very clearly and since their improvisations once they do make up their minds are utterly incomprehensible, *The Apple* becomes an exercise in mass boredom and nothing more.

With the exception of Jack Gelber, who has shown neither promise nor achievement but has received more notoriety through the shock value of his plays, the new American playwrights considered here definitely show the nucleus of a movement that, if given the chance to develop by the peculiar production economics of the New York theater, may turn out to be more lasting and more influential than the highly touted New English Dramatists movement. All in all, the prospect for a renaissance of dramatic writing in the United States is bright. The plays are being written—the only question is, will the off-Broadway theater be able to survive long enough to produce them?

3. Bernard Dukore ("The New Dramatists, 5: Jack Gelber," *Drama Survey*, II [Fall, 1962], pp. 146–57) says that Gelber is trying to show that all of us need a "connection," a "fix," to go on living in society. This seems to me to be reading things into the play. It may be what Gelber meant; it is certainly not what he succeeds in putting across.

The Spanish-Speaking Drama

FEW THINGS are more tempting and less rewarding to scholars and critics than making generalizations about a national literature based on the supposed characteristics of the nation's inhabitants. Such national generalizations tend to be facilely profound—to lend an entirely momentary air of critical insight to a remark that turns out to be only superficially clever and based ultimately on stale jokes. Thus we have the myths of the womanizing Frenchman, the stiffly upper-lipped Englishman, the brash American, the phlegmatic Dutchman, and the gay Viennese whose horizons are bounded by wine, women, song, and their palliative, psychiatry. All very amusing, to be sure; and lent an additional air of spurious authoritativeness (since life tends to imitate art far more than the reverse) by the propensity of people to try to live up to the more flattering of the several images of themselves presented to them by their artists. What is lacking, of course, is consistency: one lives up to a flattering national image when one has nothing better to do.

Spain, too, has its specious national images. There is the courtly Spaniard and there is the passionate Spaniard, both sedulously pursued in art and life. With Spain, however, generalizations about national character are more justified than with the other countries of Europe. Not, to be sure, either of the above, the former impressed on English minds by Tennyson in one of his jingoistic moments; the latter fostered largely by a misunderstanding of gypsy flamenco dancing.

What, then, are the elements of the Spanish character? As defined in its literature—and confirmed by observation—the Spanish character is something formed by the influence of the Church, the State, and the concept of *pundonor*. The latter is best defined, I believe, as self-respect carried to the point of intransigence. The perverse obsession with these three elements —the first two perforce, the third wilfully—is what defines the Spanish character and gives the literature its vitality.

Vitality originates in tension and conflict. In Spain these life-giving qualities have sprung from the situation created by a simultaneous belief in the Church and an enmity to subjugation by the State (which has always to a great extent in Spain been identical with the Church) caused by the exaggerated and even grotesque individualism implicit in *pundonor*. The paradox of this clash between an uncompromising insistence on the validity and primacy of the subjective vision and an untroubled surrender to the narcosis of the Trinitarian incense is nowhere more neatly summed up than in that most seminal of all Spanish figures, Don Quixote.

The concept of Cervantes as primarily an outraged literary critic pulverizing chivalric romance in his portrait of the Don as a lunatic unable to see reality has been sufficiently discredited. Such a theory is untenable if for no other reason than that Cervantes was clearly far too subtle a man to use such a full-scale bombardment in order to eliminate a mole-hill. But it is untenable also because Cervantes was far too much a man of his time and place—far too much a Spaniard—not to admire the stubborn idealism and cavalier contempt for mere facts that characterized the heroes of the romances which his hero set out to emulate. In his own life, Cervantes embodied the image he was to give the world: like his protagonist, he was himself a paradigm of the Spanish ethos. He combined a perfect devotion to the Church in his private life with a reckless individualism in his military exploits to produce a way of life that has been described in every civilized language ever since as "quixotic."

The second great link in the chain that leads to the contemporary Spanish drama is Ramón del Valle-Inclán. Just as no latter-day English epic poet would dream of attempting to justify the ways of God to man without first consulting Milton, so no serious contemporary Spanish dramatist would dream of writing a play without consulting Valle-Inclán. The former case is purely hypothetical: epic poets are at a premium these days, and no one would think of justifying the ways of even a putative God to man. The latter case, however, is very much alive: the influence of Valle-Inclán pervades the modern Spanish drama. Outside Spain Valle-Inclán has so far been virtually ignored—almost completely in the United States.[1] This is unfortunate because Valle-Inclán is not only one of the greatest interpreters of Spain after Cervantes, the man who has brought Cervantes' work up to date, but an author deserving of international stature in his own right. Valle-Inclán's contribution consists in perceiving the tension with which Cervantes imbued Spanish literature and in "esperpentizing" it. The "esperpento" is an art form invented by Valle-Inclán. It is a way of viewing the world as a grotesque parody of itself, like seeing "reality" as reflected in a concave mirror. This method has, of course, obvious affinities with surrealism, as well as with the view of most contemporary dramatists (e.g., Dürrenmatt) that the essential tragedy of life can be seen only indirectly, through the medium of comedy. In this method of writing the artist must rise above his subjects, must assume the position of the malicious puppeteer. Valle-Inclán himself described the method in these words:

> . . . there are three ways of observing the world artistically and aesthetically: on one's knees, standing up, and raised in the air. When one looks at reality from one's knees— and this is the oldest position of literature—the characters, the heroes, are given a condition that is superior to the human condition. . . . There are created, in a manner of speaking, beings superior to human nature: gods, demigods

1. Cf. Anthony N. Zahareas and Gerald Gillespie, "Ramón María del Valle-Inclán: The Theatre of Esperpentos," *Drama Survey*, VI (1967), 3–23 and Anthony N. Zahareas, editor in chief, *Ramón del Valle-Inclán: An Appraisal of His Life and Works* (New York: Las Americas Press, 1968).

and heroes. There is a second way, . . . and that is to look at the . . . protagonist[s] . . . as if they were our brothers, as if they were ourselves . . . And there is a third way, and it is to look at the world from a superior plane and to consider the characters of the plot as beings inferior to the author . . . with a point of irony. . . . This is a manner which is very Spanish . . . And it is this . . . that moved me to change my literature and to write the "esperpentos," the literary genre that I baptize with the name, Esperpentos.[2]

Valle-Inclán almost singlehandedly pulled Spanish drama into the mainstream of twentieth century thought. With his sardonic overview of life Valle-Inclán was able to show the grotesqueness of the contrast between the *pundonor* of the Spaniard and the circumstances of the modern world. This is, of course, exactly what Cervantes was doing for his time. Valle-Inclán brought the tension that formed the basis of Cervantes' paradigmatical work up to date by investing it with disillusionment and mockery. Cervantes, when he lost the use of his left arm as the result of wounds suffered at the Battle of Lepanto, said, with a perfect seriousness in no way tainted by the epigrammatic wittiness of the remark, that his left arm had been maimed for the greater glory of the right. Valle-Inclán also lost the use of his left arm—lost the whole arm, in fact—but the accounts that he gave of the loss were fantastic and obviously untrue. Valle-Inclán shows that the entirely honorable *pundonor* of Cervantes' Spaniard has turned to self-conscious and hypocritical attitudinizing—a psychological descent paralleling Spain's political descent—when he has *his* archetypal Spanish figure, the Marquis de Bradomín, say, on losing his arm, "My one thought was of the attitude I must henceforth adopt with women to make my disfigurement poetic. Had I but won it splendidly on valor's crimson field!"[3]

2. Quoted in Anthony N. Zahareas and Gerald Gillespie, *op. cit.*, pp. 9–10.
3. "Sonata of Winter," *The Pleasant Memoirs of the Marquis de Bradomín*, translated by May Heywood Broun and Thomas Walsh (New York: Harcourt, Brace & Co., 1924), p. 279.

The faith in the State implicit in Cervantes' action of rising from a sick bed to take a bullet through his hand at Lepanto becomes here a contempt for heroism and a translation of all motives into an obsessional pursuit of sex indicative of a decay of faith and idealism. The decadence is shown even more sharply when we read that the Marquis lost his arm in a minor skirmish during one of the petty Carlist uprisings—those fantastic epitomes of political anachronism—while leading a party to prevent a remote village priest from burning two foreigners as heretics. The expedition is a wild-goose chase since the priest turns out to have no intention of burning anyone, but the Marquis, while recuperating in a convent, manages to captivate his young attendant (whom he suspects of being his natural daughter). This is a far cry from Cervantes' burial in a Franciscan habit. We are much closer to Max Estrella's remark in Scene 2 of *Luces de Bohemia* (Lights of Bohemia): "When it comes to religious concepts, Spain is a tribe from the heart of Africa."

The three great preoccupations of the Spaniard are treated in Valle-Inclán's three most important plays: *Divinas palabras* (Divine Words), which deals with the Church; [4] *Luces de Bohemia*, which deals with the State; [5] and *Los Cuernos de Don Friolera* (The Horns of Don Friolera), which deals with *pundonor*. [6] In each of these we see the modern, sardonic, disillusioned view of these foundations of the Spanish character.

Divinas palabras is set in Valle-Inclán's homeland of Galicia, the northwest corner of Spain, with whose unique folk traditions much of his work is closely associated. Here the gloomy old sacristan of a remote village church lives married to an incongruously voluptuous woman whose character is composed equally of greed, sexual recklessness, and self-righteous

4. Translated by Edwin Williams as *Divine Words* in Michael Benedikt and George E. Wellwarth, eds., *Modern Spanish Theatre* (New York: E. P. Dutton & Co., 1968).

5. Translated by Anthony N. Zahareas and Gerald Gillespie as *Lights of Bohemia* in *Modern International Drama*, II, ii (1969).

6. Translated by Bryant Creel as *The Horns of Don Friolera* (unpublished manuscript).

respectability. The play revolves around a hydrocephalic idiot child. Mary Gaila, the sacristan's wife, fights with her sister-in-law for the privilege of exhibiting the child at local fairs, both women concealing their brutal avarice under loud pratings about charitable duties. The idiot child is killed in a peculiarly horrible manner as a direct result of this hypocritical quarrel, and Mary Gaila, caught in adultery with a vagabond in a corn-field, is pursued and stripped naked by a mob. At the end, "serene and nude," she steps over the tombstones and takes refuge in the church. Contrast is the keynote of the play's structure, the characteristic contrast between the ideal and the real that produces the vital tension of the Spanish tradition. There is the contrast between the idyllic rusticity of the setting and the sordid horror of the action, between the warmth and beauty of the background and the callousness of the actors. Valle-Inclán constantly emphasizes the calm, almost Elysian beauty of the Galician countryside and contrasts it with the pitiful squalor of the idiot child and the unfeeling mercenary attitude of the characters, climaxing in the ghastly scene in which the swine gnaw at the deformed child's dead body. The dichotomy is personified in the magnificent character of Mary Gaila as we see the coarseness inside the beauty she flaunts. The religious background pervades the whole action, but the Church is always depicted as helpless in human affairs and the people directly connected with it are depicted as grotesque. It is in the church scenes that Valle-Inclán most closely resembles the religious side of Michel de Ghelderode.[7]

In *Los Cuernos de Don Friolera* the *pundonor* ideal is "esperpentized" as we see a man forced by society to conform to the conventional code of honor and shoot his wife for having been unfaithful to him. In the event, however, he shoots his daughter by mistake. Farce and tragedy, which start out as contrasting, coincide in this play. This play about the formalization and petrification of *pundonor* is further objectified for

7. The distinguished Spanish critic Domingo Pérez Minik has pointed out that Valle-Inclán is a forerunner of Ghelderode's grotesquerie. Cf. *Teatro Europeo Contemporáneo* (Madrid: Ediciones Guadarrama, 1961), p. 206.

us by being shown as the animation of a puppet show that the two characters of the frame story see at a fair.

Luces de Bohemia is Valle-Inclán's supreme achievement. It is also one of the supreme achievements of the modern theatre. Although it is primarily a play about the corruption of the Spanish state and the Spaniard's consequent loss of patriotism, it is a panoramic, picaresque chronicle of art, life, death, and philosophy. Using the story of the last night of an aged, down-and-out, blind poet as a frame, Valle-Inclán has constructed a play that takes humanity as its subject but is at the same time archetypically Spanish. With its discussions of religion and politics the play has lost none of its bite today and it is no surprise to learn that its performance is still banned in a country whose former Minister of Propaganda reportedly boasted that 80 percent of Spanish souls were now entering Heaven as a direct result of the way in which censorship had protected their morals.

During the course of his nocturnal wanderings Max Estrella, blind and idealistic but also cynical and embittered, is guided by Don Latino de Hispalis, sneaking and pragmatic, always ready to swindle friend or foe, always looking for the main chance and missing it. First they go to a bookseller who swindles Max with Latino's connivance. Here Max conducts a superbly cynical discussion of religion while the bookseller's parrot screeches patriotic slogans. The combination constitutes as fine an objective correlative for the separation—and degradation—of Church and State as could well be thought of. Later on Max is inadvertently involved in a street skirmish and in prison meets a young striker who has been tortured and knows he is to be shot "while trying to escape"—which he is. During the discussion of politics between Max and the striker the Spaniard's love-hate relationship to his country, which for so long has given him nothing, is perfectly shown in Max's remark about the purifying destruction of Barcelona: ". . . where in hell is a bomb to disembowel this cursed Spanish plot of ground?" [8] This speech is strangely reminiscent of Ubu's re-

8. All translations are from the version by Zahareas and Gillespie published in *Modern International Drama*.

mark about razing even the ruins to the ground. At the end of the scene, when his fellow prisoner is taken out to be killed, the poet cries from impotence and rage and then relapses into a pose of Oriental meditation. The combination of these three states of mind is highly significant, for in giving them to his hero Valle-Inclán foreshadowed the basic mood of the contemporary Spanish drama. Max dies at the end, rejected and unappreciated because, as one of his gravediggers remarks, "In Spain merit is never rewarded. What's rewarded is fakery and cheapness. Everything bad is rewarded in Spain."

With Valle-Inclán as the bridge from the tradition of Cervantes we can see that the Spanish dramatists of today are the heirs of a tension composed of a belief in the value of uncompromising idealism and a realization of its uselessness; of a belief and a pride in the uniqueness and superiority of Spain and a realization of its backwardness in contrast to the rest of the Western World.

After the close of the Spanish Civil War there was, naturally, a long hiatus in the production of worthwhile dramatic art. The beginning of post-Civil War serious drama is now generally agreed to have been the production of Antonio Buero Vallejo's *Historia de una escalera* (Story of a Staircase) in 1949. Buero Vallejo was born in Guadalajara in 1916 and spent a good part of the Civil War in prison. *Historia de una escalera* is a good play—a well-written play—but it is in no sense typical of the contemporary Spanish drama. It is considered the play that began it all because it is so obviously different from and better than anything that had gone before. Well-written though the play is, it is a gauge of the provinciality of the Spanish outlook ten years after the Civil War that the play that caused an uproar among the intelligentsia because of its refreshing novelty was nothing more than a slice-of-life naturalistic drama. One can almost sense Zola peeping over Buero's shoulder. The slice of life in the play is the period 1919–1949, and the subject is a panorama of the lives of the people in the apartments opening out on a tenement staircase in a Spanish city. The construction is circular: people grow up full of hopes, the hopes become thwarted, they transfer their hopes to their children, they die; and exactly the same process starts all over again since man learns neither by experience nor by example. Buero's play is almost exclusively a psychological study; he seldom attributes human conduct to social pressures.

The post-Civil War Spanish drama began with Buero-Vallejo's *Historia de una escalera*, and it might be worthwhile to pause here and examine the most remarkable aspect of this play as a means of leading into the background against which the contemporary Spanish drama is set. Excellent though the play is as it stands, its most remarkable aspect concerns its omissions rather than anything that is in it. Although the period of the play is the thirty years from 1919 to 1949, there is no mention of the Civil War. Buero was obliged to cut out any direct allusion to the most important event to affect his characters' lives. The atmosphere in which Buero wrote is best described by quoting two recent news reports from Spain, for conditions have changed very little since 1949. The first report is from the *New York Times*:

> At exactly noon today, amid the Sunday strollers on Princesa Street, Gonzalo Arias took a pair of paper signs from beneath his suede jacket, draped them over his shoulders and set off on a walk that lasted precisely nine minutes.
>
> "In the name of the Spanish people, I respectfully ask that free elections be held for the head of state," read his sign . . . Along the sides was written in red: "Nonviolence.". . .
>
> In a book just published in London entitled, in translation, "The Sandwichmen" Mr. Arias wrote about an imaginary "Generalissimo Tranco, ruler of Trujiberia," who is forced to give way after weekly peaceful demonstrations by thousands of his subjects who wear white-paper sandwich boards asking for elections. The demonstrations are started by a single man, a printer, who steps out by himself one Sunday noon wearing a sign, and who, although immediately arrested, acquires more and more followers week by week.

Mr. Arias . . . had waited by himself in a nearby park until it was time to put on his sign. He set out slowly along the crowded, sunny sidewalk, lined with cafe tables. He had gone 50 feet before anyone noticed him. . . .

A woman news vendor interrupted a chat with a customer to wheel around and watch. "That man is totally out of his head," she said. . . .

He passed a branch of the Banco Popular and two well-dressed men broke off their conversation to stare. He passed the Vinicola Bar and four men, wineglasses in hand, tumbled out of the doorway. . . .

He crossed Alberto Aguilera, threaded his way through more crowds, and crossed the next street, Serrano Jover, four blocks from where he had started.

Then a black sedan, moving fast, swerved into the sidewalk, three doors opening simultaneously. Three husky men jumped out, surrounded Mr. Arias and asked for his papers. They did not touch him as they herded him into the car. . . . the black car made a U-turn and raced off, its siren sounding.

"He was asking for free elections and they arrested him," a well-dressed woman said rather loudly. Nobody else said anything. . . .

Fifteen minutes after Mr. Arias had set out, Felix Villamerial, a 32-year-old assistant professor of political science, put on a white cloth sign reading "no to violence" and began to walk down Princesa Street. He had passed Plaza de España—four-fifths of a mile—before two members of the gray-uniformed Armed Police stopped him, took off his sign and led him away.[9]

The quotation speaks for itself: in its quiet, understated way nothing could be a better description of an obsessively frightened officialdom spurred by its feelings of insecurity (after twenty-nine years!) to such overreaction. The second report is from the well-known French-writing, Spanish playwright Fernando Arrabal, who was imprisoned briefly in 1968 during an

9. *New York Times,* October 21, 1968, p. 2.

ill-advised visit to Spain for allegedly writing a scurrilous remark about Spain in one of his books:

> During the 24 days in Spanish prisons I spent this sum-
> mer, I learned of certain cases which I cannot let pass in
> silence without disgracing myself: in 1966 a 30-year-old
> worker was sentenced to 13 years for "illegal association and
> propaganda"; one of his comrades was given 12 years in
> prison for the same crime. An apprentice bullfighter was
> condemned to six years in prison for "injuries to the nation,"
> because in a fit of anger just after an auto accident, he
> shouted: "Spaniards are cuckolds!" After 20 years of im-
> prisonment, a worker is due to be freed: in 1947, he tried
> to organize a trade union. A progressive student, appre-
> hended with nine copies of a leftist publication, was sen-
> tenced to three years. The Captain General of the Cana-
> ries district mustered a military tribunal to judge a journalist
> "guilty" of having reprinted a poem (not at all subversive,
> taken from a book which passed the censor and is sold in
> Spanish bookstores). The author of the poem was likewise
> charged. The tribunal acquitted the defendants, finding
> nothing to condemn. The Captain General, after taking
> action against the judges, sought a new ruling from a second
> military tribunal: this time, they condemned the poet and
> the journalist. The latter, only 19, is now serving his sen-
> tence. A Madrid intellectual has been sentenced to 12 years
> in prison for having written two articles in a foreign journal.
> During my incarceration, I was in the company of intel-
> lectuals and thinkers like Marcelino Camacho, who, locked
> up for seven months, is awaiting trial (the provisional lib-
> erty he obtained was subsequently revoked); like the miners
> Garcia Gonzales and Nicholas Corte, both tuberculous and
> both suffering from silicosis, who are threatened with five
> years of prison for having written a letter claiming the right
> to strike; like Lara and Calle, brilliant young men who risk
> six years in prison for a "crime" of opinion. My case is of
> little interest compared to these. I believe I received excep-
> tionally "favorable" treatment. I could of course cite certain

irregularities of which I was a victim (but which, I'm sure, occur frequently): I was arrested at one o'clock in the morning, without a warrant issued either by executive or by judicial power; I was put into solitary confinement for five days, rather than 72 hours, as required by law (the prisoner in solitary cannot speak, or write, isn't allowed to take a daily walk, and must live and sleep in an underground dungeon constantly lit by an electric light).

I was doubtless acquitted thanks to international pressure. Without outside support, I would have spent a long time in prison, like the journalist from the Canaries or the apprentice bullfighter.

I am committed to nothing and nobody. I simply wish people to be free from injustice, and liberty to prevail. I would like to believe that all I have revealed is false, that I have been deceived, that all I saw and read this summer in Spain is only a nightmare.[10]

It should be quite easy to see from these reports that the essential thing to remember about contemporary Spanish drama is that it is written under a dictatorship. In a dictatorship the drama always has two sides: the apparent and the real. A dictatorship is an example of the quintessentially false in life, for it is the imposition of an artificial society on humanity. Perhaps the best way to describe it is in psychological terms since it is in those terms that it must ultimately have its effect, both on art and on life. It is schizophrenic, consisting of a man-made pattern grafted forcibly on to the natural life, which continues uninterrupted behind the façade. Thus drama, which reflects society, exists in two forms in a totalitarian state. In the modern, highly developed, and glossily efficient totalitarian states such as Nazi Germany and Soviet Russia, drama is recognized as a powerful didactic weapon and is used by the state for direct propaganda purposes. In such a theatre plays are written to order by servile hacks who are more interested in worming their way into favor with the authorities than with exercising whatever artistic talent they may happen to possess.

10. *The Drama Review*, XIII, i (1968), 87–88.

The drama that shows the reality of such a society is necessarily written in exile. The other type of theatre that appears in totalitarian societies is the kind that exists in Franco's Spain today. Here the theatres are privately owned and managed but are subjected to a rigid censorship. Before a play can be produced, every word is scrutinized and passed on by some official functionary. And it is this censorship that is the key to the understanding of the two Spanish theatres.

Censorship is a great temptation. And, like Oscar Wilde (though in a woefully different way), censors are able to resist everything except temptation. A censor is in a position of power; but power, as Lord Acton has pointed out to us, tends to corrupt. That has always been the crux of the censorship problem: the choice of the censor. Almost always the wrong person is chosen, but even if a capable, efficient, and impartially judicial person could be prevailed upon to accept the job, Lord Acton's dictum—one of the very few generalizations about human psychology which has, unhappily, no recorded exceptions—would take effect: the possession neither of intellectual strength nor of sincere good intentions presupposes emotional stability. Too often, indeed, the cerebral strong man juggles his mental barbells most brilliantly while the canker is creeping through his nervous system. The censor turns out to be a shining super-ego built over a raddled, pock-marked id.

The type of drama permitted by the censors in Spain is the spineless pap dribbled out by such writers as Alfonso Paso or Miguel Mihura. Both artistically and intellectually they are beneath contempt.

Fortunately there is a parallel stream of what might be called "underground" drama which deals with the reality behind the façade. I call this drama "underground," although it does come to the surface occasionally. Whenever such plays are produced, however, they have usually been emasculated by the censor. More frequently they remain unproduced in Spain and prudently withheld from the censor. We thus have the curious situation of some of the most promising playwrights of the present time working in total oblivion, for their plays are so critical of the Franco regime that they cannot be produced in

Spain—cannot even be submitted to the censor—and are as yet virtually unknown outside Spain. Many of the plays of this type will inevitably be without interest for non-Spaniards because of the obsessive single-mindedness of the political pleading, but some of them rise above their immediate interest because of the brilliance of their satire and the power of their theme, which, since it is always allegorized, may be taken to apply to any oppressive society or political system.

Buero-Vallejo has written over fifteen plays, and, together with Alfonso Sastre, has become fairly well known among Spanish scholars in the United States. His most important plays are *En la ardiente oscuridad* (In the Burning Darkness, 1950) and *El concierto de San Ovidio* (The Concert of St. Ovide, 1962).[11] Both these plays use the metaphor of blindness to indicate the plight of Spain today; both also use historical perspective and geographical distance.[12] One of Buero's more recent plays is considerably more direct. *La doble historia del Dr. Valmy* (The Double Case History of Dr. Valmy, 1967)[13] is a play about police state methods and deals with the self-realization that comes to a happily married secret policeman who becomes psychologically impotent as a result of castrating a prisoner in the course of his "duties." This and the knowledge of how deeply his wife despises him when she learns what his "work" is bring about his death at the end. Buero has accomplished the extraordinary feat of building a play around the problems of a thoroughly despicable protagonist and arousing a feeling of empathy for him at the moment of his rejoining— and simultaneously leaving forever—the human race.[14] There is another level to the action in that the play is being presented

11. Translated by Farris Anderson in *Modern International Drama*, I, i (1967), [7]–61.

12. Buero also uses blindness as a subsidiary theme in *Las Meninas*, *Las Cartas boca abajo*, and *La Tejedora de sueños* (The Dream Weaver, 1952), translated by William Oliver in Robert Corrigan, ed., *Masterpieces of the Modern Spanish Theatre* (New York: Collier Books, 1967), pp. [131]–197.

13. Translated by Farris Anderson in *Artes Hispanicas/Hispanic Arts*, I, ii (1967), [85]–169.

14. There is a strong similarity here to the theme of Fritz Hochwälder's *Der Flüchtling*. Cf. *supra*, pp. 211–215.

as a dramatization of the clinical notes of Dr. Valmy, a psychiatrist whom the protagonist has consulted about his impotence. The case of the secret policeman, Dr. Valmy tells us, is Case No. 2; No. 1 concerns a couple who live in the same building and refuse to acknowledge that Case No. 2 ever existed.

Alfonso Sastre, the other well-known "new wave" playwright, was born in Madrid in 1926. Sastre has been extremely prolific despite a great deal of discouragement. Perhaps more than any other Spanish dramatist he has suffered from censorship restrictions on his work; and he has been subjected to petty vindictiveness such as having mention of his name or of any of his works banned in all newspapers outside Madrid as well as to major vindictiveness in the form of periods of imprisonment. The interference with his life that he has had to put up with from the government is attributable to his role as a spokesman for the younger generation (he has been involved in university student protests) as much as to his plays. Sastre's theatre is extremely uneven, ranging from the very good to something that comes close to agitprop. It is his personality and his leadership as much as his artistry that has established his position in the new Spanish drama. To many members of the younger generation in Spain he has become an inspirational and charismatic figure—like Tell in his *Guillermo Tell tiene los ojos tristes* (William Tell Has Sad Eyes).*

Sastre's principal theme is revolution. This is, indeed, the principal theme of all of the new wave dramatists, but it should not be interpreted as a monotonous preoccupation with the Civil War. That war is an inevitable point of reference for them, but its function is at most to serve as a basis for the present conditions—which require social revolution *now*. In a perverse way the conditions fostered by the outcome of the Civil War provide the tension that gives the new Spanish drama its vitality. The new Spanish plays concern themselves with criticism of present social conditions and at most their concern with the war is as an explanation of how those condi-

* Published in George E. Wellwarth, ed., *The New Wave Spanish Drama* (New York: New York University Press, 1970).

tions came about. Sastre's principal concern is with the almost inevitable outbreak of violence that accompanies what is intended as peaceful reform because of the intransigence and fear of those in power. In several plays he examines how such reform movements may be driven by suppression from outside or by corruption within themselves to violence and the effect this has on the family relationships of the persons involved. In *El Pan de Todos* (Everybody's Bread, 1957), for example, David Harko,[15] a revolutionary devoted idealistically and fanatically to the cause of reform (bread for everybody), turns his own mother in when he learns that she has taken money from a corrupt official of the recently instituted revolutionary government. When she is executed, he kills himself. His idealism prevents him from shirking what he conceives to be his duty, but is not strong enough to enable him to bear up under the psychological consequences. As can be seen from this brief summary, Sastre is capable of stepping over the border of melodrama and substituting hand-wringing and hair-clutching for sustained emotion and sound thinking; he is also capable of using the same basic theme in a very good play, *Prólogo Patético* (Pathetic Prologue, 1964).[16] In this play Sastre uses a terrorist organization dedicated to the destruction of government officials. The plot revolves around the mistaken belief of one of the terrorists that he has killed his own brother during a routine bomb throwing incident. His capture gives Sastre the opportunity of writing one of the better of the many police interrogation and torture scenes in the new Spanish drama.

In *Tierra roja* (Red Earth, 1963) we have the same circumstances as in Buero's *Historia de una escalera*, but here the theme is revolutionary rather than purely naturalistic. The scene is a company mining town where the workers are evicted from their homes when they reach retirement age. A young worker just arrived in town is outraged by this and organizes

15. It is worth noting the sedulous avoidance of Spanish personal names in the new Spanish drama, as well as the universal tendency to set the plays in unspecified, imaginary, or historical countries.

16. Translated by Leonard Pronko in *Modern International Drama*, I, ii (1968), [195]–215.

resistance against the company. The workers are gunned down —all except for the young instigator who is in prison at the time. On his release he becomes a docile worker himself, even coming to believe the standard company propaganda about strikes being caused by foreign instigators because it has been dinned into him for years and he has had no means of hearing anything else all that time. At the end he is himself about to be evicted and retired when another young man, just like he was forty or so years earlier, comes along and proposes resistance; but this time the resistance will be effective because it is not isolated and instinctive but organized and controlled.

In two of his most interesting plays Sastre has been experimenting with simultaneous time technique. In *Diálogos de Miguel Servet* (Dialogues of Miguel Servet, 1965) [17] he uses the historical event as an allegory of the present. In the prologue Nazi soldiers destroy a bronze statue of Servet in order to melt it down for transformation into a cannon. This sort of mixing in of modern elements occurs unexpectedly throughout the play, drawing a parallel between the repression of Servet and contemporary repression of free thought. Thus Calvin's headquarters in Geneva are described as being fitted out with megaphones that amplify every sound in the city, even people's breathing; and the problems of censorship in France in Servet's time are discussed as a parallel to those very same problems in Spain today. In *Miguel Servet* Sastre uses the technique of historical allegory to perfection.

In *Asalto Nocturno* (Nocturnal Assault, 1964) he uses both a simultaneous time and a flashback technique to show how a series of murders in a Sicilian family vendetta spreads across the world. The vendetta began at the turn of the present century and is a microcosm of the century's violence, a fact Sastre emphasizes by news reports of whatever international violence was going on while each of the vendetta murders was committed.[18] There is no intended specific reference to Spain here,

17. This play has been neither published nor performed.
18. The similarity to Brecht's *Der Aufhaltsame Aufstieg des Arturo Ui* and to Arthur Adamov's *Paolo Paoli* should be noted, although neither of them would have been easily available to Sastre.

and, indeed, even those plays being produced by the new wave playwrights that are obviously allegorical of the Spanish situation are applicable to general political or human situations.

Buero Vallejo and Sastre were the groundbreakers of the new Spanish drama and continue, despite their unevenness, to be its leading exponents. But they are being hard pressed for preeminence by some other writers who are as yet virtually unknown. Chief of these are Carlos Muñiz, José Maria Bellido, José Ruibal, and Antonio Martínez Ballesteros.

Carlos Muñiz, born in Madrid in 1927, has written two outstanding plays: *El Tintero* (The Inkpot, 1961) and *Las Viejas difíciles* (The Unpleasant Old Women, 1963). *El Tintero* is the story of a harassed clerk, Crock, who is desperately struggling to make ends meet but is doomed to failure because he is fundamentally a misfit. Living in a world of routine, joylessness, and devotion to hierarchical obedience, he attempts to think independently and to bring beauty into his life. His indulgence in such minor sensualities as putting flowers on his desk stamps him as "unreliable" to his rule-bound superiors, and he is ultimately destroyed by his inability to adjust to the harsh reality of his milieu. Such a brief summary of the play is, of course, entirely inadequate as a means of giving an idea of its tremendous power and superbly ironic writing. Muñiz is using the office milieu with its facelessness and reliance on routine as a means of showing the barren quality of modern institutionalized life. Crock is an abstract symbolic figure living in an abstract symbolic world. The office in which he works is not real— it is a caricatured world as the barren heath of *Waiting for Godot* is a caricatured world.[19]

In *Las Viejas difíciles* Muñiz has attempted the difficult task of composing a fantastic farce that will do justice to the vicious idiocy that characterizes the atmosphere of a society under dictatorship. The suppression of freedom is here allegorized as the suppression of sex, a device that enables Muñiz to equate freedom with the deepest human desires and to show that its suppression results in the grotesque perversion depicted

19. Hazel Cazorla, "Simbolismo en el teatro de Carlos Muñiz," *Hispania*, XLVIII (1965), 231.

in the play. *Las Viejas difíciles* takes place in an unnamed city controlled by "The Association," a militant organization of old women who think all sex is evil and have passed a series of strictly enforced laws forbidding all public indulgence in it. Antonio and Julita, the "lovers" of the play, are in their late forties and have been engaged since they were young children. They have been planning to marry whenever Antonio is promoted to a better-paying job; but, as Julita points out, he never will be promoted because it is known that he has read *Don Quixote* and has published an essay in a provincial periodical. While sitting on a park bench they kiss and are immediately arrested by a policeman who has been spying on them from the bushes. In prison they are finally married and permitted to spend their wedding night together by the warden (who loses his job for this charitable act and is eventually murdered by his wife, a prominent member of "The Association"). When they are finally released, they are rejected by Antonio's two aunts, one of whom is the head of "The Association," and have to go and live with Julita's married sister in an overcrowded little room. Even here they are pursued by the vicious little old ladies of "The Association," who come in brandishing tommy-guns. One of Antonio's aunts has a change of heart, however. She turns her gun on the others and forces them to undress, thus rendering them helpless. She then helps the two to escape to the one safe place in town—a whorehouse furtively patronized and protected by "The Association." But the sordid, unreal, and impure form of freedom exercised here merely disgusts Antonio and Julita so that it is almost a release to them to be finally gunned down by the pursuing harpies of "The Association." The few critics that have commented on this play have generally failed to appreciate its tremendous power and the superbly incisive insight of its central image. One suggests that Muñiz gives love as the answer to isolation and oppressive traditions,[20] but does not see (or perhaps cannot say since he is writing in a Spanish magazine) that love is allegorical for freedom in the play. Another finds it less profound than *El Tintero* because it is cari-

20. Jaime Llabrés, "Carlos Muñiz, un representante de la nueva generación," *Papeles de Son Armadans*, XXXVII (1965), 224.

catural,[21] but does not realize that totalitarian attitudes are so ludicrous in themselves that they are incapable of being caricatured. Muñiz truly gives us a horrifying picture in this play of what Domingo Pérez Minik, referring to Spain, calls "este país crucificado." [22]

Antonio Martínez Ballesteros was born in Toledo in 1929 and still lives in that city. Almost entirely self-educated, he works as a civil service clerk and doggedly writes plays in his very limited spare time under conditions that would discourage most other men. Miguel Mihura, who, ever since he turned out his first play, the brilliant surrealist fantasy *Tres Sombreros de Copa* (Three Top Hats, 1932),[23] has been grinding out fluffy *boulevardier* comedies, maintains that people who cannot get their plays produced in present day Spain wail about restrictions to cover up their inadequacy as writers. The remark does as little credit to him as do his plays; and is easily disproved by any of Ballesteros's unproduced dramas.

Antonio Ballesteros's principal work is *En el País de Jauja*.[24] As an epigraph to his play Ballesteros uses a quotation from Leonid Andreyev: "Oh the people! They are betrayed by those to whom they give their souls; they are tricked by the very leaders who present honest faces, who mouth platitudes of unshakable loyalty and pocket the abundant gold of bribery." The play takes place in the present time "or any other" in the mythical country of Know-How. Know-How seems at first glance to be a caricatured dictatorship. But Ballesteros's powers of dramatic characterization, like Muñiz's, succeed in soon making one realize that one of the inherent qualities of a dictatorship is that it cannot be caricatured: it can always match the satirist's wildest flights of fancy with its reality. The hero of the story

21. Florencio Martínez Ruiz, "El último teatro realista español," *Papeles de Son Armadans*, XLV (1967), 184.

22. Domingo Pérez Minik, *Teatro Europeo Contemporáneo* (Madrid: Ediciones Guadarrama, 1961), p. 248.

23. Translated by Marcia Cobourn Wellwarth in Michael Benedikt and George E. Wellwarth, eds., *Modern Spanish Theatre* (New York: E. P. Dutton & Co., 1968).

24. Translated by Henry Salerno and Sevilla Gross as *The Best of All Possible Worlds* in *First Stage*, V, iii (1966), 172–193.

is the symbolically named John Poor—poor not only in being poverty-stricken because he is not a toady to the ruling *junta* but also in being the only rationalist in a society ruled solely by self-interested pragmatists. The play depicts Poor's entrapment in the bureaucratic machine, which is headed by a dictator who listens to his own speeches on the radio as if they were oracular pronouncements. This mordant comedy ends with an ironic quadruple scene showing Poor in his cell serving a twelve-year sentence, his family in miserable poverty, the dictator of Know-How and of the neighboring country of Show-How pinning medals on each other "with a rhythm that becomes more and more insane," and a former revolutionary who has been seduced by the regime stuffing himself with food.

In *El Heroe* (The Hero) Ballesteros writes about the pointlessness of "heroic" conduct and the myth-making process through which "heroes" are made. Using an interesting and skilfully handled flashback technique remarkable in an author who has never had the opportunity to test his work on stage, he tells the story of a man who has been unjustly imprisoned for ten years because he helped his fiancée and her brother— both, unlike himself, dedicated revolutionaries—to escape from the country. Now, on his release, he is hailed as a hero by the revolutionary underground and is asked to escape from the country himself in order to fight more effectively for the revolutionary movement from abroad. But José Kroll is no hero—not even in an ironic sense. He is the average man who wants to live in peace, at no matter what cost to his self-respect (he has none, anyway) and to his sense of justice. He is like an atom that has been ejected from the central mass to whirl around outside his regular orbit; and now he wants to return to the mindless inertia that is natural to him. Neither public ideals nor personal dignity mean anything to him. To his fiancée's brother, who comes to smuggle him out to a hero's welcome in the revolutionary cells abroad, he reveals the fact that he manufactured evidence against innocent men while he was in prison simply in order to avoid torture. Finally, exasperated, he kills the brother in a blind fury and is hailed as a hero by the government that imprisoned him and now preens itself on brain-

washing him from "revolutionary" to "hero." In this play
Ballesteros shows the same doubt about the spectacular revolutionaries that Sastre showed in *Prólogo patético* without letting
up in his scathing ridicule of their opponents.[25]

José María Bellido Cormenzana is in a somewhat more
favored position than his colleagues of the underground drama.
Born and brought up in the border town of San Sebastián,
where he owns a resort hotel, Bellido is fluent in at least five
languages and holds a law degree from the University of Val-
ladolid, although he does not practise because, in his own words,
he is "too busy defending himself all the time." Instead he has
tried everything but, as he puts it, "homosexuality and para-
chuting out of a balloon" in his effort to find leisure time to
write his plays.

Bellido's principal work so far is *Futbol* (Football).[26] The
political allegory being written in Spain usually takes one of
two forms: either historical allegory in which parallels to the
political situation in Spain are sought in her past history, as in
Alberti's *Noche y Guerra en el Museo del Prado* (Night and
War in the Prado Museum); [27] or fantastic allegory, in which
imaginary situations and countries are created to reflect contemporary Spain.[28] *Football* is perhaps the most elaborate and
carefully worked out example of the latter type. Bellido sets his
play in an imaginary village curiously similar to Spain: a sort
of down-at-the-heels microcosm. Thirty years before, civil war
in the form of a football (i.e., soccer) match had taken place
in this village. And now the winners lord it over the losers with
their gleaming new uniforms and their shiny, bright soccer
balls, symbols of strutting *machismo*. The losers—crushed, poverty-stricken, dressed in threadbare uniforms and bouncing de-

25. Ballesteros has written some other plays that remain unproduced
and unpublished. These include *Una Historia subversiva* (A Subversive
Story), *Los Comediantes* (The Players), and *Sancho español* (scenes from
Don Quixote). *Los Peleles* (The Straw Men) has been translated by Leon
Lyday in *Modern International Drama*, III, i (1969).

26. Translated by David Turner in Benedikt and Wellwarth, eds.,
Modern Spanish Theatre.

27. Translated by Lemuel Johnson in Benedikt and Wellwarth, eds.,
Modern Spanish Theatre.

28. The allegory is not confined to Spain, of course.

grading little rubber balls—nurse their grievances and hope for better days. Whenever they try to forget their loss and bolster their egos by carrying soccer balls, these are quickly and contemptuously deflated by the javelins of the police. All their hopes are pinned on a mystical prophecy that a divine referee will come and save them by reversing the disputed result of the fatal match. And they have one material hope, too. From the second generation of the team has come Zapatoni, the superstar, symbol of the latent strength and material potential of their village. And just as the tremendous industrial potential smoldering beneath the surface of Spain (where it has been kept untouched by the smugly complacent winners, who have been too busy preening and strutting and crowing over their fallen opponents for thirty years) is coveted by the two great opposing world powers, so in the play Nestor and Fani, caricatured Russian and American respectively, try to buy Zapatoni for their teams. Salvador, a travelling actor in costume, is mistaken for the "referee from the sky" of the prophecy because he is wearing a football referee's uniform under a monk's cassock since those are the parts he has to play the next day. Salvador becomes a parody of a Christ figure trying vainly to bring peace with his ineffectual Bible reading and humanitarian pleading. The leaders of the two football clubs combine to sell out their people; and Salvador is killed by a shot that could only have come from the church tower. Bellido deliberately leaves the origin of the shot ambiguous: it came from the direction of the church tower, but Fani enters with a rifle at the end. The members of the two clubs unite to fight for their freedom together, for they cannot trust their leaders; or the outside powers represented by Fani and Nestor; or the Church, which has blessed their football games for so long.

The principal difference between Bellido, Ballesteros and Ruibal, the three leading, most consistent and productive of the new wave dramatists, and Buero-Vallejo and Sastre, the old guard of the protest movement in the current Spanish drama, is that the latter—whose "old guard" standing by no means implies artistic weakness—are writers who concentrate either on realism or historical allegory, while the former concentrate on symbolism or abstract allegory. The problem constantly facing Buero-Vallejo and Sastre is the discovery of new historical events which in some way parallel the current Spanish situation, or the working out of new ways of depicting that situation directly without going far enough to arouse the suspicions of the censors. It is fortunately not necessary to be too explicit: years of training in the circumlocution and obliquity necessary to survival in his society have made the Spanish intellectual a man peculiarly susceptible to subtle nuances. He has been described with justice as a man chronically suspicious of direct statements—as a man who can only find information that he believes *between* the lines. Similarly, the problem constantly facing the new wave playwrights of Spain is to find new symbols to depict the plight of their country, so often repeated throughout history.

Bellido is particularly adept at creating abstract allegorical avatars. In *Tren a F . . .* (Train to H . . .) [29] he depicts an imaginary country which consists of a barren plain crossed by a train in which the inhabitants are travelling to H . . . , which could mean happiness, paradise, social progress, or everyone's private desires. All the passengers own shares in the railroad company (except, of course, the emaciated parodies of human beings stuffed into cattle cars at the rear of the train and let out only to chop the wood needed to keep the train going). Even so, the train, which is rickety and creaking in contrast to the streamlined diesels and busses streaking across the plain in the distance, frequently and inexplicably breaks down. When it does so, the passengers sing hymns in praise of the railroad company and make obsequious remarks to the unctuous conductors and ticket inspectors, who reassure them, spy on them, or reprimand them, according to the occasion. As the narrator, an incipiently rebellious young man who wants to leave the train for more modern transportation, puts it, ". . . trip after trip, century after century, that little train with its wooden cars, [stopped] for no apparent reason at improbable stations . . . lost in the immensity of the plain." What keeps the com-

29. Translated by Ronald C. Flores in *Modern International Drama,* I, ii (1968), 218–228.

pany in business is the belief of the passenger-shareholders that only the company's trains have access to the tunnel which is the only route to H . . . ; and, like one of the Church Fathers looking complacently down on the torments of the sinners in hell, they comfort themselves with the reassuring image of what they will see when they finally come to that tunnel which only the company can negotiate: ". . . thousands and thousands of vehicles . . . smashed into smithereens, crashing into the mountain . . . gigantic mounds of twisted iron on all sides of the tunnel . . . And the moaning and groaning of the dying travellers who chose to ride with our competitors." The moral could hardly be plainer, and yet so skilful is Bellido that there is nothing sufficiently concrete in the play that anyone can point to as having any specific meaning or application.

Bellido continues his mastery of the abstract allegorical form in *El Pan y el Arroz o Geometría en amarillo* (Bread and Rice or Geometry in Yellow).* Here he shows us a group of men representative of the power élite of any society: a financial manipulator, a businessman, a landowner, a military officer, and a perverted intellectual. During the conference of these men, who meet in a timeless and imaginary setting with a view to conquering the world, the intellectual "invents" patriotism, religion, propaganda, and money as a means of making people willing slaves of the power élite under the impression that they are serving their own "freedom." Their plans, however, are upset by the mysterious appearance in their midst during a sudden blackout of a beautiful, smiling yellow child. The blackouts begin occurring at seven minute intervals, and each time the number of children doubles. Meanwhile reports pour in that the whole city is inundated with these amiable and indestructible children. At the end, the rulers kill themselves in their attempt to overcome the passive resistance of the children. Bellido's theme here resembles that of Gonzalo Arias in *The Sandwichmen*, where a spontaneous demonstration begun by one man also burgeons in geometric progression.

* Published in George E. Wellwarth, ed., *The New Wave Spanish Drama* (New York: New York University Press, 1970).

When one contemplates the mechanics of totalitarian oppression, which Bellido depicts as a combination of an overriding profit motive that blots out all traditional human considerations, an irresistible attraction to a purely mischievous moral perversity, and a brutal and subhuman stupidity, one is unhappily led to think that for the most part such visions as his geometric progression of children or Gonzalo Arias's sandwichmen is so much wishful thinking. In his more lucid and pessimistic moments Bellido conceives visions of mesmerized enthusiasm like the passengers in the train to "happiness" or of hopeless apathy like the one in *Los Relojes de Cera* (The Wax Clocks), in which all the clocks in the country are made of wax and everybody pretends not to see the little men in yellow jeeps speeding around moving the hands all the time so that the tourists won't notice that time is standing still.

José Ruibal is a Galician now living in Madrid and working intermittently as a journalist. Despite the difficulties, both financial and professional, under which he lives, he is amazingly prolific. The most interesting of his plays are *El Bacalao* (The Codfish), *Los Mendigos* (The Beggars), *El Asno* (The Jackass), *Su Majestad la Sota* (His Majesty, the Jack), and *El Hombre y la Mosca* (The Man and the Fly).

El Bacalao is a wildly comic satire on governmental red tape in which two minor bureaucrats who live, as one of them puts it, ". . . in the very heart of our country . . . like the worm inside the apple" dream that they are administering justice in a land where the law of the codfish—dry and headless—reigns. Here the punishment for everything is beheading, which is seen as really merciful since "the head is the worst part of the body; ideas come out of it like putrid odors out of excrement." And once the head is off, the victim is ready to be received blissfully into the bosom of the sacred codfish.

The task of the leaders of a totalitarian society is to keep the populace quiescent, either by open repression or by drugging them into a state where they lose their consciousness of self. Ruibal treats both of these methods in his subsequent plays. In *Su Majestad la Sota* he uses the kings from the standard deck of cards as allegorical figures who are courting the princess of an imaginary country with a view to ruling it. Each has his pet system for ruling the country. The King of Spades represents militarism (the suit is Swords in Spanish) and wants to declare permanent martial law; Hearts suggests love, liberality, and permissiveness, so its king will rule by declaring the taverns national monuments; Clubs, of course wants to keep people exactly as they have always been through repressive police measures; and Diamonds proposes to rule by financial corruption and introduce a roulette table into every home. Immobility and repression, alcohol and gambling—the latter the two most effectual forms of social anaesthesia: the classic methods whereby totalitarian governments remain in power are allegorically portrayed in this play. None of the kings wins the princess, and "la sota," the knave who incorporates *all* the qualities of the kings continues to rule.

In *The Beggars* [20] an imaginary country filled with maimed beggars and overrun by camera-bearing tourists in the guise of giraffes who chatter about the "picturesqueness" of the beggars is ruled by a triumvirate consisting of a dog (who is a general), an ass (who is a Chief of Police), and a crow (who is a priest). All three of them are ineffectual, bumbling, brutal fools, however; the real power in the country is in the hands of the Minister of Propaganda, portrayed as a parrot, who veers with every wind and sells his voice to the highest bidder, but is asphyxiated by the truth at last. *The Beggars* shows the ultimate uselessness of repression, for as often as the beggars—the common people—are shot down, they rise again.

The Jackass [31] is a more cynical play, and the most stageworthy of the ones Ruibal has written to date. Here he deals with one of the same themes treated by Bellido in *Football*: commercial exploitation. As in Bellido's play, the scene is an unnamed country with a curiously Iberian flavor. An unmistakably American salesman named Mister sells the most enterprising—and most crooked—of the peddlers in a small marketplace

30. Translated by John Pearson in *Drama and Theatre*, VII, i (1968), 56–63.

31. Translated by Thomas Seward in *Modern International Drama*, II, i (1968), 33–56.

an electronic jackass which can do everything: it talks, makes stock market forecasts, cooks food, performs plastic surgery, and prints phony contracts. But while it enables its so-called owner to enslave his fellows, it, in turn, enslaves him—he is permanently in debt to the company that manufactures it.

In his latest play, *El Hombre y la Mosca*,* Ruibal comes of age as a dramatic artist. The satiric inspiration which he displayed in *The Jackass, El Bacalao, Su Majestad la Sota*, and *The Beggars* was, for all its inventiveness, essentially topical and rootless so far as style and literary antecedents were concerned. These earlier plays of Ruibal's seem to me the result of flashes of momentary inspiration and are not bolstered up by any consistent reliance upon literary tradition. They lack, in other words, literary maturity. In *El Hombre y la Mosca* Ruibal has grown up as a literary artist. This is not to imply that the earlier plays are necessarily worse than the one we are now considering. Quite the contrary. As a *play* (for staging) I think *The Jackass*, for instance, is distinctly superior to *El Hombre y la Mosca*; but as a work of *literature* the latter is of far greater significance. *The Jackass* is a brilliantly worked out stage version of a clever plot situation; *El Hombre y la Mosca*, however, is in the mainstream of modern European literature.

At the same time that Ruibal displays this immersion in the mainstream of European literature and culture, he shows in this play a distinct awareness of the tradition of Spanish literature and its most characteristic themes. There had already been signs of this in the introduction of Cervantes into *The Beggars*, where Ruibal used the technique of simultaneous time which had been worked out by Thornton Wilder in *The Skin of Our Teeth* and *Our Town* and has been carried on by Max Frisch in *The Chinese Wall*. In *El Hombre y la Mosca* the use of traditional elements from Spanish literature is far more subtle and effective. These elements are: the atmosphere of dream fantasy that pervades the play, the introduction of the supernatural and the consequent elevation of the action to a higher plane and into a different perspective, and the setting

* Published in George E. Wellwarth, ed., *The New Wave Spanish Drama* (New York: New York University Press, 1970).

of the action in an apparent unreality which is in fact a higher reality—a reality stripped of everyday accoutrements to show its quintessence. The first two of these elements hardly require elaboration for those familiar with the tradition of Spanish literature, but the last is somewhat more complicated since it demonstrates Ruibal's awareness of current trends in the drama of other nations as well. What is so interesting about this awareness is the fact that it may very well be unconscious—an independent perception of the same philosophical viewpoint since most of the literature in which it is contained is unavailable in Spain.

El Hombre y la Mosca takes place in that unnamed, mythical and symbolically representative country that is so ubiquitous in the new Spanish drama. The country has been ruled for seventy "peaceful" years by El Hombre, who is creating a double in his magnificent crystal dome to carry on his work after his death and create the myth of his immortality. In this country the people sleepwalk through their customary routines, much as they do in the so-called "realistic" plays of men like Paso, the post-*Three Top Hats* Mihura, or the journeymen plodders who supply the staple fare of New York's Broadway, London's West End, or Paris's boulevards. But the "real" reality, the reality they dare not think about is the barren plain devoid of flora and fauna, like the barren heath in Beckett's *Waiting for Godot*, in which they live and against which they have desperately thrown up psychological barriers (self-delusions, drink, social conventions, routines) and material bulwarks (technological protection, television, movies, sports). Also real, of course, is El Hombre and his magical, dazzling crystal dome. Ruibal thus shows us the quintessential reality behind the façade of life in this play.

Just as the actual central symbol of the play, the crystal dome, is an architectural construct, so is the play also. Reading this play one perceives a carefully planned structure of interlocking themes that give an overall effect of architectural cohesion and consistency. In the depiction of El Hombre and El Doble and their perverse relationship one sees a steady progression similar to that found in the structure of the ancient Greek drama. There is the sense of ineluctable fate in the realization that El Hombre cannot last and in the audience's sardonic knowledge of the vanity of his attempt to immortalize himself by reproducing himself; there is the sense of inexorable time in El Hombre's impatient efforts to complete his task of animating his puppet; and there is the sense of the culmination of destiny as we see the inevitable collapse of all these plans at the end as El Hombre's human robot falls apart, and, like Peer Gynt, whose soul Ibsen symbolized by an onion, reveals himself as all husk and no core. It is surely no accident that Ruibal has used the fly as his symbol of retribution, just as Jean-Paul Sartre did in his modernization of the Aeschylean Furies of the *Eumenides*.

The symbols are the cement in the architectural structure of this play. Besides the fly that destroys the old order at the end, we have the double symbol of the crystal dome. The dome is the place in which El Hombre has immured himself for the last seventy years and from which he rules his arid and sterile domain. As a reminder of the crystal spheres which bind and enclose the universe in the Ptolemaic system of astronomy it symbolizes the archaic system under which El Hombre lives and rules. But it is also a huge and elaborate structure whose foundations, we are told, are the bones of El Hombre's enemies; and it is planned by El Hombre as his own tomb, where, by a self-willed act, he will immolate himself and become immortal through his surrogate. As such it reminds us of the marble, granite, and porphyry tomb into which the Chief of Police descends in Genet's *The Balcony*, there to sit and wait for two thousand years until he becomes part of the matrix of universal human mythology. For El Hombre understands that he has only been in power for seventy years, an insignificant period in the context of human history, and that he would be forgotten as soon as he is gone. And so he has decided to perpetuate himself symbolically through the device of creating his own "doppelgänger," a double who will continue his work and, presumably, will create other doubles on to infinity until the image of El Hombre is indelibly imprinted on the human consciousness. The seventy-year peace of which El Hombre is so proud is also

symbolic, for it is a "peace that passeth understanding"—a
"peace" of utter sterility. The land outside the crystal dome is
like the darkness outside Ptolemy's crystal spheres—no life, no
vegetation, and no faith. Faith of a spurious kind is simulated
inside the dome, whose walls are painted to resemble stained
glass windows and are decorated with trophies of the hunt, fishing, and of war—lifelessness and sterility inside and out. Inside
the dome, also, as in Genet's Balcony—the "House of Illusions,"
as Genet calls it—everything is false. The grotesque and monstrous El Hombre does nothing but dream his vainglorious
dreams, letting papers and dust pile up, making his double
jump around like a bird in a cage, and teaching him vicious
morsels of "realpolitik" like "the lie is the only truth that can
be permitted in a constructive political system." There is one
other unconscious literary parallel in Ruibal's work, and that
is to Erich Kästner's wonderful play *Die Schule der Diktatoren*
(The School for Dictators). In this play the dictator has died,
but no one knows it except a *junta* of generals who really govern the country and keep a supply of a dozen or more doubles
on hand, constantly training more. Whenever one of the doubles playing the dictator shows a sign of independence, he is
killed off and replaced by another one from the school.

. I have spoken so far about the author's excellent command
of the devices of allegory and of fantasy and of his place in the
mainstream of current avant-garde literature. I should like to
say a few words, in conclusion, about his style and his use of
imagery. Style and imagery as satiric instruments both reach a
high point of development in this play. The passage in which
El Hombre refers to bullets as doves' eggs incubated in machine-
gun nests seems to me one of the most trenchant of modern
poetic images; and the lyric passage immediately following it
in which El Hombre pirouettes around the dome chirping about
the dove of peace perched on torpedoes, pistols, tanks, hand
grenades, and atom bombs is stage satire carried to its highest
possible level. With this play José Ruibal has joined his colleagues, Alfonso Sastre, Antonio Buero-Vallejo, José María
Bellido, Antonio Martínez Ballesteros, and Carlos Muñiz in
bringing the contemporary Spanish theatre to a point where it

can compete honorably and on terms of equality with the best theatre being written and performed in the Western World.

The writers I have mentioned in this essay are by no means the only interesting ones to be found in Spain today. There are others who are just beginning, whose works are just starting to filter out of Spain, men like Jeronimo López Mozo, Alfonso Jiménez Romero, Juan Antonio Castro, Luis Matilla, Francisco Nieva, Angel García Pintado, Miguel Romero, Carlos Pérez Dann, Ramón Gil Novales, Ricard Salvat, José Benet, Luis Riaza, Miguel Rellán, Diego Salvador, Manuel Martínez Mediero, Manuel de Pedrolo, Alberto Miralles, Jordi Teixidor, M. A. Capmany; and there are better known men whom I have not treated here like Lauro Olmo, Ricardo Rodríguez Buded, Alfredo Mañas, José Martín Recuerda, and Rodríguez Méndez. The problem is that unless writers happen to have a personal contact outside Spain, they have no hope of becoming known. It is in their courageous persistence that the *pundonor* I spoke of as being an integral part of the Spanish character survives. As an ideal form of behavior to be illustrated in literature, *pundonor* is no longer an important factor now that Spain has definitively joined the modern world; it is manifested now only in a sense of personal dignity irrespective of social class that is refreshing in contrast to the rest of the Western World. Not least of these manifestations is the stubborn insistence of the "new wave" playwrights on their principles and beliefs. The ancient Spanish tension remains but has been transformed into something more personal. The paradox of the modern Spanish drama is that in a thoroughly repressive society the Spaniard is able to maintain his individuality while in a "free" society man has become de-individualized—or "technologized," to coin a term the only excuse for which is that it will be coined sooner or later anyway.

Bibliography

French-Speaking Drama

GENERAL WORKS

Abel, Lionel. *Metatheatre*. New York: Hill & Wang, Inc., 1963.

Cohn, Ruby. "Four Stages of Absurdist Hero," *Drama Survey*, IV (1968), pp. 195–208.

————. "*Theatrum Mundi* and Contemporary Theatre," *Contemporary Drama*, I (1967), pp. 28–35.

Esslin, Martin. *The Theatre of the Absurd*. Garden City, N.Y.: Doubleday & Co., Inc., 1961.

Fowlie, Wallace. *Dionysus in Paris*. New York: Meridian Books, 1960.

Grossvogel, David I. *The Self-Conscious Stage in Modern French Drama*. New York: Columbia University Press, 1958.

————. *Four Playwrights and a Postscript*. Ithaca, N.Y.: Cornell University Press, 1962.

Guicharnaud, Jacques. *Modern French Theatre from Giraudoux to Beckett*. New Haven, Conn.: Yale University Press, 1961.

Habicht, Werner. "Der Dialog und das Schweigen im 'Theater des Absurden,'" *Die neueren Sprachen*, XVI, n.s. (1967), pp. 53–66.

Hurley, Paul J. "France and America: Versions of the Absurd," *College English*, XXVI (1965), pp. 634–40.

Knowles, Dorothy. "The French Avant-Garde Theatre," *Modern Languages*, XLII (1961), pp. 88–93, 133–36.

Parker, R. B. "The Theory and Theatre of the Absurd," *Queens Quarterly*, LXXIII (1966), pp. 421–41.

Pronko, Leonard. *Avant-Garde: The Experimental Theatre in France*. Berkeley: University of California Press, 1962.

————. "Modes and Means of the Avant-Garde Theatre," *Bucknell Review*, XII, ii (1964), pp. 46–56.

————. "The Prelate and the Pachyderm: Rear Guard and Vanguard Drama in the French Theatre," *Modern Drama*, IV (1961), pp. 63–71.

ARTHUR ADAMOV

Lynes, Carlos, Jr. "Adamov and 'le sens littéral' in the Theatre," *Yale French Studies*, No. 14 (1954–55), pp. 48–56.

Regnaut, Maurice. "Arthur Adamov et le sens du fétichisme," *Cahiers de la Compagnie M. Renaud–J. L. Barrault*, Nos. 22–23 (1958), pp. 182–90.

Weber, Jean-Paul. "Adamov (Arthur Sourenovitch), de Kislovodsk, Auteur dramatique français (1910–19——)," *Figaro littéraire* (April 3, 1960), p. 3.

ANTONIN ARTAUD

Allen, Louis. "Antonin Artaud: Cruelty and Reality," *Durham University Journal*, LVIII (1965), pp. 40–42.

Arnold, Paul. "Antonin Artaud et le théâtre de la nouvelle vague," *Revue générale belge* (January, 1960), pp. 75–83.

Bertelé, René. "*Le théâtre et son double* ou le chant d'un hérétique," *Mercure de France*, No. 352 (1964), pp. 508–14 (revue article).

Fowlie, Wallace. "New French Theatre: Artaud, Beckett, Genet, Ionesco," *Sewanee Review*, LXVII (1959), pp. 648–51.

Hahn, Otto. "Portrait d'Antonin Artaud," *Temps Modernes*, No. 192 (1962), pp. 1592–1619; No. 193 (1962), pp. 1854–82.

Knapp, Bettina. *Antonin Artaud*. New York: David Lewis, 1969.

Sellin, Eric. *The Dramatic Concepts of Antonin Artaud*. Chicago: University of Chicago Press, 1968.

SAMUEL BECKETT

Barbour, Thomas. "Beckett and Ionesco," *Hudson Review*, XI (1958), pp. 271–77.

Chadwick, C. "*Waiting for Godot*: A Logical Approach," *Symposium*, XIV (1960), pp. 199–212.

Champigny, R. "Interprétation de *En attendant Godot*," *PMLA*, LXXV (1960), pp. 329–31.

Cleveland, Louise. "Trials in the Soundscape: The Radio Plays of Samuel Beckett," *Modern Drama*, XI (1968), pp. 267–82.

Cohen, Robert. "Parallels and the Possibility of Influence between Simone Weil's *Waiting for God* and Samuel Beckett's *Waiting for Godot*," *Modern Drama*, VI (1964), pp. 425–36.

Cohn, Ruby. "The Comedy of Samuel Beckett: Something Old, Something New," *Yale French Studies*, No. 23 (1959), pp. 11–17.

———. "*Endgame*: The Gospel According to Sad Sam Beckett," *Accent*, XX (1960), pp. 223–34.

———. "Plays and Players in the Plays of Samuel Beckett," *Yale French Studies*, No. 29 (1962), pp. 43–48.

———. *Samuel Beckett: The Comic Gamut*. New Brunswick, N.J.: Rutgers University Press, 1962.

———. "*Watt* in the Light of *The Castle*," *Comparative Literature*, XIII (1961), pp. 154–66.

Dobrée, Bonamy. "The London Theatre, 1957," *Sewanee Review*, LXVI (1958), pp. 146–60.

Douglas, Dennis. "The Drama of Evasion in *Waiting for Godot*," *Komos*, I (1968), pp. 140–46.

Driver, Tom F. "Beckett by the Madeleine," *Columbia University Forum*, IV, iii (1961), pp. 21–55.

Easthope, Anthony. "Hamm, Clov, and Dramatic Method in *Endgame*," *Modern Drama*, X (1968), pp. 424–33.

Eastman, Richard. "Samuel Beckett and *Happy Days*," *Modern Drama*, VI (1964), pp. 417–24.

Evers, Francis. "Samuel Beckett, the Incurious Seeker," *Dublin Magazine*, VII, i (1968), pp. 84–88.

Fletcher, John. *Samuel Beckett's Art*. New York: Barnes & Noble, 1967.

Flood, Ethelbert. "A Reading of Beckett's *Godot*," *Culture*, XII (1961), pp. 257–62.

Friedman, M. J. "The Achievement of Samuel Beckett," *Books Abroad*, XXXIII (1959), pp. 278–81.

Frisch, Jack. "*Endgame*: A Play as Poem," *Drama Survey*, III (1963), pp. 257–63.

Gilbert, Sandra. "All the Dead Voices: A Study of *Krapp's Last Tape*," *Drama Survey*, VI (1968), pp. 244–57.

Gregory, Horace. "Beckett's Dying Gladiators," *Commonweal* (October 26, 1956), pp. 88–92.

Hamilton, Kenneth. "Negative Salvation in Samuel Beckett," *Queen's Quarterly*, LXIX (1962), pp. 102–11.

Hampton, Charles. "Samuel Beckett's *Film*," *Modern Drama*, XI (1968), pp. 299–305.

Harvey, Lawrence E. "Art and the Existential in *En attendant Godot*," *PMLA*, LXXV (1960), pp. 137–46.

Hayman, Ronald. *Samuel Beckett*. London: William Heinemann, 1968.

Hesse, Eva. "Die Welt des Samuel Beckett," *Akzente*, VIII (1961), pp. 244–66.

Hoffmann, Frederick J. *Samuel Beckett: The Language of Self*. Carbondale, Ill.: Southern Illinois University Press, 1962.

Hooker, K. W. "Irony and Absurdity in the Avant-garde Theatre," *Kenyon Review*, XXII (1960), pp. 436–54.

Hubert, Renée R. "The Couple and the Performance in Samuel Beckett's Plays," *L'Esprit Créateur*, II (1962), pp. 175–80.

Hughes, Catherine. "Beckett and the Game of Life," *Catholic World*, CXCV (1962), pp. 163–68.

Iser, Wolfgang. "Samuel Becketts dramatische Sprache," *Germanisch-romanische Monatsschrift*, XI (1962), pp. 451–67.

Karl, Frederick R. "Waiting for Beckett: Quest and Re-quest," *Sewanee Review*, LXIX (1961), pp. 661–76.

Kenner, Hugh. "Beckett: The Rational Domain," *Forum (Houston)*, III, iv (1961), pp. 39–47.

Kern, Edith. "Beckett's Knight of Infinite Resignation," *Yale French Studies*, No. 29 (1962), pp. 49–56.

———. "Drama Stripped for Inaction: Beckett's *Godot*," *Yale French Studies*, No. 14 (1954–55), pp. 41–47.

Kolve, V. A. "Religious Language in *Waiting for Godot*," *Centennial Review*, XI (1967), pp. 102–27.

La Revue des Lettres Modernes, No. 100 (1964).

Lamont, Rosette C. "The Metaphysical Farce: Beckett and Ionesco," *French Review*, XXXII (1959), pp. 319–28.

Lyons, Charles. "Beckett's *Endgame*: An Anti-Myth of Creation," *Modern Drama*, VII (1964), pp. 204–209.

McCoy, Charles S. "*Waiting for Godot*: A Biblical Appraisal," *Religion in Life*, XXVIII (1959), pp. 595–603.

Mercier, Vivian. "Samuel Beckett and the Sheela-na-gig," *Kenyon Review*, XXIII (1961), pp. 299–324.

Metman, Eva. "Reflections on Samuel Beckett's Plays," *Journal of Analytical Psychology*, V (1960), pp. 41–62.

Modern Drama, IX, iii (1966). Beckett number.

Nadeau, Maurice. "Samuel Beckett, l'humour et le néant," *Mercure de France*, CCCXII (1951), pp. 693–97.

O'Neill, Joseph. "The Absurd in Samuel Beckett," *The Personalist*, XLVIII (1967), pp. 56–76.

Pritchett, V. S. "Irish Oblomov," *New Statesman* (April 2, 1960), p. 489.

Radke, Judith J. "The Theatre of Samuel Beckett: 'Une durée à animer,'" *Yale French Studies*, No. 29 (1962), pp. 57–64.

Reid, Alec. "Beckett and the Drama of Unknowing," *Drama Survey*, II (1962), pp. 130–38.

Rexroth, Kenneth. "The Point Is Irrelevance," *Nation* (April 14, 1956), pp. 325–28.

Schoell, Konrad. "The Chain and the Circle: A Structural Comparison of *Waiting for Godot* and *Endgame*," *Modern Drama*, XI (1968), pp. 48–53.

Scott, Nathan A., Jr. "The Recent Journey to the Zone of Zero: The Example of Beckett and His Despair of Literature," *The Centennial Review of Arts and Sciences*, VI (1962), pp. 144–81.

Strauss, W. A. "Dante's Belacqua and Beckett's Tramps," *Comparative Literature*, XI (1959), pp. 250–61.

Touchard, Pierre-Aimé. "Le théâtre de Samuel Beckett," *Revue de Paris* (February, 1961), pp. 73–87.

Trousdale, Marion. "Dramatic Form: The Example of *Godot*," *Modern Drama*, XI (1968), pp. 1–9.

Walker, R. "Love, Chess and Death: Samuel Beckett's Double Bill," *Twentieth Century*, CLXIV (1958), pp. 533–44.

Weales, Gerald. "The Language of *Endgame*," *TDR* VI, iv (1962), pp. 107–17.

JEAN GENET

Barish, Jonas A. "The Veritable St. Genet," *Wisconsin Studies in Contemporary Literature*, VI (1965), pp. 267–85.

Bonnefoy, Claude. *Jean Genet*. Paris: Editions Universitaires, 1965.

Calarco, N. Joseph. "Vision without Compromise: Genet's *The Screens*," *Drama Survey*, IV (1965), pp. 44–50.

Cismaru, Alfred. "The Antitheism of Jean Genet," *Antioch Review*, XXIV (1964), pp. 387–401.

Clark, E. "The World of Jean Genet," *Partisan Review*, XVI (1949), pp. 442–48.

Coe, Richard N. *The Vision of Jean Genet*. New York: Grove Press, 1968.

Cruikshank, John. "Jean Genet: The Aesthetics of Crime," *Critical Quarterly*, VI (1964), pp. 202–10.

Dort, Bernard. "Le jeu de Genet," *Temps Modernes* XV (1960), pp. 1875–84.

Ehrmann, Jacques. "Genet's Dramatic Metamorphosis: From Appearance to Freedom," *Yale French Studies*, No. 29 (1962), pp. 33–42.

Fowlie, Wallace. "The Case of Jean Genet," *Commonweal*, LXXIII (1960), pp. 111–13.

Genet, Jean. "To a Would-be Producer." Translated by Bernard Frechtman, *TDR*, VII, iii (1963), pp. 80–81.

Jeffrey, David. "Genet and Gelber: Studies in Addiction," *Modern Drama*, XI (1968), pp. 151–56.

Killinger, John. "Jean Genet and Scapegoat Drama," *Comparative Literature Studies*, III (1966), pp. 207–21.

Magnan, Jean-Marie. *Essai sur Jean Genet*. Paris: Seghers, 1966.
Markus, Thomas. "The Psychological Universe of Jean Genet," *Drama Survey*, III (1964), pp. 386–92.
McMahon, Joseph. *The Imagination of Jean Genet*. New Haven: Yale University Press, 1963.
Melcher, Edith. "The Pirandellism of Jean Genet," *French Review*, XXXVI (1962), pp. 32–36.
Nelson, Benjamin. "*The Balcony* and Parisian Existentialism," *TDR*, VII, iii (1963), pp. 60–79.
Pierret, Marc. "Genet's New Play: *The Screens*." Translated by Rima Reck, *TDR*, VII, iii (1963), pp. 93–97.
Pronko, Leonard. "Jean Genet's *Les Paravents*," *L'Esprit Créateur*, II (1962), pp. 181–88.
Pucciani, Oreste F. "Tragedy, Genet, and *The Maids*," *TDR*, VII, iii (1963), pp. 42–59.
Reck, Rima D. "Appearance and Reality in Genet's *Le Balcon*," *Yale French Studies*, No. 29 (1962), pp. 20–25.
Sartre, Jean-Paul. *Saint Genet: Comédien et Martyr*. Paris: Gallimard, 1952.
Strem, George. "The Theatre of Jean Genet: Facets of Illusion— The Anti-Christ and the Underdog," *Minnesota Review*, IV (1964), pp. 226–36.
Taubes, Susan. "The White Mask Falls," *TDR*, VII, iii (1963), pp. 85–92.
Thody, Philip. *Genet: A Study of His Novels and Plays*. London: Hamish Hamilton, 1968.
Yeager, Henry J. "The Uncompromising Morality of Jean Genet," *French Review*, XXXIX (1965), pp. 214–19.
Zimbardo, Rose. "Genet's Black Mass," *Modern Drama*, VIII (1965), pp. 247–58.

MICHEL DE GHELDERODE

Abel, Lionel. "Our Man in the Sixteenth Century: Michel de Ghelderode," *TDR*, VIII, i (1963), pp. 62–71.
Draper, Samuel. "An Interview with Michel de Ghelderode," *TDR*, VIII, i (1963), pp. 39–50.
———. "Discovery of Ghelderode," *Commonweal*, LXXIII (1960), pp. 113–15.
———. "Michel de Ghelderode: A Personal Statement," *TDR*, VIII, i (1963), pp. 33–38.
Draper, Samuel and Lois Alworth. "Bibliography on Michel de Ghelderode," *Modern Drama*, VIII (1965), pp. 332–34.
Fraidstern, Iska. "Ghelderode's *Red Magic*: Gold and the Use of Christian Myth," *Modern Drama*, XI (1969), pp. 376–81.

Ghelderode, Michel de. "Lettres à Catherine Toth, André Reybaz, René Dupuy, Jean Le Poulain, Marcel Lupovci, Gilles Chancrin," *Revue d'histoire du théâtre*, XIV (1962), pp. 118–56.

Grossvogel, David I. "The Plight of the Comic Author and Some New Departures in Contemporary Comedy," *Romanic Review*, XLV (1954), pp. 268–70.

Hauger, George. "Dispatches from the Prince of Ostrelande," *TDR*, VIII, i (1963), pp. 24–32.

————. "The Plays of Ghelderode," *TDR*, IV, i (1959), pp. 19–30.

Herz, Micheline. "Tragedy, Poetry and the Burlesque in Ghelderode's Theatre," *Yale French Studies*, No. 29 (1962), pp. 92–101.

Stevo, Jean. "Visages de Michel de Ghelderode," *Revue générale belge* (May, 1962), pp. 45–57.

Valogne, Catherine. "Michel de Ghelderode et ses interprètes," *Revue d'histoire du théâtre*, XIV (1962), pp. 113–17.

Weiss, Aurélieu. "The Theatrical World of Michel de Ghelderode." Translated by Ruby Cohn, *TDR*, VIII, i (1963), pp. 51–61.

EUGENE IONESCO

Bonnefoy, Claude. *Entretiens avec Eugène Ionesco.* Paris: Pierre Belfond, 1966.

Bradesco, Faust. *Le Monde étrange de Ionesco.* Paris: Promotion et Edition, 1967.

Cismaru, Alfred. "The Validity of Ionesco's Contempt," *Texas Quarterly*, VI, iv (1963), pp. 125–30.

Coe, Richard N. *Eugène Ionesco.* New York: Grove Press, 1961.

Cohn, Ruby. "Bérenger, Protagonist of an Anti-Playwright," *Modern Drama*, VIII (1965), pp. 127–33.

Daniel, John T. "Ionesco and the Ritual of Nihilism," *Drama Survey*, I, i (1961), pp. 54–65.

Doubrovsky, J. S. "Ionesco and the Comic of Absurdity," *Yale French Studies*, No. 23 (1959), pp. 3–10.

————. "Le rire d'Eugène Ionesco," *Nouvelle revue française* (February, 1960), pp. 313–23.

Eastman, Richard M. "Experiment and Vision in Ionesco's Plays," *Modern Drama*, IV (1961), pp. 3–19.

Ellis, Mary H. "The Work of Eugène Ionesco," *Southern Quarterly*, II (1964), pp. 220–35.

Esslin, Martin. "Ionesco and the Creative Dilemma," *TDR*, VII, iii (1963), pp. 169–79.

Glicksberg, Charles I. "Ionesco and the Aesthetics of the Absurd," *Arizona Quarterly*, XVII (1962), pp. 293–303.

Goldstein, E. "Les précurseurs romains de Ionesco," *Bulletin des Jeunes Romanistes,* XI–XII (1965), pp. 70–74.

Greshoff, C. J. "A Note on Ionesco," *French Studies,* XV (1961), pp. 30–40.

Hughes, Catherine. "Ionesco's Plea for Man," *Renascence,* XIV (1962), pp. 121–25.

Ionesco, Eugène. "The Avant-Garde Theatre," *TDR,* V, ii (1960), pp. 44–53.

––––––. *Fragments of a Journal.* Translated by Jean Stewart. New York: Grove Press, 1968.

––––––. *Notes and Counter-Notes.* Translated by Donald Watson. New York: Grove Press, 1964.

––––––. "The Tragedy of Language: How an English Primer Became My First Play." Translated by Jack Undank, *TDR,* IV, iii (1960), pp. 10–13.

Knowles, Dorothy. "Ionesco and the Mechanisms of Language," *Modern Drama,* V (1962), pp. 7–10.

Lamont, Rosette. "Air and Matter: Ionesco's 'Le Piéton de l'Air' and 'Victimes du devoir,'" *French Review,* XXXVIII (1965), pp. 349–61.

––––––. "The Hero in Spite of Himself," *Yale French Studies,* No. 29 (1962), pp. 73–81.

––––––. "The Proliferation of Matter in Ionesco's Plays," *L'Esprit Créateur,* II (1962), pp. 189–97.

Murray, Jack. "Ionesco and the Mechanics of Memory," *Yale French Studies,* No. 29 (1962), pp. 82–87.

Pronko, Leonard. *Eugène Ionesco.* New York: Columbia University Press, 1965.

Purdy, Strother B. "A Reading of Ionesco's *The Killer,*" *Modern Drama,* X (1968), pp. 416–23.

Schechner, Richard. "The Enactment of the 'Not' in *Les Chaises* of Eugène Ionesco," *Yale French Studies,* No. 29 (1962), pp. 65–72.

––––––. "The Inner and the Outer Reality," *TDR,* VII, iii (1963), pp. 187–220.

––––––. "An Interview with Ionesco," *TDR,* VII, iii (1963), pp. 163–68.

Sénart, Phillippe. *Ionesco.* Paris: Editions Universitaires, 1964.

––––––. "Ionesco: un théâtre théologique," *Le Table ronde,* No. 192 (1964), pp. 11–25.

Smith, J. Oates. "Ionesco's Dances of Death," *Thought,* XI (1965), pp. 415–31.

Strem, George. "The Anti-Theatre of Eugène Ionesco," *Twentieth Century* (Melbourne), XVI (1962), pp. 70–83.

Tolpin, Marian. "*Chairs* and the Theatre of the Absurd," *American Imago*, XXV (1968), pp. 119–39.

Touchard, Pierre-Aimé. "L'itinéraire d'Eugène Ionesco," *Revue de Paris*, LXVII (1960), pp. 91–102.

———. "Un nouveau fabuliste," *Cahiers de la Compagnie Madeleine Renaud–J. L. Barrault*, No. 29 (1960), pp. 3–13.

Vannier, Jean. "A Theatre of Language." Translated by Leonard Pronko, *TDR*, VII, iii (1963), pp. 180–86.

Watson, Donald. "The Plays of Ionesco," *TDR*, III, i (1958), pp. 48–53.

ALFRED JARRY

Shattuck, Roger. *The Banquet Years*. New York: Harcourt, Brace & World, Inc., 1958.

York, Ruth B. "*Ubu* Revisited: The Reprise of 1922," *French Review*, XXXV (1962), pp. 408–11.

JEAN TARDIEU

Jaccottet, Philippe. "Notes à propos de Jean Tardieu," *Nouvelle revue française* (July, 1960), pp. 107–11.

German-Speaking Drama

FRIEDRICH DÜRRENMATT

Askew, Melvin. "Dürrenmatt's *The Visit of the Old Lady*," *TDR*, V, iv (1961), pp. 89–105.

Brock-Sulzer, Elisabeth. *Friedrich Dürrenmatt: Stationen seines Werkes*. Zürich: Verlag der Arche, 1960.

Carew, Rivers. "The Plays of Friedrich Dürrenmatt," *Dublin Magazine*, IV (1965), pp. 57–68.

Davian, Donald G. "Justice in the Works of Friedrich Dürrenmatt," *Kentucky Foreign Language Quarterly*, IX (1962), pp. 181–93.

Diller, Edward. "Aesthetics and the Grotesque: Friedrich Dürrenmatt," *Wisconsin Studies in Contemporary Literature*, VII (1966), pp. 328–35.

———. "Despair and the Paradox: Friedrich Dürrenmatt," *Drama Survey*, V (1966–67), pp. 131–36.

Grimm, Reinhold, Willy Jäggi, and Hans Oesch, eds. *Der unbequeme Dürrenmatt*. Basel: Basilius Presse, 1962.

Guth, Hans. "Dürrenmatt's *Visit*: The Play Behind the Play," *Symposium*, XVI (1962), pp. 94–102.

Heilman, Robert. "Tragic Elements in a Dürrenmatt Comedy," *Modern Drama*, X (1967), pp. 10–16.

Johnson, Peter. "Grotesqueness and Injustice in Dürrenmatt," *German Life and Letters*, XV (1962), pp. 264–73.

Klarmann, Adolf. "Friedrich Dürrenmatt and the Tragic Sense of Comedy," *TDR*, IV (1960), pp. 77–104.

Kuczynski, Jürgen. "Friedrich Dürrenmatt—Humanist," *Neue deutsche Literatur*, XII, viii (1964), pp. 59–89; XII, ix (1964), pp. 35–55.

Loram, Ian C. " 'Der Besuch der alten Dame' and 'The Visit'," *Monatshefte*, LIII (1961), pp. 15–21.

Muschg, Walter. "Dürrenmatt und die Physiker," *Moderna Språk* (Stockholm), LVI (1962), pp. 280–83.

Peppard, Murray B. "The Grotesque in Dürrenmatt's Dramas," *Kentucky Foreign Language Quarterly*, IX (1962), pp. 36–44.

Phelps, Leland. "Dürrenmatt's *Die Ehe des Herrn Mississippi*: The Revision of a Play," *Modern Drama*, VIII (1965), pp. 156–60.

Scherer, Josef. "Der mutige Mensch: Versuch einer Deutung von Friedrich Dürrenmatts Menschenbild," *Stimmen der Zeit*, CLXIX (1962), pp. 307–12.

Schneider, Marcel. "Friedrich Dürrenmatt, le fils prodigue de l'occident," *Revue de Paris* (August, 1961), pp. 99–105.

Temkine, Raymonde. "Friedrich Dürrenmatt," *Lettres nouvelles*, No. 7 (1960), pp. 140–45.

Usmiani, Renate. "Friedrich Dürrenmatt as Wolfgang Schwitter," *Modern Drama*, XI (1968), pp. 143–50.

Waldmann, Günter. "Dürrenmatts paradoxes Theater," *Wirkendes Wort*, XIV (1964), pp. 22–35.

MAX FRISCH

Bänziger, Hans. *Frisch und Dürrenmatt*. Bern and Munich: Francke, 1960.

Davison, Dennis. "Frisch's *Fire Raisers*," *Komos*, I (1968), pp. 147–51.

Gontrum, Peter. "Max Frisch's *Don Juan*: A New Look at a Traditional Hero," *Comparative Literature Studies*, II (1965), pp. 117–23.

Karsek, Hellmuth. *Max Frisch*. Hannover: Velber, 1966.

Livingstone, R. S. "The World View of Max Frisch," *Southern Review* (Australia), I, iii (1965), pp. 32–45.

Müller, Joachim. "Max Frisch und Friedrich Dürrenmatt als Dramatiker der Gegenwart," *Universitas* (Stuttgart), XVII (1962), pp. 725–38.

Petersen, Carol. *Max Frisch*. Berlin: Colloquium, 1966.

Waldmann, Günter. "Das Verhängnis der Geschichtlichkeit," *Wirkendes Wort*, XVII (1967), pp. 264–71.

FRITZ HOCHWÄLDER

Hochwälder, Fritz. "Über mein Theater," Wort in der Zeit, XII, iii (1966), pp. 56–64.
Loram, Ian C. "Fritz Hochwälder," Monatshefte, LVII (1965), pp. 8–16.

English-Speaking Drama

GENERAL WORKS

Abirached, Robert. "Le jeune théâtre anglais," Nouvelle revue française, XV (1967), pp. 314–21.
Brown, John R., ed. Modern British Drama: A Collection of Essays. Englewood Cliffs, N.J.: Prentice-Hall, 1968.
Gottfried, Martin. A Theatre Divided: The Postwar American Stage. Boston: Little, Brown, 1968.
Knight, G. Wilson. "The Kitchen Sink," Encounter, XXI, vi (1963), pp. 48–54.
Marowitz, Charles. "New Wave in a Dead Sea," X, A Quarterly Review, I (1960), pp. 270–77.
Taylor, John Russell. Anger and After. London: Methuen & Co., 1962.
Trilling, Ossia. "The Young British Dramatists," Modern Drama, III (1960), pp. 168–77.
Wardle, Irving. "New Waves on the British Stage," Twentieth Century, CLXXII (1963), pp. 57–65.
Weales, Gerald. The Jumping-Off Place. American Drama in the 1960's. New York: Macmillan, 1969.

JOHN ARDEN

Blindheim, John T. "John Arden's Use of the Stage," Modern Drama, XI (1968), pp. 306–16.
Gilman, Richard. "Arden's Unsteady Ground," TDR, XI, ii (1966), pp. 54–62.

JOHN OSBORNE

Barker, Clive. "Look Back in Anger—The Turning Point," Zeitschrift für Anglistik und Amerikanistik, XIV (1966), pp. 367–71.
Carter, A. V. "John Osborne: a Re-appraisal," Revue belge de Philologie et d'Histoire, XLIV (1966), pp. 971–76.
Deming, B. "John Osborne's War Against the Philistines," Hudson Review, XI (1959), pp. 411–19.

Dennis, Nigel. "Out of the Box," *Encounter*, XVII (1961), pp. 51–53 (on *Luther*).

Denty, Vera D. "The Psychology of Martin Luther," *Catholic World*, CXCIV (1961), pp. 99–105 (on *Luther*).

Gersh, Gabriel. "The Theatre of John Osborne," *Modern Drama*, X (1967), pp. 137–43.

Marowitz, Charles. "The Ascension of John Osborne," *TDR*, VII, ii (1962), pp. 175–79.

Popkin, Henry. "Williams, Osborne, or Beckett?" *New York Times Book Review*, November 13, 1960, pp. 32–33, 119–21.

Rogers, Daniel. " 'Not for Insolence, But Seriously': John Osborne's Adaptation of *La fianza satisfecha*," *Durham University Journal*, LIX (1968), pp. 146–70.

Rupp, Gordon. "Luther and Mr. Osborne," *The Cambridge Quarterly*, I (1965), pp. 28–42.

Spacks, Patricia. "Confrontation and Escape in Two Social Dramas," *Modern Drama*, XI (1968), pp. 61–72 (on *Look Back in Anger* and *A Doll's House*).

Taylor, John R., ed. *Look Back in Anger: A Casebook*. London: Macmillan & Co., 1968.

Weiss, S. A. "Osborne's Angry Young Play," *Educational Theatre Journal*, XII (1960), pp. 285–88.

HAROLD PINTER

Amend, Victor. "Harold Pinter—Some Credits and Debits," *Modern Drama*, X (1967), pp. 165–74.

Bar'.man, Katherine. "Pinter's *A Slight Ache* as Ritual," *Modern Drama*, XI (1968), pp. 326–35.

Bernhard, F. J. "Beyond Realism: The Plays of Harold Pinter," *Modern Drama*, VIII (1965), pp. 185–91.

Cohn, Ruby. "The World of Harold Pinter," *TDR*, VI, iii (1962), pp. 55–68.

Cook, David and Harold F. Brooks. "A Room with Three Views: Harold Pinter's *The Caretaker*," *Komos*, I (1967), pp. 62–69.

Dick, Kay. "Mr. Pinter and the Fearful Matter," *Texas Quarterly*, IV (1961), pp. 257–65.

Hinchliffe, Arnold. *Harold Pinter*. New York: Twayne, 1967.

———. "Mr. Pinter's Belinda," *Modern Drama*, XI (1968), 173–79.

Hoefer, Jacqueline. "Pinter and Whiting: Two Attitudes Towards the Alienated Artist," *Modern Drama*, IV (1962), pp. 402–408.

Mast, Gerald. "Pinter's *Homecoming*," *Drama Survey*, VI (1968), pp. 266–77.

Storch, R. F. "Harold Pinter's Happy Families," *Massachusetts Review*, VIII (1967), pp. 703–712.

Sykes, Arlene. "Harold Pinter's *The Dwarfs*," *Komos*, I (1967), pp. 70–75.

Walker, Augusta. "Messages from Pinter," *Modern Drama*, X (1967), pp. 1–10.

ARNOLD WESKER

Anderson, Michael. "Arnold Wesker: The Last Humanist?" *New Theatre Magazine* (Bristol), VIII, iii (1968), pp. 10–27.

Findlater, Richard. "Plays and Politics," *Twentieth Century*, CLXVIII (1960), pp. 235–42.

Goodman, Henry. "The New Dramatists, 2: Arnold Wesker," *Drama Survey*, I (1960), pp. 215–22.

Gordon, Giles. "Arnold Wesker: An Interview," *Transatlantic Review*, XXI (1966), pp. 15–25.

Jones, A. R. "The Theatre of Arnold Wesker," *Critical Quarterly*, II (1960), pp. 366–70.

Page, Malcolm. "Whatever Happened to Arnold Wesker?: His Recent Plays," *Modern Drama*, XI (1968), pp. 317–25.

Rothberg, Abraham. "East End, West End: Arnold Wesker," *Southwest Review*, LII (1967), pp. 368–78.

EDWARD ALBEE

Ballew, Leighton. "Who's Atraid of *Tiny Alice?*" *Georgia Review*, XX (1966), pp. 292–99.

Bigsby, C. W. "Curiouser and Curiouser: A Study of Albee's *Tiny Alice*," *Modern Drama*, X (1967), pp. 258–66.

———. "The Strategy of Madness: An Analysis of Albee's *A Delicate Balance*," *Wisconsin Studies in Comparative Literature*, IX (1968), pp. 223–35.

Campbell, Mary. "The Statement of Albee's *Tiny Alice*," *Papers on Language and Literature*, IV (1968), pp. 85–100.

Canaday, Nicholas. "Albee's *American Dream* and the Existential Vacuum," *South Central Bulletin*, XXVI, iv (1968), pp. 28–34.

Davison, Richard. "Albee's *Tiny Alice*: A Note of Re-examination," *Modern Drama*, XI (1968), pp. 54–60.

Dozier, Richard. "Adultery and Disappointment in *Who's Afraid of Virginia Woolf?*," *Modern Drama*, XI (1969), pp. 432–36.

Dukore, Bernard. "Tiny Albee," *Drama Survey*, V (1966), pp. 60–66.

Hamilton, Kenneth. "Mr. Albee's Dream," *Queen's Quarterly*, LXX (1963), pp. 393–99.

Knepler, Henry. "Edward Albee: Conflict of Tradition," *Modern Drama*, X (1967), pp. 274–79.

Levine, Mordecai. "Albee's Liebestod," *CLA Journal*, X (1967), pp. 252–55.

Lewis, Allan. "The Fun and Games of Edward Albee," *Educational Theatre Journal*, XVI (1964), pp. 29–39.

Markson, John W. "Albee's *Tiny Alice*," *American Imago*, XXIII (1966), pp. 3–21.

Markus, Thomas B. "*Tiny Alice* and Tragic Catharsis," *Educational Theatre Journal*, XVII (1965), pp. 225–33.

Meyer, Ruth. "Language, Truth, and Illusion in *Who's Afraid of Virginia Woolf?*," *Educational Theatre Journal*, XX (1968), pp. 60–69.

Nagel, Ivan. "Requiem für die Seele," *Neue Rundschau*, LXXIV (1963), pp. 646–51.

Nelson, Gerald. "Edward Albee and His Well-made Plays," *Tri-Quarterly*, No. 5 (1966), pp. 182–88.

Paul, Louis. "A Game Analysis of Albee's *Who's Afraid of Virginia Woolf?*: The Core of Grief," *Literature and Psychology*, XVII (1967), pp. 47–51.

Phillips, Elizabeth C. "Albee and the Theatre of the Absurd," *Tennessee Studies in Literature*, X (1965), pp. 73–80.

Roy, Emil. "*Who's Afraid of Virginia Woolf?* and the Tradition," *Bucknell Review*, XIII, i (1965), pp. 27–36.

Rule, Margaret. "An Albee Bibliography," *Twentieth Century Literature*, XIV (1968), pp. 35–44.

Rutenberg, Michael E. *Edward Albee: Playwright in Protest*. New York: DBS Publications, 1969.

Simpson, Herbert. "*Tiny Alice*: Limited Affirmation in a Conflict Between Theatre and Drama," *Forum* (Houston), VI, i (1968), pp. 43–46.

Spielberg, Peter. "The Albatross in Albee's Zoo," *College English*, XXVII (1965), pp. 562–65.

Valgemae, Mardi. "Albee's Great God Alice," *Modern Drama*, X (1968), pp. 267–73.

Zimbardo, Rose. "Symbolism and Naturalism in Edward Albee's *The Zoo Story*," *Twentieth Century Literature*, VIII (1960), pp. 10–17.

Index